AFRICAN ETHNOGRAPHIC STUDIES
OF THE 20TH CENTURY

Volume 9

CARAVANS OF THE OLD SAHARA

CARAVANS OF THE OLD SAHARA
An Introduction to the History of the Western Sudan

E. W. BOVILL

LONDON AND NEW YORK

First published in 1933 by Oxford University Press for the International African Institute.

This edition first published in 2018
by Routledge
2 Park Square, Milton Park, Abingdon, Oxon OX14 4RN

and by Routledge
711 Third Avenue, New York, NY 10017

Routledge is an imprint of the Taylor & Francis Group, an informa business

© 1933 International African Institute

All rights reserved. No part of this book may be reprinted or reproduced or utilised in any form or by any electronic, mechanical, or other means, now known or hereafter invented, including photocopying and recording, or in any information storage or retrieval system, without permission in writing from the publishers.

Trademark notice: Product or corporate names may be trademarks or registered trademarks, and are used only for identification and explanation without intent to infringe.

British Library Cataloguing in Publication Data
A catalogue record for this book is available from the British Library

ISBN: 978-0-8153-8713-8 (Set)
ISBN: 978-0-429-48813-9 (Set) (ebk)
ISBN: 978-1-138-49101-4 (Volume 9) (hbk)
ISBN: 978-1-351-03334-3 (Volume 9) (ebk)

Publisher's Note
The publisher has gone to great lengths to ensure the quality of this reprint but points out that some imperfections in the original copies may be apparent.

Disclaimer
The publisher has made every effort to trace copyright holders and would welcome correspondence from those they have been unable to trace.

Due to modern production methods, it has not been possible to reproduce the fold-out maps within the book. Please visit www.routledge.com to view them.

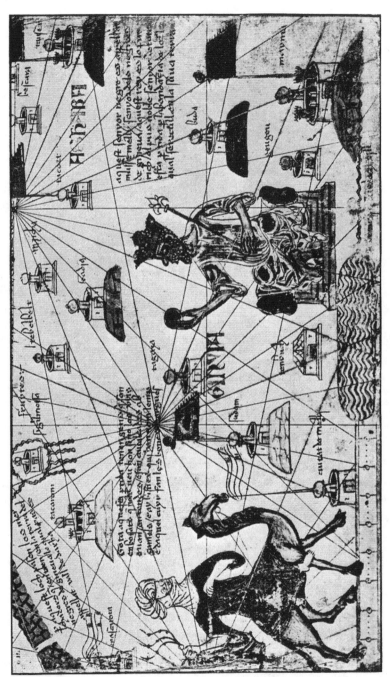

I. MUSA MALI, LORD OF THE NEGROES OF GUINEA

From a panel of the Catalan Map of Charles V (1375)

CARAVANS

OF THE

OLD SAHARA

AN INTRODUCTION
TO THE HISTORY OF THE
WESTERN SUDAN

By

E. W. BOVILL

Published for the
INTERNATIONAL INSTITUTE OF
AFRICAN LANGUAGES & CULTURES
by OXFORD UNIVERSITY PRESS
LONDON : HUMPHREY MILFORD

1933

PRINTED IN GREAT BRITAIN

TO
SYLVIA

PREFACE

THE importance to Christian Europe of the trade which it so long carried on with the Muhammadan states of the North African littoral has always been accepted, but the extent of its dependence on the desert caravan traffic with the negroid peoples of the Western Sudan has been little recognized.

The trans-Saharan trade wove ties of blood and culture between the peoples north and south of the desert, and it inspired the achievements by which, after centuries of failure, the mysteries of the remote interior were ultimately revealed to European nations.

The purpose of this volume is to outline briefly the growth of these associations and to win a measure of recognition for the part which the Western Sudanese have played in the history of civilization.

The Author's considerable indebtedness to his friends and to the works of others is briefly acknowledged in the notes. The references to the late Lady Lugard's *A Tropical Dependency*, however, are no measure of his debt to that brilliant work. It was the enthralling interest of those pages, read amid the stirring scenes which inspired them, that first urged him to explore further the field in which Lady Lugard was the pioneer.

E. W. BOVILL

LITTLE LAVER HALL,
HARLOW.
6th February 1933.

CONTENTS

INTRODUCTORY

I. THE SAHARA	. . . .	1
II. AFRICA ANTIQUA	. . . . .	13
III. RACES OF MAN	. . . . .	23
IV. MEDIEVAL ARABIC WRITERS	. . . .	32

BELED ES SUDAN

V. THE ALMORAVIDS	. . . . .	43
VI. GHANA	. . . . . .	57
VII. MALI	. . . .	67
VIII. THE RISE OF THE SONGHAI EMPIRE	. . .	82
IX. THE ASKIAS	. . . . . .	92
X. LEO AFRICANUS	. . . . . .	103

THE GOLDEN TRADE

XI. THE CRESCENT AND THE CROSS	. . . .	115
XII. THE QUEST FOR GOLD	. . . .	127
XIII. THE SEA OF DARKNESS	. . . .	137
XIV. THE MOORISH INVASION	. . . .	151
XV. THE FALL OF THE SONGHAI EMPIRE	. .	170
XVI. EL DZEHEBI	. . . . .	183
XVII. THE LATER PASHAS	. . . . .	192

THE SUDAN UNVEILED

XVIII. THE VEIL	. . . . . .	201
XIX. THE NIGER QUEST	. . . . .	210
XX. THE SOKOTO FULANI	. . . .	219
XXI. THE LIFTING OF THE VEIL	. . .	233
XXII. THE GREAT CARAVANS	. . . .	246
XXIII. SHEPHERD KINGS	. . . . .	261
CHRONOLOGY	. . . . .	270
A SELECT BIBLIOGRAPHY	. . . .	272
INDEX	. . . . . .	277

MAPS

I. Musa Mali, Lord of the Negroes of Guinea—From a panel
of the Catalan Map of Charles V (1375) . . *frontispiece*

II. Roman Africa 12

III. North-Western Africa—Tenth to Sixteenth Centuries . 42

IV. Wangara and the Upper Niger 56

V. Hausa and the Middle Niger 69

VI. North Africa in the Middle Ages 114

VII. The *Africae Tabula Nova* of Ortelius (1570) . . 129

VIII. The Discoveries of the Portuguese 139

IX. North-Western Africa—Sixteenth and Seventeenth Centuries 153

X. The *Africae Nova Descriptio* of Blaeu (1665) . *facing* 201

XI. The *Carte de la Barbarie de la Nigritie et de la Guinée* of de
Lisle (Elwe, 1792) . . . . *facing* 210

XII. The Hausa States 218

XIII. The Principal Caravan Routes of the Nineteenth Century
between pages 246 and 247

INTRODUCTORY

I

THE SAHARA

'Caelo terraque penuria aquarum.'—SALLUST

NORTHERN Africa is divided into a series of natural zones running roughly parallel to each other from west to east. Along the Mediterranean sea-board lies a narrow strip of undulating country, generally known as the Tell, which enjoys a climate similar to that of southern Europe and is peopled by an agricultural peasantry. Behind these coastal hills lie the arid uplands of the High Plateaux which, although they culminate in the peaks of the Atlas, are for the most part steppe-like in character and support a pastoral and semi-nomadic population. These highlands drop sharply into the Sahara, the largest continuous desert on the earth's surface, where extreme aridity imposes a nomadic existence on its sparse population. No natural frontier bounds the Sahara on the south. It gradually merges into steppes and these in turn give place first to savanna and then to parklands, which, like the Tell, are peopled by a sedentary agricultural population. Beyond the parklands lies the great barrier of the equatorial forest.

The broad belt of broken country separating the Mediterranean from the Sahara and extending from Tripoli in the east to the Atlantic in the west has come to be loosely termed Barbary. The great plains which lie south of the Sahara, separating it from the equatorial forest, form the Beled es Sudan, an Arabic name meaning the Land of the Blacks. It extends from the Red Sea to the Atlantic, that part which lies to the west of Lake Chad forming the Western Sudan.

Although Barbary and the Western Sudan are separated by a desert which forms one of the world's greatest barriers to human movement the cultural and economic development of both has been profoundly affected by intercourse between the two. The Sahara consequently dominates the whole of the history of the interior of northern Africa.

A slight increase in the aridity of this immense desert would produce far-reaching political consequences. It would drive the wild desert tribes into the settled uplands and plains of Barbary and the Sudan, and it would so extend the waterless stages that the caravan

THE SAHARA

routes would become impassable to camels and therefore to men. A correspondingly slight increase in rainfall would quickly multiply the water-holes and desert pastures, render man independent of the now necessary camel, and, by making his life more endurable, tame the nomad. Whether there has been any material change in the climate of the Sahara in historical times is therefore a question of great importance to the student of history.

The climate of nearly all parts of the world seems to have undergone changes in geologically recent times, and the Sahara is no exception. Long before the dawn of history, which in this region is placed in the fifth century before Christ, the northern Sahara supported a sedentary population whose abundant remains are widely scattered over areas which have since reached the extreme limit of desiccation.[1] It then probably presented no obstacle to the migration of fauna. But those conditions belonged to times long anterior to the period with which we are concerned.

There is a very widespread belief in the instability of climate and it is almost invariably of a pessimistic nature. Man is ever ready to note deterioration in his home climate, and when he travels abroad and beholds the ruins of deserted towns, dry river-beds, and extinction of wild fauna he is quick to see in them a confirmation of his suspicion that the world is not what it was. Evidence of this type is probably nowhere more obvious than in North Africa, which in consequence is generally credited with being a victim of climatic change.

The world has few more impressive monuments to offer than the vast amphitheatre of El Jem (Thysdrus), built to seat 60,000 spectators, but to-day a ruin set amid utter desolation. Or Timgad, lying like a bleached skeleton stretched on an arid plain, its deserted streets bordered by channels which we know once flowed continually with water. These and countless other ruins lie scattered over an inhospitable land which was once called the Granary of Rome. In the museums are numbers of mosaics taken from Roman villas representing a fauna now found only in tropical Africa,* and it is well known that elephants roamed North Africa in Carthaginian times. The evidence of climatic change seems to be overwhelming, and consequently it is widely believed that the desert is encroaching from the south and, as a corollary, that the Sahara itself was in historical times very much less arid than it is to-day.

---

* A striking example in the Bardo (Musée Alaoui) at Tunis illustrates Orpheus charming the animals, amongst which is a remarkable picture of the Bubal hartebeest.

THE SAHARA

As the greater part of the Sahara has reached the extreme limit of aridity it is rather to its outer fringes, where desert conditions give way to steppe, that we naturally look for signs of progressive desiccation. In Barbary the problem has been closely studied by Stéphane Gsell, the greatest authority on the history of North Africa.[2] Exhaustive research has convinced him that conditions have changed but little since the Roman period. Purely local changes caused by earth movements and other factors are admitted, but they do not alter the main argument.

Throughout Barbary stories of failing wells and shrunken springs are common enough. In nearly every case it is due to neglect by the natives. Under the Romans special engineers (*aquilegi*) were appointed to look after the springs. Everything was done to foster and maintain the water supply. Most of the springs which supplied Roman settlements still exist and for this reason French settlements tend to rise on ancient sites. Whether the springs flow as freely as they did fifteen hundred years ago cannot be proved, but there is no evidence to the contrary.

Scattered throughout the country are the ruins of reservoirs, cisterns, and wells which the Romans constructed to provide water for man and beast and for the irrigation of crops. The ruins of vast aqueducts striding across the desolate plains and piercing mountain ranges, impressive monuments to the skill of Roman engineers, are a common sight. Cirta (Constantine) drew its water from twenty miles away, Caesarea (Cherchel) from nineteen miles, and Carthage from nearly ninety miles.* All these works were destroyed or allowed to fall into decay by subsequent invaders.

The rivers to-day appear to carry as much water as they did in the past. They are navigable to the same extent and the Roman bridges were of no greater span than modern conditions require. Had the rivers been deeper many of the Roman fords would have been useless.

The modern traveller in North Africa sees little which accords with his preconceived ideas of the Granary of Rome. The crops are thin and the ears lean. Under the Emperors Africa had to supply as a tax a quantity of wheat sufficient to feed half the Roman *plebs*, estimated at about 350,000 souls. As Gautier[3] has pointed out, for a country of its size this was no great burden and in itself affords no evidence of more favourable natural conditions than those of to-day. Roman

---

* The Romans appreciated the value of good water and if local supplies were not of the desired purity they did not hesitate to look far afield for their needs.

THE SAHARA

Africa owed much of its prosperity to the cultivation of the olive. All round the Mediterranean on sites formerly occupied by the Romans are found abundant remains of *amphorae* which contained olive oil and which still bear the marks of African potters. It was the presence of immense numbers of ancient oil presses in a vast wilderness which in recent years prompted an enterprising French Director of Agriculture to plant olive trees on a huge scale in southern Tunisia and thus restore prosperity to a derelict region.[4]

During the Roman occupation there were extensive areas entirely lacking in water. Capsa (Gafsa) was surrounded by immense solitudes but it had an inexhaustible spring.[5] The provision of water for troops was a constant anxiety to their leaders, notably to Caesar[6] when fighting near Susse, or Susa, the ancient Hadrumentum, and six centuries later to Belisarius[7] in the same region.

Several Roman authors would have us believe that Barbary was in their day less favoured than at present. Sallust's famous comment has already been quoted. Other writers of the same period had an equally low opinion of the country. It was certainly subject to severe droughts. Hadrian was beloved of Africans because on his arrival in the country rain fell for the first time for five years.[8] Records of disastrous famines are numerous.

We now come to the question of extinct fauna, to which those who believe in the desiccation of North Africa attach much importance. Gsell has clearly shown that arguments based on this class of evidence, of which there is a great mass, are not conclusive.

The elephants which the Carthaginians caught and trained—an art which they had learnt from the Greeks, who were the first to use African elephants*—belonged to the same species as those which are to-day found throughout tropical Africa. They were, however, small in size, modified by isolation and environment. Wild elephants survived in North Africa far into the Christian era, their last habitat probably being the High Atlas. The belief that they had only survived under increasingly unfavourable conditions which eventually caused their extinction has no evidence to support it. There are regions in the Atlas and the Tell which are still capable of supporting elephants, though there are others such as Setif and Susse where elephants used to roam but which are now unsuited to them. A local modification

---

* The Greeks had learnt the use of elephants during the campaigns of Alexander, first at Arbela and afterwards in the Indus valley where elephants were opposed to them. They subsequently organized elephant hunts in Africa.

THE SAHARA

of climate in the latter areas has probably taken place. But climatic change seems to have been as little responsible for the extinction of the elephant as it was for that of the ostrich, which has disappeared from Barbary within living memory, or for the fast approaching extinction of the lion and leopard.

The Romans themselves were directly responsible for the extinction of the elephant, as they probably were for that of other species which to-day are found only south of the Sahara. The principal cause of the enormous destruction of African fauna was the demand for beasts to provide sport at the Games. Augustus tells us that 3,500 African animals were slain in the twenty-six Games which he gave to the Roman people.[9] Pompey showed 600 lions at a time, of which 315 were males, and Caesar 400. The elephant, however, was principally persecuted for its ivory, immense quantities of which used to be exported to Rome. According to Pliny the cartilage of an elephant's trunk was one of the particular delicacies served from Roman kitchens.[10]

The arguments for a general modification of climate in North Africa during historical times do not carry conviction. Deserted cities are found to be still habitable, rivers are much the same as they used to be, droughts seem formerly to have been as frequent as they are now, and conditions are not generally unfavourable to fauna which are now extinct.

Gsell thinks that North Africa as a whole may perhaps have enjoyed a slightly more abundant rainfall in Roman times. 'Mais, en somme', he concludes, 'si le climat de la Berbérie s'est modifié depuis l'époque romaine, ça n'a été que dans une très faible mesure.'[11]

Turning from the northern to the southern fringes of the Sahara we have to consider an entirely different type of evidence. In the Sudan records of the past are as scarce as they are plentiful in the north. There is hardly any material to enable us to picture accurately the country as it was 1,000 years ago, or even 500. The few written records confine themselves to genealogies and the bare facts of history and throw little light on contemporary conditions of life. Architectural monuments scarcely exist. Almost the sole building material has been clay, so soft and friable that an abandoned site soon crumbles into mounds of earth which vegetation quickly obliterates.

Reliable records date back only to the European occupation, scarcely a generation ago. They provide, however, a mass of evidence which places it beyond all doubt that whatever may have happened in

6 THE SAHARA

the past the present is a period of progressive desiccation. The Sahara is encroaching on the Sudan.

In Senegal desert conditions are becoming increasingly prevalent. Wells are failing and rivers are shrinking. The river-beds are being choked by drifting sand and their waters are becoming increasingly saline. Crop failures due to decreased rainfall are a constant source of anxiety to the administrative authorities. Of great significance is the tendency of the sedentary population to migrate southward in search of less arid regions, their place being taken by pastoral nomads from the desert.[12]

On the middle Niger, Lake Fagbine is drying up and the area of annual inundation is shrinking. It has been proved that in the fifteenth century, when Sonni Ali of Songhai attempted to link Walata with the lake by a canal, its shores extended much farther westward.[13] Within the Bend of the Niger a tendency among the Tuareg to migrate southward has long been noticed.

Passing eastwards into Nigeria we come to an area where much evidence of desert encroachment has been collected. The northern frontier falls roughly where the thinly populated pastures and unsettled conditions which are characteristic of the fringes of the Sahara emerge into fertile plains supporting a comparatively dense agricultural population. Along this frontier water is the limiting factor in the lives of the people who at once feel the effects of any fluctuation in the supply. In the provinces of Sokoto and Bornu dry river-beds, dwindling lakes, shrinking wells, failing crops, and a southward movement of agriculturists are unmistakable symptoms of progressive desiccation.[14] In 1826 Clapperton wrote in his diary: 'They have not been able to make the date tree grow at Soccatoo; whenever it gets a little above ground it rots and dies.'[15] To-day date palms attain a considerable size in Sokoto though they do not bear fruit. The inference is that they have benefited by increasing aridity during the last hundred years.

In northern Nigeria there has perhaps been too great a tendency to ascribe every movement of the population to desiccation. The attachment of the African native to the soil is not great and it takes little to set him moving. The causes are often political. Conscription, taxation, and irksome restrictions lead to temporary migrations across political frontiers. Natural increase in population, which has been very marked throughout Africa since Europeans put an end to tribal war and curbed the ravages of famine and disease, constantly causes

THE SAHARA

communities to outgrow the resources of their locations. When this happens the people must move.

In the Western Sudan the southward movement of the population is too general and the excuse of shrinking wells and failing crops too insistent to be ascribed to anything but some great natural cause. This is generally admitted to be progressive desiccation.

But the desiccation of the Western Sudan is not itself wholly natural. The incalculable harm which is being wrought throughout tropical Africa by the shifting cultivator is now widely recognized. The African farmer has little knowledge of crop rotation or manuring. He cultivates his land to exhaustion and then with fire and axe makes a fresh clearing in the surrounding bush or forest. In 1924 the Governor of Nigeria declared that 'the necessity for protecting the people from their own improvidence, which if left unchecked will inflict untold calamity upon posterity, is as urgent as ever . . . literally thousands of square miles of forest have disappeared since the War broke out'.[16] Agreement has never been reached regarding the extent to which forest affects climate. It is, however, the common experience of man that trees conserve moisture and that the destruction of forest impoverishes the soil and causes increased aridity. Great as is the harm wrought by the shifting cultivator, he cannot be held wholly responsible for the shrinkage of rivers, lakes, and wells on the huge scale which we find in the Western Sudan. Climatic change is undoubtedly playing its part, but man himself is aggravating the evil.

Geologists are disinclined to admit that the Sahara is encroaching on the Sudan, though they concede instances of local desiccation. They even maintain that the movement is in the contrary direction, and base their arguments on the occurrence of dead *erg* or fossil dunes in regions now lying south of the Sahara and enjoying a substantial rainfall.[17] These fossil dunes, which admittedly could not have been formed except under desert conditions, are widely distributed and point unmistakably to a former southward extension of the Sahara far beyond its present limits. Their presence, however, in no way affects the conclusion that the present period is one of increasing aridity.

It has been established that the climate of many parts of the world has been subject to pulsations of wet and dry periods since quaternary times. The Sudan was probably such a region. Neither in the existence, at some period of unknown remoteness, of desert conditions beyond their present limits nor in the overwhelming evidence of a

THE SAHARA

now existing phase of progressive desiccation is there any proof that in the Sudan the distribution of desert, steppe, and bush has changed seriously in the last 1,500 years. The Sudan affords no evidence that in historical times the southern frontier of the Sahara differed greatly from its present condition.[18]

Turning now to the Sahara itself we find that, like Barbary, it has a curious residual fauna. Crocodiles have been found in at least three parts of the desert—the Wad Mihero, the Ahaggar Mountains, and Enedi. The cobra survives in Biskra, Figuig, and Gurara. Cat-fish are a comparatively common feature of desert pools. The Ahaggar Mountains harbour Barbary sheep.[19] These and other species now surviving in the Sahara, all belonging strictly to more humid regions, provide somewhat spectacular evidence of climatic change. But, like the extensive remains of a sedentary population which once inhabited the Algerian Sahara, they have no bearing on the question of change since the dawn of history.

Throughout the rapidly growing literature of Saharan travel there are constant references to advancing sand and shrinking oases. Ancient caravan routes are being abandoned owing to failure of wells. Deserted oases are common incidents of travel, and tales of others which have been recently lost are only less frequent. The common explanation of these phenomena is desiccation due to climatic change. This seems to be a contributory factor, but that man himself is the chief cause is a conclusion at which all familiar with the Sahara eventually arrive.

The decay of the oases in the last few decades has been principally due to political unrest. Small though the population may be, the resources of the Sahara are strained to their utmost to support it. Starvation and plenty are divided by a narrow and highly sensitive margin which quickly disappears with any reduction of the already inadequate water supply.

The people of the desert are extremely virile and live permanently on a war footing. They cultivate corn and dates in the oases on a modest scale, but they are mostly pastoral nomads with highly developed predatory instincts. Their camels and their own hardihood have made them the most mobile people in the world. When the meagre desert pastures begin to fail the community starts moving and conflicts are inevitable. To the small sedentary cultivators of the oases the nomads have always been a constant menace. At any moment the dreaded *razzia* may fall upon them with the inevitable result that they lose

THE SAHARA

their crops if not their lives. This general condition of insecurity—the French have now almost put an end to it—has resulted in the cultivators abandoning to the desert all but the minimum area necessary to their needs. For the same reason there is, or was until recently, a marked reluctance to sink new wells and to repair the old ones. Under such conditions frequent opportunities occur for the desert to encroach on the cultivable areas. Often in the recent past the whole population of an oasis has been wiped out, with the inevitable result that the desert has crept in and completely enveloped the gardens. For, as the late Dr. T. F. Chipp recently pointed out, an oasis is an entirely man-made place of habitation, and it ceases to be an oasis so soon as man's control is removed.[20] A striking example of desert encroachment was afforded by the short-sighted action of the French in attempting to drive the Tuareg out of the Air Mountains after the rebellion of 1917. 'Depopulation allowed the desert to encroach,' wrote a recent traveller. 'Wells fell in, gardens went out of tillage, and the live-stock of the country, more especially the camel herds, were reduced to a fraction of what they had been.'[21]

The abolition of the slave trade has also had an unfavourable effect on the economic conditions of life in the desert. The oases used to be cultivated principally by negro labour imported from the Sudan, the Haratin of the Arabs and the Bella or Buzu of the Tuareg. With the cessation of the slave traffic the negro population of the Sahara has shrunk, and with it the oases. The decay of the caravan routes may be traced to political insecurity and to the diversion of trade to newly opened European channels. This is particularly true of the ancient salt traffic, which has lost nearly all its former importance.

The difficult task of controlling this vast desert region is one to which the French have applied themselves with vigour, and a remarkable degree of success has been attained. By enforcing tranquillity on the nomads fresh life has been infused into the oases, and even a tendency to adopt a sedentary life has been observed. That political insecurity has been the chief cause of the shrinkage of the oases is established by the fact that with the return to settled conditions not only is the encroachment of the desert being arrested but lost oases are being reclaimed.

Man, who is but a secondary cause of desiccation in the Sudan, must be held primarily responsible for the continued activity of the same process in the Sahara. In both regions climatic change is a factor of greater or less importance; but conclusive evidence that it has

THE SAHARA

produced a material change in the general character of the desert since the Romans first attempted its exploration is still wanting.

This view, which has the support of those familiar with the desert to-day, is fully confirmed by the classical authors. The present condition of the desert answers closely to the description of Herodotus, who says: 'Above the coast-line and the country inhabited by the maritime tribes Libya is full of wild beasts; while beyond the wild beast region there is a tract which is wholly sand, very scant of water, and utterly and entirely a desert.'[22] He returns more than once to the utter desolation of this region.[23] Gsell quotes similar passages from Theophrastus, Strabo, Diodorus Siculus, Pomponius Mela, and Seneca.[24]

We are very ignorant about the relationship which existed between Barbary and the Sudan during the Carthaginian and Roman periods, but, as we shall see in the next chapter, evidence is not wanting that in these very early times there was considerable traffic in the desert. There is reason to believe that it was crossed in Punic times before the camel had been introduced into Africa. It is very doubtful whether such a journey could be made under those conditions to-day. It seems likely therefore that the caravan routes were not then so ill provided with water as they are now. The slightly increased rainfall which Gsell thinks North Africa may possibly have enjoyed in Roman times perhaps extended into the desert, affording better facilities for watering and providing more extensive pastures. So much may be conceded without admitting any material change in the general distribution of desert and steppe.[25]

As our knowledge of Barbary, of the Sudan, and of the Sahara increases the more reason have we to believe that little change has taken place in any one of these regions since the dawn of history. The successive waves of invaders which swept across North Africa experienced climatic conditions closely similar to those of to-day. To each the Sahara presented an all but insuperable barrier to regular intercourse with the Sudan and at no period did man contemplate the crossing of the Sahara except as an enterprise involving grave risks and demanding the greatest hardihood.*

* The substance of this chapter was published in *Antiquity*, December 1929.

THE SAHARA

REFERENCES

1. E. F. Gautier, *Sahara Algérien*, Paris, 1908, p. 60 et seq.; Lauzanne, *Bulletin du Comité de l'Afrique Française*, 1921, p. 246.

2. Stéphane Gsell, *Histoire Ancienne de l'Afrique du Nord*, Paris, 1921, vol. i.

3. E. F. Gautier, *Les Siècles obscurs du Maghreb*, Paris, 1927, pp. 14–16.

4. Ibid., op. cit., p. 16.

5. Jugurtha, lxxix. 4.

6. *Bell. Afric.* li. 5; lxix. 5; lxxix. 1.

7. Procopius, *Bell. Vand.* i. 15, 34; *De Aedificiis*, vi. 6.

8. Hist. Augusti, *Hadrian*, xxii. 14.

9. *Res gestae Divi Augusti*, iv. 39.

10. Pliny, *Natural History*, v. 1; viii. 10.

11. Gsell, op. cit., i. 99.

12. *Annales de Géographie*, 1917, xxvi. 377 et seq.; *West Africa*, 1 April 1922; The Gambia, *Annual Report*, 1920.

13. E. F. Gautier, *Sahara Algérien*, Paris, 1908; H. S. W. Edwardes, *Geographical Journal*, 1919, liii. 206; Col. Mangeot, *L'Afrique Française*, 1922, p. 524.

14. H. S. W. Edwardes, loc. cit.; Nigeria, *Annual Report*, 1921; E. W. Bovill, *Journal of the African Society*, 1921, xx. 181–5, 259 et seq.; Sir Hector Duff, *Cotton Growing in Nigeria*, London, 1921, pp. 4, 8; Col. Tilho, *Geographical Journal*, 1920, lvi. 245; Hanns Vischer, *Geographical Journal*, 1909, xxxiii. 259.

15. Commander Hugh Clapperton, *Journal of a Second Expedition to Africa*, London, 1829, p. 219.

16. Nigeria, *Governor's Annual Address*, Lagos, 1924, p. 121.

17. E. F. Gautier, *Sahara Algérien*, Paris, 1908; R. Chudeau, *Sahara Soudanais*, Paris, 1909, pp. 244–55; *Annales de Géographie*, 1916, xxv. 455.

18. Henri Hubert, *Annales de Géographie*, 1917, xxvi. 384.

19. Conrad Kilian, *Au Hoggar*, Paris, 1925, pp. 106, 139–43, 158, 165, 178; W. J. Harding King, *Geographical Journal*, 1919, liii. 49; E. F. Gautier, *Le Sahara*, Paris, 1928, pp. 61–7.

20. *Geographical Journal*, 1930, lxxvi. 133.

21. F. R. Rodd, *People of the Veil*, London, 1926, p. 361.

22. Herodotus, ii. 32.

23. Ibid. iv. 181, 185.

24. Gsell, op. cit., i. 57.

25. E. F. Gautier, *Le Sahara*, Paris, 1928, pp. 100–3.

II. Roman Africa.

II

AFRICA ANTIQUA

'*The* Romans, *carefull Relaters of their great victories, doe speake little of the interior parts of* Affrica.'—RICHARD JOBSON.

THE earliest account of an attempt to penetrate the interior of northern Africa is a story which was related to Herodotus by some natives of Cyrene.[1]

One day, they said, when they were visiting the oracle of Ammon, the Ammonian king told them that five wild young men, sons of Nasamonian chiefs, whose country lay on the Greater Syrtis and extended some distance inland, once set out to explore the desert parts of Libya with the object of penetrating farther than any had done before. Providing themselves with a plentiful supply of water and provisions they traversed the desert in a westerly direction. After travelling for many days over the sand they came to a plain with trees laden with fruit. While they were gathering the fruit they were surprised and seized by some dwarfish negroes whose language they could not understand. They were carried away over extensive marshes till they reached a town of which the inhabitants spoke the same language as their captors. A great river containing crocodiles flowed past the town running from west to east. In due course the adventurous young men returned safely to their own country.

The Ammonian king conjectured that the river was the Nile, a view which Herodotus shared. As neither knew of any other large river in the interior no value attaches to their opinion, which must have been wrong if the Nasamonians, as the story relates, travelled in a westerly direction. That the great river flowing from west to east was the Niger is the least improbable of the many suggestions which have been made.

In the well-known story, also related by Herodotus, of the circumnavigation of Africa by certain Phoenicians under Pharaoh Necho lies the origin of the sea-route to Guinea. This idea of outflanking the Sahara is of immense antiquity and was made use of by the Carthaginians.

Herodotus relates that:

'there is a county in Libya, and a nation, beyond the Pillars of Hercules where they no sooner arrive but forthwith they unlade their wares, and, having

AFRICA ANTIQUA

disposed them after an orderly fashion along the beach, leave them, and returning aboard their ships, raise a great smoke. The natives, when they see the smoke, come down to the shore, and, laying out to view so much gold as they think the worth of the wares, withdraw to a distance. The Carthaginians upon this come ashore and look. If they think the gold enough, they take it and go their way; but if it does not seem to them sufficient, they go aboard ship once more, and wait patiently. Then the others approach and add to their gold, till the Carthaginians are content. Neither party deals unfairly by the other: for they themselves never touch the gold till it comes up to the worth of their goods, nor do the natives ever carry off the goods till the gold is taken away.'[2]

Throughout the history of northern Africa this curious custom of silent trade or dumb barter, as it is also called, has been closely associated with the gold trade of the Senegal basin. There is some reason therefore for supposing that this was the region visited by the Carthaginians, though many attempts have been made to assign a less remote situation.

Of greater interest is the famous Carthaginian expedition to West Africa under Hanno which is a well-authenticated fact of history. Its date is uncertain, but from the spectacular scale on which the expedition was planned it must at least have belonged to a period when Carthage had attained to great power.

Hanno commemorated his expedition by placing an inscription in the temple of Cronos at Carthage from which the details became well known to Greek and Roman authors. We are thus provided with a strikingly valuable piece of evidence that the expedition was an historical fact and no mere legend.

The story of the Periplus of Hanno is briefly as follows. With the object of founding Liby-Phoenician colonies beyond the Pillars of Hercules Hanno sailed with sixty vessels carrying the impossible number of about 30,000 men and women and the necessary stores and equipment. Two days' sail beyond the straits they founded the first colony which they named Thymiaterium, which has been identified with Mehedia at the mouth of the Wady Sebu. Farther westwards they came to a wooded promontory named Soloesis, probably either Cape Cantin or Cape Ghir, on which they built a shrine to Poseidon. Continuing down the coast they founded five more colonies and discovered the River Lixus where they made friends with the pastoral Lixitae.

Having obtained interpreters from the Lixitae the Carthaginians

AFRICA ANTIQUA

continued their voyage along the desert coast. After three days they came to an island which they called Cerne and here they founded a colony. Cerne is now usually believed to have been Herne Island, but there are also good grounds for identifying it with Arguin which is its traditional site.[3]

Continuing their voyage they passed a great river, the Chretes, which was probably the Senegal, and arrived at a lake where they were prevented from landing by the hostility of the natives. They then entered another large river full of crocodiles and hippopotami whence they returned to Cerne. Turning south again they sailed for twelve days along a coast peopled by Aethiopians who fled at their approach. These people spoke a strange language which was incomprehensible to the Lixitae interpreters. Coming next to some tree-clad mountains, which they skirted for two days, they entered a huge gulf which may have been the estuary of the Gambia. After taking in water they followed the coast for five days when they came to another large gulf which the interpreters called the Western Horn and was perhaps Sierra Leone. They landed on an island but were greatly alarmed at night by many fires and the sound of music. Fleeing away, but still following the coast, they came to many streams of fire flowing into the sea, the land being inaccessible on account of the heat. Again seized with fear they hurried on, but for the next four nights they could see the land covered with flames. High overhead towered a fire greater than the rest which appeared to touch the skies. By day they could see that it was a great mountain which they called the Chariot of the Gods and which was probably Cameroon Mountain.

They sailed for three days past streams of fire and then came to a gulf called the Southern Horn which may have been the Gaboon river. Here they discovered an island full of savages most of whom were women. They had hairy skins and the Lixitae interpreters called them Gorillas. They were unsuccessful in their efforts to catch some of the men, but succeeded in capturing three women. These bit and scratched so much that they had to be killed, but their skins were taken back to Carthage. Lack of supplies prevented Hanno from continuing his voyage farther along the coast and he therefore returned home.

Perhaps no voyage in history has provoked more controversy than this expedition. Not one of the many attempts which have been made to reconcile the geography of the narrative with the present

AFRICA ANTIQUA

western sea-board of Africa has been wholly successful. In the last 2,000 years the coast-line may have been modified, but if the fullest allowance be made for this it is still impossible to accept the narrative as an accurate record. It has all the appearance of having been written from memory instead of transcribed from an official log.

Whether the gorillas of the Carthaginians were apes or men is a problem so impossible of solution that it is useless to dwell here on the controversy to which it has given rise.* Of the three skins which were brought back to Carthage two were placed in the temple of Juno where they remained till the destruction of the city by the Romans.[5]

A thousand years elapsed before another effective effort was made to explore this coast. We have no certain knowledge of any such voyage between the times of Hanno and Prince Henry the Navigator. The latter was largely inspired to embark on overseas exploration by the wealth of the trans-Saharan trade which he hoped to divert to the coast to the great commercial advantage of his country. The exploratory part of Hanno's voyage may have had a similar origin, for although the ancient writers are completely silent about Punic trade with the interior of Africa, we have sufficient circumstantial evidence to infer that the Carthaginians traded overland with the Sudan.

Between the Lesser and Greater Syrtis lies one of the most arid regions on the North African littoral. Here the desert impinges on the sea, rendering the coast a singularly inhospitable region, destitute of anything conducive to human settlement or attractive to shipping.

It is, however, from this strip of coast, the Syrtica Regio of the ancients, that the Sudan is most easily reached from the Mediterranean, a circumstance which has always ensured for it a degree of prosperity out of all proportion to its immediate resources. The Carthaginians had no less than four thriving settlements on this part of the coast—Leptis, Gaphara, Oea, and Sabratha—which were linked up with Ifrikia (Tunisia) by a road which had been rendered passable only by laboriously sinking wells and building cisterns. It is difficult to believe that these towns owed their prosperity to any circumstance but their situation at the terminus of the great natural highway for trade with the Sudan.

---

* Mr. H. R. Palmer sees in the word 'gorilla' a possible connexion between the pastoral Lixitae and the pastoral Fulani of to-day, for *gorel* is the diminutive for man in the Fulfulde language.[4]

AFRICA ANTIQUA

According to Herodotus[6] thirty days from this part of the coast, which was known to him as the home of the Lotophagi, lay the country of the Garamantes, the Roman Phazania, and the modern Fezzan.

'The Garamantians', he tells us, 'have four-horse chariots, in which they chase the Troglodyte Aethiopians, who of all the nations whereof any account has reached our ears are by far the swiftest of foot. The Troglodytes feed on serpents, lizards, and other similar reptiles. Their language is unlike that of any other people; it sounds like the screeching of bats.'

The Troglodyte Aethiopians probably inhabited Tibesti where their manner of life, as in many other parts of Africa, is common enough. The name Aethiopian was used generally of the negroid races of the Sudan.

That Herodotus should have known the length of the journey from the coast to Fezzan makes it probable that this natural highway to the Sudan, the well-known Tripoli–Kawar–Chad road, was already in use as a trade route. The Carthaginians are known to have obtained carbuncles from the Garamantes and Gaetuli who also were a desert people.[7] They were, moreover, provided with gold and negro slaves. It is also recorded that a Carthaginian named Mago made three journeys across the desert.[8]

All this points to the existence of commercial intercourse between Carthage and the Sudan. If the story of Mago be true the Carthaginian merchants may themselves have been in the habit of visiting Negroland. However, from our knowledge of trans-Saharan trade in later times, it is more probable that it was in the hands of middlemen who took care that direct communication was not established between the merchants on opposite sides of the desert. This function was perhaps performed by the Garamantes who in later times acted as convoyers of caravans for the Romans. They may well have served the Carthaginians in a similar capacity.

Apart from such direct evidence as we possess, our knowledge of Punic commercial enterprise renders it probable that the Carthaginians did establish trading relations with the Sudan during the thousand years of their dominion in North Africa. They were very secretive about such matters and therefore little information may have been available to foreigners. It was probably with the object of reserving for their own use the Garamantian road to the Sudan that they so carefully fixed their eastern frontier at the Altars of the Philaeni and thus prevented the Greeks from settling in the Syrtica Regio.

c

AFRICA ANTIQUA

During the 500 years of the Roman occupation considerable interest was taken in the interior of the continent. Contemporary authors, however, are completely silent about trade. Roman writers were often guilty of a snobbish contempt for colonial affairs which they betrayed in the small notice they took of really important events at the out-posts of the Empire. To-day it is no uncommon event in North Africa to discover a Roman site of obvious importance to which no reference can be found in contemporary literature. It is therefore not surprising that the commercial affairs of Africa received little notice.

The arguments in favour of trans-Saharan trade in Carthaginian times apply with equal force to the Roman period. Sudan produce was handled in the Roman markets. The towns at the head of the Garamantian caravan road continued to flourish. Leptis in particular attained a high degree of prosperity, becoming a centre of both wealth and culture.

In 19 B.C. a military expedition under Cornelius Balbus, a native of Gades, occupied Fezzan. Amongst the places which he conquered were Cydamus (Ghadames), Tabudium (Tabonie on the Mizda–Murzuk road), Cellaba or Cilliba (Zuila in Fezzan), Rapsa (Ghat), and Garama (Jerma), which was the Garamantian capital. For this campaign a triumph was granted to Cornelius Balbus, the only foreigner, according to Pliny,[9] ever thus honoured.

Whether the effective occupation of Fezzan dates from this period is doubtful. It more probably commenced later. From inscriptions which survived till recently it seems that the Romans remained in occupation till the appearance of the Vandals under Genseric early in the fifth century. Two centuries after its original conquest by Cornelius Balbus, Cydamus was garrisoned by a detachment of the famous Third Augustan Legion from Lambaesis (Lambessa).

The absence of architectural remains in such places as Rapsa, for example, has led some to doubt whether the Roman occupation was as extensive as Pliny would have us believe. But negative evidence of this character has little value. For nearly 2,000 years the natives of North Africa have been in the habit of using Roman monuments as stone quarries for the building of their own houses. Succeeding waves of invaders have played a scarcely less important part in the work of destruction. At Ghadames the only remains of the prolonged Roman occupation are a few Doric and Corinthian columns in the two principal mosques. At Kairwan the Djama El Kebir contains about 300 marble and porphyry columns all of which must have been taken

AFRICA ANTIQUA

from neighbouring Roman or Byzantine buildings of which no traces survive. In the presence of such facts as these we can only wonder that so much still remains.

About A.D. 100 the Romans became engaged in operations against the Aethiopians, in the course of which they probably reached the most southerly limit of their penetration of the interior. The occasion is therefore of some importance to our subject.

Ptolemy, quoting Marinus of Tyre, tells us that

'In regard to the journey from the Garamantes to the Aethiopians Septimius Flaccus, when leading an army from Libya, reached the Aethiopians in three months from the Garamantes, holding a course to the south. Also that Julius Maternus (starting from) the great Leptis and marching from Garama in company with the King of the Garamantes towards (against?) the Aethiopians travelling towards the south, arrived in four months at Agisymba a district or province of the Aethiopians where rhinoceroses congregate.'

Ptolemy is reluctant to credit the length of these journeys,

'because the further Aethiopians are not separated so much from the Garamantes as to be distant a three months' journey, even these being more Aethiopians, or Negroes, than those of Agisymba, and being subject to the same king as the others, and also because it is altogether absurd that the journey made by the armies of the king should have been entirely in one direction, namely, from north to south (those people being widely spaced and scattered here and there towards the East and West).'*[10]

That Agisymba was the country of Air has found wide acceptance amongst commentators. Air has so far yielded no Roman remains and, as Mr. F. R. Rodd has shown,[11] in their absence it seems more probable that Tibesti was the region referred to. The principal objection to Air is that it is not at all easily accessible from Fezzan and would certainly not have been visited by the Romans except for some pressing need of which there is no evidence. Tibesti, on the other hand, lies close to the natural road leading southward from Fezzan to Negroland which, we believe, was then in use as a trade route and therefore would scarcely have been ignored by the Romans. When the Arabs and after them the Turks found themselves, like the Romans, in occupation of Fezzan and desirous of extending their authority southward, both penetrated to Tibesti, but neither reached Air. The same writer has also pointed out that whereas in Air there are no names similar to Bardetus and Mesche, which are mentioned

* This translation has been kindly supplied by Mr. Edward Heawood.

C 2

AFRICA ANTIQUA

by Ptolemy[12] as the names of mountains in Agisymba, there are in Tibesti a Bardai and a Miski.*

It would certainly not have required three months to reach Tibesti or even Air, which Ptolemy says it took to reach the Aethiopians from the Garamantes, but this period loses the importance which Ptolemy attaches to it when it is recalled that the occasion was a military expedition, hampered by the problems of supply and transport and probably harassed by hostile nomads. It certainly gives no justification for the supposition of some that the Romans reached the Niger. The likelihood of discovering a Roman monument somewhere in the Sudan is remote, but it is a possibility which stirs the imagination.

The Roman road to Fezzan closely followed the present route through Mizda and Gharian, which once held a Roman garrison, and over the Hammada el Homra. Barth[14] has described the numerous monuments which he found scattered along this route and extending as far south as Jerma (Garama) but no farther. The Romans at first had difficulty in keeping it open on account of predatory bands of Garamantes who used to fill the wells with sand. It seems to have been permanently opened about the time of Vespasian and was known as the *iter praeter caput saxi*,† a name which still survives among the Arabs who call it Bab Ras el Hammada, the Gate of the Head of the Desert.[16] Perhaps the effective occupation of Fezzan dates only from this time.

One of the most important events in the history of northern Africa was the introduction of the camel. Through insufficient study of the evidence available there has been much unnecessary doubt as to when this occurred. The wide distribution throughout this region of the remains of a strange quaternary camel has led some to believe that the camel of to-day has existed in Africa continuously since before the dawn of history. On the other hand, there is also a deeply rooted belief that the camel made its first appearance with the Arabs. The quaternary animal, however, did not survive into the historic period, and the Arabs found camels already in general use when they first invaded North Africa.

* Mr. Rodd's discovery in the Anu Maqaran valley of a rock-drawing which may represent oxen pulling a chariot recalls the four-horse chariots of the Garamantians and may prove to have an important bearing on this question.[13]

† Ad Garamantes iter inexplicabile adhuc fuit... proximo bello, quod cum Œensibus Romani gessere initiis Vespasiani Imperatoris, compendium viae quatridui deprehensum est. Hoc iter vocatur Praeter Caput Saxi.[15]

AFRICA ANTIQUA

The introduction of this animal indubitably belongs to the period of the Roman occupation, previous to which it did not exist in Africa. Herodotus does not mention it in his detailed account of the animals of Libya, nor is there a single reference to it in our extensive records of the Carthaginian period. Had it been in use in the early part of the Roman occupation Marius in his campaign against Jugurtha would scarcely have been so foolish as to embark on desert operations with only horse transport.

Sallust records that the first occasion on which Roman troops saw camels was not in Africa but in Asia during the campaign of Lucullus against Mithridates. Pliny,[17] who had travelled in Africa, states that the camel belonged to Asia. Evidently it was not found in Africa in Carthaginian, or even early Roman times.

The camel is first heard of in Africa early in 46 B.C., at the battle of Thapsus when the booty captured by Caesar from Juba included twenty-two of these animals.[18] They long remained scarce. Not till the middle of the fourth century do we hear of them in any numbers. In 363 Romanus demanded 4,000 camels from Leptis Magna for the supply of his army and they were duly delivered.[19] Leptis, situated as it was at the head of the Garamantian road to the Sudan, probably had greater use for camels than any other place in North Africa. It is not therefore surprising that we should first hear of them in large numbers here rather than elsewhere. In Byzantine times they were constantly referred to by contemporary writers and were evidently in general use.

Whether the Romans were directly responsible for the introduction of the camel is uncertain. It is possible that in their administration of North Africa they found themselves confronted by transport difficulties which in Asia they had solved by using this animal. They may, moreover, have perceived how greatly the economic development of Africa would be accelerated by its introduction. Either or both of these considerations might have prompted them to import camels from Asia.

The migrations of domestic animals are so frequently associated with the migrations of peoples that it is probably significant that the appearance of the camel in Roman Africa closely synchronized with the first arrival of the Zenata in the same region. These nomadic Berbers, who were destined many centuries later to give the western Maghreb the powerful dynasties of the Merinids of Fez and the Abd el Wadites of Tlemcen, came from the east by way of Cyrene.[20]

AFRICA ANTIQUA

Whether this migration was inspired or fostered by the Romans we are unable to say, but that the Zenata were responsible for bringing the camel into general use throughout Gaetulia and the steppes of the High Plateaux seems probable.

However it came about the arrival of the camel was an event of such far-reaching consequences that it marked the commencement of a new era in the history of northern Africa. The field for human endeavour broadened before men's eyes and the economic life of the whole community was affected. Man could now use the remotest pastures of the desert and exploit the fertility of the most distant oases. The desert caravan routes lost more than half their terrors and new roads were opened up for trade.

But with all these changes there appeared a type of man altogether new to Africa, the camel-owning nomad, turbulent, predatory, and infinitely mobile. Thus civilization found itself faced with a menace from which it has never since been wholly free. But the dominion of Rome was already over and it fell to the Byzantine army to combat this new enemy which the Roman legions had never known.

REFERENCES

1. Herodotus, ii. 32, 33.
2. Ibid. iv. 196.
3. H. R. Palmer, *The Carthaginian Voyage to West Africa in 500 B.C.*, Bathurst, 1931, pp. i, 14.
4. H. R. Palmer, *Sudanese Memoirs*, Lagos, 1928, iii. 67.
5. Pliny, vi. 36.
6. Herodotus, iv. 183.
7. Strabo, xvii. 3, 19; Pliny, xxxvii. 92.
8. Athenee, ii. 22, 44, 2.
9. Pliny, v. 5.
10. Ptolemy, i. 8.
11. F. R. Rodd, *People of the Veil*, pp. 318 et seq.
12. Ptolemy, iv. 9.
13. F. R. Rodd, op. cit., p. 321.
14. H. Barth, *Travels in North and Central Africa*, London, 1857–8, i, ch. v.
15. Pliny, loc. cit.
16. F. R. Rodd, op. cit., p. 323.
17. Pliny, viii. 26.
18. *Bell. Afric.* lxviii.
19. Ammianus Marcellinus, xxviii. 6, 5.
20. E. F. Gautier, *Les Siècles Obscurs du Maghreb*, pp. 192, 202.

III

RACES OF MAN

'This part of the worlde is inhabited especially by . . . the Africans or Moores, properly so called; which last are of two kinds, namely white or tawnie Moores, and Negros or blacke Moores.'—JOHN PORY.

BEFORE the Arab invasions of the seventh and eleventh centuries the interior of northern Africa was peopled by two distinct types of man, negroid and non-negroid. The latter, who were northern Hamites, were called Libyans by the Romans and Berbers by the Arabs, the last name being derived from the Latin *barbari*. The negroid peoples, infused with varying degrees of Hamitic blood, inhabited the Sahara, but they were particularly associated with the more southerly regions to which the Arabs later gave the name of Beled es Sudan, or the Land of the Blacks.

Included among the Libyans or Berbers were the Saharan races whom the Romans called Gaetuli in the north-west, Garamantes in Fezzan, and Nobatae in the Nile valley. They are believed to have belonged to an ancient Kushite stock which, long before the Christian era, had been driven from southern Arabia across the Straits of Bab-el-Mandeb into Africa. They were known as Gara. In Fezzan there survive ruins of Garama, one of their cities, from which it is apparent that they were not wholly barbarous.[1] The swift-footed Aethiopians of Herodotus, who are represented to-day by the Tebu or Teda of Tibesti, belonged to the same stock. These Gara tribes, who were later known to the Arabs as Su or So, fused with the negroes and became the ancestors of some of the Sudanese peoples such as the Mandingo tribes of Soninke and Wangara in the west and the Garawan or Guraan in the east.

Not less important than the Gara were the Libyan nomads of the desert whom we to-day call Tuareg. They were known to the Arab writers as Muleththemin. They are a tall, slender, long-faced, fair-skinned people whose children often have fair wavy hair which afterwards turns black. Their most striking characteristic is the curious custom of the men of covering the face with a *litham*, or veil, leaving only the eyes exposed. It was from this that the Arab name of Muleththemin, meaning the Veiled People, was derived. The history of the Tuareg has been traced back fairly clearly to the time of the

RACES OF MAN

Arab invasions when they were already occupying the whole of the central and western Sahara. But they are recognizable in the writings of Corippus, Ptolemy, and other early writers by their names and habits. For example the nomadic Ausuriani, Mazices, and Ifuraces, who inhabited the Garamantian kingdom, all seem to have been Tuareg. The Ausuriani of Synesius, the Arzuges of Orosius, and the Astacures of Ptolemy have all been identified with the modern Azger who for fourteen centuries have occupied very much the same region as they do now. The Ifuraces of Corippus are to-day represented by the Ifoghas, a tribe of the Azger, whose habitat is also close to that of their ancestors.

In Roman and Byzantine times the Tuareg seem not to have been veiled, for there is no mention of this most striking characteristic in the works of contemporary writers. Mr. F. R. Rodd thinks that they adopted the veil between A.D. 600 and 1000. They are divided into several groups of tribes, the most important division historically being the Sanhaja, who for a time headed a confederation of all the Tuareg, which broke up on the death of Ibn Ghania in about A.D. 1233. In each tribe the existence of two classes is recognized, Imajeghan or nobles and Imghad or serfs. Their language is Temajegh, and their alphabet, known as T'ifinagh, is partly derived from the ancient Libyan script.[2]

The Tuareg, whom the Arabs sometimes call the Christians of the Desert, are Muhammadans, but they retain many beliefs belonging to an earlier religion. There is a considerable body of evidence pointing to their having once been Christians. In spite of now being Muslims they are monogamous and their favourite motif in ornament is the cross. Their shields often bear the cross crosslet of heraldry, depicted rising out of a sea of light. Their swords are cross-hilted, the great pommels of their camel saddles take the form of a cross, and the same symbol is much used by their leather- and metal-workers. We also find it in the T'ifinagh script. Evidence of another kind is afforded by the Temajegh language which contains many words indicating a Christian origin. Two striking examples are *Mesi*, meaning God, and *andjelous*, meaning angel. The names Samuel, David, and Saul, which are rarely used by the Arabs of Africa, are common among Tuareg. It is evident that at some time during their history the Tuareg were at least influenced by Christianity. That they were themselves Christians is a theory which is receiving increasingly wide acceptance, especially among those who know them best.[3] Traces of Christianity have been noted in Bornu, especially among the Kanem

RACES OF MAN 25

tribes, and Sultan Bello of Sokoto declared that the chiefs of the Gobirawa were Copts. When we recall how deeply Christianity was rooted in North Africa and how frequently Christians were forced to seek refuge in the desert from their oppressors it would be surprising not to find some traces of the Christian religion in the interior.

In their capacity of caravan drivers the Tuareg played a vitally important part in the history of the interior of northern Africa. Four great natural roads have always linked the north with the south. These were the Sijilmasa–Walata road leading to the gold-bearing countries of the Senegal and upper Niger; the Ghadames–Ghat road to Air and the fertile Hausa country; the Tripoli–Fezzan–Kawar road to Lake Chad; and, in the extreme east, the Cyrenaica–Kufra–Wadai road. The first three of these have been controlled by the Tuareg throughout the greater part of their recorded history. The Tuareg shared, however, the Sijilmasa–Walata road with the Berabish who were Berberized Arabs, probably of Himyaritic origin. It was the Tuareg who dug and maintained the desert wells and secured them and the pastures for the use of passing caravans. They too were the transport contractors whose services were always available to merchants in the northern and southern termini of the trade routes.

To the Tuareg, who were never able to free themselves wholly from dependence on outside supplies, the maintenance of the carrying-trade of the Sahara was an economic necessity. They levied tolls and other forms of blackmail on foreign merchants using the roads they controlled, but they were careful never to impose burdens greater than the trade could afford. Although the control of wells and pastures was a frequent source of inter-tribal strife within the desert these feuds were seldom allowed to interfere with trade. That the negroid races were never cut off from the influence of Mediterranean culture and that the wealth of the far interior was always accessible to the mercantile communities of the western world were due to the Tuareg and constitute their greatest contribution to the history of civilization. But for them the Sahara might for long have proved an insuperable barrier to human intercourse instead of a highway for trade and culture.

Ibn Khaldun[4] divided the Berbers into Zenata, the nomadic people with whose arrival the introduction of the camel into Africa seems to be closely associated, and two older groups descended from two eponymous heroes, Beranes and Madghis. These two groups are perhaps represented to-day by the two distinct stocks which can still be

RACES OF MAN

recognized in many North African communities. He divides the Beranes group into several divisions of whom four—Lemta, Sanhaja, Ketama, and Auriga—he calls Muleththemin, that is to say Tuareg. The Luata or Levata, who elsewhere have been classed as Tuareg, he included in the Madghis group which is also called Botr. He introduces other divisions of Muleththemin, including Jedala or Guedala, Lemtuna—a subdivision of the Sanhaja and not to be confused with the Lemta—Utzila, Targa, Mesufa, and Zaghawa.[5]

In the sixteenth century Leo Africanus divided the Sahara from west to east into five areas. In the west were his first and second areas peopled by Sanhaja and Zanziga respectively, who, if not actually the same people, were very closely related. The third area, which included Air and Tuat, was peopled by Targa. Next on the east came the fourth area stretching from Air to Tibesti and inhabited by Lemta. Finally farthest east lay his fifth and last area, the home of the Berdeoa, between whom and the Nile valley lived Blacks. The Sanhaja, Zanziga, Targa, and Lemta were all Tuareg. Not so the Berdeoa who are to-day represented by the Tebu or Teda of Tibesti—they were Gara.[6]

The Muleththemin are believed by many to have arrived in Africa as part of a Himyaritic invasion from southern Arabia which followed approximately the same route as the much earlier migration of the Gara peoples. This belief, which seems to have originated with Ibn Khaldun, is rejected by Rodd, who believes that the Tuareg arrived in Africa from the eastern Mediterranean at a very remote date. He has satisfied himself that the Libyan captives depicted in certain Egyptian paintings and sculptures are really Tuareg. He has also pointed out the striking similarity between the names of certain Libyan tribes described in Egyptian records of the Vth and XIXth Dynasties and those of certain extant and recent Tuareg clan names. He suggests that the traditional historians of the Tuareg seized upon the memory of a Himyaritic invasion to establish a connexion for their people with the land of the Prophet, a common weakness among Muslims.[7]

The Zaghawa (the Arabic name for a people otherwise known as Shama), whom Ibn Khaldun classed as Muleththemin, now survive under that name only in Wadai, to the east of Lake Chad. They were once much more widely distributed and played an important part in the history of the Sudan. At a period probably subsequent to the first Arab invasion of North Africa they established themselves as a ruling aristocracy over the negroid descendants of the Gara from the borders

RACES OF MAN

of Abyssinia in the east to the Senegal in the west. The rise of more than one powerful Western Sudanese kingdom can be traced to Zaghawa influence. They are credited with having introduced into the Sudan the elements of metal working, and some, probably wrongly, attributed to them the introduction of the camel into the same region.[8] Throughout Hausa, Dendi, and Borgu there is a caste of artificers, metal-workers, and leather-workers known variously as Zogoran, Zugu, Zugurma, Zoromawa, and Jawambe, who are distinct from the rest of the population and are probably of Zaghawa stock.[9]

Generally speaking, modern opinion supports the view of Ibn Khaldun, and regards the Zaghawa as cognate to the Tuareg and as probably belonging to the Sanhaja group. The Zaghawa of to-day, however, appear to be a mixture of several elements.*

At the beginning of the Christian era the Jews formed a considerable element in the population of the North African littoral whence they spread far into the interior. The most important southward migration of Jewish tribes was probably that which took place in A.D. 115 after a rebellion in Cyrenaica against the Romans. The migrants followed two different routes. One body travelled southward through Air and across the Bend of the Niger to the Senegal and Futa. Here they were later joined by the other body who had taken a more westerly route through southern Morocco and the Mauritanian Adrar. As the result of these movements the Jews became widely scattered throughout the whole of the interior of northern Africa. In the oases of the Sahara Jewish communities long preserved their identity, but in the Sudan they were soon absorbed in the great mass of the native population among whom traces of Jewish blood may still frequently be noticed. Probably no people of the Western Sudan contains a greater element of Jewish blood than the pastoral Fulani who were occupying Futa when the two converging waves of migrant Jews finally met there. The subsequent eastward expansion of the Fulani carried Jewish blood to the shores of Lake Chad, which they probably reached at the end of the thirteenth century. There they founded the present Fulani settlements in Darfur, Bagarmi, and Mandara.[10]

The racial situation in North Africa was destined to be completely altered by the Arab invasions of the seventh and eleventh centuries. These, however, were preceded by the less important Vandal invasion of the fifth century, historically interesting but without much

---

* Mr. H. A. MacMichael describes the Zaghawa as a mixture of Hamitic Tebu and negro, with Libyo-Berber affinities.[9]

RACES OF MAN

permanent effect. The governor of Africa at this time was Count Boniface to whom had been entrusted the task of restoring order after the chaos caused by the excesses of the Donatists. By an unfortunate combination of circumstances he was forced into rebellion against the Empire and in 428 he invited the Vandals to come over from Spain to his assistance. They gladly responded and under their leader Genseric a rabble 80,000 to 90,000 strong landed on the shores of Africa. Boniface soon perceived the gravity of his blunder, but it was too late. Genseric was hailed as a deliverer and the whole country was thrown into turmoil. All the elements of disorder which Boniface had successfully held in check now broke loose. The Donatists eagerly sided with the invader to whom they were bound by a common hatred of the Church. Genseric marched eastwards and occupied Carthage. He secured himself against interference from overseas by an alliance with Attila. Of his administration we know little. He had, however, enough wisdom to retain the elaborate machinery of government which he found existing and thereby he succeeded in maintaining order. The persecution of the Church continued relentlessly and many Christians, as in the times of Roman oppression, sought refuge in the desert. With the death of Genseric in 477 the administration broke down and chaos supervened once more.

In 533 a Byzantine army led by Belisarius landed on the shores of the Syrtis. Like the Vandals before them, they were hailed as deliverers. The Vandals, from the first few in numbers and now enervated by ease and luxury, were no longer capable of serious resistance. Within three months of his arrival Belisarius was able to report to Justinian that Africa was Roman again. But after his return to Byzantium the Berbers began once more to assert their old love of liberty. The eunuch Solomon was next sent to reduce the country to order. To-day there are many ruined fortresses widely scattered over the country which testify to the energy and vigour of this general. But the spirit of rebellion continued to smoulder, till finally it burst into flame and Solomon was forced to seek safety overseas. For another century the country continued to be devastated by wars and Byzantine dominion shrunk till little was left but Carthage and the neighbouring sea-board. This was shortly to be swept away by the Arab flood which was about to burst upon the country.

The first advance of the Arabs westward from Egypt began in 642. Impelled no longer by religious zeal (for that had spent itself) but by sheer lust for conquest they fell upon the countries of the North

RACES OF MAN

African littoral which they called the Maghreb or the West. In 647 the Prefect Gregory, who had recently declared himself independent of Byzantium, was defeated at Sufetula (Sbeitla) and Byzantine rule in Africa practically ended. The Arabs chose for their head-quarters a site situated at the head of the sea-board road to Egypt and sufficiently far from the coast to be safe from the Byzantine fleet. Here in the heart of the central Maghreb they built the city of Kairwan.

A lull of thirty years followed during which the Muslim world was wholly occupied with schisms in its own ranks. Most of the great sects of Islam took their origin in this period. In 678 the attack on Africa was renewed under Okba ibn Nafi. The Arabs swept the whole length and breadth of the country. In the west they reached the shores of the Atlantic. Southward they occupied Fezzan and reached the oasis of Kawar, but they turned back as they were on the point of discovering the grasslands of the Sudan. Some settled in Tuat and other oases of the desert whence, after intermarriage with the Jews, they migrated farther south. Such was the origin of the Kunta Arabs of the southwestern Sahara. When the Arab triumph seemed complete the Berber love of liberty surged suddenly to the surface and produced one of those supreme national efforts which, at the moment of crisis, have so often saved the conquered from extinction. Joined at last by the Greeks they rallied under one of their own kings, Koceila, and destroyed Okba and his army near Biskra in 683. They razed Kairwan and drove the rest of the Arabs back into Egypt. 'The conquest of Africa', declared an Arab governor, 'is impossible; scarcely has a Berber tribe been exterminated when another comes to take its place.'

A few years later Hassan, the Governor of Egypt, set out resolved finally to subdue the Maghreb. He rebuilt Kairwan, destroyed Carthage, and swept the few remaining Byzantines into the sea. Once more the Berbers rallied, this time under a Zenata prophetess named Kahenah who drove the Arabs back and for long held them at bay. But in 703 she too was defeated. Five years later the Arabs under Musa ibn Noceir again swept the country from east to west. In 711, greatly reinforced by Berber converts, they invaded Spain, where they developed that wonderful civilization which was in such marked contrast with the profound ignorance prevailing throughout the rest of Europe. In Africa the Arabs achieved neither power nor culture. The history of the next three centuries, during which the Arab and Berber wrestled for supremacy in the Maghreb, is confused

30   RACES OF MAN

and obscure, but by the beginning of the eleventh century the invaders had once more been driven from the Maghreb.

In the middle of the century Africa was again invaded, this time by the Beni Hillal and Beni Soleim. These Arabs were the Bedawin, marauding nomads who had been driven from Arabia into Egypt. The Fatimite Khalif of Cairo, anxious to rid his country of such turbulent guests, urged them to make a home for themselves in the Maghreb, which he no longer pretended to control. They eagerly poured into the country, 200,000 strong, slaying and destroying and penetrating far into the interior, and this time making good their hold. This, the Hillalian invasion as it is usually called, has been likened to a swarm of locusts devouring the whole country over which it passed. As the result of the devastation wrought by these wild tribes of marauders enormous areas went permanently out of cultivation and the desert crept in. These Arabs, directly or through their herds, destroyed much of the forests of North Africa which, owing to the long rainless summer, can never have been very extensive. This caused the great shortage of shipbuilding timber which in later times became a serious embarrassment to their piratical seafaring descendants.

The persistence with which the Berbers have maintained their nationality and temperament has constantly astonished ethnologists. In spite of the introduction into their country of Phoenician, Roman, Vandal, Arab, Jewish, and Negro blood they show few traces of alien stock. Particularly striking is the way in which the Berbers and Arabs have refused to amalgamate. Although they have lived in closest proximity for over a thousand years, during which the Arab has imposed his religion, language, dress, and many of his customs on a large part of the Berber community, the latter have preserved their distinct racial type. The Arab remains essentially a herdsman, dwelling in tents, fanatical and deeply superstitious, with a feudal tribal organization. The Berber, on the other hand, is a highlander, a tiller of the soil, and a dweller in towns and villages, and essentially democratic. Although capable of fanatical outbursts he is rarely moved by religious enthusiasms.[11]

RACES OF MAN

REFERENCES

1. H. Duveyrier, *Les Touareg du Nord*, Paris, 1864, p. 279.

2. M. Reygasse, *Gravures Rupestres et Inscriptions Tifinar' du Sahara Central*, Algiers 1932; H. Duveyrier, op. cit., p. 317; F. R. Rodd, op. cit., pp. 327, 356; H. R. Palmer, 'The Tuareg of the Sahara', *Journal of the African Society*, xxxi, 1932.

3. A. Richer, *Les Oulliminden*, Paris, 1924, pp. 34–8; F. R. Rodd, *People of the Veil*, pp. 275–8; H. Barth, *Travels*, i. 227–8; O. Bates, *The Eastern Libyans*, London, 1914, ch. viii.

4. Ibn Khaldun, *Histoire des Berbères*, Paris, 1925, i. 167 et seq.

5. Ibid. ii. 64.

6. Leo Africanus, *History and Description of Africa*, Hakluyt Society, London, 1896, i. 127, 151.

7. F. R. Rodd, *The Times*, 30 March 1928.

8. H. R. Palmer, *Journal of the African Society*, xxvi (1926–7), 224; H. Barth, *Travels*, iv. 175.

9. H. A. MacMichael, *A History of the Arabs of the Sudan*, Cambridge, 1922, i. 54.

10. H. R. Palmer, *Journal of the African Society*, xxii (1922–3), 126.

11. A. H. Keane, *Man Past and Present*, Cambridge, 1920, pp. 470–2.

IV

MEDIEVAL ARABIC WRITERS

Our ancient Chroniclers of Africa, to wit, Bichri and Meshudi, knew nothing of the land of Negros but only the regions of Guechet and Cano.—LES AFRICANUS.

THE amazing development of Arab learning in the Middle Ages, which contrasted so strangely with the barbarous ignorance in which Christian Europe was still sunk, sprang from the Hellenistic culture which the Arabs had inherited from the late Roman Empire. Greek literature, which had been translated into eastern languages by the Oriental Christian Churches, profoundly influenced the intellectual outlook of the Arabs, and so stimulating did it prove that almost every branch of science still bears the impress of Arab work. To no subject did they make greater contribution than to geography. Their geographical science was based on the works of Ptolemy, which had been translated into Arabic by Christians, but it was leavened with Persian and Indian theory.

A great stimulus to geographical research and travel was provided by the vast extent and cosmopolitan character of the Islamic world in which racial differences counted for little. Throughout its length and breadth the Muhammadan traveller was sure of a welcome wherever he went. Among isolated Muslim communities in infidel lands the same hospitality awaited him. There is perhaps no more striking example of the extraordinary breadth of the Muslim horizon than the well-known incident in the life of Ibn Battuta, the fourteenth-century traveller, who, while staying at Sijilmasa in southern Morocco, discovered that his host was the brother of a man he had met some years before in western China.

A further incentive to travel and therefore to the study of geography was the *Hadj* or pilgrimage to Mecca the performance of which was obligatory on every Muhammadan who had the strength and means to perform it. Throughout the Muhammadan era countless caravans of pilgrims have annually set out from all quarters of the Muslim world to perform this pious duty. Thus men of many different nations have constantly been brought together in the holy cities, meeting there on common ground and exchanging information about each other's lands.

Trade provided yet another great stimulus to travel and geographical research. The Prophet had been a merchant and consequently in no

MEDIEVAL ARABIC WRITERS

community in the world do followers of that calling enjoy greater prestige than among Muhammadans. Their commercial enterprise took them eastwards to farther India and China and southwards into the Indian Ocean and the Sudan. Evidence of the remarkable extent of their fur trade with the north is provided by the enormous finds of Muhammadan coins on the shores of the Baltic and the note of an Arab geographer that at one of their markets the night was but an hour long.[1]

Arab writers were mostly men of wide interests who were seldom content to confine themselves to a single subject. Many of the great number who earned reputations as geographers had equal claims to recognition as authorities on other branches of learning, especially the allied subject of history. Masudi earned his reputation as the greatest of Arab geographers from a work called 'Meadows of Gold and Mines of Gems'[2] into which he claimed to have compressed everything that an educated man should know. The Arabs, like their predecessors the Greeks, based their geographical work on the reports and itineraries of travellers combined with mathematical calculations. Many of them spent years in travel for the purpose of collecting first-hand information.

Before the coming of the Arabs nothing was known of Africa south of the Sahara, and we owe practically the whole of our knowledge of the early history of the Western Sudan to a handful of Arabic authors. The chief of these were Masudi, Ibn Haukal, El Bekri, El Idrisi, Yaqut, El Omari, Ibn Battuta, and Ibn Khaldun. Our debt to these learned men is so great that a brief notice of each cannot be omitted from a volume largely based on their writings.

Masudi's contribution to our subject was not great. But he deserves our recognition because his work profoundly influenced those who came later and included extensive notices of the Sudan in their own writings. Masudi[1] was a native of Baghdad. The date of his birth has not been recorded, but we know he died in A.D. 956. He spent twenty years wandering through the countries of the Islamic world and his travels are believed to have taken him as far as China and Madagascar. He had a remarkably correct idea of the shape, size, and motion of the earth, therein showing himself to be immeasurably ahead of contemporary Christian thought. He believed the Atlantic, the Green Sea of Darkness, to be impossible of navigation. His notice of the Sudan is confined to a reference to the curious silent trade in gold.

Ibn Haukal,[3] who was almost contemporary with Masudi, was also

D

MEDIEVAL ARABIC WRITERS

a native of Baghdad. He spent twenty-five years in travel and claimed to have collected into his 'Book of Ways and Provinces' all that had 'ever made geography of interest either to princes or to peoples'. He was one of the only two medieval Arabic writers, whose works have survived, to visit the Sudan. Brief though it is, his is the earliest account we have of the Western Sudan, of which he is the first known explorer. He visited Audoghast and Ghana and saw the Niger flowing eastwards which led him to believe it to be the Nile of Egypt. He had unhappily a profound contempt for the negroes of whom he wrote: 'I have not described the country of the African blacks and the other peoples of the torrid zone; because naturally loving wisdom, ingenuity, religion, justice and regular government, how could I notice such people as these, or magnify them by inserting an account of their countries?'

The eleventh century saw the appearance of a work of supreme importance to the student of North African history. The author was Abu Obeid El Bekri,[4] an Arab of an illustrious family which had formerly enjoyed considerable power in Spain under the Ommeyads. El Bekri was born about 1028. He spent his youth in Cordova, and on the death of his father he took up a post at the court of Almina. He spent the whole of his life in Spain where he produced a remarkable series of works. They included a discourse on the divine message of Muhammad, a survey of the plants and trees of Andalusia, a notable treatise on general geography called *El Mecalek wa'l Memalek* (Roads and Kingdoms), and numerous poems. Only two of his writings have come down to us. Firstly his *Modjam*, or dictionary, of which the libraries of Leyden and Milan each have a copy; and secondly a part of his great geographical work which in its entirety filled many volumes. It contained a remarkable description of northern Africa upon which historians and geographers of all ages have drawn very liberally. His description of the Sudan is particularly interesting, for it represents the earliest attempt to give a general survey of the country. From the high degree of accuracy which is maintained throughout it is evident that the author, who never visited Africa himself, had access to documents of the first importance. The source of a great part of the information which he made known to the world is believed to have been the official archives of Cordova. He died in 1094. The British Museum has the best copy of his geographical work and there is another in the Bibliothéque Nationale in Paris.

MEDIEVAL ARABIC WRITERS

In the first half of the twelfth century there appeared a work which was the most considerable contribution to geographical science since the days of Masudi. The author was El Idrisi,[5] a Spanish Arab in the service of Roger II, the Norman king of Sicily, who himself played an important part in its production. Although Idrisi enjoyed a reputation as a great geographer in three continents we know very little of his life. No doubt Muslim writers of the period looked askance at one who had forsaken his own country to enter the service of an infidel prince, especially at a period when the Crusades had engendered the bitterest hatred between Christians and Muslims.

Idrisi belonged to a family which claimed descent from the Prophet. His grandfather had ruled as Emir of Malaga, but after being exiled to Africa his family settled in Ceuta where Idrisi was born in about 1100, during the Almoravid occupation. He was probably educated in Cordova. After travelling widely in Spain, North Africa, and Asia Minor he received an invitation from Roger of Sicily to come and help him in his geographical work.

Roger was a patron of all the sciences but geography was his ruling passion. He collected all the Arab treatises he could find on his subject, and constantly sought out travellers who might be able to give reliable accounts of countries about which he required information. After spending fifteen years amassing an immense quantity of valuable material he sent for Idrisi to reduce it to order. The work of collecting material continued under Idrisi's supervision and it culminated in 1154 in the production of the famous *Book of Roger* or, as it is sometimes called, the Rogerian Description of the World, for which the Arab was chiefly responsible. Idrisi, like Masudi, held the globular theory of the earth and he still adhered to the old custom of dividing the world into seven climates. It was, however, his accurate description of Europe and his sympathy with western thought, both products of his environment, which distinguished Idrisi above other Arab geographers.

A much abridged edition of Idrisi's *Book of Roger* was printed by the Medici at Rome in 1592, but the whole work was not published till the first half of the nineteenth century when Jaubert translated into French two manuscripts which had been acquired by the Imperial Library in Paris. The Bodleian possesses a manuscript copy which was written in Cairo in 1456.

The next Arabic author to make a contribution to our knowledge of the Sudan was Yaqut[6] of whom we know very little. His parents

36 MEDIEVAL ARABIC WRITERS

were Greeks, but when still a child he was carried off and sold as a slave to a merchant in Baghdad where he was carefully educated. He made many trading journeys in the service of his master and thereby acquired a wide knowledge of the world. His great work was a geographical dictionary based on the works of earlier geographers, but enriched with valuable material which he himself had collected during his extensive travels. His references to the Sudan are not very considerable. He died in 1200.

We possess no thirteenth-century work in Arabic of much value to us, but adequate compensation was provided by the rich output of Muslim writers in the first half of the fourteenth. The first of these was the *Geography* of Abulfeda (1273–1331), a native of Damascus whose early life was spent fighting against the Crusaders. His geographical work was based on the writings of his predecessors and is of no great interest to our present subject. Of greater importance was the work of El Omari, an Arab of Damascus, born in 1301, who entered the service of the Sultan of Egypt in 1332. After a few years in Cairo he returned to his native city where he devoted himself to literary pursuits. He died in Damascus in 1349. His *Masalik el Absar*[7] is a geographical compilation with a wide field based upon the works of earlier writers, but supplemented by material collected orally by himself. Its importance to us is the account it gives of the memorable pilgrimage of Mansa Musa, the Emperor of Mali.

Contemporary with El Omari were two far greater men of letters who will always be regarded as ornaments of Arab civilization. These were Ibn Battuta, one of the most remarkable travellers in history, and Ibn Khaldun, the famous scholar to whose work we owe so much of our knowledge of early Berber and Arab history.

Ibn Battuta was born in 1304 at Tangier where his family, who belonged to the Berber tribe of the Luata, had been settled for several generations. He received the education of a theologian and at the age of twenty-one set out on the pilgrimage to Mecca, thus receiving at an early age the stimulus which produced so many great Muslim travellers.

His pilgrimage completed, he visited the Middle East, but soon returned to Mecca where he spent three years in study and devotion. After a tour of the Arab trading stations down the east coast of Africa, Ibn Battuta set out for India with the object of sharing in the boundless hospitality with which the reigning Sultan of Delhi was attracting to his court theologians and scholars from all parts of the world. He

MEDIEVAL ARABIC WRITERS

37

followed a circuitous route through Asia Minor, which provided a welcome opportunity for visiting Constantinople, and over the steppes of Central Asia to Khurasan. During this long journey he was enthusiastically received by the local religious communities and he collected a growing throng of followers besides considerable personal wealth. His caravan must have presented an imposing spectacle as it entered India where his reputation as a scholar had preceded him. The manner of his reception was satisfying to his vanity and his immediate appointment as Malikite Qadi of Delhi scarcely less so to his purse. After spending seven years here he was sent by the Sultan on a special mission to the great Mongol Emperor of China. He set out in considerable state, but he was attacked by his enemies soon after leaving Delhi and became a fugitive.

After wandering down the Malabar coast he made his way to the Maldive Islands. The inhabitants, who can seldom have been visited by a scholar of equal eminence, welcomed him warmly and made him qadi. The zeal, however, with which he carried out his duties proved so irksome to the islanders that after eighteen months among them he found it expedient to leave their shores. We find him next in Ceylon and afterwards in Assam, visiting a famous sheikh of that country. He then set out once more for China, successfully adopting the role of ambassador. The imposture facilitated the journey to Peking which he reached safely, but he was disappointed of seeing the Emperor who was absent from his capital.

Ibn Battuta now set out on his homeward journey. Travelling by way of Sumatra, Malabar, and Syria he reached Tangier in 1349. His original pilgrimage to Mecca had been expanded into a world tour of twenty-four years during which he had had many stirring adventures and had frequently experienced the gravest peril. Though the sight of his birthplace after so long an absence brought him great joy he remained there but a short while. After visiting Andalusia he set out upon the hazardous march across the Sahara to visit the Sudan and thus complete his tour of the whole Muslim world. This, the last journey of his life, is of especial interest to us for it provided the first detailed personal narrative we have of a traveller in the heart of west-central Africa. We shall examine his account of this journey later on when recounting the history of Mali for our knowledge of which we owe Ibn Battuta no small debt.

When Ibn Battuta returned to Fez he had visited every Muhammadan country of his day besides several pagan ones, and he knew

38 MEDIEVAL ARABIC WRITERS

personally the rulers of many. He could justly claim to be the Traveller of Islam, the name by which he is sometimes known. The extent of his wanderings has been estimated at not less than 75,000 miles. He died in Fez in 1368 or 1369.

According to his contemporary Ibn Khaldun the tales of Ibn Battuta's travels were received with general incredulity at the court of Fez. Happily he was not without supporters, one of whom employed a certain Ibn Juzayy to write down the great traveller's story at his own dictation. Thus came into being a work to which we owe a great part of our knowledge of the Muslim world in the first half of the fourteenth century. The narrative was largely, if not entirely, dictated from memory with the result that it is not always accurate. Place names are sometimes confused and it is impossible to accept most of the chronology, the dates having been added later in a haphazard fashion. But having regard to the immense extent of Ibn Battuta's travels it is remarkable that more errors have not crept in. The complete text, including part of Ibn Juzayy's original autograph, was discovered in Constantine in the middle of last century.[8]

Ibn Battuta's great contemporary in letters was Ibn Khaldun, an Arab of noble descent whose ancestors occupied an influential position at Seville. They migrated to Africa at the time of the Almoravid invasion of Spain. His father and grandfather held positions of trust at the court of the Hafsids of Tunis where he himself was born in 1332.

At an early age it became evident that the child had more than ordinary talents. Happily the city of his birth, then a great centre of learning, afforded every facility for cultivating these gifts. At the age of seventeen he witnessed the occupation of Tunis by Abu'l Hassan, and he eagerly seized the opportunity which this gave of extending his studies under the eminent men of learning who had accompanied the great Merinid Sultan.

By the time Ibn Khaldun was twenty-one his considerable literary attainments were recognized and he was appointed to a responsible post at the court of the young Sultan of Tunis who had been placed on the throne after the withdrawal of Abu'l Hassan. But having formed a low opinion of his royal master's ability to retain his throne Ibn Khaldun forsook his post and migrated to Fez where he sought out the learned doctors whose friendship he had cultivated in Tunis during the Merinid occupation. He entered the service of the Sultan and quickly won for himself a position of honour at court.

Unfortunately Ibn Khaldun was ever ready to sacrifice the interests

MEDIEVAL ARABIC WRITERS

of others if he thought he could thereby secure his own personal advancement. This deplorable weakness led to a love of intrigue which in a man of such exceptional ability was a grave danger to his highly placed patrons. Under Abu Inan, who had succeeded Abu'l Hassan at Fez, he was thrown into prison for plotting with a Hafsid prince, but he was released two years later on the death of the Sultan.

Ibn Khaldun already enjoyed an established reputation as a scholar which ensured him a comfortable livelihood in any centre of Muslim learning. Such a life, however, had no attractions for him. On his release from prison he sought to satisfy his restless spirit by leading the life of a political adventurer. For the next few years we find him occupying one responsible position after another, always, according to himself, enjoying the intimacy of some royal patron who had been duped by his glittering attainments.

In 1362 we find him at the court of Granada. Three years later he returned to Africa and took up an important appointment at Bugie. Later he was at Biskra and then at Tlemcen, after which he re-entered the Merinid service under Abd el Aziz. In 1375 he returned to Tunis where he probably commenced his great work on the history of the Arabs and Berbers and other races. The introductory parts of this work form his famous *Prolegomena* and a later part the *History of the Berbers*.[9] But once again political power came within his reach and he entered the service of the Sultan of Tunis. So bitter, however, became the hostility of his rivals that Ibn Khaldun found it expedient to set out on a pilgrimage to Mecca for which the Sultan, who had begun to recognize the true character of his protégé, gladly accorded his permission.

On arrival at Cairo, where his reputation as a scholar had preceded him, he was besieged by students clamouring for instruction. In 1384 he was made Malakite Mufti and he applied himself with vigour to the difficult task of ridding the administration of justice of its many abuses. In 1387 he settled down in a village of the Fayum to a life of study and research. Here he spent many years in retirement and it was probably during this period that he compiled the greater part of his monumental historical work. During his peregrinations from one court to another he had collected an enormous mass of material which he was able to sift and digest in the seclusion of the Fayum. The scholarly character of his work is a proof of the wise discrimination he exercised in using his information. Here too, on one of the greatest trade routes of the world, he was able to collect much valuable

MEDIEVAL ARABIC WRITERS

material from passing merchants. After fourteen years of retirement he was called upon to undertake once more the important duties of Mufti at Cairo, but owing to the severity of the sentences he imposed he was not allowed to hold office for long.

In the year 1400 the great Tartar conqueror, Tamerlane, captured Aleppo, and the Sultan of Egypt, placing himself at the head of his army, hurried north to Damascus to save that city from a similar fate. Among the notables who accompanied him was Ibn Khaldun. Arriving just as the advance guard of the invaders was approaching the city the Sultan fought two engagements which were so successful that Tamerlane prepared to withdraw from Syria. But news from Egypt of a plot to seize the throne sent the Sultan hurrying home and Damascus was left at the mercy of Tamerlane who proceeded to invest it.

In spite of his advanced age Ibn Khaldun, who had been left behind by the Sultan, let himself down from the city walls by a rope and succeeded in making his way to the Tartar camp where he hoped to obtain a safe conduct to Egypt and perhaps to satisfy a historian's natural desire to meet in the flesh one of the greatest heroes of the century. The results were wholly gratifying to the aged scholar who not only obtained his safe conduct, but also enjoyed the privilege of prolonged discussion with the Tartar conqueror who had immediately recognized in his visitor a scholar of more than ordinary distinction.

Ibn Khaldun died in Cairo in 1406, recognized as the greatest Muslim scholar of his day. Though his character, judged by modern standards, was not wholly admirable, he deserves well of posterity who owe to his erudition and industry so great a part of their knowledge of early Arab and Berber history.

Besides those whom we have already noticed there were many other medieval Arabic writers who made their contributions to our subject, among them the famous historian of Egypt, Makrizi[10] (1364–1442). Several we only know of through the works of other writers, as for example Ibn Said, the geographer who died in 1286. He wrote an account of the Sudan which has most unfortunately not been preserved. But if we may judge from the frequency with which he is quoted by Abulfeda, Ibn Khaldun, and other writers his work was of the greatest interest and its loss is deeply to be regretted.

After the fourteenth century Muslim letters began rapidly to decay, but we continue to depend largely on Arabic writers for much of the later history of the Western Sudan. The more important of these will be noticed in later chapters.

MEDIEVAL ARABIC WRITERS

41

REFERENCES

1. Sir T. W. Arnold, *Travel and Travellers in the Middle Ages*, edited by A. P. Newton, London, 1926, pp. 88–103.

2. Maçoudi, *Les Prairies d'Or*, trad. Barbier de Meynard et Pavet de Courteille, 9 vols., Paris, 1861.

3. Ibn Haoukal, *Description de l'Afrique*, trad. de Slane, *Journal Asiatique*, Paris, 1842; Ibn Haukal, *The Oriental Geography*, trans. W. Ouseley, London, 1800.

4. El Bekri, *Description de l'Afrique Septentrionale*, trad. de Slane, Algiers, 1913.

5. Edrisi, *Description de l'Afrique et de l'Espagne*, trad. R. Dozy et M. J. de Goeje, Leyden, 1866; P. A. Jaubert, *Géographie d'Édrisi, Recueil de Voyages*, vols. v and vi, Paris, 1836.

6. F. Wüstenfeld, *Jacut's Geographisches Wöerterbuch*, Leipzig, 1866–70.

7. Al Omari, *Masalik el Absar*, Paris, 1927.

8. Ibn Batouta, *Voyages*, trad. Defrémery et Sanguinetti, Paris, 1853–9; Ibn Battuta, *Travels in Asia and Africa*, trans. H. A. R. Gibb, London, 1929, p. 2.

9. Ibn Khaldun, *Histoire des Berbères*, trad. de Slane, 2 vols., Paris, 1925.

10. Makrizi, *Description Historique et Topographique de l'Égypte*, trad. P. Casanova, Cairo, 1906.

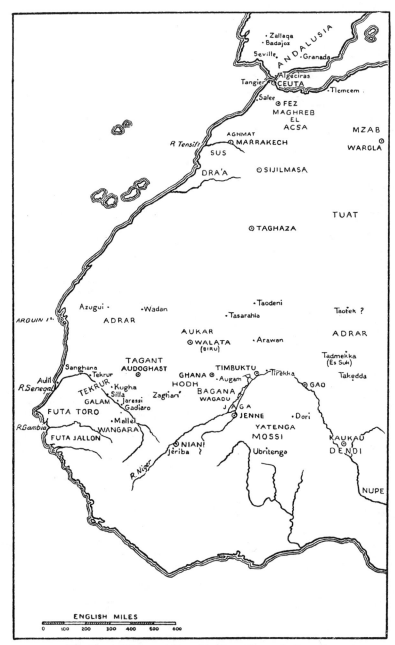

III. North-Western Africa—Tenth to Sixteenth Centuries.

BELED ES SUDAN

V

THE ALMORAVIDS

'That same plain of Morocco is a fine place to dwell in, compared with our glorious Seville! What if these barbarians have encamped there? Between us and them there lie deserts and great armies, and the waves of the sea.'—A SPANISH VIZIER.

IN the extreme north-west corner of the Sahara and at the foot of the Atlas Mountains lies the oasis of Tafilelt. Scattered for a distance of five miles along the principal watercourse, and now overgrown with rank vegetation, lie the ruins of its ancient capital, the city of Sijilmasa,[1] which, from its foundation in the eighth century to its destruction at the close of the eighteenth, was renowned through Europe for the important part it played in the trade of the Sahara. Equidistant from Fez and Marrakech and situated on the threshold of the desert at the head of the most westerly of the trans-Saharan caravan routes, Sijilmasa was one of the greatest centres for desert trade and for the fitting out of caravans. The purity of its water and the fertility of its soil ensured plenty for man and beast, and nowhere else could the merchant preparing for the hazardous journey to the Sudan find greater facilities to ensure the success of his enterprise.

One of the earliest references to Sijilmasa occurs in Ibn Haukal who, writing in the tenth century, tells us that 'it is a town of middling size . . . one cannot enter Sejelmasah but by the way of the desert, which the sand renders difficult. The town is situated near the gold mines, between them and the land of the Blacks, and the land of Zouilah. These mines are said to be of the most pure and excellent gold; but it is difficult to work them, and the way to them is dangerous and troublesome.'[2] In the following century Sijilmasa was described by El Bekri as a city of beautiful and imposing buildings inhabited by Muleththemin and remarkable for its healthy climate and freedom from flies.[3] According to Masudi, Yaqut, and Idrisi it owed its early wealth to the gold trade with Ghana, which lay two months' march to the south on the frontier of the Sudan, and with Wangara, the Land of Gold, which lay beyond Ghana.[4] But the flow of gold from the Sudan long outlived Ghana and ensured the continued prosperity of Sijilmasa for many centuries.

THE ALMORAVIDS

The merchants of Sijilmasa were also deeply interested in the salt mines of Taghaza which lay out in the desert twenty days' march down the road to Ghana. Although in most respects so richly endowed by Nature the Sudan has always lacked salt, a circumstance which from the earliest times to the present day has been exploited to the full by foreign merchants. Ghana's chief sources of supply were Taghaza and Aulil, an island near the mouth of the Senegal river, but the former was much the more important. To the people of Sijilmasa the control of these mines was a matter of great interest, for they provided a most valuable article to barter for the gold of the Sudan.

Taghaza, according to El Bekri, was constantly thronged with merchants, and work in the mines, which produced an enormous revenue, never ceased.[5] The best description of Taghaza is to be found in Ibn Battuta who stayed there on his way to the Sudan. Although his narrative was written as late as the fourteenth century, conditions at the salt mines can have changed but little during the two preceding centuries.

'After twenty-five days', he wrote, 'we reached Taghaza, an unattractive village, with the curious feature that its houses and mosques are built of blocks of salt, roofed with camel skins. There are no trees there, nothing but sand. In the sand is a salt mine; they dig for the salt, and find it in thick slabs. . . . No one lives at Taghaza except the slaves of the Massufa tribe, who dig for the salt; they subsist on dates imported from Dar'a and Sijilmasa, camels' flesh, and millet imported from the Negrolands. The negroes come up from their country and take away the salt from there. At Iwalatan (Walata) a load of salt brings eight to ten *mithqals**; in the town of Malli it sells for twenty to thirty, and sometimes as much as forty. The negroes use salt as a medium of exchange, just as gold and silver is used (elsewhere); they cut it up into pieces and buy and sell with it. The business done at Taghaza, for all its meanness, amounts to an enormous figure in terms of hundred-weights of gold-dust.'[6]

An anonymous writer of the twelfth century describing the trade with Ghana tells us that

'in the sands of that country is gold, treasure inexpressible. They have much gold, and merchants trade with salt for it, taking the salt on camels from the salt mines. They start from a town called Sijilmasa . . . and travel in the desert as it were upon the sea, having guides to pilot them by the stars or rocks in the deserts. They take provisions for six months, and when they reach Ghana they weigh their salt and sell it against a certain unit of weight of gold, and

* One *mithqal* or *mitkal* equals about ⅛ oz. of gold.

THE ALMORAVIDS

45

sometimes against double or more of the gold unit, according to the market and the supply.'[7]

The site of Ghana has been lost. Although it is impossible to reconcile the different accounts of the Arab authors, Ghana was probably situated in the desert near the present towns of Nema and Walata in the district of Aukar which lies about 300 miles west of Timbuktu.[8]

Es Sadi[9] tells us that the kingdom of Ghana existed before the *Hejira*, twenty-two kings ruling before that date and twenty-two after. They were white but of unknown origin. It is usually assumed that these early kings belonged to an ancient Jewish stock who, through fusion with Gara tribes, became later on the ancestors of the Fulani.[10] We know nothing of this white dynasty except that their subjects were Wangara or Mandingoes and that their rule ended in the eighth century after 300 or 400 years of power. They were succeeded by a negro dynasty belonging to the Soninke branch of the Mandingo race.

According to tradition the last white king of Ghana was assassinated by the Soninke[11] who placed on the throne one of their own countrymen, Kaza-Maghan Sisse, chief of the neighbouring district of Wagadu. The choice appears to have been a happy one, for we learn from Ibn Khaldun that when the Muslims conquered the Maghreb and Arab merchants first began to visit the Western Sudan they found that no negro king was more powerful than the ruler of Ghana whose dominion extended to the Atlantic.[12] Under his successors the Soninke greatly extended the limits of the state which, when it reached its apogee in the middle of the ninth century, included the greater part of Hodh and Tagant besides Aukar and Bagana. To the east it was bounded by the Niger and to the south by the Senegal and Baule rivers. During the previous dynasty many of the southern Soninke had preserved their independence, but now that one of their own blood ruled in Ghana they willingly threw in their lot with the rest of their countrymen. We are unfortunately very ill informed regarding this interesting period in the history of the negro kingdom.

Early in the ninth century Ghana became alarmed by the warlike activities of a Berber chief of the Lemtuna tribe named Tilutane. At the head of an army of 100,000 Sanhaja camelry, mostly men of his own tribe, Tilutane had already imposed his authority over nearly all the Berber tribes of the western Sahara. He had established himself in the districts of Hodh and Tagant whence he had begun to raid the neighbouring negro tribes, many of whom were vassals of the king

THE ALMORAVIDS

of Ghana. The latter, overawed by the immense strength of his war-like neighbour, dared not resist these encroachments on his kingdom. But as Tilutane was equally anxious to avoid a trial of strength with Ghana and contented himself with raiding only the outlying portions of the kingdom direct conflict between these powerful neighbours was averted.[13]

The Lemtuna capital was a town named Audoghast which lay only fifteen days' march westward from Ghana in eastern Tagant and one month's march from Arguin on the coast. It was a large and populous town with many fine buildings and was surrounded by extensive date gardens beyond which lay the sands of the Sahara. The inhabitants were Berbers, who owned great numbers of pagan negro slaves. But in it there also dwelt numbers of Arab merchants who were engaged in the caravan trade. The country people inhabiting the surrounding desert were nomadic Berbers. In the north they were fair com-plexioned but they grew darker towards the south, becoming as black as the negroes on the frontier.

Water was abundant and by means of irrigation a variety of crops were raised including dates, wheat, which was eaten only by the rich, millet, figs, vines, gourds, and henna. Cattle and sheep were abundant and cheap. Audoghast was a centre of great commercial activity carrying on trade with the Maghreb, notably with Sijilmasa. The principal exports were gold, which had the reputation of being the finest in the world, and ambergris of excellent quality which was obtained on the coast. The imports included wheat, dried fruit, brass, and robes from the north, salt from Aulil, and gold and honey from the Sudan. In the market, which was always thronged, gold dust was the currency in general use. Ibn Haukal, describing the constant pas-sage of caravans between Audoghast and the north, tells us, as an example of the large scale on which business was conducted, that he knew of a native of Sijilmasa who was indebted to a merchant of the Audoghast for so great a sum as 40,000 gold *dinars*.*

Living in the midst of so much commercial prosperity, the in-habitants had amassed great wealth. They were able to enjoy lives of ease and luxury and to cultivate the arts of civilization. Amongst the traders of the desert Audoghast was famed for the skill of its cooks and for the exquisite beauty of its white-skinned damsels on whose charms El Bekri dwells with enthusiasm. To such lengths would these young women go to preserve their looks that they preferred to recline rather

* A *dinar* was the weight of seventy-two grains of barley.

THE ALMORAVIDS

than sit lest in so doing they should distort the elegant symmetry of the more rounded portion of the body.[14]

Although Audoghast managed outwardly to preserve friendly relations with Ghana, friction between the Lemtuna and Soninke was frequent. The latter waylaid caravans from the north as they approached Audoghast and the Lemtuna retaliated by intervening in the internal affairs of Ghana and by taking part in private feuds between vassal chiefs. The Soninke, however, gradually became the dominant power. They recovered the outlying districts which had been filched from them, but they made no attempt to wrest Audoghast from the Lemtuna.

About the year 1020 the various Sanhaja tribes of the western desert agreed to unite, as in the time of Tilutane, to resist the encroachments of the Soninke in Tagant and to strike a blow at the supremacy of their rivals. They placed at their head another Lemtuna chief who changed his original name of Tarsina to Abdalla abu Muhammad on his conversion to Islam. After performing the *Hadj* he conducted a *jihad* against the negroes and certain pagan Berbers. He met his death while raiding a Jewish tribe who were perhaps a remnant of Semitic people who, after having been driven from Ghana two centuries before, had sought refuge among the Wangara or Mandingoes.[15]

Tarsina was succeeded by his son-in-law, Yahia ibn Ibrahim, of the Jedala branch of the Sanhaja, whose country lay between the Lemtuna and the Atlantic. On his way home from a pilgrimage to Mecca he passed through Kairwan where he made friends with a certain Abu Amran, a learned doctor from Fez. The latter was shocked by Yahia's deplorable ignorance in matters of doctrine and was still more deeply moved on learning that his Saharan subjects were even more ignorant than their emir. This so filled Yahia with shame that he begged his friend to find a theologian who would instruct him and his people in the orthodox religion. Abu Amran, unable to find any one suitable in Kairwan, gave Yahia a letter of introduction to a certain Wagag of Sijilmasa who might help him. The Sanhaja chief, continuing his journey, came to the home of Wagag who persuaded one of his disciples, Abdullah ibn Yacin, to brave the privations of life in the desert and accompany Yahia to his country.[16]

Ibn Yacin began his ministrations amongst Yahia's own tribesmen, the Jedala. Muslims only in name they found the austere doctrine of the ascetic from the north altogether unacceptable and strongly resented the restrictions which he tried to impose upon them. At

THE ALMORAVIDS

last, exasperated beyond endurance, they rose up, burnt his house, and drove him from their country.

Ibn Yacin, accompanied by two faithful Lemtuna followers, sought the seclusion of an island or peninsula in the Senegal river where he lived apart from the rest of mankind absorbed in devotions. No conduct was better calculated to win sympathy. The curiosity of the outside world was quickly aroused and the better elements among the neighbouring tribes began to gather round the ascetics, seeking instruction in their mysterious rites. When Ibn Yacin had collected as many as 1,000 disciples he called them together and, naming them Al Morabethin (*marabouts*), whence they became known as Almoravids, bade them go forth and compel the world to accept the reformed faith.

The Almoravids first appealed to their own tribesmen but, after the manner of prophets all the world over, they were ill received in their own land. In 1042 Ibn Yacin left the Senegal and, placing himself at the head of his followers led them in a *jihad* against the recalcitrant Jedala and the Lemtuna. They slew great numbers of their enemies and converted others. But victory was robbed of its sweetness for the Almoravids. Their austere leader forbade pillage and all the other forms of excess so dear to the heart of predatory desert nomads. He next made them build a town which was called Aretnenna where, with the object of maintaining absolute equality, the houses were all of one size. Here he submitted them to such tyranny that they rebelled against him and once more he was compelled to seek safety in flight.[17]

This time he made his way northwards to his old master Wagag who became greatly incensed on hearing of the behaviour of the Sanhaja tribes. Threatening expulsion from the community of Islam to all who should refuse obedience to Ibn Yacin he sent back the disciple to his post in the desert with orders to slay all who declared themselves against him. Ibn Yacin, who had probably collected a number of adherents in the north, rigorously carried out the master's instructions and, moreover, to such effect that before long all the tribes of the western Sahara had accepted his doctrine and were united under his leadership.

The Almoravids were now organized by Ibn Yacin into an army 30,000 strong all fired with the religious fervour of their leader. Some were mounted on camels and horses but most of them fought on foot. They were armed with pikes and spears which they used to deadly

THE ALMORAVIDS

49

effect, fighting with fanatical fury and cheerfully courting death. Although they had never before known any form of restraint they now obeyed a discipline more rigid than that of any modern army. Their ranks never broke nor were they ever seen to pursue a beaten enemy. Neither before nor since has Africa seen a more resolute force.

Ibn Yacin, already master of the western desert, now prepared to employ this redoubtable army in spreading the orthodox religion amongst the heretical tribes of the north. At this moment he received an opportune appeal from Wagag to come to the help of the unhappy Muslim population of Dra'a, who had been reduced to utter misery by the tyranny of the ruling house of Sijilmasa. The army advanced immediately and after defeating the army of Masud, the Emir of Sijilmasa, who was slain in the battle, they seized the city and massacred the remnants of the fugitive army who had sought shelter behind its walls. Ibn Yacin, having restored order and freed the people from the abuses from which they had suffered, placed a garrison in Sijilmasa and then marched back into the desert.[18]

Although Ibn Yacin could now command the allegiance of most of the tribes of the western desert the people of Audoghast, who had now fallen under the tutelage of the hated Soninke of Ghana, held aloof. The city was divided into two factions, Arab and Berber, who regarded each other with intense hatred. Profiting by this circumstance Ibn Yacin attacked Audoghast and captured it without difficulty in 1054. Resolved upon making an example of the city, he removed all restraint from his troops who massacred the citizens and violated their women.[19]

In the following year the people of Sijilmasa rose in rebellion and massacred the Almoravid garrison. Seeking to evade the retribution which they knew must follow, they laid the blame on the Zenata and besought Ibn Yacin to purge the country of these enemies of religion. Ibn Yacin had allowed his army to disperse, but he now called them together again. Those troops, however, who belonged to the Jedala tribe, jealous of the favoured position enjoyed in the Almoravid army by their hereditary rivals, the Lemtuna, refused to obey the summons and withdrew westward to the coastal region lying between the Senegal and Arguin. Ibn Yacin set out for the north with the loyal Lemtuna only, but he succeeded in re-establishing control in Dra'a and Sijilmasa. The Almoravids next assailed the great barrier of the Atlas ranges which stood between them and the rich country of Morocco. Pouring through the Glawi and Kundafi passes they swept

E

THE ALMORAVIDS

down into the plain where a few years later they were to build the city of Marrakech.

Ibn Yacin had left behind him in the desert a small force under Yahia ibn Omar, Emir of the Almoravids, whom he had ordered to remain in the mountains of Adrar, where he hoped they would be secure from the Jedala who were now in open rebellion against the rest of the sect. Yahia established his head-quarters at a fortress named Argui or Azugui. But, doubtful of his ability to resist alone the threatened aggressions of the Jedala, he implored help from the negro king of Tekrur, the Tucolor kingdom on the Senegal. His appeal did not go unanswered. But in spite of Tucolor reinforcements the Almoravids were defeated and their Emir killed.

In 1057 Ibn Yacin lost his life while fighting the Berghwata on the northern frontier. By his death there passed one of the most remarkable characters in African history. The great movement which he had fathered and directed had, by the time of his death, united into one kingdom practically the whole of the western Sahara besides the fertile northern districts of Sus, Aghmat, and Sijilmasa and its dependencies. The foundations too had been laid for a yet greater empire, extending even beyond the shores of Africa. Only a man of heroic qualities could have achieved so much.

The Almoravids elected a spiritual leader to succeed Ibn Yacin, but he died very shortly afterwards. Complete control then passed into the hand of Abu Bakr, their Emir. Establishing his head-quarters at Aghmat, within a few days' march of the site where the city of Marrakech was shortly to rise, he continued the northern campaign on which Ibn Yacin had been engaged at the time of his death.[20]

These operations were interrupted by news of trouble in the south, where quarrelling had broken out between the Lemtuna and Mesufa members of the sect. Fearing that these dissensions might cause the alienation of one or other of the parties and perhaps lead to the disruption of the Almoravid state, Abu Bakr decided that he must deal with the situation in person. Before setting out for the south he confided the command of the northern army to his cousin, Yusuf ibn Tashifin.

The personal intervention of Abu Bakr quickly restored order among his unruly followers, but he saw that unless an outlet could be found for the turbulent spirit of these desert nomads they would soon be at each other's throats again. So, placing himself at their head, he led them against the pagan Soninke who were subject to Bassi, the aged king of Ghana. Although Bassi was always friendly to Muslims this

THE ALMORAVIDS

had not saved him from the hatred of the Almoravids. Abu Bakr, however, did not allow himself and his irregulars to become involved in open war with the forces of Ghana.

Meanwhile Yusuf with a fine display of vigour and enterprise had led the northern army victoriously into the heart of the Maghreb, committed apparently to a career of conquest with almost limitless prospects. When Abu Bakr returned unexpectedly from the south he found that his lieutenant had no intention of handing back the command of the army. Abu Bakr was forced to acquiesce and after formally handing over the command of the Maghreb to his nephew he discreetly vanished into the desert.

Yusuf, with none to dispute his authority, now settled down to a career of conquest which was destined to bring him power and fame far transcending his most fanciful dreams. As he moved northward district after district submitted to him. Everywhere he proclaimed himself the champion of the masses, the liberator of the people from the cruel tyranny of corrupt princes. This popular role ensured the support of the oppressed peasantry who readily joined forces with him in the overthrow of the local tyrants.

Throughout his career Yusuf seems to have been inspired by lofty ideals and to have tried worthily to uphold the traditions of Ibn Yacin. Though none would suggest that he was free from personal ambition the interests of Islam lay next his heart, and few of those who welcomed him as a saviour lived to regret their action while he yet lived. To his enemies he was ruthless, but his administration was restrained and free from oppressive taxation. Tranquillity and prosperity marked the wake of his army.

In 1062 Yusuf founded the city of Marrakech in the upper Tensift valley at a point which commanded the approaches to the Glawi and Kundafi passes by way of which the Almoravids had invaded the country. The site was originally chosen for a camp from which the army could control the Masmuda, at that time the most formidable tribe of the Maghreb el Acsa. Presently he added a mosque and a small citadel for the storage of plunder and munitions. From this simple origin the place grew within a few years into a walled city of imposing size and became the southern capital of the country.

In the following year he entered Fez without striking a blow and from there he pushed on northwards against the Ghomara. It was not long before he found himself on the heights above Tangier which, like the neighbouring town of Ceuta, was strongly held by Andalusian

THE ALMORAVIDS

troops. Not feeling himself strong enough yet to provoke a conflict with these formidable neighbours, he turned eastward where countless small principalities offered an easy prey and abundant opportunities for a further great extension of the already vast dominions of the Almoravids.

Yusuf was beginning to find that the administrative affairs of his conquests required a great deal of attention. He had divided them into provinces, setting over each a trusted officer or one of his own relatives, but the governors were in constant need of his support and advice. Moreover the former rulers of the country were reluctant to acquiesce in their loss of power without striking a blow to recover their independence. There were consequently many insurrections which, although easily quelled, added considerably to the difficulties of administration. Perhaps the most disturbing of these outbreaks was the capture of Fez by its former king who assassinated the Almoravid governor, but lost his own life when Yusuf recaptured the city.

Time, however, was found for further conquests, especially in the east. Tlemcen, the Zenata capital and a city of considerable strategical importance, was captured and made a base for further operations. By 1082 the Almoravid Empire had been extended as far east as Algiers.

But while the Almoravid host were thus triumphantly carrying all before them and adding greatly to the prestige of Islam in Africa their co-religionists in Spain were being driven to desperation by the ever-increasing vigour of Christian aggression. Their plight was largely due to the folly of their own tyrannical Emirs, petty princes who, intensely jealous of each other, were ever soliciting Christian aid against their rivals, thus playing into the hands of Alfonso VI, King of Castile. Despairing of being able alone to stem the Christian tide the Emirs looked anxiously, but none too hopefully, towards their co-religionists in Africa for assistance.

There, close at hand, lay Yusuf with his victorious host, master of the Maghreb. A proposal to seek the aid of the wild Berber tribesmen was at first regarded by the Emirs as too desperate a measure for serious consideration. They perceived that such uncouth barbarians might well prove awkward guests if once admitted to so fair a land as Spain. The proposal, however, was supported by the theologians, who were profoundly impressed by all they had heard of the simplicity and piety of the Almoravids, and by the masses, who had nothing to lose and were unable to conceive a worse tyranny than that which they were then enduring. But desperate though the measure seemed, the

THE ALMORAVIDS

ruling princes in their distress began gradually to regard it as the only way of saving Andalusia from the Christians. Mu'tamid, King of Seville, admitted the danger, but declared: 'I have no desire to be branded by my descendants as the man who delivered Andalusia a prey to the infidels; I am loath to have my name cursed in every Muslim pulpit; and, for my part, I would rather be a camel-driver in Africa than a swineherd in Castile.'[21]

It was decided therefore that Mu'tamid should open negotiations with Yusuf and El Bekri witnessed his departure to Africa. Yusuf was invited to bring an army over into Spain, but only on condition that he should seize no state of a Muslim prince. He received the envoys coldly and sent them back with evasive and ambiguous replies, which only added to the perplexity of the Emirs. It was, however, understood that he had promised that if he came he would make no annexations.

Their perplexity quickly turned to consternation when they heard that Yusuf was already lying off Algeciras with a fleet of 100 vessels, demanding the immediate surrender of the town. Although enraged at his perfidy, which confirmed their worst apprehensions, they were unhappily in no position to refuse his demand. The wild Berber host accordingly landed at Algeciras which they proceeded to fortify and provision as a base for further operations. As Yusuf advanced inland the awed princes received him obsequiously with gifts, but the masses welcomed him with enthusiasm. Yusuf, joining forces with Mu'tamid and his Andalusian troops, marched against the Christians whom, in spite of their overwhelming superiority in numbers, he routed on 23 October 1086 at the battle of Zallaqa, near Badajoz. Alfonso VI, who had been wounded by one of Yusuf's negro guards, barely escaped with his life. Yusuf had intended carrying the war into the heart of the enemy's country, but hearing of the death of his eldest son, whom he had left sick at Ceuta, he returned to Africa with most of his army, leaving behind him only 3,000 troops whom he placed at Mu'tamid's disposal.

Yusuf left Spain a popular hero, everywhere hailed as the saviour of Islam. His piety and prowess had won the hearts of the people and even the Andalusian Emirs were less embittered than on his arrival. He had freed them for a time from the Castilians and, by lending them troops, had done his best to secure them against further aggression.

Brilliant though the victory at Zallaqa had been it was not decisive.

THE ALMORAVIDS

The Castilians, hopeful of recovering the ground they had lost, re-organized their forces and once more began to raid the Muslim lands. In spite of their Berber reinforcements the effete Emirs were still helpless against their aggressors and once more they appealed to Yusuf to come in person to their aid. So again he crossed the Straits but this time his heart was set on becoming the undisputed master of Muslim Spain.

Many Andalusians thought that the only hope of salvation for their country lay in union with the Almoravid Empire. To the masses, especially, the advent of Almoravid dominion seemed to offer much. It was their one hope of escape from the cruel exactions of their own Emirs who, while ever demanding more taxes to pay for the voluptuous extravagance of their courts, were yet unable to protect their subjects from the Castilians. It was, moreover, common knowledge that Yusuf had abolished all taxes in Africa except those sanctioned by the Quran. The theologians, who likened the frugal lives of him and his soldiers to the simplicity of the early followers of the Prophet, were ready to welcome him warmly. But the return of the Almoravids was hateful to the cultured upper classes who regarded the barbarian conqueror as little better than an uncouth savage. The men of letters too, who enjoyed privileged positions at the courts of the petty tyrants, had no reason to desire a change of masters.

As Yusuf advanced inland, welcomed by the theologians and the people, the Emirs, deeply jealous of each other and with thoughts only of self-interest, played into his hands by soliciting his aid in their personal quarrels. They received the contempt they deserved and were quickly swept away. In 1100 he entered Granada and beheld wealth greater than he had ever imagined. He distributed the treasure amongst his officers and continued the work of subjugating the country. Soon he was master of Seville, and by 1102 the whole of Muhammadan Spain had been added to the Almoravid dominions. Their empire, which now stretched from the Senegal to the Ebro, became known as The Two Shores.

The ascendancy of the Almoravids lasted only a few years. While Yusuf still lived their rule brought tranquillity, and prosperity returned to the country. But, as ever with shepherd kings, deterioration soon began to show itself among the new rulers. Transferred from the frugal life of the desert and the strenuous activity of constant warfare to positions of luxury and ease they quickly lost their simple virtues. In their vain attempts to ape the refinements of the Andalusians they

THE ALMORAVIDS 55

assimilated only the worst features of Spanish culture. As their own depravity increased their rule became cruelly harsh and tyrannical. The Christians, moreover, again took heart and fell to raiding the peasantry as of old.

The Andalusians thus quickly lost the benefits they had at first enjoyed from the change of rulers, and before long were regretting the days of their own Emirs. Driven at last to desperation they rose and massacred their oppressors. But this revulsion of feeling against the Almoravids was not confined to Spain. In North Africa a new Berber sect, the Almohads or Traditionists, drove them out. Under the brilliant leadership of Abd el Mumen the Almohads established a kingdom which stretched from the Syrtis to the Atlantic. During their enlightened rule the country enjoyed a high degree of security and prosperity and their universities became the resort of students from Europe. But this great Berber kingdom lasted only a century. From the chaos which followed its fall there emerged the dynasties of the Hafsids of Tunis, the Wabites of Tlemcen, and the Merinids of Fez.

REFERENCES

1. W. B. Harris, *Tafilet*, London, 1895, p. 283.
2. Ibn Haukal, English ed., p. 16.
3. El Bekri, p. 283.
4. Maçoudi, iv. 39; Edrisi, trad. P. A. Jaubert, i. 106.
5. El Bekri, p. 322.
6. Ibn Battuta, trans. H. A. R. Gibb, p. 317.
7. *Tohfut ul Alabi, apud* H. R. Palmer, *Sudanese Memoirs*, ii. 90.
8. M. Delafosse, *Haut-Sénégal-Niger*, Paris, 1912, ii. 12–19.
9. Abderrahman-es-Sa'di et Timboukti, *Tarikh es Soudan*, trad. O. Houdas, Paris, 1900, p. 18.
10. M. Delafosse, ii. 24; H. R. Palmer, *Journal of the African Society*, xxii (1922–3), 124–5.
11. M. Delafosse, ii. 25.
12. Ibn Khaldun, ii. 109.
13. Ibid., 65.
14. El Bekri, pp. 299, 317.
15. Gharnati, *Roudh el Qarthas*, trad. Beaumier, Paris, 1860, p. 165, *apud* Delafosse, ii. 33; El Bekri, p. 311.
16. Ibid.; Ibn Khaldun, ii. 67.
17. Ibid. 69; El Bekri, p. 313.
18. Ibn Khaldun, ii. 70.
19. El Bekri, p. 317.
20. Ibn Khaldun, ii. 71.
21. R. Dozy, *Spanish Islam*, trans. F. G. Stokes, London, 1913, p. 694.

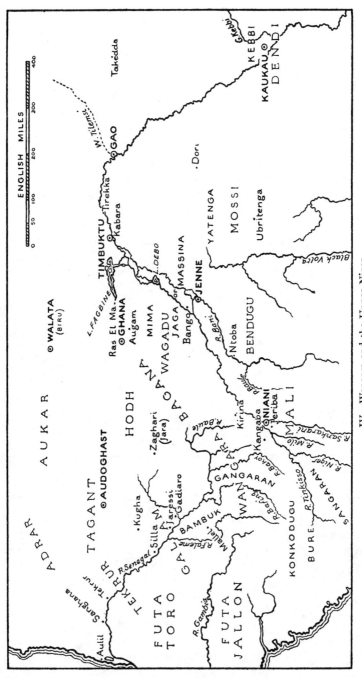

IV. Wangara and the Upper Niger.

VI

GHANA

'Mankind can live without gold but not without salt.'—CASSIODORUS.

IN the middle of the eleventh century, when El Bekri was engaged
upon his memorable description of Africa, the western Sahara was
in a ferment of political excitement over the triumphant progress of
the Almoravids. In the north the Maghreb el Acsa was already half
paralysed by the grip of Yusuf. But in the south pagan Ghana, an
object of the bitterest hatred to every member of the sect, remained
proudly independent and in full enjoyment of commercial liberty, its
thriving trade with the Maghreb seemingly undisturbed by the political upheaval which the Almoravids had wrought throughout this
whole region.

El Bekri has left us an account of Ghana which was evidently based
on information collected from the Barbary merchants who continued
to frequent that city in large numbers. His description is practically
limited to accounts of its magnificent court and of its trade, the two
aspects of life which were most likely to impress a foreign merchant.

By this time the aged Bassi was dead, and, according to a custom
designed to ensure the descent of the throne indubitably to princes
of the blood, he had been succeeded by his sister's son, Menin or
Tunka Menin. The capital consisted of two separate towns, situated
about six miles apart. The one was reserved for the Muhammadan
population and contained a dozen mosques which were the resort of
many distinguished jurists and learned doctors. The other, known as
El Ghaba or the Forest, was pagan and the seat of the court. Most of
the houses of Ghana were clay huts thatched with straw, but there were
also some finer buildings of stone.

El Ghaba took its name from the groves with which it was surrounded. These groves, which were probably little more than thickets
of thorn, were jealously guarded against all intruders, for they were
the centre of the spiritual life of the nation. Here dwelt the fetish
priests, who tended the national gods and doubtless practised many of
the gruesome rites commonly associated with West African fetishism.
Here too were the burial places of the kings and the prisons from which
none was ever known to return.

The king was the centre of a court where elaborate ceremonial and

58 GHANA

gorgeous pageantry combined to present a scene which probably did not give a greatly exaggerated impression of the wealth and resources of the kingdom. On the occasion of an audience the king, adorned in jewellery and a golden head-dress, seated himself in a pavilion around which stood ten horses in golden trappings. Behind the throne stood ten pages holding shields and golden-hilted swords. To the right were the sons of vassal princes, magnificently attired with ornaments plaited into their hair. At the feet of the king sat the governor of the city, and before him the viziers. The door of the pavilion was guarded by hounds, wearing collars and bells of silver and gold, which were the constant companions of the monarch.

Muslims held many of the court appointments, including those of Treasurer and Interpreter, and the viziers were usually Muhammadan. The commencement of the audience was announced by the beating of the royal drums called *deba*, which were made from hollowed logs.* When the king's own countrymen approached they poured dust on their heads as they knelt before him. The Muslims showed their respect by clapping their hands.[2]

The royal treasure included a gold nugget of so great a size that it became famous through a great part of the civilized world. According to Idrisi it weighed thirty pounds and the king used to tether his charger to it.[3] But popular rumour gradually raised it to fabulous proportions. By the fourteenth century, when Ibn Khaldun recorded its sale by a spendthrift prince to some merchants of Egypt, it was supposed to weigh as much as a ton.[4]

When the king died they raised a sort of wooden dome in which they laid his body, resting it on rugs and cushions. Near it they placed robes and eating utensils and supplies of food and drink. They interred with the dead king those of his servants who had been in the habit of preparing his meals. The tomb was then covered with mats and cloths over which the assembled multitude threw earth till they had formed a great mound with a ditch around it.

Of the king's negro subjects we know very little. The peasantry cultivated millet and other crops and they fished. The king frequently required them for military service against his neighbours and for slave raids. According to El Bekri he could place in the field as many as 200,000 men, of whom 40,000 were armed with bows and arrows. The people of the capital were probably wholly absorbed in commerce.

Idrisi tells us that Ghana was the largest town and the most im-

* These drums are still known as *daba* or *taba* by the Soninke.[1]

GHANA

portant market of the Sudan, and the resort of merchants from all parts of the western Maghreb. The foundation of its great prosperity was gold, which was in such abundant supply that precautions had to be taken to limit the amount coming on to the open market lest the price should fall too low. This was done by making all nuggets the property of the Crown, leaving only the gold dust available for the trade.

The people of Ghana obtained their gold from a country called Wangara, a name which for centuries remained wrapped in mystery. According to Idrisi, Wangara was an island 300 miles long and 50 broad surrounded by the waters of the 'Nile', a name which early geographers applied to every river of the interior. This 'Nile' of Idrisi flowed from east to west and was undoubtedly the Senegal. In August, the hottest month of the year, the river used to rise and flood the island. When the water receded the local negroes came to collect the gold left by the floods, and remained there till the water rose again. Wangara was a rich country with flourishing towns of which Tirekka was the most important.

Yaqut, who wrote at the end of the twelfth century, has left us a very interesting account of the gold trade of Ghana. He tells us that the people of Sijilmasa and Dra'a owed their prosperity to the circumstance of their situation on the trade route leading to the great negro city and to the goldfields of the Sudan. The Barbary merchants used to carry south easily portable trade goods, such as cheap jewellery and beads, supplementing them as they passed through Taghaza with salt for which there was always a good market among the negroes. They also obtained in the desert a certain resinous wood used for sweetening water which had been carried long in skins. On their tedious and painful journey across the Sahara the water supply was a constant source of anxiety, and much forethought had to be exercised to secure a sufficiency.

In Ghana the merchants were met by their agents who were familiar with the curious market customs of the south, and together they travelled on for twenty days over more desert till they reached the Senegal. The scene which followed recalls the account which Herodotus gave of how the Carthaginians used to barter for gold on the African coast.

When the merchants of Barbary arrived at the river they beat on big drums to summon the local natives, who were completely naked and lived in 'holes in the ground'. From these holes, which were

GHANA

doubtless really the pits from which they dug the gold, they refused to emerge in the presence of the foreign merchants. The latter, therefore, used to arrange their trade goods in piles on the river bank and retire out of sight. The local natives then came and placed a heap of gold beside each pile and withdrew. If the merchants were satisfied they took the gold and retreated, beating their drums to signify that the market was over.[5] Yaqut tells us that according to Ibn el Faqih the gold grew in the sand of Wangara like carrots and was gathered by the natives each day at dawn, and a similar statement was later attributed to Mansa Musa.[6]

On one occasion the foreign merchants tried to discover the source of the gold by treacherously capturing one of the shy negroes. They secured one prisoner but he pined to death without divulging any information. As the result of this act of perfidy the gold trade was interrupted for three years, at the end of which their craving for salt compelled the negroes to resume it.

Masudi, writing in the tenth century, tells us that in his day this silent trade in gold was well known in Sijilmasa.[7] Late in the fifteenth century Cadamosto was informed by Arab and Sanhaja merchants that it was still the custom of the gold trade. It was also described by later travellers, but these may only have been quoting from the narratives of their predecessors. It is certain, however, that for many centuries silent trade, or dumb barter as it is sometimes called, was a distinctive feature of the gold traffic with Wangara.

Although Wangara is now generally used as a name for the Muslim Soninke and Jaula branches of the Mandingo race it still survives in variant forms as the name of a rather obscure district. Between the Faleme and the upper Niger lies the auriferous region of Bambuk and Bure, a small portion of which is to-day variously called Gbangara, Gwangara, Gangara, or Gangaran.[8] There seems no reason to doubt that Bambuk and Bure are the Wangara of history. They conform with striking accuracy to the several accounts which have come down to us. This region is not an island, such as Idrisi described, but it is hemmed in on all sides by rivers—on the north by the Senegal, on the west by the Faleme, on the east by the Niger, and on the south by the Tinkisso—which gives it an appearance of insular form. Alluvial gold, moreover, is widely scattered throughout the region, and deposits are still worked between the rise and fall of the floods, as described by Idrisi 800 years ago. The Senegal answers closely to the description of the river on the banks of which the gold market was held. Salt,

GHANA   61

which was always a favourite article for bartering for gold, has still to be imported and forms a staple article of trade.

Silent trade is no longer practised, but the Malinke gold-diggers are a deeply superstitious people who, in a slightly earlier stage of development, may well have shunned contact with their neighbours. They sink their pits between the months of January and May, but their operations are strictly controlled by the whims of priests or sorcerers. They recognize the neighbouring mountains as the real source of the gold from which it is washed by the rains, but they never venture to exploit the rich veins which they know there exist, believing them to be jealously guarded by ferocious devils.[9]

The curious custom of silent trade was for long so striking a feature of the gold trade of West Africa that it is often regarded as peculiar to that region, and its occurrence in many other parts of the world has sometimes been overlooked. It usually arose through ignorance of language or mistrust, and was apt to occur where one or other of the parties was reluctantly compelled to trade by dire necessity, as in the case of Wangara, where salt was the supreme need of the people.

Pomponius Mela, writing in the first century of our era, described the practice of silent trade in the Himalayas. At the same period it was a feature of the silk trade which the Romans carried on with the Chinese on the banks of a river beyond Parthia.[10] Fa-Hien, the Chinese explorer of the fifth century, recorded its occurrence in Ceylon.[11] Cosmas of Alexandria, writing a century later, gave a long account in his *Christian Topography* of the gold trade in Abyssinia, which was conducted on lines very similar to those practised in Wangara.[12] Many other examples could be quoted.[13]

The custom seems now almost to have died out in Africa. It is still practised by the Pygmies of the Congo[14] and till recently was to be found in both West and East Africa. In 1830 the two Landers witnessed silent bartering for yams on the lower Niger, the proceedings being presided over by an old woman.[15] As recently as 1907 Mr. E. J. Arnett came across an interesting example of it in the Zaria Emirate of Nigeria.*

* The scene was a pagan hill-town called Kinuku which had always stubbornly refused any intercourse with the outside world and was only approachable by a defile so narrow that a few armed men could easily defend it against a host. 'My informants of the neighbouring tribe to the west,' Mr. Arnett writes, 'with whom friendly relations had been established, were emphatic in stating that no person of another tribe was permitted to enter Kinuku or to have any personal contact with the people of Kinuku. They said that their people and others from the south sometimes traded

GHANA

The unusual method by which Ghana obtained its gold added greatly to the mysteriousness of the situation of Wangara, the discovery of which later became the cherished ambition of European adventurers. This quest, which occupied men's minds for a thousand years or more, will demand our attention in later chapters.

The principal buyers of the Wangara gold were merchants from the Maghreb el Acsa and from Wargla, the capital of Mzab. But there was another object in their long and painful journeys across the Sahara. Besides gold the foreign merchants used to take home with them negro slaves for whom there was always a good sale in the north. The slave market of Ghana was kept supplied by constant raids on the primitive forest tribes beyond the southern frontier. These people were known to the Arabs as Lemlem or Demdem.* They were armed with bows and arrows and with clubs cunningly carved in ebony; fishing was one of their principal occupations. Their chief towns were Mallel and Daw or Dao.†[17]

Other imports of Ghana were salt from Taghaza and from Aulil, an island which was probably situated near the mouth of the Senegal, and dates from the western Maghreb and Mzab. Brass was imported from the north and also great quantities of cheap jewellery for which there was an enormous demand among the unsophisticated tribes of the south as well as in Ghana itself. The chief industry of Ceuta in Morocco was the cutting and polishing of coral beads for Ghana and the Sudan.

The king of Ghana collected a tax of one golden *dinar* on each load of salt coming into the country and two *dinars* on each going out.

---

with Kinuku, a statement which appeared startlingly inconsistent with their previous assertions of absolute seclusion until they explained that any one who wished to trade with Kinuku halted and deposited his goods at the entrance to the defile and shouted to the sentry on watch, if he had not already been challenged. The would-be traders would then retire beyond bow-shot and wait until the Kinuku people had inspected the goods and retired to the town. The traders would then advance and find beside their goods what was offered in exchange. If the goods offered were acceptable, they were free to take them in exchange for their own. If not acceptable they would retire again leaving the articles of both parties untouched and hope that an increased offer would be made. Trade under these circumstances was a lengthy and laborious, but probably profitable, process. The survival of such a primitive method of intercourse and the determined seclusion from the world which dictated it, were all the more surprising since two marches away was the great market of Zungon Katab, well known throughout Hausaland for many generations as a spot where a good slave could be had in exchange for a very poor horse.'[16]

* Nyam-Nyam is to-day a common name for cannibals generally in the Western Sudan. † The site of Daw has not been identified.

GHANA

Every load of brass paid five *mitkal* and all other merchandise ten. The goldfields too were taxed. Foreign merchants, El Bekri tells us, suffered greatly from the climate of Ghana, particularly at the time of the harvest when sickness used to cause many deaths.[18]

Besides the capital there were other important markets. The chief of these were Gadiaro and Jaressi on the Senegal which probably owed their importance to their proximity to Wangara. North of these, on the western frontier, lay Kugha, also an entrepôt for the gold trade.

To the west of Ghana and athwart the Senegal lay the important kingdom of Tekrur. This name was sometimes loosely applied by the Arab geographers and others to the whole of the Western Sudan. For example the kings of Mali, the heirs to the greatness of Ghana, were known in Egypt as kings of Tekrur.[19] The name too is that by which all natives from the west are still known in the Eastern Sudan. In the eleventh century Tekrur was the home of the Tucolors. When the Berbers later advanced to the Senegal from Adrar these people were pushed south and west from Tekrur into their present home in Futa, where they are still known as Tekarir by their neighbours.

The principal towns of Tekrur were all on the Senegal. In the west was Sanghana* which was probably near the sea; Tekrur, the political capital, was situated near the present town of Podor; higher up the river, on the frontier of Ghana, was Silla. The last seems to have been the commercial capital and, like the neighbouring Ghana towns of Jaressi and Gadiaro, probably owed its importance to its proximity to the goldfields. The king usually resided in his capital and ruled firmly but justly, and gave his country peace. The negro people of Tekrur were converted to Islam as early as the first half of the eleventh century.

Tekrur, like Ghana, was a country of much commercial activity. The salt of Aulil came by boat up the river to Silla, whence it was distributed over a great part of the Western Sudan. Brass, wool, and jewellery were imported from the Maghreb. The chief exports were gold, slaves, and whips made from the hide of the hippopotamus. The principal industry was the weaving of a coarse cloth called by El Bekri 'chigguiya', doubtless the same *shigge* which Barth purchased in Timbuktu in the middle of last century.[20] The people of Tekrur, like those of Ghana, obtained their slaves by raiding the Lemlem.

El Bekri mentions two tribes of Lemlem whose country lay adjacent to Tekrur, the Zafcu and the Ferawi. The former worshipped an

---

* It has been suggested that the Senegal river took its name from Sanghana.

GHANA

enormous reptile. The Ferawi being as much in need of salt as they were well provided with gold were willing to exchange the one for the other weight for weight. They also possessed a plant of remarkable aphrodisiac properties the use of which was permitted only to their king.[21] Such were the strange tales which drifted through to the Maghreb concerning the obscure tribes which lay beyond the two comparatively civilized and commercially very important kingdoms of Ghana and Tekrur.

To return to our story, it will be recalled that when the small body of Almoravids under Yahia ibn Omar, whom Abu Bakr had left behind him in Adrar, sent to Tekrur for assistance against the Jedala their appeal did not go unanswered. This incident subsequently led to an alliance which was destined to effect the overthrow of Ghana.

In 1062, when Abu Bakr returned to the south after surrendering to Yusuf the command of the northern army, he devoted himself to spreading the reformed religion by force of arms among the negroes. The forces at his disposal were small, but he found a valuable ally in Lebbi or Ibrahim Sal, the same king of Tekrur who had ineffectually aided the ill-fated Yahia some years previously.

The persistence of Ghana in its adherence to paganism and its continued commercial prosperity stood as a constant challenge to Almoravid supremacy. The downfall of Ghana may have been an ambition cherished by Abu Bakr, but he can scarcely have expected to accomplish it. We unfortunately know nothing of his activities at this period, except that they eventually brought him into direct conflict with the forces of Ghana and that the triumphant outcome of a prolonged struggle, in which Tekrur played an important part, was the capture of the Soninke capital in 1076, fourteen years after Abu Bakr's return. The city was looted, many of the Soninke inhabitants were massacred, and the rest were forced to apostatize or to flee. The king of Ghana was permitted to retain his throne, but he became tributary to the Almoravids. His kingdom was shorn of all its dependencies which, including the goldfields of Ghana, passed into the hands of the conquerors.

Great though their triumph had been, this new hegemony of the Almoravids in the Sudan was short lived. Tribal feuds and petty jealousies made union impossible, and without concentration of their scattered forces the sect could not stand. The Lemtuna of Adrar, from the first the backbone of the movement, still remained faithful to the Emir. The Jedala held aloof. The Mesufa, Lemta, and several

GHANA

lesser tribes participated in raids, but they would never consent to regular service under a Lemtuna chief. In 1087 Abu Bakr was himself killed and what little organization was left now collapsed. His successors still claimed to be Emirs of the Almoravids, but they were never really more than chiefs of the Lemtuna and exercised no authority, either spiritual or temporal, outside that tribe.

The break up of the Almoravid sect enabled the Soninke of Ghana to regain their independence. But each of the small principalities, which united had formerly given the kingdom its strength, was now eager for autonomy and none would surrender its new found freedom for the common good. Under these circumstances it was impossible for Ghana to recover the predominant position it had formerly occupied.

Of these independent principalities the most important was the kingdom of the Susu,* a Soninke tribe whose country lay in the south between the Baule and the Niger. It had been the refuge of those who escaped from the massacre in Ghana and seems to have derived from these fugitives some of the enterprise and virility of the old Soninke capital. The Susu gradually grew in strength and power till in the year 1203, under their king, Sumanguru, they seized and occupied Ghana.

The fortunes of Ghana declined still further under the Susu. Finally in 1224 it was robbed of the last tattered shreds of its old commercial fame by a great exodus of its principal citizens. In that year the Arab merchants and the remaining rich Soninke families, despairing of ever being able to build up again their trade in Ghana, marched out into the desert under a sheikh from Mecca and settled at a camping ground of caravans called Biru† or Walata, a hundred miles to the north. The town they built there became the centre of the caravan trade which had formerly belonged to Ghana and it quickly attained a high degree of prosperity. The Soninke settlers seem to have taken with them some of their old pagan customs, for as late as the sixteenth century Leo Africanus reported that there were fire-worshippers in Walata.[22]

Sixteen years later the little that remained of Ghana was destroyed by Sundiata, the great Malinke chief who had made himself master of the Susu and had thereby founded the fortunes of the Mali Empire. Thereafter the ancient metropolis of the south-western Sahara ceased to exist. In the fourteenth century it was referred to by Abulfeda and

* Susu is a re-duplicated form or Su or So, the name by which the ancient Gara peoples were known to the Arabs. † Biru means in Soninke 'the tents'.

66 GHANA

Ibn Khaldun as if it still survived in their day.[23] But they probably confused it with Walata which Marmol two centuries later described as 'Gualata quo otros llaman Ganata'.[24]

REFERENCES

1. M. Delafosse, ii. 43.
2. El Bekri, pp. 328–31.
3. Edrisi, trad. Dozy et de Goeje, p. 8.
4. Ibn Khaldun, ii. 115.
5. Al Omari, p. 83.
6. Yaqut, *apud* Delafosse, ii. 45; El Omari, p. 71.
7. Maçoudi, iv. 93.
8. M. Delafosse, i. 55.
9. J. Meniaud, *Haut-Sénégal-Niger*, Paris, 1912, ii. 174.
10. M. P. Charlesworth, *Trade Routes and Commerce of the Roman Empire*, Cambridge, 1926, p. 107.
11. Fa-Hien, *Travels*, ch. xxxviii.
12. Cosmas, *Christian Topography*, Hakluyt Society, London, 1897, p. 52.
13. P. H. Hamilton Grierson, *The Silent Trade*, Edinburgh, 1903.
14. Sauzey, *La Géographie*, XLVI, 1926, p. 31.
15. Richard and John Lander, *Journal of an Expedition to Explore the Niger*, London, 1833, iii. 161.
16. E. J. Arnett, C.M.G., letter to the author.
17. Edrisi, trad. Dozy et de Goeje, p. 4.
18. El Bekri, pp. 328–31.
19. Al Omari, p. 53; Makrizi, *apud* Al Omari, p. 89.
20. H. Barth, *Travels*, iv. 443.
21. El Bekri, p. 327.
22. Leo Africanus, iii. 820.
23. Charles Monteil, *Les Empires du Mali, Bulletin du Comité d'études historiques et scientifiques de l'Afrique Occidentale Française*. Paris, 1930, p. 90.
24. Marmol, *apud* Delafosse, ii. 59.

VII

MALI

'The people of this region excell all other Negros in witte, ciuilitie, and industry.'—
LEO AFRICANUS.

THE virile peoples of the Western Sudan have always been distinguished for commercial enterprise, martial ardour, and aptitude
for the art of government. From the happy combination of these
qualities there sprung a number of political states to which the
grandiose style of empire is often loosely assigned. None, however,
can challenge the fairness of its application to the great Mandingo
kingdom which is known as the empire of Mali or Mande, and is
sometimes called the Mellestine.

Mali was distinguished above other Sudanese states by its great
territorial extent, and by the prestige which attached to its name, not
only in Africa but also in Europe. Its wide recognition as a power was
largely due to the regular observance by its rulers of the religious duty
of the *Hadj*, which resulted in the formation of many foreign friendships. The trade of the empire was greatly stimulated by these far-
flung associations and attracted to the capital all manner of foreign
merchants to whose reports may probably be traced the keen interest which, in later years, Christians, especially the Portuguese,
showed in the Mandingoes.

The empire of Mali is a subject on which we are unhappily very ill
informed, our knowledge being practically limited to fragments
scattered through the writings of a handful of Arab authors, of whom
Ibn Battuta was the only one to visit the Sudan. Our great need
is for a chronicle written by a native of the country, similar to Es
Sadi's invaluable history of Songhai, and till some such record comes
to light our knowledge will be limited to the roughest outline of its
story.

In its origin Mali was a small Mandingo kingdom extending eastwards from the upper Bakhoy across the Niger. The capital was Jeriba,
where extensive ruins have been found.[1] Of its history before the
thirteenth century all we know is that one of its rulers, named Baramendana, was converted to Islam by an uncle of Yusuf ibn Tachifine*
in the early days of the Almoravid movement. Baramendana made

* Possibly Omar, the father of Yahia and Abu Bakr.

F 2

68   MALI

a pilgrimage to Mecca and thus set an example which was regularly
followed by his successors.[2]

At the beginning of the thirteenth century the Mandingo kingdom
had become sufficiently powerful to excite the jealousy of the Susu,
who, flushed with their successful capture of Ghana, were in no mood
to permit a rival, though of the same Mandingo race as themselves, to
interfere with their own aspirations. The Susu king, Sumanguru,
sought to undermine the growing strength of Mali by striking a suc-
cession of blows at their ruling house. He succeeded in putting to
death eleven brothers, all heirs to the throne of Mali, but he spared
the twelfth, a cripple child named Sundiata. But as the weakling grew
he became cured, and on attaining manhood he revealed himself as
a leader with remarkable qualities which enabled him to lay the
foundations of a great empire. To this day he is regarded by the
Mandingoes as their national hero.[3]

On his accession Sundiata, or Mari Jata as he was now called, found
his hold on the throne precarious. He was unable to rely on the loyalty
of his subjects, by whom he was feared but not liked. He surrounded
himself with a guard of hunters and desperadoes on whom he could
depend for personal protection and support. With them he crossed
the Tinkisso and fell unexpectedly on the neighbouring kingdom of
Sangaran over which one of his uncles ruled. The latter very quickly
accepted the suzerainty of his assailant and placed his own warriors,
with himself at their head, under his arrogant nephew's banner. With
his force thus strengthened Sundiata next fell on Labe in Futa Jallon
in the west where he was again successful and acquired yet another
army. He now turned eastwards and, crossing the Niger and the
Sankarani, he fell upon some insurgent Bambaras whom he reduced to
obedience. A series of successful expeditions into different parts of
the kingdom followed, and as the result of these he consolidated and
extended his dominions and placed beyond question his authority over
them. With the security of the throne thus assured he returned to
Jeriba in 1234 and made a triumphant and impressive entry into the
capital.

In their victorious progress the armies of Sundiata had encroached
on Susu territory. This decided Sumanguru to take the field against
Mali before his rival became too powerful to be resisted. The Susu
and Mali forces met at Kirina, which was probably just north of the
modern town of Kulikoro. The result of the battle, which took place
in 1235, was a complete victory for Sundiata. Sumanguru was killed

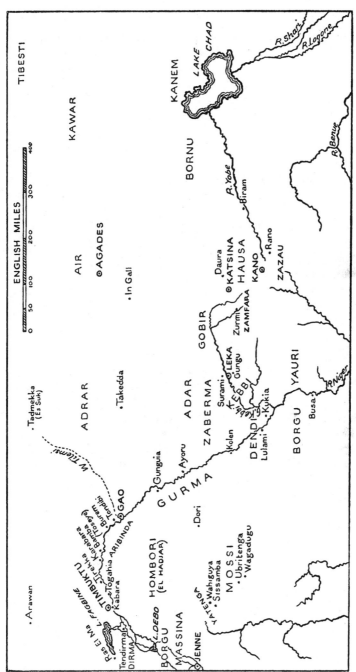

V. Hausa and the Middle Niger.

MALI

and his kingdom was absorbed. This constituted the first great territorial acquisition of Mali which now extended northwards beyond Aukar. Five years later, as we have already seen, he destroyed all that remained of the city of Ghana. The name survived as that of a district and, according to El Omari, its chief was the only vassal of Mali allowed to call himself king,[4] a concession to the past glory of the fallen kingdom.

Sundiata now moved his capital from Jeriba southwards to Niani where a village of the same name still survives.[5] The city which he built there was often known as Mali or Mande, after the state of which it was the capital. During the rest of his life Sundiata made the economic development of the country surrounding Niani his special interest. He never again took the field with his troops, but under their own leaders they continued to extend the frontiers of his empire. They were particularly active towards the west where they reached the Gambia river and the marches of Tekrur. The goldfields of Wangara had been acquired some years previously. According to El Omari, attempts were made to convert the pagan gold-diggers, but as these efforts always resulted in a cessation of the output of gold it was decided to leave them in peace so long as they remained loyal and continued to pay the tribute which had been levied on them.[6]

Sundiata died in 1255. During his reign of twenty-five years he had transformed his petty kingdom into a powerful empire with his own dynasty firmly established at its head.

He was succeeded by his son Mansa Ule, or Sultan Ule, a lover of peace who made a pilgrimage to Mecca during the time of the Mamluk Sultan Ed Daher Bibers.[7]* In spite of the unwarlike disposition of the king the frontiers of Mali were further extended during his reign. The commanders of the army, who had been trained in the brilliant campaigns of Sundiata, were loath to resign themselves to lives of inactivity under his less enterprising successor. Three of them established themselves as petty kings over the districts of Bambuk, Konkodugu, and Gangaran which thus became apanages of Mali.

Mansa Ule was followed by three kings of whom we know very little. In 1285 the throne was seized by a freed slave of the royal house, named Sakura, who proved himself worthy of the position to which he had aspired. He made several successful expeditions against his neighbours, notably the Tucolors of Tekrur in the west and the

---

* Ibn Khaldun derived his information about Mali from a certain sheikh of Ghana whom he met passing through Egypt in 1393-4 on his way to Mecca with his family.

MALI

71

Songhai of Gao, who were becoming a power on the middle Niger, in the east. In his time Mali was commercially very prosperous and was visited by merchants from the Maghreb el Acsa and Ifrikia.

Sakura died in 1300 on his way back from Mecca. He was not returning by the customary route through Cairo, but through Eritrea and the Eastern Sudan, following what has now become the great pilgrim road of West-Central Africa. He was assassinated by the Danakil on the coast of Tadjurah as he set foot on African soil.

The joint reigns of the next three occupants of the throne, Gau, Mamadu, and Abu Bakr II, lasted only seven years. Abu Bakr* was a son of a sister of Sundiata and will always be remembered as the father of Mansa Musa who succeeded him in 1307. With the possible exception of Sundiata, his grandfather, Mansa Musa was the most illustrious of the Mandingo kings and was even renowned in Europe.

The fame of Mansa Musa, sometimes called Kankan or Gongo Musa by French writers,† was primarily due to the manner of his pilgrimage to Mecca. The spectacular scale on which it was conducted caused such a sensation in Cairo and other places which witnessed the passage of his splendid caravan, that the name of the Mandingo Emperor quickly became familiar throughout a large part of the civilized world. He set out across the desert in 1324, the seventeenth year of his reign, accompanied by a great host of followers. He rode on horseback preceded by 500 slaves, each carrying a staff of gold weighing 500 *mitkal* or about 6 pounds. In his baggage train of camels were 80 to 100 loads of gold each weighing 3 *kantar* or about 300 pounds. The magnificent caravan passed through Walata and Tuat and thence to Cairo. Musa's piety and open-handed generosity and the fine clothes and good behaviour of his followers quickly made a favourable impression. His pale complexion, usually described as red or yellow, gave the negro monarch a distinctive appearance which perhaps contributed to the sensation he caused. The sole object of his journey was the performance of a religious duty and, in spite of the pomp with which it was carried out, seems to have been free from political motives. Only with the greatest difficulty was he persuaded to interrupt his spiritual exercises in order to pay a formal visit to the Sultan of Egypt. When the time came to continue the journey to Mecca the Sultan made

---

* El Omari relates how Abu Bakr organized two expeditions to explore the Atlantic and lost his own life at sea while leading the second.[8]

† Kankan, his birthplace, was not necessarily the well-known modern town of that name in French Guinea.

72 MALI

elaborate arrangements to ensure the utmost comfort for the negro potentate.

El Omari, who was in Cairo twelve years after Mansa Musa had left it on his homeward journey, found the townspeople still loud in his praises. His popularity was chiefly due to his unprecedentedly lavish distribution of gold among the hordes of petty Egyptian officials. The masses had also benefited from the highly profitable trade which they had done with his followers, simple folk who would readily pay five *dinar* for a garment worth only one. Fine clothes and female slaves were what appealed to the negroes most, and these commodities represented the bulk of their purchases. In consequence of Mansa Musa's visit so much gold came into circulation that its value in Egypt fell considerably and even in El Omari's time the price had not recovered.[9]

Mansa Musa did not confine to Cairo this prodigal display of wealth. Wherever he went he showered gold. In the holy cities he was particularly generous in his charitable gifts. It is not therefore surprising to learn that by the time he had returned to Cairo he had come nearly to an end of his immediate resources. Needless to say there was little difficulty in finding accommodation for the monarch of a country which produced gold on a scale which had already dazzled so many eyes.

On his homeward journey he was accompanied by a poet of Granada, generally known as Es Saheli, to whom he had become attached in Mecca. In the desert he was joined by El Mamer, the friend of Ibn Khaldun to whom we owe much of our knowledge of Mali. These two men travelled with him to the Sudan, treated as honoured guests and freely enjoying the royal favours.

While he was still in the desert Mansa Musa heard of the capture of Gao, the Songhai capital, by Sagmandia, one of his generals. Songhai was the powerful riverain kingdom which extended the whole length of the middle Niger from the frontier of Mali to Dendi, a distance of 1,000 miles. The news of this enormous extension of his empire decided Mansa Musa to turn aside from his homeward route and visit Gao. He made an impressive entry into the city and received in person the submission of the Songhai king. To ensure the fidelity of his new vassal he took with him to Mali as hostages the latter's two sons, Ali Kolen and Sulayman Nar.

While he was in Gao Mansa Musa entrusted to Es Saheli the task of building a mosque better suited to the worship of God than the mean structure of mud and straw which the Songhai had found

MALI

73

sufficient. The talented Andalusian constructed an imposing edifice of burnt bricks, the use of which had till then been unknown in the Sudan. This mosque, with its minaret, was still standing in the middle of the seventeenth century.

Mansa Musa, continuing his homeward journey up the Niger, came next to Timbuktu which, after the capital, was the most important Songhai town. Timbuktu was originally the meeting place of those who travelled by land and those who travelled by water, that is to say of the nomads from the desert and the Sudanese who navigated the Niger. Here they met to exchange salt and dates and the merchandise of the Maghreb for the grain, kola nuts, and gold dust of the Sudan. In about 1100 the tents began to give place to straw huts and these in turn to more permanent structures of clay. Two centuries later the merchants of Jenne made Timbuktu an entrepôt for their trade with Walata and it quickly became an important market with a port of its own at Kabara on the Niger which was only five miles away. Its geographical situation close to a navigable waterway which tapped so great a part of the Western Sudan gave it a great advantage over the neighbouring markets of Walata and Tirekka the trade of which it gradually captured. Walata had long enjoyed a reputation as a centre of learning which it owed to its Jedala scholars who had come there from Ghana when the latter began to decline. When Walata also began to lose its trade they moved on to Timbuktu which very soon became commercially and intellectually the most important city of the western interior. Probably the most eminent scholar it ever produced was Ahmed Baba, the Jedala historian whom Es Sadi so frequently quotes. At the time of the Mandingo occupation Timbuktu was already flourishing. Marmol tells us that in the thirteenth century merchants of Barbary and Egypt used to go to Timbuktu for the gold of *tibar*, or gold dust, a trade which had once been controlled by Ghana.[10]

Mansa Musa, considering that Timbuktu, like Gao, was worthy of a finer place of worship than it then possessed, ordered Es Saheli to build a new mosque there also and a palace for himself.

Under Mansa Musa's patronage the city attained greatly increased importance, both as regards trade and culture. It was regularly visited by caravans from Egypt, Aujila, Fezzan, Ghadames, Tuat, Dra'a, Sijilmasa, Fez, and Sus. With trade there came the rich and the cultured and the learned divines of many lands. Its great mosque of Sankore, which produced many distinguished men of letters, became famous as a seat of learning.

MALI

Mansa Musa died in the year 1332. He left behind him an empire which in the history of purely African states was as remarkable for its size as for its wealth, and which provided a striking example of the capacity of the negro for political organization. From Tekrur in the west it spread eastwards to Gao and perhaps to Air, but whether the latter was a dependency of Mali is not certain. According to Ibn Khaldun a great but indefinite part of the Sahara recognized Mandingo suzerainty. Southwards the empire extended into the forests. Curiously enough, however, the little town of Jenne, situated only a few days' march from Niani, but admirably protected by a network of waterways, still preserved its independence.

Mansa Musa's reign had seen a great expansion in the foreign trade of his empire. This development was due to the assiduity with which he cultivated foreign relations. Apart from the friendships with Egypt and Mecca, which had resulted from his famous pilgrimage, his relations with the Merinid Sultan of Fez were particularly cordial. Interesting evidence of the prestige which now attached to the Mandingo Empire as a result of the foreign associations developed by its great ruler is provided in the *mappae-mundi* of European cartographers who, at this period, were making their first serious attempts to represent the interior of Africa. What perhaps is the first cartographical reference to Mali occurs on a *mappa-mundi* of Angelino Dulcert of Majorca, dated 1339, in which a road passing through the Atlas Mountains is described as leading to the king of the gold mines, *rex melli*.[11] In one edition of the *mappa-mundi* of the Pizzigani of Venice, dated 1367, the Atlas range is broken by a col called the Valley of Sus, 'through which passes the merchandise coming from the King of Mali'. On the famous Catalan atlas of Charles V, to which we shall have occasion to refer again, we find depicted in the desert a veiled man on a camel riding towards a monarch seated on a throne. The latter holds a sceptre in one hand and in the other a nugget of gold which he is offering to the rider. 'This negro lord', reads the inscription, 'is called Musa Mali, Lord of the Negroes of Guinea. So abundant is the gold which is found in his country that he is the richest and most noble king in all the land.' The fame of the great negro ruler persisted for some time and many even believed him to be no less a personage than the mythical potentate Prester John. As late as 1502 we find the single name 'Musa Mali' blazoned across the desert on the *mappa-mundi* of Caneiro. By 1574 it had disappeared, replaced by the misshapen forms of giraffes and lions.[12]

MALI
75

Mansa Musa was succeeded by his son Maghan, an effete monarch who in a brief reign of four years permitted the great empire which he had inherited to suffer two severe blows to its prestige. In 1333, shortly after his accession, the warlike Mossi of Yatenga on the upper Volta raided Timbuktu, routed the Mandingo garrison, and burnt the city. The Mossi, who with their neighbours and relatives the Gurmanche represent a very ancient stock, had two kingdoms, Yatenga and Ubritenga, of which Wahiguya and Wagadugu afterwards became the respective capitals. Although formidable warriors the Mossi never sought territorial expansion, contenting themselves with raiding their neighbours. The Mossi of Yatenga were the more enterprising, sometimes raiding, as we shall see, even farther afield than Timbuktu.

But a still more unfortunate incident was to follow. Maghan had incautiously permitted complete freedom to the two Songhai princes whom his father had retained as hostages after the capture of Gao. The young men were not slow to perceive that the change of ruler provided an opportunity for their countrymen to regain their freedom. They both escaped to Gao, and Ali Kolen, proclaiming himself king, successfully freed the old Songhai capital from the Mandingo yoke.

Maghan was succeeded by his uncle Sulayman, a brother of Mansa Musa, who did much to repair the damage which the empire had suffered under his nephew. He failed to recover Gao, but he restored control over the rest of his dominions and re-established Mandingo prestige in the north. In 1351 he made the pilgrimage to Mecca which gave him an opportunity of re-asserting Mandingo authority in some of the more distant parts of his empire through which he had to pass.

The most important place on the pilgrim route across the desert was the town of Takedda, at this time a thriving centre of the caravan trade and one of the most valued apanages of Mali. Its situation has never been determined, but it is generally agreed that it lay somewhere between Gao and Air. Ibn Khaldun placed it seventy days' march south-west of Wargla with which it enjoyed very friendly relations. According to the same authority, each year a caravan of 12,000 camels used to pass through Takedda on its way from Cairo to Niani.[13] The foundation of its commercial importance was its copper mines, from which Barbary, Egypt, Mali, Hausa, and Bornu drew their supplies. Mansa Musa declared that from no other source did he derive so great a sum in taxes as from the copper trade of Takedda.[14] It is curious that no trace of these important mines has yet come to light.

The event of Sulayman's reign of most interest to us was the visit

76   MALI

of the renowned traveller Ibn Battuta, to whose narrative we owe so much of our knowledge of the Muslim world in the first half of the fourteenth century. He was sent to the Sudan on a mission by Abu Inan, who had seized the Moroccan throne from his father Abu'l Hassan. Setting forth in 1352, Ibn Battuta fitted out his caravan in Sijilmasa and travelled south through Taghaza. From there his caravan had an arduous journey to Tasarahla where they halted three days, mending and refilling their water-skins.

It was from Tasarahla that they sent out the *takshif*, the Mesufa messenger who used to go ahead, to Walata to announce the approach of a caravan and to get water sent out to meet it in the desert. If, as sometimes happened, the *takshif* failed to arrive the caravan was in danger of perishing in the desert.

On this occasion the *takshif*, who was paid a hundred gold *mitkal* for his services, was almost blind. The point is not without interest. Leo Africanus tells us of a caravan losing its way and being saved by a blind guide who 'riding foremost vpon his camell, commanded some sand to be giuen him at euery miles end, by the smell whereof he declared the situation of the place'.[15] Blind guides who found their way over the desert by their sense of smell are also mentioned by Pellow[16] and Jackson.[17] The *takshif* piloted the caravan successfully, and Ibn Battuta records the pleasure with which on the seventh day out from Tasarahla he and his companions saw the fires of those who had come out to meet them.

In Walata, which was reached two months after leaving Sijilmasa, the travellers presented themselves before the negro governor who was the official representative of the Emperor of Mali. They were received in so insolent a manner that Ibn Battuta began to regret ever having set out for the Sudan.[18]

He stayed in Walata fifty days. He tells us that the inhabitants were mostly Mesufa, who wore garments of fine Egyptian fabrics, that mutton was plentiful and the women of surpassing beauty. He thought the important social position accorded to the women and the liberty they enjoyed very extraordinary and he was greatly puzzled by the custom of uterine descent.

He set out for Niani, which was twenty-four days' march from Walata, with only three companions and a guide, the safety of the road making it no longer necessary to travel in a company. Neither had they to carry provisions, nor gold nor silver. With salt, beads, and aromatic goods for barter they were able to obtain food in variety at

MALI

each village they came to. They passed through Zaghari—identified by Delafosse with Jaga[19]—which was inhabited by Wangara traders and a colony of Ibadites who were perhaps merchants from Mzab. Shortly afterwards they came to the 'Nile' or Niger which Ibn Battuta believed to be the Nile of Egypt, and described as flowing past Timbuktu, Gao, 'Muli, in the land of the Limis' which may have been Dendi, and thence to Yufi, which is usually identified with Nupe in Nigeria. 'From Yufi', he tells us, 'the Nile descends to the land of Nuba, who profess the Christian faith, and thence to Dunqula (Dongola), which is their chief town.'[20]

Ibn Battuta found himself in Niani amongst fellow countrymen by whom he was hospitably entertained. He had the misfortune to fall ill directly he arrived and was attended by an Egyptian doctor. He was laid up for the first two months he was in the capital, which did not incline him to a less critical attitude towards the Sudan, his contempt for which he makes no effort to conceal.

Ibn Battuta describes at some length the ceremonies at the court of Sulayman.[21] The scenes seem to have closely resembled in their pageantry those which took place at Ghana. People who sought audience presented themselves before the *pempi* clothed in rags and pouring dust on their heads. Applause was signified by the twanging of bow strings. Two goats were present to give protection against the evil eye.

Among the visitors to Sulayman's court were negro cannibals from Wangara. 'The sultan received them with honour, and gave them as his hospitality-gift a servant, a negress. They killed and ate her, and having smeared their faces and hands with her blood came to the sultan to thank him. I was informed that this is their regular custom whenever they visit his court.'[22]

As he grew better acquainted with the Sudanese Ibn Battuta began to recognize some of their good qualities. In common with many other travellers he particularly appreciated their love of justice and the security of their roads.

'The negroes', he wrote, 'possess some admirable qualities. They are seldom unjust, and have a greater abhorrence of injustice than any other people. Their sultan shows no mercy to any one who is guilty of the least act of it. There is complete security in their country. Neither traveller nor inhabitant in it has anything to fear from robbers or men of violence. They do not confiscate the property of any white man who dies in their country, even if it be uncounted wealth. On the contrary, they give it into the charge of

MALI

some trustworthy person among the whites, until the rightful heir takes possession of it. They are careful to observe the hours of prayer, and assiduous in attending them in congregations, and in bringing up their children to them. . . . Among their bad qualities are the following. The women servants, slave-girls, and young girls go about in front of every one naked, without a stitch of clothing on them. Women go into the sultan's presence naked and without coverings, and his daughters also go about naked. Then there is their custom of putting dust and ashes on their heads, as a mark of respect. . . . Another reprehensible practice among many of them is the eating of carrion, dogs, and asses.'[23]

Ibn Battuta left Niani at the end of February 1353, after spending eight months there. Being unable to afford a horse, which would have cost him a hundred gold *mitkal*, he rode a camel. Travelling down the Niger he next visited Timbuktu, but he says little about it. He tells us that the inhabitants were mostly of the Mesufa tribe and he mentions the tomb of Es Saheli, the poet-architect from Andalusia. From Timbuktu he continued his journey by water in a dug-out canoe, stopping every night at Songhai villages where he bought meat and butter in exchange for salt, spices, and glass beads. At one of these stopping places he was presented by the chief with a slave boy who was still with him when he wrote the history of his travels.

He followed the Niger as far as Gao and thence travelled eastwards to Takedda.

'The inhabitants of Tagadda', he tells us, 'have no occupation except trade. They travel to Egypt every year, and import quantities of all the fine fabrics to be had there and of other Egyptian wares. They live in luxury and ease, and vie with one another in regard to the number of their slaves and serving-women. The people of Malli and Iwalatan do the same. They never sell the educated female slaves, or but rarely and at a high price. . . . The copper mine is in the outskirts of Tagadda. They dig the ore out of the ground, bring it to the town, and cast it in their houses. . . . The copper is exported from Tagadda to the town of Kubar, in the regions of the heathens, to Zaghay, and to the country of Barnu which is forty days' journey from Tagadda.'*[24]

While he was here Ibn Battuta received a command from the Sultan of Fez to return home. He set out at once with a caravan of 600 women slaves travelling by way of Air, Tuat, and Sijilmasa.

We have an interesting account of the organization of a commercial house of Tlemcen which was trading with the Sudan at this period. The firm consisted of five brothers, named Al Makkari, who were

---

* Kubar is Gobir, but Zaghay has not been satisfactorily identified.

MALI

79

co-equal partners. Two of these were established in Walata where they collected ivory and gold. One of them visited the Mali capital in 1352. The brothers in Walata were kept supplied with European trade goods by two other brothers who remained in Tlemcen for the purpose. The fifth brother, the head of the firm, had settled in Sijilmasa, the chief centre of the Saharan caravan trade, where he was able to watch the markets closely and keep his brothers advised of price fluctuations.[25] Abu Hammen, who had been king of Tlemcen at the beginning of the century, had wished he could banish all merchants except those who traded with the Sudan, for whereas the latter brought great wealth to his kingdom the others merely impoverished it.[26]

On the death of Mansa Sulayman in 1359 Mali was rent by civil war. His son Kamba who succeeded him had a formidable rival in a son of Maghan. After much bloodshed Kamba was killed and his rival thereafter ruled as Mari Jata II. The new monarch hastened to establish friendly relations with Fez, the good will of which the Mandingoes were always anxious to retain for commercial reasons. Among the presents which Mari Jata sent the Sultan was a giraffe which caused a sensation on its arrival in Morocco.

According to Ibn Khaldun, whose informant was a native of Sijilmasa who had spent some time in Mali, Mari Jata ruined his empire by his extravagance, and he attributes to him the sale of the famous nugget of Ghana to some merchants of Egypt. After a life of excess he died in 1374 of sleeping sickness which at that time was a common disease among those occupying high positions.[27]

Mari Jata was succeeded by his son Musa II, who inherited all the vices of the father and allowed the control of the State to pass into the hands of his principal minister Jata. The latter was happily a man of abounding energy and enterprise who re-organized the army and conducted a series of successful campaigns in the east. His activities led him into the country beyond Gao where he came to blows with Omar ben Idris, the Sultan of Bornu.[28]

By the beginning of the fifteenth century Mali had lost much of the power which it had enjoyed under the illustrious rule of Mansa Musa. Its territorial extent was nevertheless still very considerable. According to Delafosse it included Timbuktu, Aukar, Mima, Bagana, Jaga, Jara, and perhaps part of Galam.[29] Any control, however, which the Mandingoes may have exercised in the past over Tekrur had probably been lost. They perhaps still regarded the Songhai as vassals but there

MALI

is no evidence that the independence of the latter, except around Timbuktu, was other than complete. The extent of Mandingo influence over the Sahara has always been doubtful. According to Ibn Khaldun the great Sanhaja confederation of Muleththemin still paid tribute to the king of Mali, whom he calls the *Malik es Sudan*—King of the Land of the Negroes*—and he tells us they furnished troops for the Mandingo army. From our knowledge of the proud Berber desert folk we may well doubt whether this represented the true relationship existing between them and the negro Mandingoes.

With the accession of Magha III in 1390 Ibn Khaldun closes his account of the Sudan. We are dependent for the later history of Mali on the *Tarikh es Sudan* and on the narratives of a few Portuguese explorers. But these sources are so barren that it becomes difficult to follow the history of the empire in the period of its decay.

REFERENCES

1. Vidal, *Bull. du Comité d'études historiques et scientifiques de l'Afrique Occidentale Française*, 1923. See also C. Monteil, *Les Empires du Mali*.

2. El Bekri, p. 333; Leo Africanus, iii. 823; Ibn Khaldun, ii, p. 111. *Tarikh et Fettach*, pp. 54-60.

3. M. Delafosse, ii. 175.

4. Al Omari, p. 59.

5. M. Delafosse, *Bull. du Comité d'études historiques et scientifiques de l'Afrique Occidentale Française*, 1924; Vidal, loc. cit.

6. Al Omari, p. 58.

7. Ibn Khaldun, ii. 110.

8. Al Omari, p. 74.

9. Ibid., p. 79.

10. Marmol Caravajal, *L'Afrique*, trad. Perrot d'Ablancourt, 3 vols. Paris 1667, ii. pp. 29, 125.

11. Charles de la Roncière, *La Découverte de l'Afrique au Moyen Âge*, Cairo, 1924, i. 123.

12. Ibid., p. 169.

13. Ibn Khaldun, ii. 116.

14. Al Omari, p. 81.

15. Leo Africanus, iii. 802.

16. *The Adventures of Thomas Pellow*, London, 1890, pp. 195–99.

17. J. G. Jackson, *An Account of the Empire of Marocco*, London, 1809, p. 240, and *An Account of Timbuctoo and Housa*, London, 1820, p. 5.

18. Ibn Battuta, trans. H. A. R. Gibb, p. 320.

19. M. Delafosse, ii. 195.

* The hereditary title of the Emir of Kontagora in Nigeria is *Sarkin Sudan* which is Hausa for *Malik es Sudan*.

MALI

20. Ibn Battuta, trans. H. A. R. Gibb, p. 323.

21. See also Al Omari, p. 65.

22. Ibn Battuta, trans. H. A. R. Gibb, p. 332.

23. Ibid., pp. 329–31.

24. Ibid., pp. 335–6.

25. Abbé Bargès, *Mémoire sur les relations commerciales de Tlemçen avec le Soudan* (*Revue de l'Orient*), Paris, 1853 (*apud* de la Roncière).

26. Abbé Bargès, *Tlemcen, ancienne capitale du royaume de ce nom*, Paris, 1859, p. 208 (*apud* de la Roncière).

27. Ibn Khaldun, ii. 114–15.

28. M. Delafosse, ii. 206.

29. Ibid. 207.

VIII

THE RISE OF THE SONGHAI EMPIRE

'*That which Nilus is to Aegypt, the same is Niger to the land of the Negroes.*'—LEO AFRICANUS.

BETWEEN the modern French Sudanese towns of Bamako and Kulikoro the Niger is interrupted by the rapids of Sotuba and Kénié. It is similarly obstructed at Busa in the British Protectorate of Nigeria. Between these two points lie 1,000 miles of perennially navigable waterway which formed the controlling geographic factor in the history of the Songhai people.

Below Kénié the Niger splits up into several channels and combines with its confluent the Bani to form the great lacustrine region which lies to the south and west of Timbuktu. The waters of the two rivers here become dissipated over a very large area, forming an elaborate series of lakes which are linked with each other by innumerable waterways. A little above Kabara, the port of Timbuktu, the waters are again united to form a single stream flowing far into the desert. The river varies in breadth from one to three or more miles, till at Tosaye it is forced violently through a narrow gorge of great depth. Below Tosaye the river again widens and flows steadily towards the south-east with a gentle current, interrupted here and there by shelves of hard rock. It is navigable for canoes as far as Busa where perilous rapids form an effective barrier to almost every form of craft.

Throughout the greater part of its course the middle Niger is fringed with a luxuriant growth of *borgu*, a highly nutritious aquatic grass to which the natives bring their cattle from great distances. The river banks are much broken by creeks and inlets, while the main stream is frequently interrupted by small islands. Throughout the turbulent history of the middle Niger these reed-grown creeks and obscure inlets, no less than the easily defended islands lying far out in midstream, have been havens of refuge and the resort of the oppressed. The river banks, lying for the most part in arid regions, are almost destitute of timber and in consequence we find here the same lack of boat-building material which constantly handicapped Babylonia. For several hundred miles down-stream from Jenne the only available timber is the fan palm, of which perforce practically all the canoes of the middle Niger are built. Had better boat-building material been

THE RISE OF THE SONGHAI EMPIRE

at hand this great water-way might have played a still more important part than it did in the political history of the region.*

The Songhai are a negro people whose traditional home is Dendi, which lies to the north-west of the confluence of the Gulbin Kebbi and the Niger and not far above the Busa rapids. Over 1,000 years ago they spread from this region northwards up the Niger as two distinct and mutually hostile clans—the Sorko, who were fisher-folk, and the Gabibi, who were agricultural peasantry. The Sorko, with the independence characteristic of their calling, ranged far up and down the Niger. They named the left bank Hausa and the right Gurma after the countries which lay adjacent to each shore. They entirely dominated the less mobile Gabibi, raiding their granaries and pillaging their villages.

Meanwhile the Gabibi fell under the domination of Zaghawa invaders from the north. These were Lemta whom Ibn Khaldun later classed together with the Sanhaja, Ketama, and Auriga as Muleth-themin, and who are to-day represented by the Aulimmiden and other Tuareg. The Lemta chief, Za Aliamen, according to Es Sadi, slew the tyrannical river-god which the Gabibi worshipped in the form of a fish with a ring in its nose. The fish of this legend probably symbolizes the oppressive Sorko (who perhaps wore nose rings) from whose tutelage the Gabibi were freed by the Lemta. Za Aliamen settled in Kukia, the capital, and became the first of a long line of Berber kings of the Songhai.

The situation of Kukia, the ancient Songhai capital, has long been a subject of controversy, and continues to present a problem to which no wholly satisfactory solution has been propounded. Our only guide among the medieval writers is Idrisi, who himself was doubtful of its situation.

Idrisi tells us that the Kukia was situated on a river flowing from the north which some said was a tributary of the Niger. He was certain, however, that the river on which the city stood, after flowing for some distance, disappeared into the sands of the desert 'like the Euphrates, which flows through Irak and is lost in the Bataïh'.[1]

Desplagnes,[2] who has been followed by other French writers, placed it on the island of Bentia between Gao and Tilaberi. Idrisi's description of Kukia on an intermittent stream flowing through desert recently set Mr. H. R. Palmer looking for it on one of the dry water-

---

* In the reign of Askia Daud the timber necessary for the building of a new mosque in Timbuktu had to be supplied from Gao.

84 THE RISE OF THE SONGHAI EMPIRE

courses which fall into the Niger on its left bank between Illo and Say, that is to say, in Dendi, the traditional home of the Songhai. His inquiries led to the discovery of the ruins of an ancient city called Kaukau to the north-west of Argungu and not far from the present town of Beibei. It is probable that this was the site of the ancient Songhai capital. It is on a branch of the big wadi called the Dallul Mauri,* which was probably once a river, a situation which, he claims, entirely corresponds with Idrisi's description.[3]

On the arrival of the Lemta invaders the Sorko fisher-folk, proud and mobile, retreated up the Niger. One powerful section, led by a certain Faran Ber, founded an independent kingdom at Gao which was situated on the left bank of the Niger at the point where it is joined by the great Wadi Tilemsi. Another section, the Fono, moved still farther upstream and established themselves on the crest of the Bend of the Niger, probably in the neighbourhood of Bamba.

There was a constant state of war between the Sorko of Gao and the Lemta of Kukia. A prolonged conflict culminated in the capture of Gao by the Lemta in about the year 890. After this disaster the Sorko withdrew farther up the Niger till at last they reached the distant shores of Lake Debo. Here they came into conflict with the Soninke and Bozo, but they eventually succeeded in establishing themselves as masters of the lacustrine region with liberty to navigate the Bani. Although so far removed from their own country they continued to call the right bank of the river Gurma and the left Hausa, and these terms are still commonly used on the Niger all the way from Dendi to Lake Debo.[4]

At the beginning of the eleventh century and in the reign of Za Kossoi the Lemta-Songhai capital was moved from Kukia to Gao and in 1009 or 1010 the king became a Muhammadan. These two important events were probably not unconnected. Gao was a commercial centre much frequented by merchants from the Maghreb and probably had a considerable Muhammadan community. On the conversion of the king it became a more suitable place for the capital than Kukia, which was far removed from the caravan routes linking the Sudan with the Mediterranean littoral and from the important markets which had sprung up at Tadmekka and Takedda.

The earliest reference to Gao occurs in Ibn Haukal, but his contempt for all negro countries did not permit him to do more than merely mention its name. Happily El Bekri, writing in the eleventh

* See Map XII, p. 218.

THE RISE OF THE SONGHAI EMPIRE 85

century, has left us a short description of it.[5] According to him Gao was composed of two quarters, the one inhabited by Muslims, which was no doubt the foreign quarter, the other the pagan or native quarter, where the king or *kanda* resided. The natives wore loin cloths or aprons of skins and they worshipped idols. When a new king, who had to be a Muslim, came to the throne he was given a seal, a sword, and a Quran which was said to have been especially provided by the Khalif in confirmation of his investiture. El Bekri tells us that the inhabitants of Gao were called by the Arabs Buzurganiyin or Basur-Kayin. The reference here is evidently not to the natives, but to the foreign merchants who were North African Semites comparable to-day to the so-called 'Arab' merchants of Kano and the Wasuri of Bornu. It is thought that they were originally Syrians or Phoenicians of Tur or Tyre, whence they acquired the name Turawa by which white men are widely known in the Western Sudan.[6] The currency of Gao was salt from Taotek which lay in the desert six days' march beyond Tadmekka.

Tadmekka was situated at the head of the Tilemsi valley in the mountainous district of Adrar and up till the sixteenth century it was one of the most important markets in the Sahara. It is usually called Es Suk, the Market, the name by which it was known to the Arabs. To-day only ruins mark the site, but these are sufficiently extensive to indicate the former existence of a town of considerable size. El Bekri tells us that it was a finer town than either Ghana or Gao. The inhabitants were Muleththemin and their market was Koceilata, a name which recalls the hero of Berber emancipation. They ate flesh, milk, and burr grass or *karengia* and they obtained millet and other cereals from the negroes. Their women were of exquisite beauty and very free with their favours. Their currency was unstamped gold. The nomadic Berbers who inhabited the surrounding desert were known as Saghmara. They still survive as a section of the Tadmekket. Tadmekka traded with Gao and Ghana and also with the distant cities of Kairwan and Ghadames. The road to Kairwan passed through Wargla, which was fifty days' march away. There were two desert roads to Ghadames, which was forty days' march. On one of these were some mines of agate and other stones, the principal market for which was Ghana. This is all we know of Tadmekka, but it leaves no room for doubt that in the eleventh century it was a place of considerable commercial importance trading over an immense area.[7]

On the road from Tadmekka to Ghana there was another important

86 THE RISE OF THE SONGHAI EMPIRE

market called Tirekka. It was situated on the Niger in the neighbourhood of Timbuktu which, although unknown at this time, was destined eventually to capture its trade. Tirekka was described by Idrisi
as a large and populous unwalled town and was evidently a favourite
meeting place for merchants from Ghana and Tadmekka. It was noted
for its enormous tortoises. From Tirekka the road to Ghana followed
the northern shore of Lake Fagbine.[8]

We have no certain knowledge of the history of the Songhai people
previous to the beginning of the fourteenth century, when Gao was
captured by Mansa Musa and they became subject to the Mandingoes. In 1335, as we have already seen, Ali Kolen and Sulayman
Nar, who had been held as hostages, escaped to Gao. Ali Kolen
was placed on the throne of his Lemta ancestors with the title of
Sonni and successfully threw off the Mandingo yoke. He was succeeded by his brother Sonni Sulayman Nar.

In 1353 Gao was visited by Ibn Battuta who spent a month there.
He described it as 'a large city on the Nile, and one of the finest towns
in the Negrolands. It is also one of their biggest and best provisioned
towns, with rice in plenty, milk and fish, and there is a species of
cucumber there called *inani* which has no equal. The buying and
selling of its inhabitants is done with cowry-shells, and the same is the
case at Malli.'[9]

Of the following century, during which the Songhai were ruled by
sixteen successive descendants of Ali Kolon, we know practically
nothing. The kingdom retained its independence of Mali, which was
now in its decline, but the frontier continued to be confined to the
narrow limits of the district immediately surrounding Gao.

The period was an eventful one for Timbuktu. With the decline
of Mandingo power the city had become the constant prey of desert
Tuareg whom Es Sadi calls Maghcharen.[10] The Mandingo garrison
was powerless to keep these raiders out of the city, and to attempt to
carry the war into the enemy's own country, in which none but they
could live, was futile. Finally in 1433, Akil ag Malwal, the chief of the
Maghcharen, actually drove out the garrison and he remained master
of the city for the next thirty-five years. Akil, with the nomad's
hatred for town life, confided the government of the city to a Sanhaja
from Adrar, named Muhammad Naddi, who previously had been
Timbuktu-Koi under the Mandingoes of Mali.

Muhammad Naddi was succeeded as Timbuktu-Koi by his son
Omar. Before long trouble arose between Omar and his overlord,

THE RISE OF THE SONGHAI EMPIRE   87

Akil the Targui. The principal emolument of the governor was a third of the taxes, the other two-thirds being distributed among his retainers and supporters. After Muhammad Naddi's death Akil took to descending on the city when the taxes were coming in and carrying off the governor's share for himself. Not content with this, the Tuareg then started forcing their way into the houses of the citizens and violating their women. Omar, exasperated by the conduct of Akil and his followers, secretly sent a message to the Songhai offering to hand the city over to them.

The king of Songhai at this time was Sonni Ali, an able and ambitious ruler who was not slow to seize the opportunity which Omar offered. Placing himself at the head of his cavalry he set out for Timbuktu. He marched up the right bank of the Niger so as to keep the river between himself and the Tuareg who had not yet begun to occupy the country to the south. When he reached a point nearly opposite Timbuktu he was sighted by Akil and Omar. The former, greatly alarmed at the formidable spectacle which the Songhai host presented, immediately fled to Walata accompanied by the *literati* of the Sankore university among whom were many distinguished scholars.[11] Omar who expected to be richly rewarded was at the last moment also seized with panic and joined in the exodus across the desert. Sonni Ali entered Timbuktu in January 1468 and put a great number of its citizens to the sword.[12]

The people of Timbuktu, who prided themselves on their Berber blood and their superior culture and learning, regarded the negroid Songhai as no better than uncouth savages. The Songhai king, in spite of his Berber descent of which probably little apparent trace remained, was an object of the most passionate hatred to Es Sadi. He constantly calls him such names as master tyrant, libertine, and scoundrel, and he presents him as one who especially gloried in the massacre of the learned and pious.

Possibly Sonni Ali merited much of the opprobrium which the historian of the Sudan heaped upon him. Although professing Muhammadanism his religion sat lightly upon him. Tradition in the Sudan is insistent that he practised pagan rites. He excused his ruthless treatment of the people of Timbuktu on the ground of their friendship with the Tuareg, who were the hereditary enemies of the Songhai. From the earliest times the riverain villages had been a constant prey to the predatory nomads, against whose incursions they were defenceless and whose desert haunts they could not assail. That

88 THE RISE OF THE SONGHAI EMPIRE

Timbuktu should have received such harsh treatment is not therefore difficult to understand. Sonni Ali, according to Es Sadi, continued for two years to vent his hatred by the most cruel persecution of its cultured inhabitants.

Sonni Ali's second triumph was the capture of the rich city of Jenne which had, according to tradition, successfully withstood ninety-nine assaults by the kings of Mali. Jenne had been founded in 1250 by the Soninke Sono on a backwater of the Bani and on the site of an earlier Soninke settlement. It was the metropolis of the *Podo*, which is the name the natives call the great region of lakes, rivulets, and swamps through which the waters of the Niger and the Bani are dissipated above Timbuktu. The governors of the city right down to modern times have all belonged to the family of the original Soninke chief.[13] Es Sadi described it as one of the great markets of the Muslim world where one met salt merchants from the mines of Taghaza and those who brought gold from the mines of Bitu (Bonduku) which had no equal in the whole world. 'It is because of this blessed town', he tells us, 'that caravans come to Timbuktu from all points of the horizon, from the east, from the west, from the south and from the north.'[14] Such words from Es Sadi, who was intensely jealous of the reputation of his own city of Timbuktu, are a convincing tribute to the importance of Jenne.

The world-wide fame which Timbuktu has enjoyed for several centuries (thanks to the highly coloured picture painted by Leo Africanus in the sixteenth century, and to the scarcely less flamboyant effusion of a more recent writer) has obscured the claims of Jenne to recognition as a commercial and intellectual centre of the first importance. Whereas Timbuktu was devoid of natural defences and at the mercy of any invader, Jenne was surrounded by a network of waterways which, besides making it easily accessible, gave it the security which for 800 years attracted the merchants and men of letters of the Maghreb. In Timbuktu trade and learning were constantly interrupted by desert politics; in Jenne they took deep root and formed a nucleus from which the culture of the northern littoral was constantly being spread into the surrounding country.

Sonni Ali only prevailed over Jenne at the cost of a trying siege of several years. The investing army was constantly forced to change its position by the rise and fall of the waters which till then had always successfully prevented the capture of the city. Famine afflicted the besiegers and besieged alike, but just as the former had reached

THE RISE OF THE SONGHAI EMPIRE 89

the limit of their endurance and were about to withdraw the city capitulated. The date of this event is in doubt, but it is usually placed in the year 1473. On this occasion Sonni Ali displayed his good qualities in his treatment of the vanquished who, not being friends of the Tuareg, had not incurred his special hatred. The young king of Jenne was honourably received and treated as an equal by the victor, and the city escaped the bloodshed and looting of which Timbuktu had been the victim. After marrying the queen-mother Sonni Ali withdrew to the north ravaging the country of Dirma which lay between Jenne and Timbuktu, its capital being Tendirma. After successfully raiding the pastoral Fulani of Farimake, to the west of Lake Debo, he began to harry the people of a country called Borgu* which lay farther south and to the west of Mopti, but he here met with a reverse. In 1476 he returned to Gao after an absence of ten years from his capital.[15]

The success of Sonni Ali's western campaign had excited the jealousy of the Mossi of Yatenga to whose enterprising raid on Timbuktu, shortly after the death of Mansa Musa, reference has already been made. In the year 1480, with even greater daring, they marched under their great warrior king, Nassere, north-westwards into the desert and attacked Walata which capitulated after a month's siege. Having sacked the town they withdrew, carrying off a great number of women and children and an immense quantity of booty. Omar, the former governor of Timbuktu, organized a pursuit and recovered most of the captives.[16]

Meanwhile Sonni Ali had come west again and had established his head-quarters at Ras el Ma, the most westerly point of Lake Fagbine. He was apparently still anxious to wreak his vengeance on Akil and the *literati* of Timbuktu who had eluded him by fleeing to Walata. Although this remote desert city had so recently been sacked by the Mossi, Sonni Ali determined to add it to his empire. To accomplish his end he conceived the amazing project of digging a canal from Lake Fagbine to Walata. It has been pointed out that in the fifteenth century the lake probably extended as far west as Bassikunu[17] thus reducing the distance considerably. But even so it is surprising that a man of Sonni Ali's intelligence should have conceived such a fantastic

---

* Borgu is the name given to at least two districts in the Niger basin. Besides the one here mentioned there is the more famous Borgu on the western frontier of Nigeria. Both districts probably take their name from the aquatic grass called *borgu* which provides such valuable grazing for cattle.

THE RISE OF THE SONGHAI EMPIRE

scheme. We can only suppose that his long campaigning in the lacustrine region had so convinced him of the military advantages of a navigable water-way that he thought that a canal would be the only effective way of making Walata permanently an integral part of his empire. Whatever his reasons the gigantic task was put in hand, but in 1483, before the work had proceeded very far, it was interrupted by the reappearance of the Mossi under Nassere who had again marched northwards and were threatening his rear.[18] Sonni Ali, abandoning his canal for good, defeated the Mossi just south of Lake Debo and pursued them back into their own country of Yatenga. On his way back he made an unsuccessful attack on the Tombo of the Hombori Mountains.

After this defeat the Mossi were content to concentrate their martial enterprise against the unhappy Mandingoes of Mali who, already fully engaged in staving off the Songhai in the north and the scarcely less aggressive Fulani of Futa in the west, vainly appealed to the Portuguese for help. The latter were now well established on the coast and were trading with the Mandingoes. They had also succeeded in penetrating from their distant northern base at Arguin as far inland as Wadan where, with Sonni Ali's permission, they had established a trading factory. From Wadan, as we shall see later, they sent a mission to Timbuktu.

Sonni Ali now returned to Timbuktu where he began once more to harass its unhappy inhabitants. Again there was an exodus of *literati*, who on this occasion chose Aukar as their refuge and there they remained in exile till the death of the impious monarch. For this they had not long to wait. He was drowned in 1492 while crossing a river during a raid on the Zaghrani and Fulani of Gurma.

During a reign of twenty-six years Sonni Ali had transformed a petty kingdom into a formidable empire and at the time of his death his people had become the greatest power in the Western Sudan. Apart from his amazing energy and enterprise there is little to admire in a character of which brutality seems to have been one of the chief attributes. His worst crimes, however, were usually followed by deep remorse and he was said to have been sometimes capable of generous actions. On one occasion after capturing a number of beautiful Fulani girls he presented them as concubines to the notables of Timbuktu to whom he usually could show nothing but cruelty. Some of these girls became the legal wives of their masters, and Es Sadi, by whom Sonni Ali was so bitterly hated, was descended from one such union.

THE RISE OF THE SONGHAI EMPIRE 91

Sonni Ali was succeeded by his son Bakari Da'a who, shortly after his accession, found himself confronted with a formidable rival for the throne. This man was a Muslim Soninke named Muhammad Ture who had been one of Sonni Ali's principal lieutenants and therefore commanded the support of a considerable military force. Bakari was victorious in his first conflict with his dangerous rival, but in a subsequent battle at Angoo near Gao he was hopelessly defeated and remained a fugitive for the rest of his life. Thus terminated in the year 1493 the Za dynasty of Lemta kings, who had ruled over the Songhai for eight centuries.[19]

REFERENCES

1. Edrisi, p. 13.
2. L. Desplagnes, *Plateau Central Nigérien*, Paris, 1907, p. 75.
3. H. R. Palmer, *Sudanese Memoirs*, ii. 9–13, 20–3.
4. M. Delafosse, i. 238–44; ii. 60–3.
5. El Bekri, p. 342.
6. H. R. Palmer, op. cit., ii. 10.
7. El Bekri, p. 339; A. Richer, op. cit., pp. 47, 61.
8. Edrisi, p. 10; El Bekri, p. 337.
9. Ibn Battuta, trans. H. A. R. Gibb, p. 334.
10. *Tarikh es Soudan*, p. 37.
11. Ibid., p. 106.
12. Ibid., p. 105.
13. M. Delafosse, ii. 275.
14. *Tarikh es Soudan*, p. 22.
15. Ibid., pp. 26, 104; M. Delafosse, ii. 80.
16. *Tarikh es Soudan*, p. 112.
17. Col. Mangeot, *L'Afrique Française*, 1922, p. 524.
18. *Tarikh es Soudan*, p. 114.
19. Ibid., p. 117.

IX
THE ASKIAS

Abuacre Ischia, *hauing . . . conquered many large dominions, . . . concluded a league with all nations.*—LEO AFRICANUS.

AFTER the battle of Angoo Muhammad Ture entered Gao and proclaimed himself King of the Songhai. According to tradition, when the daughters of Sonni Ali heard this they cried out '*a si kyi a*', meaning in the Songhai tongue, 'he shall not be'. Muhammad ordained that this should be the royal title of himself and his successors. Thus he became Askia Muhammad I, afterwards known as Askia the Great, and the founder of the negroid Soninke dynasty whom we know as the Askias.

The new monarch had many exceptional qualities of which the most striking were a genius for political organization and a profound respect for religion and learning. Conscious of his own limitations, he did not hesitate to seek the advice of men more erudite and more experienced in affairs than himself. This gave the cultured classes a prestige which they had never before enjoyed. From being the most oppressed section of the community they now became the most favoured. The learned doctors of Timbuktu, who had for so long been in exile in Walata, now returned to their native city, and Omar once more became Timbuktu-Koi, the post he had held at the time of Sonni Ali's accession.

The revival of Muhammadanism in a country which was still largely pagan gave rise to a series of constitutional problems. Askia Muhammad wisely sought the advice of the great reformer, Muhammad Abd el Kerim el Maghili, sometimes known as El Baghdadi. This eminent divine was a native of Tlemcen, but he had spent his early years in Tuat where he had instigated a massacre of Jews. But the austerity of his teaching was so unacceptable to the people of Tuat that they eventually drove him out. He fled southward, preaching as he went. He visited Air, Takedda, Katsina, and Kano where he added greatly to his reputation as an apostle of Islam. He then travelled westwards to Gao, which he reached in 1502. While he was there he received news that the surviving Jews of Tuat had avenged themselves by murdering his son. In his rage and grief he tried unsuccessfully to persuade Askia to put to death the Israelites of Gao, who had sought refuge there from the massacres in the north.[1] He died between 1530 and 1540. He is remembered as the greatest religious teacher in the history of the Western Sudan, and many are the places which men still

THE ASKIAS

hold sacred because El Maghili prayed there. In the answers he gave to the problems set him by Askia the preacher revealed himself as a wise counsellor with a keen appreciation of the responsibilities of government. The negro monarch greatly respected him and remained much under his influence.

Askia quickly took in hand the reform of the administration. He introduced a system of organized government which had never before been seen in the Western Sudan, but which thereafter became almost traditional throughout a region which extended beyond the widest limits of Songhai. Wiser than most contemporary European rulers, he realized the folly of depending for military force on the impressment of unwilling peasantry. He formed a standing army which enabled him always to have troops ready for immediate service.

He divided the kingdom into provinces with a governor in charge of each. The most important offices were those of Gurma-Fari, Dendi-Fari, Aribinda-Fari, Hombori-Koi, and Bango-Fari. The last, whose province included Lake Debo, enjoyed the exceptional privilege of being allowed to enter Gao with drums beating. The cities of importance had their mayors, of whom the Timbuktu-Koi and the Jenne-Koi were the principal. Other important officers were the Balama or Chamberlain, the Hi-Koi or High Admiral who was naturally always a Sorko, the Fari-Mondio or Treasurer, the Kore-Farima or High Priest of the Pagans, the Sao-Farima or Chief Verderer who controlled all matters relating to the forests and the chase, and the Ho-Koi or Chief Fisherman. An elaborate code of court etiquette carefully defined the precedence, uniform, and privileges, such as numbers of drums, of each officer.

In 1495 Askia set out on a pilgrimage to Mecca. His escort consisted of 500 cavalry and 1,000 infantry, and he carried with him 300,000 pieces of gold from the treasure left by Sonni Ali. Of this sum 100,000 pieces were set aside for the charitable foundations of the Holy Cities. In the Hedjaz he met the Abbassid Khalif of Egypt, El Motawekkel, who confirmed him in his royal rank and appointed him to be his official representative in Songhai. He returned to Gao in 1497, strengthened in his faith, with lustre added to his name and, according to Leo Africanus, in debt to the extent of 150,000 ducats. Thereafter he was known as Askia Muhammad el Hadj.[*][2]

On his accession Askia's kingdom comprised all the countries

---

[*] In Hausa Askia is always referred to as Sarkin Musulmi or Amir ul Muminina, a title probably conferred on him by the Khalif.

THE ASKIAS

conquered by Sonni Ali, but he was destined greatly to extend these already considerable limits. Es Sadi tells us that his dominions stretched northwards to Taghaza and westwards as far as the Atlantic. There is, however, no evidence that he conquered Tekrur, which renders it highly improbable that his rule ever reached the coast.

In the year after his return from Mecca Askia led a *jihad* against the Mossi of Yatenga, which was conducted on the most orthodox lines. He first of all summoned Nassere, the Morho-Naba or Mossi king, to embrace Islam. The envoy returned with the message that between the Mossi and the Songhai there could be only war. Askia's army accordingly marched against the Mossi, slew a great many of them, devastated the more accessible parts of their country, and carried off a number of slaves. The Mossi, however, still retained their independence.[3]

Askia next went to Tendirma, from whence he sent an expedition against the governor of Bagana which was an apanage of the decaying empire of Mali. Although assisted by the Fulani, the Mandingoes were defeated and Bagana became a province of Songhai. In the following year Askia moved to the eastern extremity of the empire, where he captured Ayoru on the Niger, which had been the place of refuge of Bakari Da'a, the son of Sonni Ali.[4] Bakari Da'a presumably favoured the old Lemta dynasty and perhaps still cherished a hope of its ultimate restoration.

In 1500 Askia renewed his attack on Mali and launched an expedition under Omar Komdiago against the country to the west of Bagana. But the troops met with an initial reverse and it was not till Askia himself came to their aid that they were successful. They devastated the country and carried off a large number of women, one of whom became the mother of Askia's son Ismail. He then returned to Gao where he remained for the next three or four years.

In 1504–5 he marched down the Niger to Say and attacked Borgu, where he captured many prisoners, one of whom became the mother of his son and successor Musa. But Askia learnt, like many other leaders during the following centuries, that an attack on the warriors of Borgu was an enterprise not to be lightly undertaken. The expedition proved very costly in troops, the heaviest losses being suffered by the contingent from Zaberma, a country east of the Niger and close to Dendi. Askia affected not to regret the loss of these men on whose loyalty he could not depend. As they came from a part of the empire which was closely associated with the Lemta, it is probable that their sympathies were with the old dynasty rather than the new.[5]

THE ASKIAS

95

Another expedition against Mali advanced the western frontier of Songhai to the borders of Tekrur. But this was followed by an insurrection in the same region fomented by a Fulani chief named Tindo Galadio. The latter was eventually defeated and killed at Jara, near Nioro. But his son, Koli, made good his escape and fled to the Jolof kingdom of Futa, where he founded a Fulani dynasty which lasted into the eighteenth century.

Askia next turned his energies towards extending the eastern frontier of his empire, which marched with the rich country of Hausa and with the semi-desert kingdom of Air or Asben. Hausa, which extended eastwards from the Niger towards Lake Chad, was inhabited by peoples of varied origins, all speaking the same language and calling themselves *Hausawa*. It was divided into the kingdoms of Kano, Zazau (Zakzak, Zegzeg, or Zaria), Daura, Gobir, Katsina, Biram, and Rano, which were known as the *Hausa Bokwoi* or Seven Hausa States, Daura being the most ancient.

The Hausa States were greatly influenced by, and were in part long subject to, the people of Bornu, an ancient kingdom which extended from Hausa to the north and east of Lake Chad. The first Bornu dynasty were Muleththemin, probably Zaghawa. Their capital was in Kanem which El Bekri described as difficult to reach and the home of idolaters, amongst whom was a settlement of Ommayyads.[6] Later they conquered and intermarried with the negroid Tebu who eventually became the predominant element, though they are still known as Beri-beri or Berbers.[7] The general mass of the population were negroes. The Muhammadan religion was probably introduced in the eleventh century when trade was being actively carried on with Cairo. Early in the thirteenth century the Bornu Empire was extended under the warrior king Mai Dunama Dabalemi to Kawar and Tibesti in the north and into the districts south-west of Lake Chad. There then followed a long period of war with a race of giants known as the So, who probably represented the aboriginal stock of the country. On the accession of Ali Ghaji Dunamami, towards the end of the fifteenth century, Bornu was again organized into a powerful kingdom and was closely allied with some of the Hausa States.[8]

We unfortunately know very little about Askia's two eastern campaigns. Es Sadi merely tells us that in 1513 he made an expedition against the Hausa city of Katsina, and in the following year another against Agades, the capital of Air.[9] Happily we are able to glean a little more information from Leo Africanus, who travelled through

96   THE ASKIAS

the country almost in the wake of the Songhai armies. The first
campaign, during which Askia was accompanied by Kanta, King of
Kebbi,* whose capital was at Leka, resulted in the conquest of the
greater part of the Hausa States and the extension of his empire to the
frontier of Bornu. First Gobir fell. Its king was killed and his sons
were gelded and added to the number of Askia's eunuchs. He then
captured Zamfara and treacherously slew the kings of Katsina and
Zaria to whom he had posed as a friend. Kano, however, was only
captured at the cost of a long siege and it is pleasing to learn that its
gallant king received chivalrous treatment. After being made to
marry one of Askia's daughters, he was restored to his kingdom on
condition that he paid to Songhai a third of his taxes. Officials were
appointed to reside in Kano in order to collect the tribute.[11] The
Hausa campaign thus resulted in the acquisition of a very considerable
province which was equally distinguished for its fertility and for the
industry of its inhabitants. They did not, however, remain long under
the Songhai yoke.

These new conquests inevitably brought the Songhai into conflict
with their hereditary enemies the Tuareg, who habitually raided the
industrious Hausa peasantry. Accordingly in 1515 Askia, again accompanied by Kanta, set out across the desert to attack Al Adalet, the
Tuareg Sultan of Agades, which was at that time very prosperous with
a flourishing foreign trade.

The first Tuareg to come into Air belonged to the Lemta division
of the Muleththemin. They had been driven from an early home in
Fezzan and Ghat by the Arab invasion of the eighth century. Travelling down the Kawar road towards Lake Chad they settled in Bornu,
where in the ninth century they established themselves as shepherd
kings. After ruling there for several generations they were forced out
by Arab and Kanuri infiltration from the east—a movement probably
arising from the Hillalian Arab invasion of the eleventh century.
They migrated to Air which was then inhabited by the negroid
Gobirawa,† with whom they lived peacefully. They were later joined

---

* Whether Kanta, whom Muhammad Bello in his *Infakul Maisuri*[10] describes as
a slave of the Fulani, was an independent ruler or only a governor appointed by
Askia is uncertain. The site of his capital, Leka, lies two miles west of Gande and is
now occupied by the hamlet of Kulala.

† The Gobirawa capital was T'in Shaman, close to the site of Agades, the later
capital of Air. Mr. Rodd has drawn attention to the close analogy between the names
of T'in Shaman or Ansaman and Nasamones, the tribe of caravaneers described by
Herodotus.[12]

THE ASKIAS

by other Tuareg, notably Kel Geres and Sanhaja, by whom the Gobirawa were either driven out or absorbed. The Tuareg of Air established an independent kingdom with an Amenokal, or Sultan, at its head.

According to themselves when they first wanted an Amenokal, and could not agree on whom they should appoint, they sent a deputation to Stambul asking the Khalif to send a prince to rule over them. In due course a prince arrived and took over the administration. It is fairly certain, however, that the first Amenokal was appointed very early in the fifteenth century, that is to say prior to the capture of Constantinople by the Muslims. The Tuareg appeal must therefore have been addressed to a Christian emperor instead of a Muhammadan Khalif. That the first Amenokal of Air was a Byzantine prince may sound very improbable. But when we learn that his name was Yunis or John, and that his wife was Ibuzahil or Isabel, it becomes less difficult to credit.[13]

Askia captured Agades and drove out the greater part of its Tuareg inhabitants. Their place was taken by a Songhai colony which Askia planted there. He remained a year in Agades and imposed upon it a yearly tribute of 150,000 ducats. Although Leo was in Agades immediately afterwards he makes no mention of this important event in its history. He merely tells us that it was tributary to Gao.[14]

Nowhere have the effects of Songhai conquest been more lasting than in Air. The inhabitants of Agades, the Emagadezi as they are called, are a preponderantly negroid people although they show traces of Tuareg blood, and they are not regarded as natives of Air by the rest of the inhabitants of the country.[15] In the middle of the last century Songhai was the language of its people and it is still spoken there and at In Gall. Agades in fact remains an outpost of the Songhai people.[16]

Kanta, who returned with Askia from Agades in 1516, was dissatisfied with his share of the spoils. The Songhai governor of Dendi warned him that if he dared to complain to Askia he would undoubtedly be treated as a traitor. Finding, however, that his followers were prepared to give him their enthusiastic support, he revolted and, after defeating the Songhai forces, declared himself independent. Askia sent an expedition against him, but Kanta held his own and stubbornly preserved his independence. He later moved his capital from Leka to Gungu, which is thirty-seven miles west of the modern Sokoto, and from there to Surame which he built on a site ten miles

98   THE ASKIAS

north-west of Gungu. The seven stone walls of Surame are wonder-
fully preserved and still present an imposing appearance. They seem
to be the work of people other than those who at present inhabit the
country.[17]

Kanta is said to have ruled over 'Katsina and Kano and Gobir and
Zazau and the town of Ahir and half of the land of Songhai',[18] but
this may refer only to his campaigns as a subordinate of Askia the
Great. He was attacked in Surame by Mai Ali, Sultan of Bornu, who
was acting as an ally of the Sarkin Air. But Mai Ali, who had marched
north of Daura and Katsina and south of Gobir, was unable to capture
Kanta's imposing stronghold and he withdrew with the Kebbawa in
pursuit. Kanta next scored a series of victories over the Beri-Beri,
but on the return journey to his own country he met with resistance
at Katsina and was mortally wounded. He died at Zurmi, and they
carried his body to Surame for burial. The name Kanta became the
hereditary title of the kings of Kebbi, the Lekawa, who gave their
people prosperity and were never conquered.

The story of Kanta's spirited defiance of the great Songhai monarch
remains the most cherished tradition of his people. His brazen canoe,
they claim, still lies in the marsh below Birnin Kebbi. Kanta's
descendants inherited some of the great qualities of their illustrious
ancestor. When, early in the present century, the British finally
conquered the Sokoto Empire they were welcomed by the gallant old
Sarkin Kebbi Samma of Argungu, a descendant of Kanta, who was
still sturdily holding his own against the repeated aggressions of the
Fulani, whose twin capitals of Sokoto and Gwandu lay but a few miles
from his own.[19]

Soon after the trouble with Kanta, Musa, a son of Askia, rebelled
against his father and attempted to form an independent kingdom
at Kukia, where he was supported by two of his brothers, Daud and
Ismail. Askia, now an old man worn out with service to his country
and quite blind, summoned his brother Yahia to his aid and sent him
to reduce Musa to obedience, but he ordered him to deal leniently
with his sons. Yahia had hoped to bring the rebels to reason without
resorting to violence, but the latter, determined to fight for their
independence, made the avoidance of bloodshed impossible. Yahia was
mortally wounded in the encounter and he died vainly imploring his
nephews to become loyal and dutiful sons once more.

The rebel leaders now marched into Gao where they forced their
unhappy father to abdicate in favour of Musa. Thus ended in the

THE ASKIAS

year 1528 the reign of perhaps the greatest monarch that ever ruled in the Western Sudan. Although Askia the Great had given to his kingdom a territorial extent greater than at any other time in its history, his greatest service to his people was to teach them organized government by which alone could security and prosperity be achieved. These two conditions of life were found wherever he ruled. Leo Africanus has left us a graphic description of the Sudan in his reign to which we will return in the next chapter. Unhappily for Askia the Great he had still before him more years to live, years of misery, degradation, and despair.

Musa ruled as a bloodthirsty tyrant for three years, at the end of which he was assassinated by his exasperated subjects. He was succeeded by Muhammad Bengan Korei who led a disastrous expedition against Kanta, which ended in the rout of the Songhai troops and the ignominious flight of the Askia. This was the last attempt that was made to conquer Kebbi. On his accession Askia Bengan Korei brutally evicted Askia the Great from the royal palace, where he had been in honourable confinement, and banished him to an island on the Niger infested with mosquitoes and frogs.

Bengan Korei was succeeded by Ismail whose first action was to rescue his unhappy father from his miserable plight, but the old man died the following year in Gao. Military expeditions, notably against Dori and the pagans of Gurma, occupied most of Ismail's brief reign of two years. The frequent change of ruler had greatly weakened the central government and consequently expeditions against rebel tribes had become increasingly necessary. So numerous were the captives taken during Ismail's expeditions that the price of slaves in Gao fell to the absurd sum of 300 cowries each.

In 1543 Askia Ishak, who had succeeded Ismail, marched against Ntoba in Bendugu, in the extreme west, and the following year against Dendi. This was followed by a successful attack on Mali, which resulted in the capture of the Mandingo capital, but no attempt was made to occupy it permanently.

At this time the valuable salt mines of Taghaza were included in the Songhai dominions. The control of these mines was, as we have already seen, very important to the Sudanese, who were largely dependent on them for the salt which their own country so signally lacked. About the year 1546 Mulay el Aarejd, the Sultan of Morocco, perceiving how great a hold he would have on the valuable Sudan trade if he could possess himself of these mines, invited Askia Ishak to

H 2

THE ASKIAS

cede Taghaza to Morocco. Ishak sent a defiant reply and followed it up by dispatching a force of 2,000 Tuareg to raid the country of Dra'a, which lay to the south of Marrakech.

Ishak died in 1549 having to some extent strengthened the central government and restored the foreign prestige of his empire. He was succeeded by Daud, brother of Ismail and son of Askia the Great. The early part of his reign was occupied in war with the Mossi and with the Fulani of Massina. In 1552 he quarrelled with Kebbi, but he concluded a treaty of peace with that kingdom in the following year. Having thus secured his flank, he dispatched, according to Es Sadi, an incredibly inadequate raiding party of twenty-four resolute horsemen, led by the Hi-Koi, to attack the Hausa city of Katsina. It is related that they recklessly hurled themselves on a body of 400 Katsina horsemen, who killed fifteen of their number, including the Hi-Koi, and wounded and captured the remaining nine. But so great was the admiration of the Katsinawa for the courage of the Songhai that they sent their prisoners safely back to Askia Daud with the message that men of such incomparable valour did not deserve to die.[20] In 1554–5 Daud sacked Busa on the lower Niger and later he invaded Mali and routed a Mandingo army.

Meanwhile the people of Morocco had taken their revenge for Ishak's raid on Dra'a by killing the Songhai governor of Taghaza as well as a number of Tuareg who were engaged in carrying salt to the Sudan. The survivors sought Daud's permission to abandon the mines and to exploit others which they knew of in the same region. Thus in 1557 they began to dig salt at a point between Taghaza and Taodeni known as Taghaza el Ghizlan or Taghaza of the Gazelles.

In 1578 the throne of Morocco passed to a ruler of great enterprise and ability. This man was Mulay Ahmed El Mansur whose accession was destined to alter the whole course of history in the Western Sudan. El Mansur had not long been on his throne before he asked Askia Daud to lease to him for a year the salt mines of Taghaza, which were once again being worked by the Songhai. The request, which was accompanied by a present of 10,000 pieces of gold, was granted, and friendly relations were established between the two courts.

Askia Daud died in 1582. He was succeeded by his son, Muhammad El Hadj, who seized the throne in the absence of his elder brother, Muhammad Bengan. Soon after the new Askia's accession an embassy from Mulay Ahmed El Mansur arrived in Gao bearing costly presents. The Askia, deeply flattered by the compliment and little suspecting

THE ASKIAS

that its real purpose was a military reconnaissance, accorded the mission a magnificent reception and sent them back to Morocco laden with presents which consisted principally of slaves and eunuchs, and greatly exceeded in value those sent by El Mansur.

Es Sadi tells us that shortly after this El Mansur sent an expedition of 20,000 men across the desert to attack Wadan, in south-eastern Mauritania, and from there to seize the region of the upper Senegal and attack Timbuktu. According to the *Tarikh es Sudan* this Moorish army perished miserably in the desert before reaching its first objective and only a few survivors made their way back to Morocco.[21] This remarkable story has never been corroborated, but that it had a basis of truth is not wholly improbable in the light of subsequent events.

In 1585 a force of 200 Moorish musketeers seized Taghaza and drove out the Berabish and Mesufa, who worked the mines for the Askias, and they also seized Taghaza el Ghizlan. This led to the discovery of the well-known salt deposits of Taodeni. The Songhai temporarily recovered the Taghaza mines, but Taodeni became for the future the chief source from which they obtained their salt.

Askia Muhammad III was succeeded by his brother Muhammad Bani who was followed two years later by Ishak, another son of Daud. Askia Ishak II was a popular prince, but from the moment of his accession he was beset with intrigue and peril which finally, through little fault of his own, brought unparalleled disaster upon his people. Civil war, which had now become customary with every change of ruler, first swept the country and peace was not restored till every possible claimant to the throne had been destroyed. But no sooner had Ishak secured himself on his throne than he received grave news from Morocco where greed for the gold of the Sudan had set on foot one of the most remarkable enterprises in the whole history of Africa.

Before proceeding to the stirring events which followed, it will be necessary to turn first to Leo's memorable account of the Sudan in the time of Askia the Great, and then to review briefly the growth of Christian enterprise in the African field. The marked development in trade between Barbary and the Sudan, which had taken place under Askia the Great and his successors, had not escaped the notice of the western world. The Moors were not the only people whose cupidity had been excited by the golden wealth of the interior.

THE ASKIAS

REFERENCES

1. Ibn Meriem, *apud* Delafosse, i. 219; A. G. P. Martin, *Les Oasis Sahariennes*, Algiers, 1908, pp. 142 et seq.

2. *Tarikh es Soudan*, p. 119.

3. Ibid., p. 121.

4. Ibid., p. 124.

5. Ibid., p. 125; M. Delafosse, ii. 91.

6. El Bekri, p. 29.

7. H. R. Palmer, *Mai Idris of Bornu*, Lagos, 1926, p. 4.

8. H. R. Palmer, *op. cit.*, pp. 1–3; C. K. Meek, *The Northern Tribes of Nigeria*, London, 1925, i. 78–80.

9. *Tarikh es Soudan*, p. 129.

10. E. J. Arnett, *The Rise of the Sokoto Fulani*, Kano, 1929, p. 13.

11. Leo Africanus, iii. 828–30.

12. F. R. Rodd, *People of the Veil*, p. 365.

13. C. Jean, *Les Touareg du Sud-Est l'Aïr*, Paris, 1909, p. 89; F. R. Rodd, op. cit., p. 101.

14. Leo Africanus, iii. 829.

15. F. R. Rodd, op. cit., pp. 117, 410.

16. H. Barth, *Travels*, i. 418; M. Abadie, *La Colonie du Niger*, Paris, 1927, p. 189.

17. *Tarikh es Soudan*, p. 129; C. K. Meek, op. cit., i. 57.

18. E. J. Arnett, op. cit., p. 13.

19. Ibid.

20. *Tarikh es Soudan*, p. 169.

21. Ibid., p. 193; M. Delafosse, ii. 110.

X

LEO AFRICANUS

'Moreouer as touching his exceeding great Trauels *. . . I maruell much how euer he should haue escaped so manie thousands of imminent dangers. . . . How often was he in hazard to haue beene captiued, or to haue had his throte cut by the prouling Arabians, and wilde Mores? And how hardly manie times escaped he the Lyons greedie mouth, and the deuouring iawes of the Crocodile?'—*JOHN PORY.

LEO had many engaging qualities of which frankness was not the least. 'For mine owne part,' he wrote, 'when I heare the Africans euill spoken of, I wil affirme my selfe to be one of Granada: and when I perceiue the nation of Granada to be discommended, then will I professe myselfe, to be an African.' In actual fact he was born in Granada probably in the year 1494–5. His Moorish parents, of whom little is known, named him Al Hassan Ibn Muhammad. His father evidently occupied the good position which in those times wealth assured, and an uncle was sufficiently important to be employed by the Sultan of Fez on a diplomatic mission to the Sudan. The mention of another relative in Fez, who was ruined by alchemy, completes the family record.

Our knowledge of Leo's life is principally derived from passing allusions to himself in his great work, *The History and Description of Africa*,[1] supplemented by the casual references of contemporary writers. Granada had capitulated to Ferdinand and Isabella some while before his birth. The terms of the surrender were remarkably generous to the Moors. They were permitted either to cross over into Africa or to remain in Spain with complete freedom in matters of religion and in full enjoyment of their civil rights. Like many of the wealthier classes Leo's father elected to seek a new home in Barbary, but he did not leave till after the birth of his son. The family settled in the neighbourhood of Fez and there continued to enjoy the advantages of their social rank.

At this time Morocco, in an unstable condition politically, was embarrassed by the ever-increasing propinquity of the Portuguese, who were in occupation of a great part of the coast. The intellectual life of Fez and Marrakech, however, continued undisturbed by the turmoil of the outside world, and their libraries remained the resort of the most brilliant Arab scholars of the day. Indeed the exodus of so many educated and wealthy Moors from Spain tended to stimu-

LEO AFRICANUS

late the African centres of Muslim learning. To the child, therefore, Fez offered unrivalled opportunities for education of which he took full advantage. Here he studied 'rhetorick, philosophie and other ingeneous sciences', including Muslim law. Either in Fez, or later in Italy, he became acquainted with the classics.

At an early age Leo set out into the world to seek his fortune. As he wandered from town to town his knowledge of the law brought him plenty of work. At the age of fourteen or fifteen he was called upon to act as Qadi, an office which he afterwards frequently filled. But his principal employments appear to have been with merchants or government officials to whom he acted as clerk or notary. Occasionally he traded on his own account. At times he served the Sultan on diplomatic missions or as a soldier; at others he followed the humble calling of a hawker of verses of his own composition. His manner of life brought him adventures and took him far afield. Many coastal voyages and inland journeys in the company of merchants familiarized him with the length and breadth of Barbary.

In 1513, when seventeen years old, he made his memorable journey to Timbuktu and West-Central Africa. This was undertaken with an uncle, who was acting as envoy from the Sultan of Fez to Askia the Great. There was nothing remarkable in the journey itself for, in spite of its arduous nature, it was regularly performed by the great numbers of merchants who were at this time engaged in the Sudan trade. But it became memorable for the information which Leo then collected and afterwards published to the world.

Leo's journeys, however, were not confined to Africa. At some time in his youth he travelled widely in Asia, reaching Tabriz in Persia, and he made more than one journey to Constantinople. In about the year 1520, when returning from one such journey, he was captured by Christian corsairs off Jerba, the Island of the Lotus Eaters. When they discovered their captive was a man of some distinction the pirates carried him to Rome and presented him to the Pope. The Pope was the Medici Leo X, the son of Lorenzo the Magnificent, and a patron of the arts who delighted in his much travelled slave. Given his freedom and a pension, Leo contentedly settled down in Rome to a life of ease and, ever guided by considerations of personal interest, became an easy convert to Christianity. From the Pope, who was his godfather, he received the names of Giovanni Leone. He spent many years in Rome enjoying the society of intellectual companions and free access to fine libraries. Here he

LEO AFRICANUS

wrote in the Italian language his famous work on Africa. It reflects an alert and observant mind and a pleasant wit.

Little is known of these years spent in Rome or of his after life. There is reason to believe that he carried out his expressed intention of returning to Africa, and that he died in Tunis in the year 1552 after reverting to the Muslim faith.

. . . .

In Leo's day trade between Barbary and the Sudan was extraordinarily active. His frequent references to Barbary merchants carrying on 'great trafficke unto the land of the negroes' lead one to suppose that he was particularly interested in the Sudan, but that this was not so is apparent from the shortness of the passage in his book devoted to the interior of Africa. His constant references to the Sudan trade in his account of Barbary are therefore all the more striking.

That this trade was abnormally prosperous in Leo's day is not surprising. The rise of Songhai power on the Niger had brought political stability to a vast area, and this had naturally stimulated the caravan traffic. Increased security beyond the Sahara tempted greater numbers of Barbary merchants to venture upon the hazardous desert crossing in search of the rich rewards which attached to the Negro trade. Leo complains, however, that the negroes are 'vtterly vnskilfull in trades of merchandize, being destitute of bankers and money-changers: wherefore a merchant can doe nothing among them in his absence, but is himselfe constrained to goe in person, whithersoeuer his wares are carried'.[2]

Throughout Barbary, from the Atlantic coast to Tripoli, nearly every inland town of importance was engaged in this traffic. The most notable of these markets were Fez, Sijilmasa, Tlemcen, Wargla, and Ghadames, but fully a score are mentioned by Leo. That almost every one of these was an inland town is a striking fact, which throws light on the marked ignorance of the interior which was common to the host of Christians who were actively engaged in trading with the African coast. The sea-ports acted as feeders of European trade goods to the merchants of the interior, who alone were principals in the Sudan trade and who rigorously protected themselves against interlopers.

The principal goods exported to the Sudan were European cloth, sugar grown in Sus in southern Morocco, wearing apparel, brass vessels, horses, and books. These were exchanged for various merchandise,

LEO AFRICANUS

the chief of which were gold, slaves, and civet. Leo mentions a present given by the Sultan of Fez to a mountain chief which consisted almost entirely of produce of the Sudan. The following are the details of this costly gift which Leo happily took the trouble to record:

'Fiftie men slaues, and fiftie women slaues brought out of the land of the Negros, tenne eunuches, twelue camels, one Giraffa, sixteen ciuet-cats, one pound of ciuet, a pound of amber (amber-gris), and almost six hundreth skins of a certaine beast called by them Elamt,* whereof they make their shieldes, eurie skin being woorth at Fez, eight ducates; twentie of the men slaues cost twentie ducates a peece, and so did fifteene of the women slaues; euery eunuch was valued at fortie, euery camell at fiftie, and euery ciuet-cat at two hundreth ducates: and a pound of ciuet and amber is solde at Fez for threescore ducates.'[3]

The relative values are interesting for they indicate the extent to which the negro races of Central Africa were at this time being enslaved to meet the demands of the northern markets.

Although in Leo's time Saharan traffic was exceptionally heavy, there is no reason to infer that conditions differed greatly from those of, say, the nineteenth century. Wells were perhaps more numerous, but of the hazardous nature of the desert march there is no lack of evidence. Describing his own experiences between Sijilmasa and Timbuktu, on one of the most frequented of the Saharan routes, Leo writes: 'For sometime being sore a thirst, we could not find one drop of water, partly because our guide strayed out of the direct course and partly because our enemies had cut off the springs and chanels of the foresaid pits and wels.'[4]

In common with other authorities Leo is content to indicate only roughly the main caravan routes of the Sudan traders. The most important of these was the most westerly, which ran south from Sijilmasa to Timbuktu. This was the road travelled by Leo on his mission to Songhai. Its importance was due to its linking Morocco with the rich gold-bearing regions of the Sudan. Leo tells us that there were goldsmiths and artificers in 'all the regions lying in the way from Tombuto to Fez'.

The gold traffic formed the most important part of the Sudan trade. In the north it was centred in Sijilmasa which had been particularly associated with this commodity from early times. The minting of gold and silver coins was an important local industry and

* Addax gazelle.

LEO AFRICANUS

in after years it was here that the gold which flowed so abundantly northward was turned into coin. In Leo's time there was a mint at Fez. This city was noted for its goldsmiths, and some sort of government control appears to have been exercised here over gold and silver, for they both had to be hall-marked. Muslims were debarred by law from becoming goldsmiths on account of the nefarious practices they introduced into the trade which was consequently mostly in the hands of the Jews.

From Sijilmasa the Sudan traders travelled due south, reaching the Taghaza salt mines after about three weeks. Leo spent three days there and, in common with other travellers, was greatly impressed by the extreme desolation of the place and by the misery of its inhabitants, who, he tells us, were foreign labour imported from the Sudan. They were entirely dependent for foodstuffs on passing caravans and should these be delayed in coming the miners were likely to die of starvation. Elsewhere we learn that so bad was the water that none lived long at the mines.

Beyond Taghaza lay a vast region of intense desolation from which there was no relief till Walata was reached. On the way toll had to be paid to the Sanhaja at the rate of a piece of cloth worth a ducat for every camel load. Walata was an important junction of caravan routes. On the west it was linked with the Atlantic coast by a road running through Wadan to Arguin, but as the factory which the Portuguese had established at Wadan in 1487 is not mentioned by Leo it had probably been abandoned before his day. Roads running to the south and east connected Walata with Jenne, Mali, and Timbuktu, all important markets.

Another notable caravan route ran south from Tlemcen to Tuat, where it divided into two, one branch leading to Timbuktu and the other to Agades. Farther west was the important Wargla–Agades route which was fed with European trade goods from Constantine, Kairwan, and Tunis by the ancient Roman road running south through the El Kantara gorge, Biskra, and Tuggurt. The Air or Asben trade, which was centred in Agades, brought great wealth to Wargla.

The fourth important Saharan route ran from Ghadames through Kawar to Bornu. The Sudan trade of the ancient Tripolitan town goes back to early times. During this long association the Ghadamsi merchants won for themselves a predominant position in the commercial affairs of Negroland, all the way from Bornu to Timbuktu.

LEO AFRICANUS

Although the desert trade is dead they may still be found occupying their own quarter in Kano and other cities of the Sudan. In Leo's day they were in league with the warlike Tebu, who permitted to them alone safe passage through their country, a privilege which virtually gave them a monopoly of the traffic on this road.

Leo appears to have known personally only the Fez–Timbuktu route. After visiting Mali, Jenne, and Timbuktu, he travelled down the Niger striking eastwards across the Hausa country to Bornu, following a well-known route.

'I my selfe saw fifteene kingdoms of the Negroes . . .', he wrote. '. . . Their names therefore (beginning from the west, and so proceeding Eastward and Southward) are these following: Gualata, Ghinea, Melli, Tombuto, Gago, Guber, Agadez, Cano, Cafena, Zegzeg, Zanfara, Guangara, Borno, Gaogo, Nube. These fifteene kingdomes are for the most part situate vpon the riuer Niger, through the which merchants vsually trauell from Gualata to the citie of Alcair in Egypt. The journey indeede is very long, but yet secure and voide of danger.'[5]

Like Ibn Battuta before him, and the great European explorers of later years, Leo was much impressed by the safety of travel in the Sudan.

Leo commences his account of the land of the Negroes with a description of Walata. Although still an important junction of caravan routes, Walata had lost most of its commercial prosperity as the result of its destruction first by the Mossi and afterwards by Sonni Ali, and also through the competition of Timbuktu. Leo found it inhabited by friendly Songhai.

There is some doubt as to the route he followed after leaving Walata. At the beginning of his work he tells us he travelled from Timbuktu to Jenne and Mali,[6] but in his description of the Sudan, which has all the appearance of being a chronological record of his journey, he describes Jenne and Mali before describing Timbuktu. This would have been quite a natural itinerary. But we should expect a diplomatic mission to the Askia, such as Leo was engaged upon, to have gone straight to Timbuktu, where the monarch was residing, before visiting less important places. This is a point to which we shall return later for it may have some bearing on Leo's notorious blunder about the course of the Niger.

Jenne, he tells us, was 'called by the merchants of our nation Gheneoa, by the natural inhabitants thereof Genni, and by the Portugals and the other people of Europe Ghinea'. The people of

LEO AFRICANUS

Jenne, who used a gold currency, were doing an active trade with merchants from Barbary in cotton which they bartered for European cloth, brass, and arms of war. Leo also mentions the summer floods during which merchandise had to be conveyed between Jenne and Kabara, the port of Timbuktu, in dug-out canoes. Continuing his journey to Mali he was favourably impressed by the wealth and culture of the old Mandingo capital.

Timbuktu made a profound impression on his mind. At the time of his visit it was the head-quarters of Askia the Great, and accordingly Leo's uncle had here to discharge the duties of his mission. The pageantry and elaborate ceremonial with which every Sudanese ruler loves to surround himself doubtless assumed most extravagant forms at the court of the great negro monarch. Leo was certainly dazzled by the display of wealth with which he and his uncle were surrounded. Here, too, they found numbers of their own countrymen grown rich in importing European cloth and horses. A gold currency was in circulation, but cowries were used for small values. Cattle, corn, milk, and butter were abundant, but there was a great scarcity of salt, which was imported from Taghaza. Leo saw a camel load sold for eight ducats. He admired the mosque and palace which had been built two centuries previously for Mansa Musa by Es Saheli, the poet of Granada. These buildings of burnt brick must have been in striking contrast to the thatched huts of the rest of the city. Here, too, he found 'great store of doctors, iudges, priests, and other learned men, that are bountifully maintained at the kings' cost and charges. And hither are brought diuers manuscripts or written bookes out of Barbarie, which are sold for more money than any other merchandize'. But, as the result of El Maghili's teaching, Askia so hated all Jews that they were forbidden to enter the city and, Leo tells us, 'whatsoeuer Barbarie merchants he vnderstandeth haue any dealings with the Jewes, he presently causeth their goods to be confiscate'.[7] Thus the persecution of the Jews had spread from its original focus in Spain as far as the Sudan. But in Gao, as we have already seen, they were still tolerated.

At the time of Leo's visit Timbuktu was enjoying the exceptional prosperity which the conquests of Askia had given to Songhai. Doubtless no pains were spared to impress the Moroccan envoys with a display of power and wealth and, if we may judge by Leo's narrative, this end was successfully accomplished. Although the glamour which the name of Timbuktu so long enjoyed in Europe was partly due to

LEO AFRICANUS

its importance as a centre of learning and a source of gold it owed a great deal to Leo's extravagant description of the city.

Leo next travelled to Gao, the Songhai capital, where he again found himself surrounded by all the outward signs of wealth and prosperity.

'It is a woonder', he wrote, 'to see what plentie of Merchandize is dayly brought hither, and how costly and sumptuous all things be. Horses bought in Europe for ten ducates, are here sold for fortie and sometimes for fiftie ducates a piece. There is not any cloth of Europe so course, which will not here be sold for fower ducates an elle, and if it be anything fine they will giue fifteene ducates for an ell: and an ell of the scarlet of Venice or of Turkie-cloath is here worth thirtie ducates . . . but of al other commodities salt is most extremelie deere.'[8]

Gold was in such abundant supply that often it could not be sold, and the negroes would have to return home with a third or a half of what they had brought.[9]

Continuing his journey westwards, Leo passed through Gobir on his way to Agades. In Gobir he noticed the skill of the weavers and leather-workers, and he described the method of cultivating rice which is still actively carried on in the valleys of the Gulbin Rima and the Gulbin Kebbi. 'At the inundation of the Niger,' he tells us, 'all the fields of this region are overflowed, and then the inhabitants cast their seede into the water onely.'[10] Such was the innocent origin of the magnificent *Lacus Guber* of Ortelius and other sixteenth-century cartographers. Corrupted into *Lacus Guarde* or *Lac de Guarde*, it survived on maps of Africa to the end of the eighteenth century. Leo also mentions 'a certaine great village containing almost sixe thousand families, being inhabited with all kinde of merchants'. The identity of this town is not certain, but it may refer to Birnin Zamfara, a ruined town some eleven miles in circumference, the remains of which may still be seen close to Isa.[11]

Leo describes Agades as principally populated by foreign merchants. It was carrying on a vigorous trade with Kano and Bornu, but payed tribute to Songhai. From Agades he travelled southwards along the well-known caravan route to the Hausa States. He found Kano suffering from the effect of the recent Songhai conquest, but it boasted many rich merchants. A similar depression had settled down on Katsina, Zamfara, and Zazau, all of which had been swept by the same invading tide.

LEO AFRICANUS

In his description of this region (Leo never uses the name Hausa, and he calls the language of the country 'guber')[12] he introduces the kingdom of Wangara which 'adjoineth south-easterly upon Zanfara' and south of which lay a region 'greatly abounding with gold'.[13] Leo's wording is ambiguous. It might mean either that Wangara was to the south-east of Zamfara or that Zamfara was south-east of Wangara, and it confused the cartographers from Ortelius in 1570 to De Lisle in the eighteenth century, some reading it one way and some the other. It is quite evident that Leo thought this was the Wangara of the Arab geographers, which we now know was a thousand miles farther west and not far from places Leo had visited on his first arrival in the Sudan. It is surprising therefore to find him placing it in Hausa. A probable explanation is that while in Zamfara he heard of a settlement of Mandingoes or Wangara in the south, perhaps near Gwari where there was gold, and that he mistook this for the famous Wangara of history. Since the fourteenth century there had been Wangara throughout the Hausa country. In Barth's time they were the principal merchants in Katsina,[14] which is not far from Zamfara, and they may well have been important people locally in Leo's day. However the blunder arose, cartographers continued to place Wangara in Hausa for the next 300 years on the authority of Leo.*

In Bornu he found the Sultan carrying on an active trade in horses with Barbary. In spite of the fact that gold was in general use at court, even the royal hounds wearing chains of gold, the Sultan refused to make payment for horses in anything but slaves which were in abundant supply on account of the constant war which he waged against his neighbours. As many as fifteen or twenty slaves would be given for a single horse, but this human currency appears to have disgusted the Barbary merchants who much preferred gold. Later, as we shall see, they came for slaves only and would accept no other form of payment.

Leo completes his description of the Sudan with accounts of the kingdoms of 'Gaoga', or Kuka, and 'Nubia', both of which had commercial relations with Cairo. In these regions ivory, which

---

* Mr. F. de F. Daniel suggests that Leo's Wangara was Gwozaki, an ancient town 80 miles south of Katsina. Included in Gwozaki territory is a village called Gangara, a common place-name in north-west Hausa, expressing a declivity. Mr. H. R. Palmer, on the other hand, suggests this Wangara was in the district of Katsina Laka, north-west of Zaria.[15]

LEO AFRICANUS

Leo does not elsewhere mention, was an important article of commerce.*

Leo's account of the Western Sudan was a valuable contribution to geographical knowledge of the day, but it was marred by a blunder of almost incredible magnitude. To him was given the opportunity of establishing for good and all the direction in which the Niger flowed. Since the days of Herodotus there had been doubt. Leo stated quite definitely that it flowed into the Atlantic on the west. Pory mistranslated the essential passage which, according to the Hakluyt Society editors, should read:

'The Niger rises from a very large lake in the desert of Seu in the east, and flows westward into the Ocean; and our Cosmographers assert that it is a branch of the Nile, which flows underground, and on issuing forms the Lake referred to. Others assert that this river rises in some mountains in the West, flows East and forms a lake. Such, however, is not the case for we navigated it with the current from Timbuktu to Ghinea and Melli which are to the west of Timbuktu.'[16]

This last sentence possibly provides a clue to the mystery of how Leo came to commit such a blunder. In his account of the Sudan, which, as we have already remarked, has the appearance of being a chronological record of his journey, he describes Jenne and Mali before describing Timbuktu. The statement quoted above comes from an introductory passage at the beginning of his work. His recollection of the interior may then have been less clear than later on when he was concentrating on his description of the Sudan. If, for the moment, he was deceived by his memory into thinking that he had visited Jenne and Mali after Timbuktu, but recollected never having navigated the Niger against the current he might well have credited the river with a westerly course. This, moreover, would have accorded with the opinions of the 'Cosmographers' of Rome, by whom he was surrounded, and perhaps influenced, when compiling his work and who probably believed the Senegal and the Niger to be the same river.

There are two objections to this suggestion. Firstly, the improbability of the mission on which Leo was engaged not going straight to Timbuktu, and, secondly, the possibility that his description of the Sudan was not a chronological record of a journey, but a description of the principal places of interest taken in order from west to east. It does, however, provide an explanation of an otherwise

* See note ·p. 146 below.

LEO AFRICANUS

inexplicable blunder. There does not at any rate seem to be any reason to accept the suggestion of the learned editors of the Hakluyt Society that this passage rendered Leo's 'claim to having visited Ghinea and Melli very doubtful'. To accept this view is to question whether he ever saw any other part of the Niger for which there is no room for doubt.

For nearly 300 years cartographers continued to give the Niger a westerly course on the sole authority of Leo. He was not found to be wrong till Mungo Park, in the moment of exultation, drank its water at Segu in 1796. The supreme importance of Leo's work was that from the beginning of the sixteenth century to the end of the eighteenth geographers depended almost entirely on his *History and Description of Africa* for their knowledge of the interior of the western part of the continent.

Apart from his extraordinary blunder over the Niger no comment on Leo's work seems more apt than his own condescending reference to Pliny: 'He erred a little in some small matters concerning Africa: howbeit a little blemish ought not quite to disgrace all the beautie of a faire and amiable bodie.'

REFERENCES

1. Leo Africanus, *The History and Description of Africa, done into English by John Pory*, edited by Dr. Robert Brown, 3 vols., The Hakluyt Society, London, 1896.
2. Ibid. i. 186.
3. Ibid. ii. 309.
4. Ibid. i. 174.
5. Ibid. 128.
6. Ibid. 124. iii. 1096.
7. Ibid. iii. 825.
8. Ibid. 827.
9. Léon l'Africain, *Description de l'Afrique*, trad. Jean Temporal, Paris, 1830, ii. 156.
10. Leo Africanus, iii. 828.
11. F. de F. Daniel, letter to the author.
12. Leo Africanus, i. 134.
13. Ibid. iii. 831.
14. H. Barth, *Travels*, ii. 82.
15. F. de F. Daniel, letter to the author. H. R. Palmer, *Journal of the African Society*, xxxvi (1927–8), 218.
16. Leo Africanus, i. 124; iii. 1096.

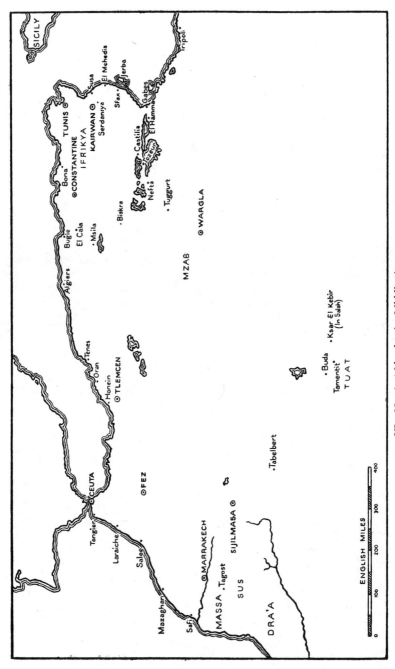

VI. North Africa in the Middle Ages.

THE GOLDEN TRADE

XI

THE CRESCENT AND THE CROSS

'Thou shalt surely find the most violent of all men in enmity against the true believers to be the Jews, and the idolaters: and thou shalt surely find those among them to be the most inclinable to entertain friendship for the true believers, who say, We are Christians.'—QURAN, *Sura* v. 82.

WHEN the Arab hordes first invaded Africa most of their religious fervour had already evaporated. Though not wholly forgetful of the duty of proselytizing imposed upon them by their Prophet, the real impulse of their westward movement was desire for conquest. The native Berbers were free to resist and fight, or to accept Islam, or to pay tribute. People who had produced such fanatics as the Donatists and Circumcelliones, and who could boast as many as 500 bishoprics were obviously capable of religious enthusiasms. But their convictions were never profound, and once their resistance had been broken by the invaders they made little difficulty of apostasy. But there were those of sterner mould who clung stubbornly to their beliefs. Some of these sought seclusion in the desert, others retired to the less accessible parts of their native mountains and some fled overseas. Probably at this period the Christian religion became widely disseminated through the northern Sahara, where, as we have already seen, we still find evidence that certain tribes of the Muleththemim at one time practised the Christian religion.

The Christian Berbers who took to the highlands continued, as long as they paid tribute to their conquerors, to enjoy civil and religious liberty. They never lost touch with Rome, and the Popes used to send priests to minister among them without fear of molestation by Muslims. How strangely the toleration of the Arabs compares with the fanatical fury of Charlemagne, who at this very time was offering the alternatives of death or baptism to the barbarous Saxons of the Elbe and Weser! The Church in Africa grew in strength till at the end of the ninth century there were nearly forty episcopal towns in the Arab provinces, Carthage still being the seat of the Primate of All Africa. Sometimes distress or famine would drive

THE CRESCENT AND THE CROSS

uncouth African clergy across to Italy, where their strange ways, not the least of which was their refusal to regard celibacy as a virtue, caused considerable embarrassment to the Popes.

Circumstances, however, were against the survival of these scattered Christian communities. Deprived of any opportunity of recruiting their numbers from outside, it was inevitable that they should ultimately be absorbed in the great mass of the Muslim population which surrounded them. Tolerated but ignored, they gradually became a depressed class to whom apostasy, affording as it did the only hope of worldly advancement, made a strong appeal. One of the most vigorous of these Christian communities was El Cala, near Sétif, which by the twelfth century had become so influenced by the language and customs of the Arabs that its bishop—the last purely African bishop of whom we have any record—was known to his flock by the name of Khalif.[1] Another important Christian community was that of Tlemcen, whose church is mentioned by El Bekri.

As the result of war and piracy numbers of Christian captives were constantly brought to the shores of Africa where they were sold as slaves. Some succeeded in purchasing their freedom, and most of these returned to their own country. A few, however, were content to remain in Africa, where they either found employment in the ports or, very occasionally, banded together to form agricultural settlements in the interior. One such colony was established near Kairwan by some natives of Sardinia.[2] Near Tozeur there was a similar but larger colony, known as Castilia. These colonies eventually adopted the language and religion of the country and became absorbed in the Muslim population. Traditions of a Christian origin, however, survived till the middle of last century among the inhabitants of the Tunisian towns of Tozeur, El Hamma, and Nefta.

But these scattered communities of Christians, whether of pre-Arab or later origin, played a negligible part in the life of the Maghreb. Gradually, however, two other classes of Christians began to make their influence felt. These were the mercenaries and the merchants, both of whom were destined to become very powerful factors in the political and economic life of the country.

No feature of the relationship between Europe and Africa in the Middle Ages is so striking as the extent to which Christian mercenaries were employed in the Maghreb. The custom apparently began in the twelfth century, when both the Almoravids and Almohads

THE CRESCENT AND THE CROSS

used Christian troops. But their worth was soon more widely recognized. Before long the Frankish militia or *Frendji*, as they were called, became an established institution throughout the length and breadth of Barbary.

The first care of nearly every Sultan was to provide himself with a personal bodyguard of *Frendji*. They were everywhere regarded as a *corps d'élite*, and there was never any question of their being required to apostatize. On the contrary, churches and priests were provided for them, and they were usually led by officers of their own race and creed.* The Popes constantly interested themselves in the welfare of these mercenaries, and sometimes made themselves ridiculous by the extravagance of their demands for special privileges for them.

Far from being the rabble of renegades and fugitives from justice we might expect, these Christian corps were highly disciplined and well-organized bodies of troops in the ranks of which were to be found many honourable men of noble birth. It will be recalled that the Knight in Chaucer's *Canterbury Tales* had once served in Barbary. Many were disappointed men, who had come to Africa as soldiers of fortune, or disgruntled princes and knights who, together with their followers, had left their ungrateful countries to seek more congenial service under the African Sultans. Such were Frederick of Castile and Frederick Lanza, whom St. Louis found fighting against him with many other Christians when he landed in Tunis in 1270.[4]

Italians, French, Castilians, English, and Germans were to be found serving in the armies of the various African Sultans, notably at Marrakech, Tlemcen, Bugie, and Tunis. They were regularly recruited in Europe by arrangements with the Christian monarchs concerned and with the full approval of the Holy See. In 1228 El Mamun, the Almohad, obtained 12,000 Castilian horsemen from Ferdinand III for service against the Almoravids. But it was understood that he should give in exchange ten fortified towns near the Castilian frontier, and that on the capture of Marrakech, for which these troops were especially required, a church should be built for them with the exceptional privilege of being allowed to ring its bells at the hours of prayer.[5] So large a body of Christian troops was probably quite exceptional, but the kings of Tlemcen and Tunis regularly maintained forces of 2,000 to 3,000 *Frendji*. At Tlemcen

---

* It should be noted, however, that Leo, writing early in the sixteenth century, tells us that 'The King of Tunis hath fifteene hundred most choise soldiers, the greatest part of whom are Renegadoes or backsliders from the Christian faith'.[3]

THE CRESCENT AND THE CROSS

they eventually acquired so much political power that they had to be disbanded.

In courage and discipline the Christian militia were greatly superior to the native troops, but they were chiefly valued for their unfailing loyalty to their masters. Like foreign mercenaries in Europe, they were much used as personal body-guards by rulers whose lives were constantly endangered through political jealousies and tribal disputes, which were of no interest to foreigners. The conduct of the Christian militia was usually in happy contrast to that of the undisciplined mob of Arabs and Berbers, who formed the greater part of the armies, and they could be depended upon to stand fast long after the other ranks had broken.

The importance of the *Frendji* to the political life of Barbary greatly strengthened the ties which linked Europe and Africa. They helped to ensure the observance of the numerous commercial treaties which from the twelfth century onwards were constantly being negotiated between Christians and Muslims for the advancement of their mutual commercial interests. In this connexion the officers of the militia were often required to act as interpreters and as witnesses to the signatures of the plenipotentiaries.

During the long struggle between Berbers and Arabs large areas of the Maghreb had gone out of cultivation, and this caused disastrous famines, especially in years of drought. Europe being the only quarter which had corn available for export to Africa, the Arabs found themselves under the necessity of reopening the ancient trade which had for so long been carried on between the opposite shores of the Mediterranean. Another consequence of the devastation they had wrought was a shortage of timber suitable for shipbuilding. As soon as the Arabs began to take to a seafaring life they were forced to turn to the richly wooded hills of the northern shores of the Mediterranean for the supplies they needed. But the confidence of Christian merchants was not easily restored. In the seventh and eighth centuries maritime trade in the Mediterranean was almost at a standstill.

A marked change took place in the reign of Charlemagne, whose friendship with the Khalifate of the east was as cordial as his hatred for that of the west was bitter. This served to increase the rift in the Muslim world and to hearten Christian seamen, who again ventured forth and, by their superior seamanship, made the Mediterranean once more a Christian sea. When Harun el Raschid's ambassador to Charlemagne arrived in Pisa from Africa he was accom-

THE CRESCENT AND THE CROSS 119

panied by an officer representing the governor of Ifrikia, whose presence cannot have been without a political significance. Later the governor of Carthage sent Charlemagne the bones of St. Cyprian. Africa next gave him an elephant, which had come from Baghdad.[6] These gestures could scarcely be ignored. Gradually confidence was restored and Christian merchants discovered that they were again welcome in Barbary ports.

The tenth century was a period of great prosperity in the Maghreb. Large areas which had fallen derelict were, thanks to the introduction of elaborate systems of irrigation, once more under cultivation. The olive was again cultivated on a very large scale. Kairwan was producing sugar, Msila cotton, Sebab indigo, Gabes silk. The manufacture of cotton and woollen cloths and pottery was restoring to Tripoli, Sfax, and Tunis their former prosperity. In the west the coral fisheries of Ceuta and Tenes were again active. But probably the most profitable trade was that which the Maghreb was carrying on with the Sudan, whence slaves, ivory, ebony, and gold dust were imported.

Ibn Haukal, describing the country at this time, tells us that 'the Maghreb is chiefly remarkable for black slaves . . . (the white slaves come from the quarter of Andalus) . . . and coral, and ambergris, and gold, and honey, and silk, and seal-skins'.[7] In the east there was an enormous demand for slaves—Christian, negro, and mulatto—and for eunuchs, which were chiefly supplied from Constantinople and the Maghreb. Most of the African trade in slaves passed through Kairwan, the richest city in the land.

So much prosperity inevitably attracted Christian merchants, who soon discovered that great profits were to be derived from the African trade. The galleys of Naples, Venice, Genoa, Pisa, Marseilles, and Castile were regularly to be found in the ports of Barbary, especially at Bona, Tunis, Sfax, and Tripoli, where they bartered their manufactured goods for slaves, olive oil, coral, and other produce. But the Italians were by far the most active. The great commercial prosperity of the Arabs of Barbary at this period has been attributed largely to the traffic with Italy on the one hand and with the Sudan on the other.[8]

The upheaval caused in the eleventh century by the invasion of the Maghreb by the wild Hillalian Arabs led to a period of war between Europe and Africa which for a time seriously interrupted trade. The failure, however, of the Arab Sultans to pursue a single policy

THE CRESCENT AND THE CROSS

in their relationship with Christendom prevented war becoming general, and consequently trade between Europe and Africa probably never completely ceased.

The Crusades, on the other hand, which greatly embittered the relationship between Christians and Muslims in Syria and Spain, had a stimulating effect on the Barbary trade. The Arabs of Africa had lost their nationalism and with it all desire for further conquest. Now thoroughly Berberized, they were well content with the land of their adoption. Having no interest in the political affairs of their co-religionists in Syria, Egypt, or Spain, they took little heed of the repeated demands of Damascus and Cairo for reinforcements and subsidies. This greatly strengthened the confidence of European merchants carrying on business with Barbary. Even when the Popes found it necessary to forbid Christians to trade with Muslims, or to serve in their fleets and armies, an exception was made in favour of the Arabs of Barbary. The trade now became sufficiently advanced to be based largely on mutual trust. Credit was readily given, and every nation maintained permanent establishments in Africa, and many also had their own Consuls. The protection of the interests of foreign merchants was one of the chief duties of the head of the Arab Customs in each port.

In the second half of the twelfth century the Almohads completed their conquest of the Maghreb. All the country from El Mehedia in the east to the Atlantic in the west became subject to Abd el Mumen, their warrior Sultan, who had always disapproved of the presence of so many Christian galleys in African harbours. As the result of his measures Christian trade with Barbary received another check. Although generally hostile to Christians, whose ships his seamen always attacked, Abd el Mumen was not ill disposed towards the Genoese, to whom, to their very great advantage, he granted a treaty of peace. Genoa at once set about reorganizing her African trade. In order to develop to the full this unexpected monopoly, her merchants, bankers, and shipowners formed themselves into joint-stock companies. The voyages of their ships were carefully planned and the proceeds of these trading expeditions were divided amongst the stock-holders.

But Genoa did not long enjoy her privileged position. The death of Abd el Mumen in 1163 gave the Pisans an opportunity of re-entering the field in which they had formerly been predominant, and of competing with their hated enemies the Genoese. Some years

THE CRESCENT AND THE CROSS

later the Normans of Sicily, between whom and the Almohads there had been bitter war for twenty years, recovered their old privileges in Africa, and soon afterwards the Barbary ports were again thrown open to practically all Christians.

When Christian trade with Africa first became general and the numbers of Europeans engaged in it greatly increased, those who had been first in the field sought to secure the advantageous positions, which they had won for themselves by their own enterprise, by negotiating treaties with the African Sultans. Most of the concessions granted them had been mere verbal arrangements. Among the first Christians to enter into formal treaties with the Muslims of Africa were the Norman kings of Sicily. At the end of the eleventh century they strengthened their commercial ties with the Maghreb by entering into binding contracts with the Sultans of El Mehedia and Kairwan. The Pisans and Genoese, quickly perceiving the advantage which had been gained by the Normans, set about negotiating similar treaties in order to safeguard their own privileges.

Such treaties, which always guaranteed the personal safety of the nationals of the contracting parties in each other's ports, were as much to the advantage of Muslims as of Christians, and they were often initiated by the former. In 1133 the Almoravids sent two galleys to Pisa seeking a treaty, which was readily granted. Pisa, at this time enjoying the predominant position at sea which had formerly been held by her rivals of Amalfi and Naples, was carrying on a very large trade with Tunis. She also had over a hundred vessels trading with Morocco, where her merchants had been allowed to establish their own trading factories. Similar privileges were granted to the Genoese and later to the Marseillais, who, however, were required to give an undertaking that their corsairs, who showed little discrimination in their war with the Saracens, would refrain in future from interfering with Moroccan galleys. Gradually the whole of the African trade became regularized by a vast number of commercial treaties between the European and African trading ports.

The increased sense of security which these treaties inevitably gave permitted a very much more elaborate organization of Christian interests on the African coast. Practically every nation had its own Consul in each of the African ports with which it traded, and most had also their own factories, or *fonduks*, within the walls of which the Consul resided. The Consul's duties were to settle disputes between his nationals, to see that they were fairly treated by the

THE CRESCENT AND THE CROSS

Arab Customs, to act as an intermediary between them and the Sultan, to safeguard the estates of deceased merchants, and to protect the interests of those who were absent. The Consul, who held office for a limited term, was required to maintain an establishment worthy of the nation he represented, and his household always included a chaplain.

The *fonduk* was usually situated in the town, but sometimes in a suburb. The warehousing of goods was only a small part of its functions. Within its walls were the offices of the different merchant houses trading with the port, and here also they conducted their business. The *fonduk* invariably included, besides the Consul's living quarters and a garden, a church and a cemetery, which were provided for in every treaty to ensure to the Christians complete freedom in the exercise of their religious rites.

In the early days of their trade with Europe the Arabs had sometimes granted trade monopolies. But they were not long in realizing the folly of a practice which was only harmful to their own interests, and it became customary to give every one equal opportunities. An exception was made in favour of the Venetians, who for long continued to enjoy the sole right of exporting lead from Barbary. The Arabs also took steps to prevent any one nation making a 'corner' in any article of trade. Duty was payable on all goods entering and leaving an African port, the amount, which was fixed by treaty, varying slightly from port to port and with different nations, but it was usually about 10 per cent. *ad valorem*. The Sultans, all of whom were active traders on their own account, enjoyed the right of pre-emption and could requisition in the public interest any foreign vessels lying in their ports.

Apart from liability to frequent interruption by political disturbances, to which North Africa has been subject throughout its troubled history, Christian trade with Barbary was carried on with singularly little difficulty. Piracy was the chief cause of friction. Although the parties to every treaty always undertook to forbid piracy and to indemnify each other against loss from this cause, and although it was to the interest of every one engaged in the African trade to stamp it out and, furthermore, in spite of the fulminations of Christian princes and the Holy See, piracy thrived throughout the Middle Ages. Always an intensely popular form of lawlessness among the maritime peoples of southern Europe and irresistible to the predatory instincts of the Arabs, it was a force which none could control. Not till the

THE CRESCENT AND THE CROSS

coming of strong central governments and powerful navies centuries later did the evil begin to abate.

Arab pirates enjoyed certain advantages over their Christian rivals. In Africa great prestige attached to piracy, which was encouraged by the Sultans (who were deeply interested in its success) and, as long as it was directed against Christians, by religion. It was a popular and well-organized industry and, directly and indirectly, engaged the activities of a large part of the population.[9] In Europe, speaking generally and leaving out of account the wicked little Italian republics who were always a law unto themselves, Church and State and public opinion were against piracy. The Christian corsairs, however, had better vessels and were better seamen than their rivals, and were fully able to hold their own.

If Christians seem more often to have been the victims than the authors of piracy, it is because their coasts were less easily defended, because their trade was greater and therefore more vulnerable, and because their history is better known than that of the Arabs. The superior seamanship of the Christian corsairs, moreover, made them more formidable than their Muslim rivals, who did not gain the ascendancy till the Turks came and organized them on a national basis.

The Genoese, Pisans, and Provençals were all inveterate pirates. But none of these attained to the rapacity of the Greeks of the Ægean islands who for centuries were the scourge of the eastern Mediterranean and who taught the dreaded Turkish corsairs of later times the mysteries of their nefarious trade. Although the activities of Christian pirates were usually directed against Muslims, they frequently attacked Christian vessels. In very early times certain Italian republics, notably Amalfi, were even known to join forces with Arab corsairs in raids on other Christians. The profits were very considerable, and in times of trade depression it was no unusual thing for an otherwise perfectly respectable Christian merchant to have an occasional 'flutter' in piracy.

The Crusades, by encouraging war against Muslims and popularizing seafaring life, gave a great stimulus to Christian piracy. The course of trade consequently was frequently disturbed by regrettable incidents on the high seas in which the Arabs, as often as not, were the injured party. But it was to every one's interest to make as little as possible of these unfortunate affairs, and very often the most flagrant acts of piracy were overlooked by mutual consent.

124 THE CRESCENT AND THE CROSS

The goods handled in the ports of Barbary covered a very wide field. In spite of the ban of the Holy See and the proscription of the sale of captives under the terms of innumerable treaties, slaves, both white and black, continued to be exported to Christian Europe, where Pisa and Genoa were the chief centres of the iniquitous trade. From the planispheres of the fourteenth century it is evident that the gold trade of Morocco was of considerable importance at that time. The export trade in gold seems to have been centred in the port of Massa, the ancient Temest. The Pisans and Venetians were those most interested in this trade. Later in the same century we first hear of malaguetta pepper, which was then being imported into Nîmes and Montpellier from the Sudan through Barbary. The Italians, puzzled by the mysterious origin of this strange product, called it Grains of Paradise, by which it later became widely known and from which the Grain Coast of Guinea derived its name.* The Sudan also supplied ivory, ebony, and 'Morocco' leather, all required for sale to the Christian merchants, the gaily-coloured leather being particularly popular in the markets of England and Normandy.

In exchange for these products Europe sent to Africa a wide range of goods many of which were required for the trans-Saharan caravan trade. Of the metals, copper was especially required for re-export to the Sudan, where its bright colour made it popular. The principal glassmakers of Venice had their representatives in Barbary where, till recent times, there was always an enormous demand for glass beads for the Sudan trade. European cloth also commanded a ready sale south of the Sahara. Wine from France, Spain, and Greece was sold publicly throughout Barbary, where its use was not by any means restricted to the Christian communities. The Almohads reproached the Almoravids with being wine-drinkers, but that they themselves were open to the same reproach is proved by the surviving records of the medieval wine-shippers of Marseilles. In spite of numerous laws which made it illegal for Christians to sell ships or ship-building materials to Muslims[11] the great shipyards of Venice and Genoa regularly built vessels for the African market. These craft were very superior to those of Arab build, and so anxious were the Sultans to encourage their use that sales of Christian vessels in African ports were exempt from duty.

* In the sixteenth century, according to Pory, the Portuguese did their utmost to keep it out of Europe as its popularity interfered with their trade in East Indian pepper.[10]

THE CRESCENT AND THE CROSS 125

Their vigorous trade familiarized the Christian galleys with every inch of the Barbary coast. It kept busy a score of African ports, in nearly all of which the Christian merchants maintained permanent establishments. But the interior was closed to all but a very few, and Europe for long remained in profound ignorance of what lay beyond the greater part of the coast. Individual merchants occasionally penetrated to Marrakech, Tlemcen, Constantine, and Kairwan, but it was very rare during the Middle Ages for European traders to secure a permanent footing in these or in any other of the important markets of the interior. An early fourteenth-century Italian cartographer mentions on one of his maps that the source of certain information was a Genoese doing business at Sijilmasa with merchants trading with Walata and Guinea.[12] Christian merchants also probably maintained establishments at Tlemcen, which was always an important entrepôt for the Sudan trade, but very near to the coast.[13] Generally speaking the activities of Christian merchants were restricted to the maritime towns.

From Leo we gather that the native merchants of the ports had little to do with the trade of the interior, which was in the hands of middlemen who naturally resented intruders, whether Muslim or Christian. Consequently any enterprising European merchant who attempted to extend his activities to the interior was likely to find his treaty rights of little avail among people who regarded him as an unwelcome intruder. Trade was made impossible for him, and he very soon wished himself safely back in the neighbourhood of his own *fonduk* on the coast. Early in the thirteenth century a Venetian ambassador obtained permission for his countrymen to travel with their caravans wherever they liked throughout the dominions of the Sultan of Tunis, but there is no evidence that they derived much benefit from the privilege. It was a great deal easier to secure the good will of a Sultan than that of jealous native traders.

The failure of Europeans to penetrate Africa during the Middle Ages was in striking contrast with the extraordinary journeys which they were then making into the remotest parts of Asia. Merchants and ecclesiastics brought back a certain amount of vague information about the nearer *hinterland*, but the far interior, where immensely rich countries were known to exist, remained wrapped in an alluring atmosphere of mystery.

THE CRESCENT AND THE CROSS

REFERENCES

1. Mas Latrie, *Relations et Commerce de l'Afrique Septentrionale ou Maghreb avec les Nations Chrétiennes du Moyen Âge*, Paris, 1886, p. 125.
2. El Bekri, pp. 70, 156.
3. Leo Africanus, iii. 724.
4. Mas Latrie, p. 268.
5. Ibn Khaldun, ii. 235, n. 1.
6. Mas Latrie, p. 20.
7. Ibn Haukal, English ed., p. 16.
8. Mas Latrie, p. 22.
9. El Bekri, p. 118.
10. Leo Africanus, i. 78.
11. A. E. Sayous, *Le Commerce des Européens à Tunis*, Paris, 1929, p. 36.
12. De la Roncière, i. 113.
13. Abbé Bargès, *Revue de l'Orient*, Paris, 1853.

XII

THE QUEST FOR GOLD

'Beating and laying open the way where and how this Golden Trade should rise.'—
RICHARD JOBSON.

DURING the greater part of the Middle Ages it was, as we have
seen in the previous chapter, practically impossible for Christians
to obtain any first-hand knowledge of the interior of Africa, but they
found in the Jews a valuable source of information.

From very early times the Jews have formed an important element
in the population of the Maghreb. Like other foreigners they were
regarded with contempt and were frequently treated with contumely.
But they played a very active part in the trade of the country and
they sometimes rose to occupy high official positions, especially in
Morocco. From the Maghreb they spread, as we have already seen,
into the oases of the Sahara and into the Sudan. The *mellahs* of
Barbary consequently became the repository of a great deal of information about the interior of the continent, but it was long before
any of this became available to the outside world.

Late in the fourteenth century Majorca produced a valuable series
of maps of Africa which represented a modest but definite advance in
geographical knowledge. These maps were the product of a colony
of Jews who, originally noted as makers of clocks, astrolabes, quadrants,
and other instruments, were now acquiring considerable fame as
cartographers. Their maps were commercial rather than political,
from which it is evident that they were based upon information
supplied by their co-religionists in Africa. The African trade of
Majorca was at this time very prosperous owing to the friendly
relations, cemented by various commercial treaties, which existed
between Aragon and Barbary. The Jewish cartographers of Majorca,
therefore, were very well placed to obtain first-hand information
about the trade routes leading to the Sudan.

Of these Jewish maps the so-called Catalan map, which was made
for Charles V by Abraham Cresques of Majorca in 1375, has become
world famous and represents the highest achievement of the age in
the cartographer's art. The most prominent geographical feature of
Africa on this map is the Atlas Mountains which are depicted as a
single formidable range dividing the whole of Barbary from the

THE QUEST FOR GOLD

Sahara. This range is broken by two gaps or cols, one in the west and the other in the east. The westerly col is described on the map as 'the Valley of the Dra'a, through which pass the merchants who travel to the Land of the Negroes'. (Another map of the same period tells us that 'merchandise bound for the country of the King of Mali' passed this way.) The easterly col, we are told, was that used by pilgrims going to Mecca. Blazoned across the middle of the Sahara is the imposing figure of a white skinned Targui, mounted on a camel, turbaned and veiled and carrying in one hand a whip of knotted cords. 'All this region', reads the accompanying inscription, 'is occupied by people who cover their mouths: only their eyes are visible. They live in tents and travel in caravans with camels. There are also beasts called Lemp whose hides make good shields.' The Targui is riding towards the still more imposing figure, which has already been described, of Mansa Musa whose land was so rich in gold that he was 'the richest and most noble King in the land'. In the prominence given to the great westerly caravan route across the desert and the emphasis laid on the golden wealth of the Sudan we see reflected the deep interest of the Moroccan Jews in the gold trade.

South of the Atlas range we find the town of *Tagost*, where we know there was a large colony of Jews. It is here described as the largest city in the province of Sus, containing 8,000 households and making large quantities of cloth for export to Timbuktu. From Sijilmasa a road leads by Tabelbert and Tuat through Taghaza to *Tenbuth* (Timbuktu). In the Sudan we find the cities of *Mali*, *Geugeu* (Gao), and *Mayma* which some, without apparent justification, have sought to identify with Niamey. There is also a place called *Zogde*,* the position of which has misled many into believing it to be Sokoto which, however, did not exist before the beginning of last century.

The gradual advance in knowledge of the Sahara may be seen in the beautiful map produced in 1413 by Mecia de Viladestes, a converted Jew. It shows two of the Tuat oases—Tamentit and Buda—also the district of M'zab where, Leo tells us, merchants from Algiers and Bugie came to trade with those from Timbuktu. We also find Tuggurt, Ksar el Kebir, Ahaggar, and In Ziza all on, or served by, one of the great caravan routes.

But the interest of the Jewish cartographers in Africa was not allowed to continue very long. The end of the fifteenth century saw

---

* *Zogde* does not appear on the panel of the Catalan map reproduced on the frontispiece. It is on an adjoining panel, due east of *Mayma*.

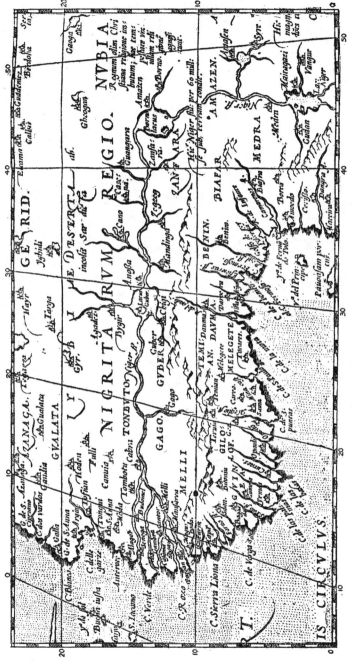

VII. The *Africae Tabula Nova* of Ortelius (1570).

THE QUEST FOR GOLD

a wave of Jewish persecution spreading from its original focus in Spain across into Africa and through the Sahara to the Sudan. The cruel massacre instigated by El Maghili in Tuat was only one of many similar incidents at Tuggurt and in other oases. At that time, it will be recalled, Askia the Great banned all traffic with Jews in Timbuktu. The effect of this widespread persecution is clearly seen in the Jewish maps of the period, which betray a loss of knowledge of Africa.[1]

The Majorcan school had brought about a considerable advance in European cartography, especially in Italy which produced much good work. These Italian maps all show a keen interest in the interior of Africa, which was doubtless largely due to the intimate commercial relations then existing between the Barbary States and the petty Italian republics. The ignorance of Europeans, however, was still profound.

The closing years of the fourteenth century are memorable for the great westward movement of the Seljukian Turks. They reached Tunis in 1390 and gradually spread to the Maghreb el Acsa. At first the trade between Europe and Africa, accustomed by centuries of experience to adapting itself to every sort of political upheaval, was little affected, though it was destined later to be utterly destroyed by the intolerable menace of Turkish piracy. In the Levant and eastern Europe the Turkish conquest was politically disastrous, but its early effect on the trade of the Mediterranean seems, in the light of recent research, often to have been exaggerated.

By the beginning of the fifteenth century the demands of an enormous foreign trade and a period of disastrous wars had largely denuded Europe of her stores of precious metals. Owing to the limitations of camel transport the bulky wares of the west could not bear the heavy cost of land carriage to the east. Payment for the valuable produce of India, China, and the Spice Islands—all of which came overland—had, therefore, usually to be made in gold or silver, though coral was sometimes used in their place. The supply of precious metals was unequal to the demand, and in consequence a period of financial stringency settled down on Europe.[2]

In the past Europe had depended chiefly on her own mines, but from early times her merchants had traded with Barbary in the gold of Guinea. It was therefore natural that when faced with a shortage of the precious metal she should turn first to Africa for relief from an embarrassing economic situation. The scarcity of gold in Europe resulted in determined efforts to penetrate the interior of the continent.

THE QUEST FOR GOLD

The universal admiration excited by Spanish and Portuguese enterprise at the close of the century has hitherto obscured this interesting phase of African exploration. A fresh light has recently been thrown on it by the diligent researches of M. de la Roncière, and recognition has at last been won for travellers whose achievements would never have been overlooked had they not so closely preceded the most glorious period in the history of geographical discovery.

The history of the exploration of the interior during the fifteenth century opens with the romantic story of Anselm d'Isalguier. A native of Toulouse of noble birth, he set out on a long journey in the year 1402. We next hear of him in the very heart of Africa, at Gao, the capital of Songhai.

How d'Isalguier came to reach so remote a spot remains a mystery. De la Roncière suggests that he may have been the Christian slave who, according to the *Tarikh el-Fettach*,[3] was at about this time in Gao after having escaped from the Canaries. At Gao the lonely Frenchman married a Songhai princess who, eight years later, was persuaded to return with him to France. Accompanied by their mulatto daughter, aged six years, and by a suite of three negro eunuchs and three negresses, they crossed the Sahara in safety. They were less fortunate in the Mediterranean, where they were attacked by corsairs and shipwrecked. But Marseilles was eventually reached, and d'Isalguier with the whole of his party re-entered his native town in the year 1413, finding France sunk in the gloom of the Hundred Years War.

The return of the wanderer with so unusual a *ménage* caused some stir in Toulouse, where he settled down to a life of ease made possible by his wife's rich dowry of gold and jewels. Public interest was well sustained by the subsequent birth of two more daughters. One was white, but the other black, like the eldest child, who had by now grown to great beauty.

Meanwhile Aben Ali, one of the eunuchs, had set up as a medical practitioner in the town. The sinister rites of the Sudanese witch-doctor made a strong appeal, and Aben Ali built up a practice lucrative enough to excite the violent jealousy of the more orthodox though less successful physicians of the town. Even the Dauphin Charles summoned the negro doctor to attend him when he fell ill after his triumphal entry into Toulouse in 1420. Aben Ali set the crown on his medical career by restoring the royal patient to health, for which he was richly rewarded. Such is the story of d'Isalguier

132   THE QUEST FOR GOLD

and his family according to the recently discovered narrative of a local historian who dallied with the pretty daughter, was attended by the negro physician, and read the remarkable traveller's own narrative of his adventures.

In the middle of the century Genoa entered the field of African exploration. Occupying a predominant commercial position, this city suffered inevitably by the chaotic conditions of continental exchanges, and was intimately affected by the bankruptcy of France which had resulted from the Hundred Years War. In 1445, greatly concerned at the depreciation of her own currency, she appointed a committee of experts to seek solutions to her economic problems. After deliberating for two years the committee was reluctantly persuaded by the wisest of its members, a certain Benedetto Centurione, to advise the adoption of a gold standard. Accordingly the Genoese bankers were compelled to make payments in gold, and all bills drawn on foreign countries were henceforward based on the new standard.

In forcing the new measure on Genoa in the face of universal opposition a notable personal triumph had been secured by Benedetto Centurione, who represented one of the greatest financial houses of the late Middle Ages. From their head-quarters in Genoa members of the Centurione family had gone out and opened branches in many distant countries. At various times they maintained establishments in the Crimea, Majorca, Lisbon, Rouen, Antwerp, and Bruges. In later years the young Christopher Columbus was employed by Luigi Centurione, nicknamed the Scot, in his trade with Britain. The sugar business gave the firm interests in Madeira, and we may assume that they participated in the important African trade.

It was perhaps characteristic of the commercial enterprise of the house that in the very year that Benedetto Centurione forced a gold standard on Genoa one of its agents was already in the heart of the Sahara engaged upon inquiries regarding the mysterious source of the African gold supply.

This man was a certain Antonio Malfante, the only record of whose travels is the report he sent home from Tuat in 1447.[4] From this fragment we learn that he landed at Honein, the port of Tlemcen much frequented by the galleys of Venice and Genoa, and from there travelled southward with a corn caravan. In describing this country not many years later, Leo Africanus wrote, 'A man shall seldome trauell safely through this kingdome: howbeit here are great store of merchants, perhaps either because it adioneth to Numidia, or else

THE QUEST FOR GOLD

for that the way to the land of the Negros lieth through it.'[5] Without doubt Malfante was bound for the Sudan, but he travelled this part of his road in safety. He reached Tamentit, the chief town of the oasis of Tuat, and there lodged with the Sheikh. He found the town to be an important market with a well-organized municipality, and so well guarded were the interests of merchants that they there enjoyed greater security than in such important places as Tlemcen and Tunis. Although he was the first Christian to be seen in Tuat, Malfante was treated with respect and suffered no greater inconvenience than the idle curiosity which his presence naturally excited. The common people were mostly negroes, but the prosperous trade of the oasis was in the hands of a peace-loving community of Jews, many of whom he regarded as men of the highest integrity.

Malfante found that in spite of the presence of considerable wealth, the restricted resources of Tamentit imposed a life of poverty on every one. As no cereals could be raised, dates were the common fare. Meat was unobtainable except for camel flesh, and even this was scarce and dear. A little grain was brought every year by the Arabs with whom he had travelled. The houses were built of rock-salt and the surrounding desert was peopled by 'Philistines', in describing whom Malfante gives a very good picture of Tuareg. Their veil excited his curiosity, but his inquiries regarding its use proved no more fruitful than those of recent travellers.

Malfante set about collecting information regarding the countries which lay to the south, and his report contains the following list of the principal Muslim states of the Sudan. 'Thora, Oden, Dendi, Sagoto, Bofon, Igdem, Bembo, omnes istas civitates maximas et privates provintiarum. . . .'

M. de la Roncière has been bold enough to identify these place-names with Tekrur, Wadan, Dendi, Sokoto, Bornu, Ghadames, and Bamba, respectively.[6] With the exceptions of Wadan and Dendi, it is difficult to agree with him. The assumption that Sagoto was Sokoto is definitely a blunder, for little more than a hundred years ago the Fulani capital was a mere hunters' camp at the foot of a tamarind tree, nor had it inherited the name of a more ancient town. It may be noted, however, that the three names of Sokoto, Sagoto, and Zogde (from the Catalan map of 1375) have all been connected with Zaghawa, the generic name by which the Arabs knew the Shama tribes of this part of Africa.

Malfante described the Niger flowing past Timbuktu, but, sup-

134 THE QUEST FOR GOLD

posing it to be the Nile, he declared that were it not for certain rapids there would be through communication with Cairo. He completed his account with a lively picture of the horrors of the pagan country lying beyond the Sudan.

Although Malfante took an intelligent interest in everything he saw and heard, it is apparent that his chief concern was with trade, and more particularly with the trade in gold. He found in Tuat a demand for many different kinds of goods, but the chief articles of commerce were copper and salt, the former being imported from Alexandria for sale to the Sudan, though what the negroes could want with it he was at a loss to understand. Gold was imported in quantities from the south and exchanged for merchandise. There was also a considerable trade in cattle and camels. He reported Tamentit to be a good trading centre because it was the meeting-place of merchants from north and south. He deplored, however, the rapacity of the local merchants who would not trade without 100 per cent. margin. His own efforts at trading resulted in a loss of 2,000 doublloons, the doubloon being the gold 'sarrasin' or 'African coin' of Genoa, and then worth three *lire*.

Malfante's host, the Sheikh of Tamentit, was credited with having amassed a fortune of 100,000 doubloons during thirty years spent in Timbuktu. It was from this sheikh, whom he regarded as trustworthy, that Malfante collected most of his information. But regarding the principal object of his inquiries he could never get a satisfactory answer. To the oft-repeated question of where all the gold came from he always got the reply: 'I spent fourteen years in the negro country and never heard nor saw a man who could say of certain knowledge, "This is what I saw, this is how they find and collect the gold". Also it is to be presumed that it comes from afar, and, in my opinion, from a very circumscribed area.' Although this answer did not give satisfaction it is probable that the old sheikh spoke the truth, for even in the Sudan the source of the gold was surrounded with mystery, and was known only to certain members of the trade.

Malfante concludes his report with a list of the distances of Tuat from the chief markets of the Maghreb and he leaves the reader with the impression that his inquiries were not at an end. Of his subsequent history we know nothing. It is evident that he was a man of education and a worthy representative of the great merchant house by whom he had been sent on so hazardous a journey. Tuat was probably but the first step in an expedition which had the Sudan

THE QUEST FOR GOLD

as its objective. Presuming that he continued his journey southward it is not improbable that his quest for gold cost him his life. At all times the middlemen of the Sahara strongly resisted any effort of a Christian to intervene in the Sudan trade, but the secrets of the gold trade they guarded with particular jealousy. Although Malfante was kindly treated in Tuat, it is significant that he was given no opportunity of trading except at a loss.

In the middle of the fifteenth century the Florentines began to interest themselves in Africa. By her geographical position Florence had long been precluded from competing with Venice and Genoa for sea-borne trade. She had probably felt little need for such expansion, for the astuteness of her great banking houses had won for their city a position in European affairs with which they could well afford to be content. Although hampered by the aggressive domination, first of Pisa and then of Siena, and constantly rent with civil strife, the city nevertheless maintained its predominant position in the financial world.

In 1407 Florence seized the port of her Pisan rivals and from this new base her merchants vigorously applied themselves to overseas expansion. They were particularly successful in North Africa where they negotiated several very advantageous commercial treaties by which they acquired monopolies in Tunis, Bona, Bugie, Algiers, and Oran, to the exclusion of all other Christians. In Tunis, as we have already noted, they gained the exceptional concession of being allowed to trade in the *hinterland*.

The Florentines, succeeding where others had failed, profited from the opportunity of exploring the interior of Africa which their new privileges afforded them. We know little of their activities in this sphere, the only record being a passing allusion to what to-day would be considered a noteworthy journey performed by a great Florentine traveller. This man was Benedetto Dei, who travelled widely in the interests of Florentine trade. He was the agent of the Portinari, a great merchant house which in its wide foreign interests may be compared with the Centurioni of Genoa.

Dei's mission appears to have been to establish trade with the east by outflanking the Turks, but his thoughts were not all of trade. In Beirut he collected a serpent with a hundred teeth and four legs. From Jerusalem, which moved him to loftier thoughts, he sent home a mass of holy relics. In Carthage he secured a chameleon 'which lived on air'. Tunis he found remarkable for its crickets. Sfax roused

136   THE QUEST FOR GOLD

him to meditation on the Punic wars, but he was brought back to earth in Archudia, where his interest was aroused by the sight of monkeys being sold like chickens with their legs tied together. He subsequently went to Paris, and then, in 1470, to Timbuktu, a visit which he lightly dismissed as a mere incident of travel. 'I have been', he wrote, 'to Timbuktu, a place situated beyond Barbary in very arid country. Much business is done there in selling coarse cloth, serge, and fabrics like those made in Lombardy.'[7]

To one with so strong, if somewhat eccentric, a bent for zoology, Timbuktu must have been disappointing, but it is to be regretted that the first recorded visit of a European to that remote city should be passed over so lightly. It has been suggested, and with reason, that by 1470 there was nothing very remarkable in this journey and that Dei had been preceded by others of his countrymen. We know that only a few years after Dei's journey the Portuguese established a factory at Wadan whence they sent a mission to Timbuktu, but these incidents belong to the romantic story of the maritime exploration of the western coasts of the continent.

REFERENCES

1. De la Roncière, i. 167.
2. A. H. Lybyer, *English Historical Review*, 1915.
3. De la Roncière, iii. 2, *Tarikh el-Fettach*, p. 111.
4. De la Roncière, i. 143 et seq., iii. 15 et seq.
5. Leo Africanus, ii. 660.
6. De la Roncière, i. 154.
7. Ibid. i. 161 et seq.

XIII

THE SEA OF DARKNESS

'You cannot find a peril so great that the hope of reward will not be greater. . . . Go forth, then, and . . . make your voyage straightway.'—PRINCE HENRY THE NAVIGATOR.

IN classical times no feature of the known world conveyed so perfect an impression of infinity as the boundless ocean of the west. In all other directions great land masses held promise of discovery and expansion. Neither the frozen *tundra* of the north nor the unhabitable deserts of the south inspired the same degree of terror as that with which men contemplated the boundless ocean which beat incessantly upon the rugged western shores of their world. The Arab geographers had long called it the Green Sea of Darkness and their notions persisted till the close of the Middle Ages. Ibn Khaldun described it as a vast and boundless ocean on which sailors dared not venture for fear of being lost in mist and vapour.

The Canaries had been discovered as early as 1270. A few years later the Genoese had sent out an expedition to search for a sea route to India. They had passed Cape Nun and then disappeared for ever. In 1341 another voyage was made to the Canaries, but terror of enchantment prevented a landing. Five years later some Catalans sent a galley to seek out the mysterious River of Gold where the silent trade was carried on, but when the Catalan map was made in 1375 nothing more had been heard of them.

In 1402 a Norman expedition under de Béthencourt conquered and colonized the Canary Islands. In embarking on this enterprise de Béthencourt had to some extent been influenced by the possibility of getting news of the mysterious Prester John whom some vaguely identified with the king of Mali. It had also been his intention to discover the River of Gold, which tradition placed 150 leagues south of Cape Bojador and which had been marked on the Portolano Mediceo of 1351, the Pizzigani map of 1367 and also on the Catalan map.[*1] He failed in these quests, and the discovery of Prester John and of the River of Gold remained to figure prominently in the ambitions of the Portuguese who, under the brilliant leadership of

---

[*] On the Pizzigani map, in a latitude a little south of the Canaries, is shown a river Palolus and in the middle of its course an island with the inscription 'The island Palola: here gold is gathered'.

138   THE SEA OF DARKNESS

Prince Henry the Navigator, were the next to enter the field of exploration.

We are fortunate in having in *The Chronicle of the Discovery and Conquest of Guinea* by Gomes Eannes de Zurara, or Azurara,[2] a full account of the early Portuguese voyages down the coast of Africa, written by one who was personally acquainted with many of the principal actors in the stirring incidents which he so graphically describes.

Henry was the third son of King John I of Portugal and Philippa of Lancaster, daughter of John of Gaunt and niece of Edward III of England. He was born in March 1394. As a boy he had often heard of the great caravans coming out of the Sahara laden with gold dust, and at an early age his thoughts turned towards the exploration of Africa. The resolve to make this his life's work dated from the capture of Ceuta by the Portuguese in 1415, where, at the age of twenty-one, he won his spurs. While in Africa he gathered from the Moors much valuable information regarding the caravan routes of the interior and this was supplemented by reports from a merchant of Oran with whom he corresponded. He had doubtless already familiarized himself with the Majorcan and other maps. He returned from Africa resolved to seek the golden land of Guinea by way of the sea, and on this he concentrated all his thoughts and resources.

Whether the project of discovering a sea route to India was uppermost in Henry's mind from the first is open to doubt, but that it eventually became his most fondly cherished ambition is certain. As one discovery led to another the likelihood of reaching India became increasingly probable, the idea growing as the work of exploration progressed. The works of Herodotus and other classical authors had certainly convinced Henry that the sea route existed. Its rediscovery meant the capture of the Levant trade, which had brought greatness to Venice and Genoa, and was a prize rich enough to inspire mariners to the highest endeavour. Henry's immediate objective, however, was the discovery of Guinea and the capture of the rich desert trade which kept the ports of Barbary filled with Christian galleys. To the motive of imperial expansion and the development of foreign trade Henry, who was Grand Master of the Order of Christ, added that of proselytizing in a new field.

Moreover, there was great hope of establishing communication with the mysterious Christian priest-king, Prester John, and of enlisting his services in the holy war against the heathen. The origin

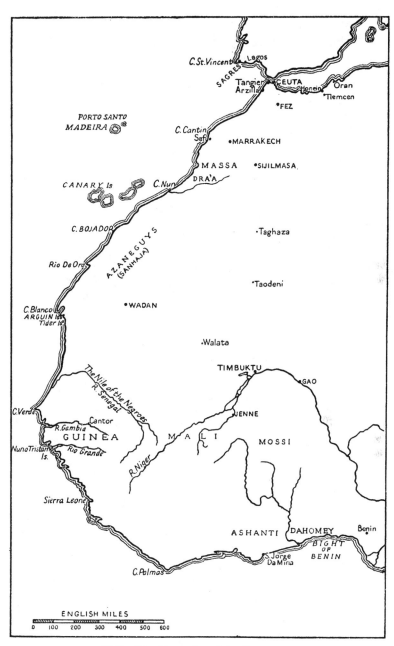

VIII. The Discoveries of the Portuguese.

140 THE SEA OF DARKNESS

of the legend of Prester John is not known, but it probably long preceded the twelfth century to which the earliest documentary records belong. In that century men's minds were greatly occupied with the identity of this 'Johannes Presbyter' who was generally believed to be an Asiatic monarch. This belief was based upon vague knowledge of the existence of Nestorian Christians in Central Asia and China, where they had been established since very early times. But by Prince Henry's time the name of Prester John had become associated with Abyssinia.

Some Dominicans had recently succeeded in establishing themselves in Abyssinia and an Ethiopian embassy visited Venice and the court of Aragon. Thenceforward Prester John was generally regarded as the title of the Negus of Abyssinia whose kingdom was keenly sought by the Portuguese. In later years, as they extended their discoveries eastwards along the coast of Guinea, the hope of finding the kingdom of Prester John increased and it came to be regarded as a step towards their ultimate objective which was India. Like de Béthencourt many of the Portuguese mariners imagined that Prester John was the ruler of Mali.

After his return from Ceuta, Henry withdrew from political life to the secluded head-quarters which he built himself at Sagres on the headland of Cape St. Vincent and close to the old naval arsenal of Lagos. The latter he enlarged and re-equipped for the building of the ships necessary for his enterprise. At Sagres he led the life of a student and from there he directed the work of exploration. With the assistance of the men skilled in the arts of the sea whom he had collected about him, he greatly advanced the science of cartography and improved the nautical instruments of the day, besides perfecting the design and structure of his caravels. No doubt the Jewish instrument makers and cartographers of Majorca were well represented at Sagres, but history has preserved the name of only one, a certain Maistre Jayme, whose services as a teacher of cartography were engaged by Henry in 1438.

The high degree of success achieved by Prince Henry in geographical exploration was due to the well-reasoned and systematic methods he employed to attain his object. He was the first to show what could be accomplished in the field of discovery by carefully thought out plans pursued with dauntless determination. In his contempt for superstition and his development of organized research he was much ahead of his time. Although he lived to see but a part

THE SEA OF DARKNESS

of his plans carried to a successful conclusion the great events of discovery in the Old and New Worlds which closely followed his death were directly due to the principles he taught at Sagres.

At first the work of exploration went forward slowly. Porto Santo, Madeira, and the Azores were rediscovered and colonized. But after ten years of exploration Cape Bojador, which had been marked on the Catalan map of 1375, was still the 'farthest south' of Christian knowledge. Men began to scoff at the Prince and to complain of the wanton extravagance of his fruitless schemes. Henry, roused to greater efforts, resolved at all costs to pass the Cape. But its conquest was not easily achieved. Time and again the caravels were turned back by the turbulent seas breaking upon the headland. At this time, Barros tells us, the nautical experience of the Portuguese was limited to coasting in sight of land and they feared to venture sufficiently far to seaward to round the shoals off the Cape.

To the terror of the Sea of Darkness, with its treacherous winds and currents, was added the superstitious dread inspired by legends of the tropics. It was believed that the man who passed Bojador would turn black, and that the tropical sea was the home of monsters waiting to lure the mariner to his doom. The land, moreover, was regarded as the home of devils and unhabitable by man who, should he intrude, would be destroyed by liquid fire.

When Gil Eannes, one of his own squires, returned with lame excuses Henry lost patience and, scoffing at his superstitious fears, he ordered him to go back and pass the Cape at all costs. Gil Eannes was now determined to succeed, and in 1434 he triumphantly rounded Cape Bojador and was agreeably surprised to find beyond it none of the terrors he had anticipated. He returned in triumph to report his success to Henry. 'And since, my lord,' he concluded, 'I thought that I ought to bring some token of the land since I was on it, I gathered these herbs which I here present to your grace; the which we in this country call Roses of Saint Mary.'[3] Simple as this rounding of the Cape had proved when approached with determination, it was one of the most important events, not only in Henry's career, but in the whole history of geographical discovery, for it demonstrated for good and all the absurdity of the superstitious terror with which mariners regarded the unknown.

Gil Eannes accompanied by Baldaya, Henry's cup-bearer, made another voyage to the African coast and returned with the sensational news that fifty leagues beyond Cape Bojador the footprints of men

142   THE SEA OF DARKNESS

and camels had been found. Baldaya was sent back to find out who
the strange people might be and if possible to bring home a captive
to be trained as an interpreter. He discovered an inlet which, in the
first proud moment of success, he took to be the mouth of the mysterious River of Gold, and ever since this part of the coast has been
known as the Rio d'Ouro, or Rio de Oro.* A landing party located
some natives whom they attacked, but no capture was made.

In 1441 an expedition under Antam Gonçalvez returned with the
first prisoners. They were Sanhaja Tuareg and the Portuguese called
them Azaneguys. He returned from a second voyage with more
slaves and a little gold dust. A little later Nuno Tristam passed Cape
Blanco and discovered the island of Arguin which, by reason of its
good water and safe anchorage, was destined to become an important
entrepôt for the trade of the interior. Tristam returned with another
cargo of captives who were sold into slavery.

The return of ships laden with gold and slaves had wrought a
marked change in public opinion in Portugal. Henry's service at
once became extraordinarily popular and volunteers pressed eagerly
forward to man his ships. But an unfortunate change now took place
in the character of the voyages down the coast. Discovery was now
only appreciated as a means to personal gain. Men had soon learnt
that wealth could be quickly won by the enslavement of Africans.
In a short time the slave trade became an established and flourishing
industry with a demand far in excess of the supply. Buccaneers made
regular raids upon the coasts, ruthlessly shooting down with their
cross-bows all who resisted and carrying off the remainder. The
slaves appear to have been well enough treated in Portugal where
they adopted the religion of their masters and led, for the most part,
peaceful lives.

Prince Henry has been hardly judged for the part he played in
these unhappy episodes, but it is certain that he at least was not
influenced by consideration of personal gain. At first it seemed to
him that the only means by which the salvation of the souls of the
heathen could be effected was by their enslavement, and he regarded
the raids as acts of Christian charity. But he very soon began to see
that the cause of evangelization could be better served by the peaceful
intercourse of trade, and we next hear of him sending out three
caravels under responsible captains with orders 'to see if they could

---

* According to Barros it was so named because here was obtained the first gold
dust from this coast.

THE SEA OF DARKNESS 143

bring the Moors of that part to treat of merchandize . . . and if with the aforesaid pretence they could guide them into the way of salvation'. The expedition was not very successful. 'They were not able to accomplish aught or do business with them, except in the matter of one negro.'

The expedition, however, was chiefly notable for the enterprise shown by one of its members, a certain John Fernandez, who elected to be left behind at the Rio d'Ouro to learn what he could of the country and its inhabitants. This hardy adventurer was well qualified for the hazardous task he had undertaken, for he had already acquired a knowledge of Arabic as a slave in the hands of the Moors of Barbary.

In 1445 Nuno Tristam set out for Africa resolved upon making some fresh discovery, nor was he disappointed. He sailed far south till the desert was past and a new land revealed, 'covered with palms and other green and beautiful trees, and it was even so with the plains thereof'. Although the surf prevented a landing, Nuno Tristam approached close enough to the shore to see that the natives who stood there beckoning to him were negroes. The Sudan, or Guinea as the Portuguese called it, had at last been reached by sea, and negroes, hitherto known only to Christendom as the slaves of others, were for the first time seen enjoying a free life in their own country. The discovery was important for it proved that not only was there a limit to what had seemed a boundless desert, but that beyond it there lay a well-favoured land which offered promise of rich reward to mariners engaged in the work of exploration.

Dinis Diaz made the second voyage to Guinea. He discovered the mouth of the Senegal river, which he believed to be the Nile, and then Cape Verde. His successful capture of some local natives, remarks the *Chronicle*, 'was no small honour for our Prince, whose mighty power was thus sufficient to command peoples so far from our kingdom, making booty among the neighbours of the land of Egypt'.[4]

The Nile and the Senegal were closely associated in men's minds at the time. The Senegal, which Ibn Said, the Arab geographer of the thirteenth century, had described as the Nile of Ghana,[5] was believed by the Portuguese to be the Niger of Herodotus, Pliny, and Ptolemy, and a western branch of the Nile of Egypt. Through this it came to be known as the Nile of the Negroes. The Portuguese regarded the Senegal as the frontier between the Sanhaja (Azaneguys) or Tawny Moors and the Negroes or Black Moors, and therefore as

THE SEA OF DARKNESS

the northern boundary of Guinea,* a name which they loosely applied to the whole western extremity of the Sudan. In the previous century it had been given even a wider application and included Cape Bojador.

It is often said, probably on the authority of a statement made by Leo,† that the name of Guinea is derived from Jenne, the important market town of the upper Niger, but a very similar name was used by the Arab geographer Zohri to designate the Western Sudan over a century before Jenne was built.[6] That it was connected with the more ancient name of Ghana is less improbable. Its modern application to the coast rather than the interior dates from 1481. In that year the Portuguese built a fort at Elmina (San Jorge da Mina) and their king, John II, was permitted by the Pope to style himself Lord of Guinea, a title which was retained until the recent abolition of that monarchy.

In discovering the sea route to Guinea Prince Henry had accomplished the first great task which he had set himself to perform. The second, which was to capture its overland trade, had yet to be accomplished. So far the intercourse which his captains had established with the natives of the coast had not borne much fruit. Only a few negro slaves and a little gold dust had been brought back to Portugal; the caravan traffic with Barbary had in no way been interrupted, nor was there yet any indication of its probable diversion to the coast. Henry keenly felt the want of more information about the interior without which it would be difficult to turn to account the considerable discoveries which he had already achieved. Adahu, the Sanhaja chief, had proved less helpful than had been expected.

While the work of discovery was being carried forward John Fernandez, the gallant adventurer who had been left on the Rio d'Ouro, had not been forgotten. Antam Gonçalvez, with whom he had originally sailed, obtained from Henry permission to go in search of the lonely explorer and by a piece of extraordinary luck he succeeded in discovering him on the coast. During his seven months' sojourn in the desert Fernandez had been treated reasonably well by the Sanhaja and had collected a good deal of information about the trade of the interior which must have been particularly welcome to Henry.

---

* According to the Portuguese pilot who wrote the *Navigation of the Island of St. Thomas*, published by Ramusio in 1558, Arguin marked the dividing line between Barbary and Negroland.　　　　　　　　　　　　　　† See p. 108 above.

THE SEA OF DARKNESS 145

But the progress of discovery was slow. Men preferred to turn to their own advantage the discoveries which had already been made rather than to carry forward Henry's plans for continuous exploration. On the coast of the Sahara slave-trading had taken the place of raiding, for the Sanhaja had learnt that by keeping the Portuguese traders supplied with negro slaves they could secure themselves against molestation. Farther south, on the coast of Guinea, the old methods of violence were still in favour. But the negroes, by reason of their greater courage and of the deadliness of the poison of their arrows, were found to make far more formidable foes than the Sanhaja had ever been. A series of reverses set men wondering whether the risks they ran in attacking the negroes in their own country did not outweigh the possible advantages to be gained, and they became less inclined to brave the hazards of discovering new lands without certainty of profit. But Henry could still command the services of men with stout hearts. Among his devoted followers was a certain Alvaro Fernandez who proudly brought Henry a pipe of water from the Senegal, where he had carved on a palm tree the Prince's arms and his motto, *talent de bien faire*. 'Of a surety I doubt', comments Azurara, 'if since the great power of Alexander and of Caesar, there hath been any prince in the world that ever had the marks of his conquest set up so far from his own land'.

The Senegal, or 'river of Nile', was believed to be the gateway to the interior, and its discovery by Dinis Diaz had inspired great hopes. Manuscript maps of the period show the mouth of the river marked with two palm trees. These were a landmark for which the mariner eagerly watched. 'And when the men in the caravels', says Azurara, 'saw the first palms and lofty trees as we have related they understood right well that they were close to the river of Nile, at the point where it floweth into the western sea, the which river is there called the Senegal.'[7]

By the end of 1448, when Azurara brings his *Chronicle* to a close, the Portuguese had established regular and peaceful trade with the coast as far south as Cape Verde. 'For after this year', he writes, 'the affairs of these parts were henceforth treated more by trafficking and bargaining of merchants than by bravery and toil in arms.'[8] Negro slaves, obtained in barter with the Sanhaja Tuareg, still formed an important part of this traffic, and seals, valued for their skins and oil, formed another. Gold dust was probably scarce, and ivory seems to have been regarded only as a curiosity, the principal market for it

146

THE SEA OF DARKNESS

being the eastern Mediterranean in which region Portuguese traders did not operate.* The wealth of the African fishing fields had already been discovered, and under Henry's licence they were being exploited.

Madeira had become an important victualling station for the West African fleets, and Cape Blanco was much used as a place of assembly. Close by lay Arguin Island with a good water supply and a safe anchorage. In fact so important had the trade of Arguin with the mainland become that Henry built here a fort for the protection of the merchants and their interests. At this period we begin to hear of the important desert market of Wadan with which, either now or a little later, the Portuguese factory at Arguin established commercial relations.

In 1454 a Venetian vessel bound for Flanders arrived off Cape St. Vincent and was there held up by contrary winds. Hearing of their arrival Henry sent out to the Venetians inviting them to enter his service and make the Guinea voyage. The only response came from a young Venetian named Cadamosto who thought that Guinea might offer greater opportunities for fame and fortune than Flanders. A few months later Cadamosto sailed for Guinea in a new caravel of ninety tons burden provided by Henry. From the account of his African voyages, which he afterwards published in Venice, it is evident that by this time Arguin had developed into an important trading centre which was successfully tapping the trans-Saharan slave traffic which passed northwards through Wadan. He gives an account of the salt trade of Taghaza and the silent bartering of salt for gold in the distant south. Although the discovery of the Gambia seems to have been the principal object of his voyage, an important part of his mission was to collect information regarding the unexplored interior.

From Arguin he sailed southward till he reached the Senegal

---

* Thus Azurara writes: 'I learnt that in the East of this part of the Mediterranean Sea the tusks of one of these elephants were well worth 1,000 doubloons.'[9] Similarly Leo Africanus, at the beginning of the next century, found that it was only the negroes of the Central Sudan who traded in ivory, Cairo being the market to which they sent it. Some, however, was exported from the central Maghreb.

It is interesting to note that at about this time John Fernandez, returning from Dra'a in southern Morocco, where he had been ransoming Moors for negroes, 'brought to the Infant a lion, which he afterwards sent to a place in Ireland which is called Galway, to a servitor of his who dwelt in that land, for they knew that never had such a beast been seen in that part'.[10]

THE SEA OF DARKNESS

where he spent four weeks trading horses, silk, and other merchandise for slaves. He then set out to look for the Gambia river which, according to Henry whose information had probably come from the natives of the Senegal, was very rich in gold. On the way he fell in with two more Portuguese caravels and together they sailed triumphantly into the mouth of the Gambia. The natives, who had probably heard from their neighbours on the Senegal of the ways of Christian slave raiders, boldly resisted their entry into the river and could by no means be brought to trade. Cadamosto wished to sail on up the river in search of less hostile tribes, but the crews gave trouble so he had to put back to sea homeward bound.

Next year Cadamosto again visited the Gambia and succeeded in penetrating far up the river. With some difficulty the natives were persuaded to trade, but gold was scarce and dear. Sickness among the crew soon forced Cadamosto to return to the sea, but he continued his voyage some distance down the coast till he reached the Rio Grande and from there he returned home.

This was his last African voyage. Judged by the new discoveries he made his achievement was not remarkable. But an alert and observant mind combined with a happy facility for making friends with primitive tribes enabled him to make a very substantial contribution to geographical science.

Shortly after Cadamosto's return another important voyage was made to the Gambia by three caravels under Diego Gomez. His orders from Prince Henry were to sail as far south as he could. It was evidently expected that the sea route to India might at any time be discovered, for the expedition was accompanied by an Indian interpreter. Diego Gomez reached the Gambia and sailed up to Cantor which was the highest point to which he could navigate. Here, he wrote,

'the natives came together from all quarters, viz. from Tambucatu in the north, from Sierra Geley in the south, and there came also people from Quioquun,* which is a great city, surrounded by a wall of baked tiles, and where I understood there was abundance of gold, and that caravans of camels and dromedaries crossed over thither with merchandise from Carthage or Tunis, from Fez, from Cairo, and from all the land of the Saracens, in exchange for gold.'[11]

They further told him of a great river running westward and of a

---

* Probably Gao or Kukia which Gomez confused with Mali.

L 2

148   THE SEA OF DARKNESS

great lake which were probably allusions to the Niger and the lakes above Timbuktu.

'I questioned the negroes at Cantor', continues the narrative, 'as to the road which led to the countries where there was gold, and asked who were the lords of that country. They told me that the king's name was Bormelli, and that the whole land of the negroes on the right side of the river was under his dominion, and that he lived in the city Quioquia. They said further, that he was lord of all the mines, and that he had before the door of his palace a mass of gold just as it was taken from the earth, so large that twenty men could scarcely move it, and that the king always fastened his horse to it, and kept it as a curiosity on account of its being found just as it was, and of so great size and purity.'*

This was the last important voyage of Prince Henry's life which was now drawing to an end. He died in the year 1460 at the age of sixty-six. Great as were the advances in geographical discovery which had resulted from his life work, they were of small importance compared to the supreme service which he rendered to mankind in laying the foundation of scientific oversea exploration. Through his dauntless spirit the unknown had been divested of terror and the high seas had come to be recognized as a field for glorious achievement. It was his teaching and example which enabled the nations of western Europe to make the great world discoveries which closely followed his death, and, in so doing, to turn the Sea of Darkness into the premier trade route of the world.

Prince Henry's death was not allowed to interrupt the work of exploration, which was now carried on by John II. With the discovery of a sea route to India as the supreme object in view, frequent expeditions continued to be sent out to Africa. Shortly after Henry's death Pedro de Cintra discovered Sierra Leone. In 1481 the Portuguese founded the first European settlement in Guinea at San Jorge da Mina, the Elmina of the present day. Soon afterwards voyages were made into the Bight of Benin, whence native envoys were brought home to Lisbon. They told John II that the King of Benin was a vassal of a certain Ogane, a powerful monarch of the interior, who was probably the Awni of Ife in the Niger delta. They happened also to mention that he wore a cross round his neck which was quite sufficient to convince the Portuguese that Ogane must be Prester

---

* Further evidence of confusion in the mind of Gomez. The reference is obviously to the famous Ghana nugget which, according to Ibn Khaldun, had been sold to Egyptian merchants in the previous century.

THE SEA OF DARKNESS   149

John.[12] This was the beginning of the long association of the Portuguese with Benin, where, instead of discovering the Priest King, they had to content themselves with trading in malaguetta pepper.

Spurred perhaps by the activities of rivals in the same field, the Portuguese made a fresh effort to penetrate the Sahara from their base at Arguin. In 1487 they succeeded, with the permission of Sonni Ali of Songhai, in establishing a factory at Wadan, the important entrepôt for north and south caravan traffic which lay a few days' march to the east of their sea-board settlement. From Wadan they should have been able to participate more freely in the trade of the interior, but Barros, our only authority, is characteristically reticent regarding this desert outpost. He tells us that the Portuguese governor, besides keeping Arguin supplied with Sudan produce, sent a mission to Timbuktu.[13] Of the eight persons who composed the mission only one returned, a certain Pero Reinel, who, we are told, was already well acquainted with the Sudan.

In 1488 the Portuguese governor at Arguin sent home to Lisbon a Jolof prince named Bemoy, who gave much valuable information to John, particularly regarding the Mossi. According to Bemoy, the Mossi people were neither Muslim nor pagan, but conformed in many ways to the customs of Christians. John now leapt to the conclusion that after all the Mossi king, 'El rey dos Moses', must undoubtedly be Prester John.

The name of the Mossi was already familiar to the Portuguese. The fame of their powerful and warlike kingdoms was well known on the coast and Portuguese help, as we saw in an earlier chapter, had already been vainly sought by their enemies, the Mandingoes of Mali. Convinced that the king of Mossi was the Priest King, the Portuguese now attempted to get into touch with him, but there is no evidence that they were successful.

After the death of John II and the discovery of the Cape route to India by Vasco da Gama in 1497, Portuguese interest in Africa began to evaporate. The wealth and pageantry of the east offered far more alluring prospects than the fever-stricken forests and wild savages of Guinea. The Portuguese did not abandon their West African trade, but it was carried on without enthusiasm, and only on a scale sufficient to maintain their sovereign's claim to the suzerainty of Guinea and their consequent right to exclude all other nations. Their forts extended all along the coast from Arguin to the Bight of Benin. Not till Barros, their great national historian, became Governor-

150 THE SEA OF DARKNESS

General at Elmina some years later did interest in the interior revive. In 1534 he sent an ambassador, named Peroz Fernandez, to the king of Mali who gave a cordial welcome to the mission.[14] In 1550 the Portuguese discovered the gold mines of Bambuk, the Wangara of history, but unfortunately no account of this incident nor of the Fernandez mission to Mali has been preserved. The discoverers of Wangara either killed each other or were murdered by the natives.

Europe added greatly to her knowledge of Africa during the fifteenth century, but by its end interest in the continent had already been largely lost. The stirring events of the discovery of America and the opening up of the Cape route to India had revealed to men so vast a field for oversea enterprise and such stores of wealth that Africa came near to being forgotten.

REFERENCES

1. J. de Béthencourt, *The Conquest of the Canaries*, edited by R. H. Major, Hakluyt Society, London, 1871, pp. 100–6.

2. Gomes Eannes de Azurara (Zurara), *The Chronicle of the Discovery and Conquest of Guinea*, Hakluyt Society, 2 vols., London, 1896, 1899.

3. *The Chronicle of Guinea*, i. 34.

4. Ibid. i. 100; ii, chs. lx, lxi.

5. Aboulfeda, *Géographie*, Paris, 1848, ii. 45.

6. M. Delafosse, ii. 277.

7. *The Chronicle of Guinea*, ii. 177.

8. Ibid. 289.

9. Ibid. 180.

10. Ibid. 278.

11. R. H. Major, *The Life of Prince Henry of Portugal, surnamed the Navigator*, London, 1868, p. 290.

12. J. de Barros, *Da Asia*, Lisbon 1778, 1 Dec., Book III, ch. i, p. 154; P. Amaury Talbot, *The Peoples of Southern Nigeria*, Oxford, 1926, i. 155.

13. Barros, op. cit., 1 Dec., Book I, ch. 3, p. 29.

14. Ibid., p. 257.

XIV

THE MOORISH INVASION*

'The golden trade of the Moores of Barbary . . . was the incourager and beginning of this business.'—RICHARD JOBSON.

IN August 1578 Europe received from Morocco news so grave that it profoundly shocked the whole of Christendom. Earlier in the year Sultan Muhammad XI, a mulatto and therefore sometimes called the Black Sultan, had appealed to Dom Sebastian of Portugal to help him recover the throne which his uncle, Abdul Malek, had usurped. Dom Sebastian, on the understanding that he should be allowed permanently to occupy the coast, landed 17,000 troops at Tangier. The expedition was regarded in the nature of a crusade and the eyes of all Europe were upon the young Portuguese king as he led his troops into the interior. Abdul Malek was mortally ill at the time but, placing himself at the head of his army, he fell on the invaders at El Ksar el Kebir. The Christians, amongst whom were many Germans and Italians and several hundred papal troops under an Englishman named Stukeley,† were destroyed. Dom Sebastian and Muhammad were killed and Abdul Malek died in his litter in the hour of victory.‡ The elated Moors, as the people of Morocco were now called in Europe, having flayed the body of

---

* We have four contemporary accounts of the Moorish invasion of the Sudan. Firstly, that of Es Sadi, the author of the *Tarikh es Sudan*, who was a native of Timbuktu. Secondly, that of Mahmud Kati who also lived in Timbuktu. He died in 1593, but his grandson completed the work up to the year 1599. Their narrative is of particular value as it was written by men who were intimately affected by the scenes they described, and for this reason is the most readable. The third account is that of El Ufrani, a native of Morocco.[1] We also have a very interesting account of the opening phase of the Moorish campaign in an obscure and anonymous Spanish narrative dated 1591.[2] These four accounts are in general agreement about the essential points of the campaign. In some important details there are discrepancies and dates constantly differ, but to no serious extent.

† While on their way to aid a rebellion in Ireland they had put into Lisbon, whence they had been diverted to Tangier.

‡ A curious legend was widely accepted in Europe that Dom Sebastian had not been killed but had escaped secretly from the battle. First he was thought to have sought refuge with Prester John; later he was reported to be in Persia and then in Europe. For many years the people of Portugal eagerly awaited his return and no less than four impostors claimed to be the *rei encuberto*, the 'hidden king'.

THE MOORISH INVASION

Muhammad and sent his stuffed skin on a tour of their principal cities,*³ placed a younger brother of Abdul Malek on the throne.

Mulay Ahmed El Mansur was less than thirty years of age when he so unexpectedly found himself at the head of the only Muhammadan state which could claim without fear of contradiction equal footing with European powers. Moorish arms had proved themselves not less redoubtable than Turkish, and Europe began to desire alliances with El Mansur. Not only was he acclaimed the hero of the Muhammadan world, but his favours were sought by an obsequious Christendom. Muslim princes and Christian monarchs sent their ambassadors to his court, bearing costly presents and the felicitations of their royal masters. Of especial magnificence was a propitiatory offering from Portugal which included a sumptuous bed-of-state of cloth of gold, a dagger set with rubies, and precious works of art from China and the Indies.⁵

Spain sent treasures which included emeralds worth 100,000 ducats. The King of France and the Sultan of Turkey sent embassies. Elizabeth of England, who had secretly attempted to negotiate an alliance with Morocco as far back as 1577 and whose subjects were trading actively with the country, carried on a lively correspondence with the young Sultan. But the Queen, true to her character, refused to be dazzled and behaved with greater dignity than the other Christian rulers. She graciously conceded permission for her merchants to sell him ship-building timber, which was felled in 'the counties of Sussex and Southampton', in return for its equivalent in salt-petre, which she sorely needed in her arsenal.†⁶

Not unnaturally the young man's head was slightly turned. His insolent treatment of the Ottoman ambassador provoked the enmity of the Khalif who, with Lepanto fresh in his memory, was not inclined to excessive jubilation over the rout of infidels by a section of Islam not subject to Stambul. An expedition had already set sail with orders to humble the Moorish Sultan when the Khalif yielded to the rich presents and abject apologies of El Mansur and recalled the fleet.

---

* Leo Africanus in describing the customs of Cairo writes: 'But rebels or seditious persons they flea aliue, stuffing their skins with bran till they resemble mans shape, which being done, they carrie the saide stuffed skins vpon camels' backs through euery street of the citie, and there publish the crime of the partie executed.'⁴

† At this time Catholics had been forbidden by the Pope to trade with the Barbary States in timber suitable for ship-building which was rightly regarded as a munition of war. El Mansur therefore had difficulty in obtaining the supplies he needed.

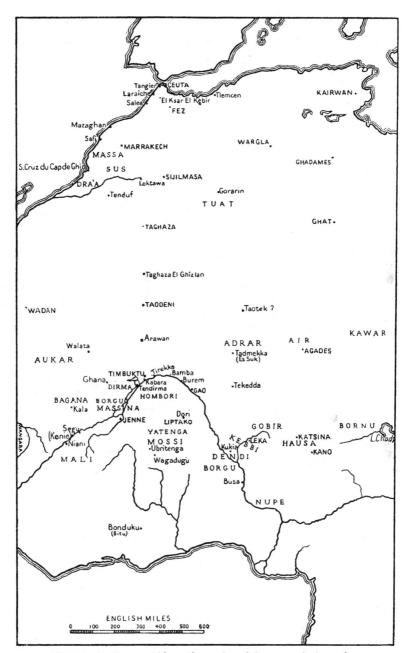

IX. North-Western Africa—Sixteenth and Seventeenth Centuries.

THE MOORISH INVASION

Having narrowly averted the catastrophe of a war with the Turks, the young and ambitious Sultan looked about him for more profitable fields in which to employ his victorious troops. The army was not sufficiently strong to risk a trial of strength with such formidable neighbours as Spain, which had annexed Portugal after the disaster of El Ksar, or with the Turks of Algiers who were a constant menace on his eastern frontier. Hemmed in on the north and east by these powerful states and on the west by the Atlantic, El Mansur was forced to contemplate the forbidding wastes of the Sahara as the only direction in which imperial expansion was possible.

Beyond the Sahara lay the rich countries of the Western Sudan the vast natural wealth of which was well known to every merchant of the Maghreb. During the sixteenth century a strong central government had conferred upon the peoples of the middle Niger the supreme blessing of tranquillity which, as we have already seen, had attracted large numbers of foreign merchants. Consequently the Western Sudan was enjoying a high degree of commercial prosperity. It will be recalled that at the beginning of the century Leo's mission had returned from the Sudan profoundly impressed by the wealth and culture of Timbuktu, which they had chanced to find at the very zenith of its prosperity. Inspired by motives very similar to those which had first prompted Prince Henry the Navigator to explore the Guinea coast, El Mansur conceived the bold project of conquering these rich negro countries.

At the time of El Mansur's accession the most powerful kingdom of the Western Sudan was Songhai. Although it had lost much of the glory of the days of Askia the Great its power still dominated the whole of the great Bend of the Niger. To the east of Songhai lay the small but proud kingdom of Kebbi and the Hausa States, the latter divided by petty jealousies and incapable of combined action. To the west lay arid and sparsely populated plains, and beyond them the Senegal basin, the tribes of which were powerless to resist a determined invader. The old Mandingo empire of Mali, the former greatness of which had long since passed to Songhai, was confined to the unhealthy swamps and forests of the upper Niger. To conquer Songhai, therefore, was the first step towards becoming master of the Western Sudan.

It will be recalled that ever since 1546 the salt deposits of Taghaza had caused trouble between Morocco and Songhai. Situated in the northern desert within a few days' march of Marrakech and therefore very vulnerable to attack, these mines were a constant temptation to

THE MOORISH INVASION

155

the Moors who wanted the salt for the gold trade. The rapid growth of prosperity which had followed the battle of El Ksar had greatly stimulated the demand for gold and this had revived interest in the salt mines.

In 1585 El Mansur seized Taghaza, but, as on previous occasions, the Moors failed to hold it. He then demanded a royalty from Askia Ishak of a *mitkal* of gold on every load of salt exported to the Sudan, but he received a defiant refusal.

In 1589 there arrived in Marrakech a Songhai negro named Uld Kirinfil. This man, having incurred the displeasure of Askia Ishak, had been banished to the mines of Taghaza, whence he had escaped to Marrakech where he secured an audience with El Mansur. The negro claimed to be the elder brother of Askia Ishak, who, he said, had usurped his throne. He appealed to El Mansur to restore to him his kingdom, representing the project as simple to achieve and promising a rich reward once he was restored to power. The man's story was accepted and served to strengthen El Mansur's determination to invade the Sudan.

The Sultan summoned a council of the principal officials and wise men of his kingdom and announced his intention of attacking the Prince of Gao, whom he described as Lord of the Sudan. He dwelt upon the great wealth of Songhai and he pointed out that as Askia Ishak was not of the tribe of the Quraysh he had no right to the throne he occupied. In spite of the faintly religious flavour which the Sultan sought thus to impart to his scheme the announcement was received in cold silence by the Elders. On being pressed for an answer they unanimously condemned the project as reckless. To them the desert was an insuperable obstacle. They dwelt upon the horrors of waterless solitudes and they reminded El Mansur, without strict regard for truth, that such powerful and illustrious dynasties as the Almoravids, the Almohads, and the Merinids had never meddled in the affairs of the Sudan. They pressed him to be guided accordingly, boldly declaring 'the people of to-day are no wiser than those of the past'.

El Mansur laughed at their fears and reminded them of the defenceless merchants who were constantly traversing the desert. His eloquence was not without effect. Not only did he succeed in winning their consent, but he even fired them with some of his own martial zeal. The Council broke up obsequiously murmuring—in the French of M. Houdas—'Les esprits des princes sont les princes des esprits.'

THE MOORISH INVASION

Energetic preparations for the expedition were at once put in hand. A great part of the force raised was composed of Elches and Andalusians. The Elches were Christian troops who, unlike the *Frendji* of earlier times, were renegades. The Andalusians were renegades from Islam from the mountains of Granada. The fighting men included 2,000 infantry, half Elches and half Andalusians, armed with the harquebus, 500 horsemen, similarly armed, and 1,500 lancers who alone were natives of Morocco. The artillery was composed of six large cannon[*] and various smaller pieces. The artillerymen were European gunners, who used to be drawn from English and other ships which frequented Moorish ports or from among the Elches of the army. The cannon balls and other munitions had largely been supplied from England. They were obtained in exchange for saltpetre and sugar in which a large trade was done with London. There were also 600 pioneers and 1,000 camelmen. The transport consisted of 8,000 camels and 1,000 pack-horses. Large quantities of military stores, including 300 quintals of powder, were also carried. The personnel of the army was largely European, and Spanish was its official language.[†]

The command of the expedition was given to a blue-eyed Andalusian eunuch, named Judar, who had been brought up in the royal palace from infancy. He was a young man without military experience, but as a successful gatherer of taxes he had been marked out for high preferment. Most of the Kaids were also of European origin. The army was divided into three divisions, each under a Lieutenant-General. One division came from Fez, another from Marrakech, and the third, which was the weakest, from Cheraga.

On 23 June 1590 El Mansur wrote to Queen Elizabeth of England regretting his inability to deal promptly with certain matters she had brought to his notice, owing to the preparations for the Sudan expedition which, he said, would start in a few days.[8] However, it was not until 16 October, at the time of year most favourable for crossing the Sahara, that Judar Pasha, surrounded by a body-guard of seventy Christian harquebusiers, marched out of Marrakech at the head of his army. He crossed the Atlas and descended into the rich valley of the Dra'a, halting at Lektawa, where they used to mint the gold from the Sudan. Here he collected supplies of wheat, barley, and dates. Everything being at last complete, the bullock-skins were filled with

---

[*] In 1536 French renegades were casting cannon for the Moors.[7]

[†] Of the Spanish words of command which were afterwards remembered in the Sudan, Es Sadi mentions 'Kor li kabissa' or *cor te le cabeza*, meaning 'cut off his head'.

THE MOORISH INVASION

157

water and loaded on to the camels. The hazardous march began and the expedition disappeared into the Sahara.

It has been said that under modern conditions it would have been impossible for Judar to transport a whole army overland to the Sudan. This is probably correct, but not because the geographical conditions were materially different. The route he followed was a great trade route which probably carried as much traffic in the sixteenth century as at any other period, and to maintain this trade wells, most of which have since been lost, were then both numerous and well tended. But even so the march was hazardous enough and there is no reason to belittle Judar's achievement.

Unfortunately we have no record of the experiences of the Moorish army during their trans-Saharan journey. The route, for a large part of the way, was undoubtedly that of the gold traders which ran southward from Sijilmasa through Taghaza to Walata, skirting Arawan; but we have no details of the road and we do not know where Judar abandoned the main caravan route. He may have split up his force into two or more columns so as to make use of alternative routes, as was done on a later occasion owing to the insufficiency of water on the trunk road. From our records of Saharan travel and of the later experiences of the Moors we may assume that the loss of life was heavy. We have the unsupported testimony of an Englishman resident in Morocco that of the original force, which he placed as low as 1,700 men, a third perished in the desert.*[9]

As Judar passed near Arawan he commandeered some camels. The aggrieved owner went to lay his complaint before the Sultan at Marrakech and was the first man to bring news of the arrival of the Moors in the Sudan. On 28 February 1591 Judar Pasha halted his army on the left bank of the Niger at an obscure place called Karabara.†

* Mahmud Kati believed the original strength of the Moorish army to be 3,000 or 4,000, but he only mentions 1,000 Moorish troops as being engaged at the battle of Tondibi. This is scarcely sufficient to justify the assumption of some commentators that all the rest had perished in the desert.

† Col. de Castries confuses Karabara (sometimes spelt Kabara) with Kabara, the well-known port of Timbuktu, evidently misled by the Spanish narrative which states that the Moorish army, having crossed the Sahara, marched on Gao leaving Timbuktu on the left hand—'a mano izquierda'.[10] All authorities agree that the Moors avoided Timbuktu, which they could not have done if they went to Kabara, its port, which lay less than five miles to the south, and we know that they were unable to cross the Niger. El Ufrani's statement[11] that on reaching the Niger Judar camped in the neighbourhood of Timbuktu is too vague to be of value, quite apart from the fact that the writer had little knowledge of the geography of the Sudan.

THE MOORISH INVASION

It lay near the present town of Bamba, the southern terminus of several caravan routes which converge on this point where the Niger is more easily crossed than almost anywhere else on the Bend. Karabara moreover was a place of considerable strategic value to the Moors, for it lay halfway between Gao and Timbuktu. Here there was little risk of their being forced to fight a decisive engagement before they had had an opportunity of recovering from the rigours of the desert march, and at the same time they were in a position to interrupt communication between these important centres.

The people of Songhai were ill prepared for the invasion of their country. The recurring friction over the salt mines cannot have left room for doubt concerning the hostile intentions of the Moors, but the Songhai leaders, like the timorous members of El Mansur's council, regarded the Sahara as a bulwark which made invasion from the north impossible. It must be conceded in their favour that they derived their false sense of security from one of the most formidable geographical frontiers in the history of the world, and that the enterprise of the Moors had been rewarded with success where disaster seemed almost inevitable.

On hearing of the approach of the invaders, Askia Ishak rushed all his available forces to Kala, which lay beyond Massina, evidently expecting invasion from the west. On the receipt of fuller information he returned to Gao, where he summoned a council of war. The meeting was fraught with indecision. There was still uncertainty as to the objective of the invaders. At first it was thought to be Timbuktu and later Gao. Although there was a standing army sufficient to quell the frequently recurring rebellions within the borders of Songhai, there was no machinery for dealing with a danger of the magnitude which now threatened the state. We are told that the council broke up without accomplishing anything except the arrest of a man suspected of being an enemy agent. The Askia, however, sent orders to the desert chiefs to fill in the wells and harry the Moors on the dispersal of their army, which, it was hoped, would result from lack of water. Unfortunately for the Songhai these orders were sent too late. Ishak's attempt to mobilize a large force failed on account of the apathy of the people, who refused to credit the gravity of the situation. It was only when the Moors had reached the Niger and had been seen by the scared riverain peasantry that the Songhai forces began to assemble.

Judar celebrated his arrival on the Niger with a banquet, and he allowed his troops a short respite. In a few days they were again on

THE MOORISH INVASION

the march, moving down-stream towards Gao, following the left bank of the Niger. They encountered some Tuareg who habitually preyed upon caravans passing between Gao and Timbuktu. These they drove off, but farther on the Moors found some of their victims, four wounded negroes, who turned out to be the messengers sent by Ishak to the desert chiefs, and upon them were found the orders to fill in the wells. Had these messengers been sent a few weeks earlier every Moor might well have perished in the desert.

Judar, giving orders that non-combatant natives were to be respected, continued his march to Gao. A party of Songhai coming up the river in their canoes by night made an attack under cover of darkness, but they were quickly driven off. The entire lack of timber prevented the Moors from making boats, but they constructed rafts with their water-skins which enabled them to raid numerous island villages from which they replenished their stores with rice and other foodstuffs.

As he approached Gao Judar, learning through his scouts that the Askia was preparing for battle, made a fruitless appeal to the Songhai ruler to surrender to El Mansur and thus save unnecessary sacrifice of human lives. This was mistaken for a sign of weakness and only served to hearten the Songhai. On the following day the negro army was sighted near Tondibi, about fifty miles from Gao, the approach to which it barred. Judar resolved to give battle on the morrow and he cheered his troops with the promise of the sack of the capital.

Estimates of the strength of the Songhai army vary considerably. The most conservative is that of Mahmud Kati who placed it at 18,000 cavalry, and 9,700 infantry. According to Es Sadi the army was composed principally of archers but there were a few thousand cavalry armed with spears. Although firearms had already been introduced into Bornu,[12] the Songhai had no knowledge of their use. In spite of their conversion to Islam they retained many of their pagan beliefs, and were accompanied into battle by the customary band of magicians and sorcerers. Before the engagement the Songhai drove a mob of cattle before them with the object of throwing the invading army into confusion. The Moors, however, opened their ranks and allowed the cattle to pass through without doing harm. The battle then opened.

From the first there was no hope for the negroes against the superior arms of their adversaries. Never was the issue in doubt, although the Elches temporarily lost one of their banners. The greater part of the

160 THE MOORISH INVASION

Songhai army was a mere rabble, but there was a nucleus of very highly disciplined troops forming the advance guard, whose extraordinary courage is recorded in each of the four accounts of the battle which have come down to us. On the approach of the Moors they knelt on one knee and lashed the shin to the thigh, after the manner of hobbling camels, thus rendering themselves unable to rise. There they remained, firing arrows, till mown down by the Moors. The object of this strange manner of fighting was to inspire the less disciplined troops with courage and to prevent panic. In spite of their courageous resistance the Songhai were utterly routed and they left many dead whom the Moors eagerly stripped of their gold ornaments.*

Askia Ishak, seeing that his capital must inevitably fall into the hands of the invaders, sent orders to the people of Gao to seek safety across the Niger in Gurma, where they would be secure from immediate pursuit. He and the shattered remnants of the army also fled across the river. There were not sufficient boats for the townspeople, and in the panic many lives and much valuable property were lost in the river. There were distressing scenes of distracted mothers imploring the boatmen with bribes to take their children over the water to safety.

Ishak had sent similar instructions to Timbuktu, which shared with Gao the misfortune of being situated on the same side of the river as the invading army. But the people of that city arrived at Kabara only to find that their cowardly harbour-master had already fled upstream with all the craft. Some returned resignedly to their homes, but others fled into the desert.

Judar continued his march and entered Gao unopposed. He found that only the poorest of the inhabitants had remained in the capital, together with some foreign students and a number of Barbary mer-

---

* The various translations by Houdas have caused some confusion regarding the date of the battle of Tondibi. Es Sadi gives 17 Djomada which Houdas in 1900 translated as 12 April; El Ufrani gives the 16th of the same month, translated by Houdas in 1889 as 16 February. The *Tarikh El Fettach* gives 2 Djomada which Houdas translated in 1913 as 1 March.

According to De Castries (in *Hespéris*) the date of El Mansur's manifesto to the Sheriffs announcing the victory was 8 Chaban which he translates as 2 June, but in the Public Record Office in London there is a manuscript dated 1591 and signed by Richard Tomson stating that in a letter dated 24 April (presumably from Morocco) Don Custoval reported to Don Antonio news of the battle and that Ishak's head had been sent to Morocco and shown to the Turkish Ambassador![13]

THE MOORISH INVASION

chants who welcomed their victorious fellow countrymen. As we have already seen, the trade between the Mediterranean littoral and the Sudan, of which Gao was one of the principal markets, had brought great wealth to the merchants of the Maghreb. On this account Judar, in common with most of the Moors, had been misled into believing that the Songhai capital was an imposing city of great wealth. When he and his troops found themselves amid huts of mud and thatch and saw the humble dwelling of Ishak, surrounded by the usual squalor of a Sudanese town, they were filled with disappointment. What little of value the place had ever contained had been carried off in the general exodus and not an article of gold remained. Amongst the few things left behind by the fugitives were a cannon bearing the Portuguese arms, which the Songhai did not know how to use, a statue of the Holy Virgin, and a crucifix.

Although the victory at Tondibi had been easily won by the Moors they must have suffered severe privations when crossing the Sahara. They entered Gao fully expecting to be well rewarded for all they had endured and they felt their disillusionment keenly. To add to their despondency disease began to spread in their ranks and it carried off many lives.

Meanwhile Ishak, who was reorganizing his forces in the security of Gurma, opened negotiations with Judar. He undertook to recognize the suzerainty of El Mansur and offered to pay Judar 100,000 *mitkal* of gold and 1,000 slaves, if he and his army would return to Morocco. Ishak also offered the Moors certain trade concessions by which they were to be allowed to import salt and cowrie shells into the Sudan.

Judar, disillusioned and despondent, was ready enough to accept the settlement proposed by Ishak, but he had no authority to make terms. It was decided, therefore, to refer the matter to the Sultan. Judar prepared the necessary dispatch and, fervently hoping to win El Mansur's acceptance of the terms, he added a vivid description of all their sufferings and dwelt on the extent to which the wealth of Songhai fell short of their anticipations.

Disease was still rife amongst the Moors. In about a fortnight 400 of the troops had died and Judar himself was ill. Heavy losses amongst the transport animals added to the general gravity of the situation. Ishak, with whom a truce of a remarkably amicable nature had been established, recommended a retirement to the more salubrious climate of Timbuktu. In order to expedite their departure he offered to

THE MOORISH INVASION

provide the Moors with a large number of horses. In his anxiety to recover his capital he was prepared to sacrifice Timbuktu to the invaders.

Judar conferred with his Kaids and decided to act on Ishak's advice. After a march of twenty-nine days he made a peaceful entry into Timbuktu, but he was irritated by the sullen behaviour of the inhabitants. Here he settled down and while awaiting the return of his messenger he set the slaves of the town to building a fort in the flourishing quarter of the Ghadamsi merchants, many of whose warehouses had to be destroyed for the purpose.

The envoy bearing Judar's dispatch arrived in Marrakech in June 1591. His arrival had long been preceded by the news of his approach, which, directly he arrived in Dra'a, had flashed through the country with lightning speed. It was eight months since the departure of the expedition and during all that time no news had been received from the Sudan, excepting the report of the desert chief that the Niger had been reached.*

The news of the victory at Tondibi caused intense excitement amongst the populace of the capital. The contents of the dispatch, however, produced a very different effect upon El Mansur who regarded the terms submitted by Judar as too contemptible to be considered. He was particularly enraged that the Pasha had returned from Gao without either leaving a garrison in the capital or obtaining hostages from the enemy, and he simply refused to credit the unfavourable report on the wealth of Songhai. There could be no doubt that gold in vast quantities was to be found somewhere in the Sudan. For centuries it had been obtained in the natural course of trade. The Sultan resolved that the source of the gold supply must be sought at any cost, and that all the resources of his kingdom must be strained to that end.

El Mansur, seeing that great demands on his unfortunate subjects would be necessary, took care that no shadow which might lessen their enthusiasm should be cast over their jubilations. He issued a dithyrambic manifesto proclaiming the triumphant crossing of the Sahara, the glorious victory over the Songhai army, and the extraordinary wealth discovered in the Sudan.† No reference was made to the heavy

---

* In a letter to Queen Elizabeth of England, dated 12 March 1591, El Mansur only mentions that he had invaded the kingdoms of 'Gyney and Tureg' from which it is evident that no news had then reached him from the Sudan.[14]

† The text of El Mansur's proclamation has recently been discovered,[15] but

THE MOORISH INVASION 163

loss of life in the desert and from disease in the Sudan, nor to the rest of the unpalatable information contained in Judar's dispatch. The proclamation produced the desired effect and the victory of Moorish arms was celebrated in all the towns of the kingdom.

The Sultan now looked about him for a new leader of greater enterprise and vigour who would wring from the negroes their stores of gold. He chose Mahmud ben Zergun, a son of a renegade and the Kaid of all the Elches of the kingdom. Like Judar he was a eunuch who had been brought up since childhood in the royal palace. The news of his appointment, which soon leaked out, caused misgivings. Some thought Judar was dead, but those who were better informed suspected that he had merely fallen from grace.

Mahmud Pasha, with an escort of forty renegades and twenty followers to mind the transport, left at once for the Sudan. Some concern was felt for their safety for the season was most unfavourable for the Saharan march. The heat was intense, the levanter was blowing, and water was known to be more than usually scarce. They were ordered to march only at night.

El Mansur next gave orders for a body of irregulars to be raised amongst the Arabs of Sus for dispatch to the Sudan in the autumn. He also ordered boats for the navigation of the Niger to be built in Dra'a. They were to be constructed in sections which could be carried across the Sahara on camels and assembled on the Niger where Judar had been so gravely handicapped by lack of water transport, but there is no evidence that they were ever built.

An anonymous Spaniard has left us a valuable record of contemporary opinion in Marrakech concerning the Sudan venture. Some people saw in the Moorish victory over Songhai the promise of great wealth and the assurance of a glorious future for their country. Others, for whose judgement the Spaniard had greater regard, held contrary opinions—they were probably better informed than El Mansur intended concerning the true state of affairs in the Sudan. While not denying the initial success of the expedition they feared that exhaustion and ruin would result from El Mansur's determination to exploit his victory to the utmost. It was apparent that to retain only that which had already been conquered would necessitate the maintenance of a large garrison in the Sudan. Predatory nomads, a constant menace to communications across the desert, would waylay

unfortunately it contains no information of value which, having regard to its purpose, is not surprising.

164 THE MOORISH INVASION

small bodies of troops at the wells and cut them to pieces, as apparently had already happened. The ravages of disease in the unhealthy climate would demand a constant supply of reinforcements. This the country could ill afford, for none but harquebusiers were suitable and these were all Andalusian renegades on whom alone could the Sultan depend for the safety of his throne. Too many had already been sent to the Sudan, and it was not expected that they would ever come back.

But the Sultan, they remarked, not content with what he had achieved, was already planning fresh conquests for which more and more troops would be required. The more cautious doubted whether he would ever reach the gold-bearing region which they shrewdly believed was still far off, and they feared that financial ruin would result from the enormous cost of the campaign. The pay of the troops alone would absorb the Songhai tribute. Their principal concern was for their own trade, which they saw being ruined. In the past the negroes had been ready enough to go and fetch gold in order to barter it for salt and the trade goods of the Mediterranean, but if their only reward was to be confiscation by the invader they would soon cease to fetch it.

'Ainsi les revenus du Roi,' concludes the French translation of the narrative, 'seront sensiblement diminués, et ses sujets perdront aussi beaucoup, par la mévente de leurs marchandises; ce qui tournera au préjudice du Roi, car les rois maures sont maîtres absolus de la fortune de leurs sujets, puisque quand ils le veulent, ils la leur prennent librement.'[16]

Mahmud Pasha, for whose safety there had been some anxiety, arrived in Timbuktu about seven weeks after his departure from Marrakech. He immediately took over command from Judar. The harbour-master was still in hiding and there were no boats on the river. Mahmud, however, felled and cut into planks the few large trees which grew in the arid vicinity. With these and the door frames of the houses he managed to build two boats which were launched within a few days of his arrival. Leaving a small garrison in Timbuktu he set off with the army down the left bank of the Niger in search of Askia Ishak, taking Judar with him. The boats followed.

Ishak had meanwhile reorganized his forces and had, to some extent, restored their confidence. Hearing of the approach of Mahmud he quitted Gurma and marched against the enemy, whom he encountered at Bamba. This, his second, engagement with the Moors was not more

THE MOORISH INVASION

fortunate than the first. Again he was forced to fly across the river with a beaten army at his back. Mahmud, with his boats to help him, carried the pursuit into Gurma and built a fort at Gungia.

The Songhai rabble continued their flight southward into western Dendi where they ungratefully turned upon their unhappy monarch. Ishak fled, and, failing in an attempt to reach Kebbi, was forced in desperation to throw himself on the mercy of the pagans of Gurma. The latter had long suffered from Songhai oppression, and they avenged themselves by putting the Askia and his companions to death.

Ishak's Balama, or Chamberlain, Muhammad Gao, was elected to succeed him, but the choice was an unhappy one. At the moment of his accession several men of influence deserted to the enemy, and this so unnerved the new Askia that he promptly offered to swear allegiance to the Sultan of Morocco. The year was one of famine throughout the Western Sudan, and Mahmud, finding great difficulty in feeding his troops, was reduced to eating his transport animals. He therefore called upon the Askia to prove his sincerity by sending him supplies. Muhammad Gao ordered the crops on the Hausa, or left, bank of the river to be reaped and brought over to the Moorish camp. He himself was bidden to the enemy head-quarters to swear the oath of allegiance. On arrival in the camp he and his companions were treacherously seized and dispatched by boat as prisoners to Judar at Gao. A messenger was sent all the way to Morocco to inquire of the Sultan what should be done with them, but long before an answer could be received they were murdered. The Moors excused themselves for this act of perfidy on the ground that it was a reprisal for the alleged massacre of 400 of their troops, when on the road to the Sudan from Morocco, an incident of which no record survives.

Having put to death Askia Muhammad Gao the Moors asserted their sovereignty by appointing an Askia of their own with Timbuktu as his capital. Henceforward there was an Askia of the North, who was always the puppet of the Moors, and an independent Askia of the South. The Moors wisely interfered as little as possible with the system of government which they found existing in the Sudan and by appointing an Askia to govern the natives of the occupied territories they prevented the collapse of this valuable administrative machine.

There now arose amongst the Songhai a brilliant national leader who rallied their broken forces and fired the people with some of the zeal with which they had risen to oppose the invader when he first set foot in their country. This man was Nuh, a younger brother of

166 THE MOORISH INVASION

Muhammad Gao, and the Songhai now made him their Askia. Mahmud Pasha had already shown himself a leader of enterprise and energy, but Askia Nuh was soon to prove himself a match for the Moorish general. In spite of the miserable equipment of his much-reduced forces he maintained the field against the well-armed invaders for the next four years. This he achieved by never letting pass an opportunity for inflicting loss upon the enemy, at the same time taking care never to become engaged in a decisive action. As a guerrilla leader he was extraordinarily successful, and in his appreciation of the natural advantages of the country he displayed remarkable tactical ability. His commanding personality and martial zeal held together and inspired the broken remnants of his people. While the Moors continued to support a puppet Askia of their own, Nuh maintained Songhai independence in the south-west. The fall of the empire of Gao was followed by the rise of the kingdom of Dendi.

Mahmud Pasha did not delay to strike hard at the new leader. Nuh awaited the onslaught on the frontier of Dendi, choosing his own ground for the encounter. The issue was undecided, but the Moors were held at bay for a whole day and the Songhai force ultimately retired unbroken. Nuh withdrew southward, seeking thick bush in which alone he could hope to wrestle successfully with the Moors. Mahmud followed and built a fort at Kolen near the present town of Say. After thus consolidating his position he foolishly allowed himself to be drawn still farther south. Here he was quickly beset with grave difficulties, and the initiative passed to the Songhai general.

The opposing forces were now in that part of Dendi which to-day we should call Borgu, and which lies just south of the twelfth parallel of north latitude. Here the wastes and savannas of more northern latitudes give place to parklands which rapidly thicken into dense forest as the coast is approached; rainfall is abundant, filling the depressions with swamps and bogs. The small daily range of temperature and damp atmosphere combine to produce an unhealthy and enervating climate. The struggle between Nuh and Mahmud is believed to have centred chiefly in the desolate Mekron river district where to-day the ruins of deserted villages are the only evidence left of human occupation, the depopulation of the country being due solely to the ravages of the tsetse-fly.[17]

Borgu had never formed a part of the Songhai empire, though war had been unsuccessfully waged against its pagan inhabitants by such redoubtable monarchs as Sonni Ali and Askia the Great. It was the

THE MOORISH INVASION

proud boast of the Borgawa that they had never been conquered. Their country was easily defensible, and none knew better than themselves how to utilize its natural advantages. When in the closing years of last century Europeans first attempted to penetrate their country by force of arms they found that the Borgawa had lost none of their skill in the arts of war. Lord Lugard has attributed their successes to two causes.

'First to their reputation for a knowledge of witchcraft and of deadly poisons which renders their poisoned arrows very dreaded. Second to their fighting tactics. So far from dreading to separate their forces their custom, I am told, when they attack by day is to make a feint of attack simultaneously on front and rear, reserving the bulk of their strength for a strong attack on the centre of a long caravan. This mode of attack by ambush would generally succeed in dividing their enemies' forces and inducing panic. They, however, love most to effect a night surprise.'[18]

So typical were Nuh's methods of those employed by these bellicose pagans that it seems fairly certain that he secured their active support. Although the Borgawa never had any love for the Songhai they were probably ready enough to join forces with the latter to drive out the common enemy.

Having lured the Moors into this inhospitable region Nuh was able, with the assistance of a distinguished lieutenant named Muhammad uld Benchi, to inflict upon them severe losses. The Moors, entirely without experience of bush fighting, were unable to counter the guerrilla methods of their enemies. Ambushes, surprise attacks, and lightning raids were the methods of attrition to which Nuh subjected them. These tactics, combined with a persistent refusal to offer battle, denied to the Moors the superiority which their firearms had given them in their first engagements. Even in recent years highly disciplined troops with the most modern equipment have suffered the same humiliating experiences in similar country at the hands of natives no better armed than the Songhai and their Borgawa allies.

The Moors had not been long in Borgu before its bad climate caused another serious outbreak of disease in their ranks. The humid bush, lack of suitable food and bad water took heavy toll. While malaria and dysentery destroyed the troops, tsetse-fly killed all the horses of the cavalry. In short the Moors were experiencing those same conditions which have combined at all times to prevent the effective occupation of the forests by the predatory slave-raiding tribes of the Sudan. Their difficulties were those which had set a limit

168　THE MOORISH INVASION

to the southward expansion not only of the Songhai, but also of the older empires of Ghana and Mali, and which afterwards arrested the triumphal progress of the Fulani and other Sudanese peoples. Their afflictions, too, were those which till recent years effectively closed the interior of West Africa to the old European trading settlements scattered up and down the Atlantic seaboard.

For two years the Moors continued their fruitless struggle with the Songhai army. Exhaustion at last compelled Mahmud to recognize the futility of continuing the contest. He wrote to the Sultan reporting the condition of his troops and their painful experiences in Dendi and Borgu. But, fearing to lose touch with the enemy till he had received instructions from El Mansur, he did not withdraw.

When Mahmud Pasha watched the messenger bearing his dispatch setting out for the far-distant north he cannot have failed to recall the effect produced on the Sultan by the discouraging report which his predecessor had sent back to Morocco. El Mansur, however, received the dispatch of the gallant Mahmud in a spirit very different from that in which he had read the contemptible letter of Judar. Probably he was not altogether unmindful of Mahmud's devotion to duty nor of the hardships endured by his troops. He received his report with sympathy and proved his appreciation of all that his troops had done by sending out strong reinforcements to assist them. Fifteen hundred infantry and fifteen hundred cavalry with five hundred spare horses were immediately got ready and sent to join Mahmud. They were followed shortly afterwards by two small columns, four hundred strong altogether. Probably these and most subsequent reinforcements were natives of Morocco.

But Mahmud realized that even with the help of these fresh troops it would be hopeless to continue the struggle with Nuh. At the end of 1593 he retired up the Niger. He left Judar with a garrison at Gao, built a fort at Bamba, and arrived back in Timbuktu at a time when the presence of a strong man was greatly needed in that city.

THE MOORISH INVASION

REFERENCES

1. Mahmoud Kati, *Tarikh el-Fettach*, trad. O. Houdas et M. Delafosse, Paris, 1913. El Ufrani, *Nozhet-Elhadi*, trad. O. Houdas, Paris, 1889.

2. Lt.-Col. H. de Castries, *Hespéris*, Paris, 1923, pp. 433 et seq.

3. El Ufrani, p. 135.

4. Leo Africanus, iii. 887.

5. Public Record Office, *State Papers, Foreign, Barbary States*, vol. xii, *apud* de Castries, *Sources Inédites de l'Histoire de Maroc*.

6. Hatfield House, Cecil MSS., vol. xi. 95, *apud* de Castries, op. cit.

7. Leo Africanus, iii. 991.

8. H. de Castries, op. cit.

9. Richard Hakluyt, *Principal Navigations of the English Nation*, Glasgow, 1904, vii. 101.

10. *Hespéris*, 1923, p. 459.

11. El Ufrani, p. 164.

12. H. R. Palmer, *Mai Idris of Bornu*, p. 11.

13. De Castries, *Les Sources Inédites de l'Histoire de Maroc*, Première Série, Angleterre, Paris, 1918–25, ii. 65.

14. Ibid. ii. 69.

15. *Hespéris*, 1923, p. 478.

16. Ibid., p. 477.

17. *Renseignements Coloniaux*, Paris, 1929, p. 139.

18. *Geographical Journal*, vi (1895), p. 219.

XV

THE FALL OF THE SONGHAI EMPIRE

Neither shall the Arabian pitch tent there; neither shall the shepherds make their fold there. ISAIAH xiii. 20.

NO quality in the character of the Western Sudanese so excited the admiration of the early Arab and European explorers as their love of peaceful pursuits. Nevertheless the population contained many subversive elements. The great number of mutually hostile tribes springing from many different stocks, the varying degrees of civilization, a diversity of religious beliefs, a widely diffused predatory instinct, and an almost total absence of natural geographical boundaries were some of the factors which combined to throw the country into turmoil directly the restraining hand of a powerful central authority was removed.

It is not surprising to find, therefore, that the immediate sequel to the defeat of the Songhai army by Judar at Tondibi was a general outbreak of anarchy and brigandage. The news of the flight of Askia Ishak and his shattered forces let loose all the turbulent elements and produced chaos throughout those parts of the tottering empire which had not yet felt the direct impact of the invader. The tribes who had been under the tutelage of Songhai, flushed with the excitement of their unexpected liberation, abandoned themselves to orgies of licence and excess. The Fulani and the Zagrana (who have not been identified with certainty) flung themselves upon the Songhai peasants of the lacustrine region above Timbuktu. The rich province of Jenne was ravaged from end to end by hordes of pagan Bambara, whose especial object was the abduction of Muslim women. The Tuareg, who had held the Songhai in respect, grew bolder in their raids on the riverain peasantry. 'Security gave place to danger,' wrote Es Sadi, 'wealth to poverty, distress and calamities and violence succeeded tranquillity. Everywhere men destroyed each other; in every place and in every direction there was plundering, and war spared neither life nor property nor persons. Disorder was general and spread everywhere, rising to the highest degree of intensity.'[1]

The presence in Timbuktu of Judar Pasha with an army at his back had saved that city from the general turmoil. This comparative tranquillity ended in September 1591 when Mahmud, soon after his arrival in the Sudan, departed for the distant south in pursuit of Askia Nuh.

THE FALL OF THE SONGHAI EMPIRE 171

Throughout the history of Songhai there hovered on its northern frontier uncontrolled bands of Tuareg, mostly Idenan and Immedideren to whom the foundation of Timbuktu has been attributed. These predatory nomads, for centuries a menace to the sedentary peoples of the middle Niger, at all times regarded the commercial prosperity of Timbuktu with a jealous eye. Lying on the threshold of the desert it was a constant prey to their raids. Even to-day, under French administration, the immediate vicinity of the city is not free from an occasional *razzia*. So sudden and unexpected were these descents that it became customary to conduct business indoors instead of in the open air. There was not, however, constant enmity between the nomads and the townspeople. Sometimes there were prolonged periods of friendly intercourse, and it was during one of these tranquil spells that the Moorish invasion occurred. Amongst those who had fled the city and sought refuge in the surrounding desert on the approach of the Moors was a certain powerful Tuareg chief named Yahia. Shortly after Mahmud's departure for the south, Yahia and his followers returned and attacked the small garrison which had been left behind in the city under Kaid El Mustapha. Yahia was killed and the troops triumphantly paraded his head through the streets. The townspeople, incensed by the ill treatment they were receiving from the Moors, killed seventy-six of the hated harquebusiers and drove back the remainder into their fort and laid siege to it. A fresh band of Tuareg, acting with treachery peculiarly characteristic of desert nomads, now suddenly proclaimed themselves partisans of the Moors and fired the city.

The rebellion continued till the end of the year when the besieged garrison was relieved by Kaid Mami ben Barun, who had come out as Mahmud's secretary and was to prove himself one of the ablest men El Mansur sent to the Sudan. He had been ordered back from Borgu with over 300 harquebusiers to stamp out the rebellion and he handled the difficult situation with dexterity. His arrival spread terror in Timbuktu and there was again an exodus into the surrounding desert. Although Mahmud had told him to slay every living soul in the city if he thought it necessary Mami acted with restraint. Indeed he showed such moderation that his sympathies would seem to have been on the side of the rebels rather than with El Mustapha.

He showed every mark of respect for Abu Hafs Omar, the venerable Qadi of Timbuktu, and begged his pardon for the inexcusable excesses of the troops. He slew with his own hand a soldier whom he found

172   THE FALL OF THE SONGHAI EMPIRE

robbing a townsman and took steps to see that everything supplied to the troops was paid for in cash. These measures quickly resulted in happier relations between the garrison and the town, and public confidence was restored. The fugitives began to return from the desert and even the timorous harbour-master of Kabara reappeared with the boats. The people swore allegiance to El Mansur, the trade routes were reopened, and life in the city became normal once more.

Mami, having restored peace, embarked upon a punitive expedition against the tribes who, under the leadership of Yahia, had originally caused the outbreak. He was as ruthless to them as he had been merciful to the people of Timbuktu. Of the prisoners taken, the men were put to death and the women and children were sold as slaves. This heavy flooding of the market caused a slump and slaves changed hands at the equivalent of a few pence apiece.

Meanwhile the scholars and merchants of Jenne, who notoriously quailed at the sight of blood, hearing of the unexpectedly generous treatment which Timbuktu had received from the invaders, hastened to tender their submission to the Moors. On the completion of the necessary formalities, which included placing the affairs of the city in the hands of officers appointed by Mami, and the assessment of its tribute at 60,000 pieces of gold, the people of Jenne again resumed their peaceful callings.

The tranquillity which they thought they had now secured was rudely broken by the spirited governor of Bagana, Bokar by name, the son of a former Askia. Under the pretext of wishing to tender his submission he obtained leave to enter the town, where, rallying round him the turbulent spirits, he plundered the merchants' stores and robbed the newly-appointed officials. At last Mami arrived with a strong force and rid Jenne of her unwelcome guest by putting him to death.

Meanwhile the incapable El Mustapha, left alone in Timbuktu, had again got himself into trouble with the nomads of the desert, this time with the Sanhaja Tuareg. The latter, having surprised and massacred the Moorish garrison at Ras-el-Ma, had advanced on the city itself, where that ever unhappy governor found himself with but a single horse and unable to mount his men and lead them out into the desert to ward off the threatened attack. When the raiders were only a short distance from the city, news reached El Mustapha, who was in an agony of despair, of the approach of

THE FALL OF THE SONGHAI EMPIRE 173

the reinforcements which El Mansur had sent from Morocco to assist Mahmud. In response to an urgent appeal the leader of the column hurried some horses forward to Timbuktu where they arrived in time for El Mustapha to mount his men and disperse the Tuareg.

Shortly afterwards, at the end of 1593, Mahmud returned from Borgu. His mood after two years of bush fighting, as exhausting as it had been barren of results, boded ill for Timbuktu. Several sensational executions were immediately ordered, but the reprieve of innocent victims was effected by astutely directing the wrath of Mahmud against the Tuareg who had been responsible for the massacre of the Ras-el-Ma garrison. The guilty Sanhaja were almost annihilated.

Since his first arrival in Songhai Mahmud had enjoyed little opportunity for plundering the enemy. What little had been left behind in Gao had fallen into the hands of Judar, and the Borgu campaign can have produced little or no loot. He therefore decided to squeeze what he could out of Timbuktu. Too war-weary to plunder the city by mere force of arms he resorted to cunning. He first sent a crier through the streets announcing that on the morrow there would be a house to house search for arms, but that an exception would be made of houses belonging to descendants of the sainted Sidi Mahmud, who had been Qadi of Timbuktu for fifty years. Every man who could boast acquaintanceship with a descendant of the venerable Qadi rushed to deposit with him his valuables, which he had little doubt would all be stolen during the search for arms if allowed to remain in his own more humble dwelling. Their cunning was only inferior to that of the Pasha into whose hands they were playing. After their homes had been searched they were summoned to the Sankoré mosque to receive the oath of allegiance. The descendants of Sidi Mahmud were next summoned, but the doors of the mosque were closed behind them, and while they were held prisoners the soldiers plundered their homes, which contained all the wealth of Timbuktu, and violated their women. Much of the loot was distributed amongst the troops, but 100,000 pieces of gold were set aside for the Sultan. The prisoners were sent to the fort in two parties; one party arrived in safety, but the other was foully massacred by its escort.

Meanwhile Askia Nuh, relieved of the presence of the Moors in Borgu, had been meditating fresh aggressions. News soon reached Timbuktu that he had invested the distant river post at Kolen, and that the garrison was in grave danger. Mami, no doubt a little weary of getting other people out of trouble, was at once dispatched

174   THE FALL OF THE SONGHAI EMPIRE

down the Niger to their relief. He arrived just in time. The garrison was extricated only with great difficulty and brought safely back to Timbuktu.

During Mahmud Pasha's long absence in Borgu there had been constant trouble in Timbuktu between the townspeople and El Mustapha. In the end Abu Hafs Omar, the Qadi, was driven to sending envoys to Morocco to lay before the Sultan the grievances of the citizens. The envoys were much gratified by the cordiality of their reception at the Moorish court, and especially by El Mansur's prompt action in righting their wrongs. He sent them back with Bu Ikhtiyar, a Kaid, described as a renegade son of a Christian prince, who carried instructions for the better treatment of Omar and his people.

Bu Ikhtiyar took with him 1,200 reinforcements who crossed the Sahara in two columns and reached Timbuktu in safety. But the Kaid and the Qadi's envoys found that they had been preceded by a messenger from El Mansur, who had brought very different instructions. These orders were for Abu Hafs Omar and the *literati* of Timbuktu to be sent in chains to Morocco, together with all their books and treasures. As these people belonged to the most cultured and the wealthiest section of the community they were the least suited to the physical exertion which such a journey entailed, especially as most of them had been greatly weakened by five months in gaol. Nevertheless they were now compelled to set out with their unhappy women and children on the ghastly trans-Saharan march. We have no record of their sufferings in the desert nor of how many survived. Amongst the latter, however, were Abu Hafs Omar and Ahmed Baba the distinguished historian so frequently quoted in the *Tarikh es Sudan* and other works. During the journey Ahmed Baba fell from his camel through the weight of his chains and broke his leg. When Omar first sighted Marrakech he cursed its people. 'O Allah!' he cried, 'as they have tormented us and driven us from our country, let them too be tormented and driven from theirs!' Men afterwards declared that this was the commencement of an era of calamities for the city. Omar was liberated in 1596.[2] But Ahmed Baba remained a prisoner in Marrakech till he was released by Mulay Zidan in 1607; he returned at once to Timbuktu where he died the same year.

El Mansur, furious that his share of the loot of Timbuktu was only 100,000 *mitkal*, dispatched Kaid Mansur ben Abderrahman to the Sudan with orders to supersede Mahmud and put him to death.

THE FALL OF THE SONGHAI EMPIRE 175

The Pasha, meanwhile, was carrying on the campaign against Askia Nuh with his accustomed energy.

The Niger all the way from Jenne to Gao was in the hands of the Moors. Gao, the most distant of the Moorish outposts since the fall of Kolen, was strongly held by Judar, who, since his removal from the supreme command, had become a less complacent leader. Nuh, forced to leave the valley of the Niger, led his forces into the district of El Hadjar, or Hombori, the home of the Tombo. This mountainous region lies within the Bend of the Niger in close proximity to the populous and fertile plains around Lake Debo and within striking distance of Timbuktu itself.

Mahmud Pasha, who had come south in pursuit of Nuh, was entangled with his army in the El Hadjar hills when he received from Abu Fares, a son of the Sultan, a kindly warning of the fate which awaited him at the hands of Kaid Mansur, who was due soon to arrive. Perceiving there was no escape Mahmud decided that he would die in arms against the enemies of his country. He accordingly resolved to attack the formidable rocks of Almina Walo, an enterprise of such a hazardous nature that few would follow him. Under cover of darkness and accompanied by a handful of men he advanced against the pagan stronghold and there found the death he sought. The exultant pagans severed his head and sent it to Askia Nuh. The trophy was forwarded on to the king of Kebbi, 400 miles away, who set it up in the market-place of Leka. Through his own folly El Mansur had lost his best general.

Askia Sliman, the puppet Askia of the Moors, withdrew the troops to the river. On reaching Timbuktu Mansur, assisted by Judar, returned with the army to El Hadjar and concluded the campaign by inflicting a severe defeat on Askia Nuh, who fled and was heard of no more. We unfortunately have no record of how the defeat of this gallant and able leader was accomplished.

In the history of the Moorish campaign in the Sudan no leaders served their respective countries better than Mahmud Pasha and Askia Nuh. For nearly four years they remained at the head of the opposing armies. As long as they held the stage the campaign was conducted in a spirit of high resolve which was so markedly absent in its earlier and later stages. It was many years after the final defeat of Nuh in 1595 before the Songhai forces were again able to take the field against the Moors. Though death robbed him of this final victory Mahmud was the most successful of the Moorish Pashas and

176 THE FALL OF THE SONGHAI EMPIRE

his loss was only less serious to his country than that of Askia Nuh to the Songhai.

Mansur and Judar returned with their victorious troops to Timbuktu where, owing to the Sultan having omitted to appoint a successor to Mahmud, a serious quarrel broke out between them. Judar refused to recognize the authority of Mansur, and the two became rivals for the control of the Sudan. They decided, however, to refer their quarrel to El Mansur, but the consequences of his decision were even worse than those of his original omission. He appointed Mansur commander-in-chief of the army and Judar was made civil governor-general, both men being warned against impeding each other in their respective duties. This foolish attempt at dual control was foredoomed to failure. The two leaders became implacable enemies, each concentrating on defeating the measures of the other. Finally Mansur fell ill and died in circumstances which suggested he had been poisoned by Judar.

El Mansur now gave the Pashalik of the Sudan to Muhammad Taba, an elderly Kaid who had been mellowed by twelve years in gaol. On arriving in Timbuktu with 1,000 fresh troops, half cavalry and half infantry, he relieved Judar of his command and was promptly murdered. Judar next dealt with El Mustapha, the effete governor of Timbuktu, whose final act of folly was an attempt to oust Judar from command of the army. With reckless disregard for the consequences they decided to allow the army to settle their dispute. The troops chose Judar for their leader, and from that day they knew themselves to be their own masters and this eventually cost Morocco her new dominion.

El Mustapha was strangled. Nothing seemed more probable than that Judar would next defy the Sultan and declare himself the independent ruler of the Sudan. But he had no such ambition. Actuated by the highest motives his sole desire was to administer the country in the best interests of the Sultan and without interference from others. El Mansur, for his part, saw the futility of sending out more Pashas to be murdered by Judar who was displaying a persistence of which he had never been suspected and which might yet be turned to good account. Indeed Judar's high-handed actions so won the admiration of El Mansur that he recalled him to quell some serious disturbances which were causing much anxiety in Morocco. But Judar's self-confidence knew no bounds. He refused to return till a competent governor had been appointed to carry on the administration of the

THE FALL OF THE SONGHAI EMPIRE

Sudan. When two civilian Kaids, one of whom was a Portuguese, arrived to relieve him he still refused to go. He wrote to El Mansur insisting on the need for a Pasha, a military governor, who would be capable of dealing with a critical situation which had arisen owing to a threatened Mandingo invasion and preparations for rebellion in Massina.

El Mansur, again acquiescing in Judar's demand, sent out Ammar Pasha, a young eunuch of Portuguese descent who had already had an unfortunate experience in the Sahara when conducting 1,000 reinforcements to the Sudan. He had divided them into two columns each following a different route, the one composed of 500 Elches and the other 500 Andalusian Moors. The former had reached Timbuktu in safety, but the whole of the Andalusian column had perished in the desert.

In March 1599, when Ammar arrived, Judar at last consented to return to Morocco. Eight eventful years had passed since his first arrival in the Sudan. He appears to have convinced others, as he had convinced himself, that the crimes of which he was guilty were committed in the best interests of the Sultan.

Jasper Tomson, an Englishman who was in Morocco at the time, has left us an interesting account of Judar Pasha's homecoming.

'Six dayes past,' he wrote in a letter dated 4 July 1599, 'here aryved a nobleman from Gago, called Judar Basha, whoe was sent by this kinge 10 yeares past to conquere the said contrye, wherein many people of this contrye have lost theire lyves. He brought with him thirtie camels, laden with tyber, which ys unrefyned gold (yet the difference ys but six shillinges in an ownce weight betwene yt and duccattees); also great store of pepper, unicornes, hornes and a certain kynde of wood for diers, to some 120 camel loades; all which he presented unto the Kinge, with 50 horse, and great quantitye of eanuches, duarfes, and woeman and men slaves, besydes 15 virgins, the Kinges daughters of Gago, which he sendeth to be Kinges concubines. Yow must note all these be of the cole black heyre, for that contrye yeldeth noe other.'[3]

In a postscript Tomson adds that the thirty camel-loads of gold may have amounted to £604,800. The evident trouble which Judar took to render the occasion of his return agreeable to El Mansur was not wasted. He was received with honour and continued to serve his country with distinction for several more years.

A month after Judar's departure from the Sudan the anticipated

178   THE FALL OF THE SONGHAI EMPIRE

Mandingo invasion burst upon the country. Reinforcements were rushed up to Jenne by boat, but only just in time. They succeeded in forcing their way into the city, but the enemy closed in behind them. The greatest danger was from the surrounding tribes who were known to be disaffected and ready to rise in sympathy with the Mandingoes. Such a combination would inevitably put an end to Moorish rule on the upper Niger. It was therefore necessary to force an immediate decision with the army of Mali. Only a few hours after the investment of the city the garrison made a desperate sortie. The Mandingoes, quite unprepared for so sudden a counter, were routed, and the neighbouring tribes dared not rise and help them.

Ammar Pasha, who had taken no part in the defeat of the Mandingoes, soon proved himself unfitted to administer the country. He was succeeded by Sulayman Pasha, the last, and perhaps the best, selection for this appointment made by El Mansur. Sulayman, who brought 500 fresh troops with him, was an enlightened and energetic administrator, but it was as a disciplinarian that he rendered most valuable service. The army had grown impatient of control and the spirit of indiscipline which so quickly breeds disruption and ruin had already begun to spread in its ranks. Sulayman endeavoured to arrest its growth by reorganizing the army and subjecting the troops to a severity of discipline which they had not known since Mahmud's time. He moved them to a camp outside Timbuktu and thus freed the civil population from the constant thieving and petty tyrannies of foreign soldiery.

In August 1603 Mulay Ahmed el Mansur died of plague and was buried in a magnificent tomb in Marrakech. The moment of his accession had been auspicious, but he had not failed to turn to account the singular advantages which he enjoyed. His reign was accounted peaceful by his people who for centuries had been bred and born to turbulence and strife and were probably easy to satisfy in this respect. He had dazzled Europe by his wealth, and when we come to examine the results of the campaign for which he will always be remembered, we shall see how richly the Sudan contributed to his exchequer.

Sulayman Pasha heard of El Mansur's death shortly after his arrival in the Sudan. He kept the fact to himself till he was able to proclaim it simultaneously with the news of the accession of Mulay Abu Fares. He thereby avoided that dangerous period of public licence which was apt to occur between the death of one Moorish Sultan and the acces-

THE FALL OF THE SONGHAI EMPIRE 179

sion of the next.* Seldom did the throne fall vacant without several claimants, backed by mobs of armed partisans, trying to seize it. In Morocco there were no less than three different Sultans in the six weeks which followed El Mansur's death.

The new Sultan recalled Sulayman from the Sudan and appointed Mahmud Lonko to succeed him. No more unfortunate choice could have been made, for the new Pasha was incapable of controlling his subordinates. Officers aspiring to sole command of the army sought to realize their ambitions by canvassing the troops who now seized the reins of power and became virtually their own masters. Henceforward no Pasha could be appointed without the consent of the army. For a time Mahmud Lonko was permitted to retain the title of Pasha, but the command of the army, which carried with it the administration of the country, passed first into the hands of El Hassan, the Treasurer, and then into those of Ali et Tlemcani, one of the Kaids. The latter remained in command for over four years, during which he maintained sufficient control of the troops to enable him to offer some opposition to the rising tide of native rebellion which was ever threatening to destroy the surviving remnants of Moorish rule.

Thirteen years had elapsed since the final defeat of Askia Nuh by Mansur and Judar. During this period the Moors had been principally occupied in domestic dissensions which cost them much of the prestige they had enjoyed as conquerors. The Tuareg had reverted to their old practice of raiding the riverain tribes and the Moors were powerless to prevent their incursions. The pagan tribes of Hombori, who had never lost their independence, continued to support every movement hostile to the Moors.

While Mahmud Lonko yet remained the titular Pasha the smouldering embers of Songhai nationalism again burst into flame. The work of Askia Nuh had been carried on by other leaders under whom the armed forces had been freshly recruited. They now took the field again, first marching against those tribes of the upper Niger who had submitted to the Moors. Their advance was successfully arrested by Ali et Tlemcani, but, conscious of the weakness of his position, the Kaid was compelled to make very conciliatory terms, especially with the disaffected Fulani of Massina who had played a prominent part in the rebellion.

A year later the Songhai army again marched westward to raise

---

* For an interesting parallel in recent times see Walter B. Harris, *Tafilet*, London, 1895, p. 346.

180   THE FALL OF THE SONGHAI EMPIRE

a revolt on the upper Niger. Jenne had promised her active co-operation, but her ever faint-hearted citizens failed to honour their engagements. The Songhai general turned northwards and encountered the Moorish army under Ali. Both sides lost heavily in the sanguinary conflict which ended in the defeat of the Moors.

The Songhai victory was productive of many revolts, and it even put heart into the timid scholars and merchants of Jenne openly to defy the invaders. Communications with Timbuktu were severed and lawless bands looted Moorish boats and attacked detachments of their troops. The Fulani again rose in open rebellion. Although Ali recovered control of this region and caught the instigator of the rising, he dared not put him to death on account of his popularity amongst the surrounding tribes who were ready to seize any pretext for a fresh outbreak.

In 1612 the Songhai army advanced north-westwards from its headquarters in Dendi and encountered Ali somewhere between Dori and Hombori. The armies turned aside to avoid an engagement, and it was popularly supposed that the Songhai leader was bribed by the Moors to withdraw. Having regard to the extreme weakness already displayed by Ali the story seems not improbable. In corroboration it was related that gold was found concealed in the clothes of the Songhai general who was afterwards executed by the Askia.

On his return from this expedition Ali contrived the removal of Mahmud Lonko, and on 11 October 1612 he openly defied the Sultan of Morocco and had himself proclaimed Pasha in Timbuktu.

Ali's coup occurred when Morocco was being rent by one of those periods of chronic civil strife which have so constantly afflicted her. Mulay Zidan, the reigning Sultan, was too much occupied with these disorders to concern himself with the affairs of Songhai. Since the death of El Mansur there had been a strong feeling that the time had come for Morocco to abandon her commitments in the Sudan. For five years nothing was done to recover control of the Niger territory, but eventually Ammar Pasha, who was accompanied by a French slave named Paul Imbert, was sent out to see what could be done.

The presence of the European slave is not without interest. An anonymous French writer of this period, describing the difficulties of a journey across the Sahara, tells us that 'to steer your course, you must make your observation from the rising and setting of the Sun, and the Stars and the Compass must (if there be occasion) direct you. They

THE FALL OF THE SONGHAI EMPIRE 181

always take care to have some or other in the *Caphille* (caravan), who understand these matters, as Paul Imbert did, who was a Mariner, and well-beloved, and cherisht by his Master, the *Alkayde Hamar*, who was a *White* Eunuch, by Nation a *Portugal*, a very worthy and noble person'.[4] The value of astronomical instruments in the Sahara had been recognized also by Mulay Ahmed. In 1600 a London instrument maker was advised by his correspondent in Marrakech that his 'instrument of declination would be commodious for a yeerely voyage, which some make for the King over a sandy sea (wherein they must use needle and compasse) to Gago. If you question about the matter, and shew them some instrument serving for this purpose, it will give great content'.[5]

On arrival in the Sudan Ammar Pasha found the situation so hopeless that there was nothing to be done except to punish Ali et Tlemcani whom he tortured to death. Beyond this he could achieve nothing. He returned home to report the utter disruption of the Moorish forces and a state of general chaos throughout Songhai. With the return of Ammar in 1618 the costly enterprise to which El Mansur had committed his country twenty-eight years previously was finally abandoned.

It was principally the remoteness of the Sudan which had made it impossible for Morocco to hold her newly won dominions. The Sultans had tried to exercise direct personal control over the Pashas by forbidding them to make important decisions without reference to the central government. But at least four months, and often as much as six, were required to obtain a reply from Morocco, and the Pashas were frequently forced to act on their own initiative. Official approval for decisions made under such circumstances could not be easily withheld and so the Pashas grew more and more into the habit of acting independently. As long as the Pashalik of the Sudan was entrusted to a man as loyal as Judar this increasing spirit of independence served to strengthen the administration and was therefore an advantage. But when the local government passed into the hands of men of less integrity the ties with Morocco weakened, the administration grew increasingly corrupt, and the troops became so arrogant that a large measure of political power passed into their hands. It was inevitable that sooner or later some ambitious demagogue, with a large following in the ranks of the army, would defy the Sultan and take the government of the country into his own hands.

182   THE FALL OF THE SONGHAI EMPIRE

REFERENCES

1. *Tarikh es Soudan*, p. 223.
2. Ibid., p. 266.
3. Public Record Office, *State Papers, Barbary States*, vol. xii, *apud* de Castries.
4. Mons. A. ✱✱✱✱, *A Letter concerning the Countrys of Muley Arxid, King of Tafiletta*, Englished out of French, London, 1671, p. 15.
5. Samuel Purchas, *Purchas His Pilgrimes*, Glasgow, 1905, vi. 59.

XVI

EL DZEHEBI

'This king of Morocco is like to be the greatest prince in the world for money, if he keeps this country.'—ANTHONY DASSEL.

MULAY ZIDAN declared there were records showing that in El Mansur's reign alone the Sudan had consumed 23,000 Moorish troops. A few had returned to Morocco, but all of these had afterwards died from the diseases they had contracted in the tropics. Es Sadi would have us believe that the enormous expenditure of men and material had largely been in vain, but from other sources a very different impression is gained. El Mansur became generally known as El Dzehebi, the Golden, and it is nowhere suggested that the name was not well deserved. Owing to the auspicious circumstances of his accession he had commenced his reign with a well-filled Treasury, but his Sudanese conquests increased his already considerable riches to enormous wealth.

'A la suite de la conquête des principautés du Soudan,' wrote El Ufrani, 'le sultan marocain reçut tant de poudre d'or, que les envieux en étaient tout troublés et les observateurs fort stupéfaits; aussi Elmansour ne paya-t-il plus ses fonctionnaires qu'en métal pur et en dinars de bon poids. Il y avait à la porte de son palais 1,400 marteaux qui frappaient chaque jour des pièces d'or, et il y avait en outre une quantité du précieux métal qui servait à la confection de boucles et autres bijoux. Ce fut cette surabondance d'or qui fit donner au sultan le surnom de Eddzehebî.'[1]

In August 1594 Laurence Madoc, an Englishman residing in Morocco, wrote to a friend in London, '. . . not ten dayes past here came a Cahaia of the Andoluzes home from Gago, and another principall Moore, whom the king sent thither at the first with Alcaide Hamode,* and they brought with them thirty mules laden with gold. I saw the same come into the Alcasava with mine owne eies: and these men themselves came not poore, but with such wealth that they came away without the king's commandment.'

In a second letter he wrote

'the rent of Tombuto is 60 quintals of gold† by the yeere; the goodness whereof you know. What rent Gago will yeeld, you shall know at the Spring,

---

* Mahmud ben Zergun.

† In the middle of the seventh century gold dust was worth about 50s. an ounce. A quintal is about 100 lb.

184   EL DZEHEBI

for then Alcaide Hamode commeth home. The rent of Tombuto is come by the cafelow or carovan, which is, as above is mentioned, 60 quintals. The report is, that Mahomed bringeth with him such an infinite treasure as I never heard of: it doth appeare that they have more golde than any other part of the world beside. The Alcaide winneth all the country where he goeth without fighting, and is going downe towards the sea coast.'[2]

Besides gold great numbers of slaves and quantities of valuable produce, such as civet and ebony, were sent back to the Sultan.[3] In 1593 Morocco was astounded by the arrival of an elephant from the Sudan, and its negro keepers, who had achieved a remarkable triumph in conducting the animal across the Sahara, are said to have introduced the use of tobacco into the Maghreb.[4]

However much Mulay Zidan may have deplored the costliness of the campaign to which El Mansur had committed his country the revenue of Morocco continued for many years to be swelled by tribute from Timbuktu and Gao. A Frenchman, writing from Morocco in 1607, reported that treasure amounting to 4,600,000 livres of gold, *or de tibre*, was shortly expected from these two cities.[5] Although the flow of gold became irregular it was long before it wholly ceased. As the power of the army weakened the ancient trade in salt and gold was gradually resumed and this served to supplement the dwindling tribute.

Nevertheless the campaign was not popular in Morocco. Great disappointment had been caused to all classes by the failure to discover the prolific mines which yielded such abundant wealth. All had looked forward to the discovery of this El Dorado. As we have already seen, the mines were beyond the reach of the invaders. Wangara, Bonduku, and Ashanti, each of which contributed their quota to the gold exports of Gao and Timbuktu, lay in the unconquerable pagan belt. Although the Sudan was rich in other products, their worth was greatly depreciated by the cost of transport across the desert. Gold alone was free from this disability and was the only standard by which the enterprise was measured.

The needs of the campaign, moreover, imposed a severe strain on the resources of Morocco. The merchants were impoverished by loss of trade, and the peasantry were oppressed by the intolerable burden of increased taxation and the constant demand for recruits to fill the wasting ranks of the army. Neither the reduced circumstances of the merchants nor the general poverty of the peasants were relieved by the quantities of gold which poured into the country. All

EL DZEHEBI

was concentrated in and about the court and mostly spent on palaces and fortresses.

El Mansur built in Marrakech the vast palace known as Dar el Bideea which was destroyed a century later. At Fez he raised the two forts still known as El Besatin, or the Bastions, the name given them by the Europeans, either slaves or renegades, who built them. At Laraiche and in other Moorish towns there are other forts dating from the same period.[6]

Enormous sums were expended upon the decoration of the royal palaces for which skilled craftsmen were imported from Europe. Philip II purchased the release of Portuguese noblemen captured at El Ksar by sending Spanish painters and architects to decorate the Sultan's palaces and the public buildings.[7]

Capt. John Smith of Virginia, who was in Morocco soon after El Mansur's death, tells us that

'in all his kingdome were so few good artificers, that hee entertained from England, Goldsmith, Plummers, Carvers, and Polishers of Stone, and Watchmakers, so much he delighted in the reformation of workmanship, hee allowed each of them ten shillings a day standing fee, linnen, woollen, silkes, and what they would for diet and apparell, and customs free to transport, or import what they would; for there were scarce any of those qualities in his Kingdoms but those, of which there are divers of them living at this present in London.'[8]

Much of the marble required for his palaces came from Italy and some from Ireland, and was paid for in sugar, it is said, weight for weight.[9]

The oversea trade of the country was greatly stimulated by this unprecedented prosperity. In Marrakech and in other Moorish towns there were large foreign mercantile communities representing principally England, France, and the Low Countries. Since the middle of the century the English merchants had held the predominant position, and they enjoyed almost a monopoly of the trade passing through Santa Cruz du Cap de Ghir (Agadir) and Safi whence the Portuguese had been driven by the Moors in 1541.

The Portuguese held only the ports of Ceuta, Tangier, and Mazaghan, and bitterly resented the loss of the valuable southern Moroccan trade. They claimed that under the famous bull of Pope Alexander VI, which granted to Portugal all lands discovered east of a line drawn north and south through a point 370 leagues west of Cape Verde, they alone had the right to trade with Morocco and every other part of Africa. This was the subject of a long controversy with the

186 EL DZEHEBI

English. England finally agreed to surrender her claims over Guinea, where she had traded since 1553, but she stubbornly refused to abandon her very lucrative trade with Morocco. Another cause of bitterness was that the greater part of the trade of the English, and to a lesser extent of the French, consisted in supplying the Moors with munitions of war which were chiefly required for driving the Portuguese out of Africa. In 1562, roused by a recent reverse in Morocco, the Portuguese vigorously protested against this iniquitous trade which long since had been banned by the Popes. In contravention, they declared, of the laws of God and man, the English had shipped such quantities of munitions to the Moors that they had become better armed than the Christians.

The difficult Barbary coast was so much better known to English seamen that the ships of other nations trading with Morocco often carried English pilots. In 1577, when the Easterlings or Hansa merchants first proposed to trade with Morocco in munitions, they decided to 'hier certen Englishe masters and pilottes as best acquainted with that coast to conduct other shippes thither'.[10] On representations being made by the Portuguese, who had heard with concern of this proposed extension of the nefarious traffic, the Privy Council took steps to prevent English seamen entering the Hansa service for African voyages.

The goods shipped by the English to Morocco were mostly weapons, armour, metal for casting cannon, ship-building materials and every sort of marine gear. These munitions were all sold to the State. Great quantities of cloth of various kinds were shipped for private trade. The principal exports to England were gold, sugar, saltpetre, copper, hides, and skins. The gold was mostly *tibar* from the Sudan, but through the medium of Moroccan Jews great quantities of Moorish sequins were sent to London where they were reminted into coin of the realm. Sugar had been grown in southern Morocco for centuries and there were many State-owned sugar mills continually working at high pressure to meet the demands of the European markets. In the same region there were also large deposits of saltpetre of which Christian monarchs, especially Queen Elizabeth, were in constant need for their arsenals. For the same reason that the Popes banned the traffic in munitions, the Moors had conscientious objections to supplying Christians with this essential ingredient of gunpowder, but their scruples were as easily overcome as the papal ban was ignored.

Interest in the gold trade of the interior of Africa had been stimu-

EL DZEHEBI

lated by the publication in 1573 of Marmol Caravajal's *Descripcion de Africa* which was widely read in Europe during the next few decades. Marmol was a Spaniard who, like Leo Africanus, was born in Granada and forsook his native land for Africa. But whereas the Moor found himself amongst his co-religionists by whom he was received with honour, the Spaniard spent his seven years in Africa as a slave. The description of Africa written after he recovered his freedom confirmed his predecessor's account of the activity of the trans-Saharan trade.[11]

Europe was at this time drawing regular supplies of gold from the numerous trading factories scattered along the coast between Cape Verde and the Bight of Benin. But the inconsiderable quantities received from this source and the tendency for the Moorish gold trade to increase rather than to diminish left no doubt in men's minds that mines of fabulous wealth hidden in the obscure interior had yet to be discovered. The prospect of such a discovery seemed remote, and many still played with Prince Henry's idea of capturing the Moorish overland trade in gold by tapping it from the western coast of Guinea.

In a letter dated from Arguin on the Gum coast (as it was now called) in January 1591, while the expeditionary force under Judar Pasha was on its way to the Sudan, a certain Melchior Petoney submitted a proposal of this nature to a prominent member of the Spanish court. If Philip II, he wrote, would send every year to Arguin two or three caravels

'with Flanders and Spanish commodities, as bracelets of glasse, knives, belles, linnen-cloth, looking-glasses, with other kinds of small wares, his Highnesse might do great good here. For 50 leagues up into the land the Moores have many exceeding rich golde mines; insomuch that they bring downe their golde to this castle to traffique with us; and for a small trifle they will give us a great wedge of gold. And because here is no trade, the sayd Moores cary their golde to Fez, being 250 leagues distant from hence, and there doe exchange the same for the foresayd kindes of commodities. By this meanes also his Majesty might stop that passage, and keepe the King of Fez from so huge a masse of golde. Scarlet-clothes and fine purples are greatly accepted of in these parts.'[12]

When European nations heard of the unbounded wealth which his Sudan expedition was bringing to El Mansur their interest in the gold trade was again excited, and men began once more to speculate on the inexhaustible source of the gold of the Moors. In 1600 a Dutchman

EL DZEHEBI

declared that few negroes on the Guinea coast knew where the mines were and that no Portuguese or Netherlander had ever seen or been near them. His own inquiries in Guinea only indicated that the gold was alluvial and dug out of pits.[13]

In 1603 Henry Roberts, who had formerly been an agent of the chartered Barbary Company in Marrakech and had subsequently served Elizabeth in the same capacity, placed before James I a scheme for the conquest of Morocco and its conversion to Christianity. The capture of the gold trade was the great inducement. 'And your Ma[tie] haveinge possessed this countrey,' he wrote, 'you may invade and goe as farre as you please into Genney, which is very rich both in goulde and other great riches comodities.' After humbly beseeching His Majesty to bestow on him a small pension or a 'poore knights roome in Windsor, to relieve him now in his olde aidge' Henry Roberts disappears from history and we hear no more of his project.[14]

In 1618 some London merchants, fired by accounts of the heavily laden gold caravans, formed themselves into a 'Company of Adventurers for the countries of Ginney and Binney' with the purpose of 'discovering the golden trade of the Moores of Barbary'.

The Gambia river, which was by now well known, seemed to the Adventurers to offer the most likely route to that part of the interior where the gold mines were supposed to be situated. According to a contemporary French writer, men believed that the Sudan gold mines were near Gao which was known to be on the Niger. As they also believed that the Senegal and Gambia rivers were the outlets through which the Niger found its way to the sea, they argued that if either of these was followed from the coast into the interior it would be found to lead ultimately to the long-sought mines from which the Moors obtained all their gold.

'The *English*, more than any other Nation,' he wrote, 'have these imaginations, and it is not to be believ'd that they have possess'd themselves of the Mouth of the River Cambaia, and taken either by force or treaties those Fortifications, which the Duke of *Curland* and the *Dutch* had there, only to enjoy a small Trade of some *Raw-hides*, *Wax* and *Elephant-teeth*: This was neither the design of the English, nor of Prince *Rupert*, who did these famous exploits there some years since: Their principal design was to mount up the River *Niger*, nay, perhaps to the very Head, and so by consequence to the Gold of *Gago*.'[15]

The Adventurers sent out a ship called the *Catherine*, commanded by a certain George Thompson, 'a man about fifty yeares of age, who

EL DZEHEBI 189

had lived many years a Marchant in Barbary'. Thompson, who took with him trade goods valued at nearly £2,000, was ordered to explore the upper reaches of the Gambia through the medium of trade. On arrival in the lower river he anchored the *Catherine*, and he himself proceeded upstream with a few companions. During his absence some Portuguese and their mulatto associates seized the vessel and cut the throats of the crew. When news of the disaster reached England the Adventurers sent out a relief ship to Thompson, but he elected to remain on the Gambia, asking only for a further supply of trade goods. He sent home a message to his employers, assuring them that they 'should no wayes doubt of a hopefull discovery, where the Moores of Barbary traded, and a valewable returne for their losses sustained, promising in the meane time, with such company as he had left with him, being in all onely eight persons, in his small boate to search up the River'.[16] He did not live to make the discovery which he anticipated, for shortly afterwards he was murdered by one of his own men.

The Adventurers next sent out Richard Jobson, who sailed with 'a shippe called the *Syon*, burthen 200. tunne, and the *S. John*, a pinnace of 50 tunne', in 1620, to carry on the work which Thompson had begun. He travelled a considerable distance up the river and, like his predecessor, constantly believed himself to be on the point of meeting Moorish traders from Barbary, and was ever ready to seek refuge from the attack which he anticipated their discovery of him would provoke. Although he heard reports of Moorish traders in the interior he never met any of them.

The towns of Timbuktu and Gao were special objects of his inquiries, but he could obtain no certain information about either. He heard, however, of a great lake near Gao.[17] According to the natives, the most important market of the interior was a town named Jaye, which Jobson thought might be Gao, but it was more probably Jenne. He heard of houses covered with gold and was told that 'not farre from Jaye, there were a people who would not bee seene, and that the salt was carryed unto them, and how the Arabecks, had all their gold from them, although they did never see them'.[18]

After giving an account of the silent trade according to the description of earlier writers, Jobson adds the following curious note of his own.

'The reason why these people will not be seene, is for that they are naturally borne, with their lower lippe of that greatnesse it turnes againe, and covers

EL DZEHEBI

the greater part of their bosome, and remaines with that rawnesse on the side that hangs downe, that through occasion of the Sunnes extreame heate, it is still subject to putrifaction, so as they have no meanes to preserve themselves, but by continually casting salt upon it, and this is the reason, salt is so pretious amongst them: their countrey beeing so farre up in the land, naturally yeeldes none.' * [19]

Jobson's expedition was a failure, both as regards exploration and trading, but he returned to England still full of confidence in the ultimate success of the Company's project. His employers, however, had grown weary of repeated assurances of the imminence of a triumphant and profitable discovery, and consequently Jobson's efforts to persuade them to pursue their venture were ill received. Too much money had already been lost, and the Adventurers abandoned their enterprise.

Posterity owes a debt of gratitude to Jobson for the delightful account of the Gambia which he published in 1623, under the title of *The Golden Trade, or A Discovery of the River Gambra, and the Golden Trade of the Aethiopians.* His lively description of the strange men and beasts which he saw deserves to be more widely known. Of particular interest is his opinion regarding the mystery which surrounded the gold trade. The Moors, he tells us, followed this trade 'with such great dilligence and government, that amongst themselves, none are admitted but principall persons, and by especial order, without entertaining any other nation, what respect or familiarity so ever they have gained amongst them'. His experience like that of others had led him to believe that the traffic in gold was in the hands of a close 'ring' of merchants who carefully concealed the secrets of their trade.

* The reference is evidently to a tribe using the pelele.

EL DZEHEBI

REFERENCES

1. El Ufrani, p. 167.
2. R. Hakluyt, op. cit., vii. 99–101; *Purchas His Pilgrimes*, vi. 60.
3. El Ufrani, p. 169.
4. Ibid., p. 264.
5. Paul Masson, *Histoire des Établissements et du Commerce Français dans l'Afrique Barbaresque*, Paris, 1903, p. 92.
6. El Ufrani, p. 260.
7. Dr. Robert Brown, *Leo Africanus*, Introduction, vol. i, p. xvii.
8. *Travels of John Smith*, Glasgow, 1907, ii. 163.
9. El Ufrani, p. 261.
10. Public Record Office, Privy Council Register, Elizabeth, vol. III, f. 142; *apud* de Castries.
11. Marmol Caravajal, *L'Afrique*, trad. Perrot d'Ablancourt, Paris, 1667, ii. 29.
12. R. Hakluyt, op. cit., vii. 88.
13. William Bosman, *A New and Accurate Description of the Coast of Guinea*, Eng. trans. London, 1721, pp. 63 et seq.
14. British Museum, Additional MSS. 38139, f. 33; *apud* de Castries.
15. Mons. A. ✱✱✱✱, op. cit., p. 19.
16. Richard Jobson, *The Golden Trade*, Teignmouth, 1904, p. 7.
17. Ibid., p. 18.
18. Ibid., p. 128.
19. Ibid., p. 131.

XVII

THE LATER PASHAS

The sons of the alien shall be your plowmen and your vinedressers.—ISAIAH lxi. 5.

ABDERRAHMAN ES SADI, the author of the *Tarikh es Sudan*, was born in Timbuktu in 1596. He belonged to an aristocratic family and from early youth was accustomed to moving in influential circles. He was intensely proud of his native city and in his *Tarikh* he constantly reverts to its importance as the metropolis of Negroland. His first public appointment was that of notary at Jenne, where he afterwards became Imam, a post which he later filled at Timbuktu. He played an active part in political life and received the title of Katib or Secretary to the Government in recognition of his public services. He carried his *Tarikh* down to the year 1655 which was probably not long before his death.

The first traveller to bring back to Europe any precise information about the *Tarikh es Sudan* was Henry Barth who had the good fortune to see a copy in Gwandu in 1853. He attributed its authorship to the renowned Ahmed Baba for which, as for most of the few other mistakes made by this remarkable traveller, there was considerable excuse. Of the three existing manuscript copies of the *Tarikh* of Es Sadi two are in the Bibliothéque Nationale in Paris.

The first part of the *Tarikh*, which covers the history of the rise of the Songhai empire and the early years of the Moorish occupation, was compiled from various sources and is very dull reading. Probably much of it was oral tradition, but Es Sadi drew largely on earlier writers whose works have not come down to us. He mentions only two of these, the famous Biographical Dictionary of Ahmed Baba and a work entitled *El Kheber*.

Ahmed Baba, who died in Timbuktu in 1607 after several years of captivity in Marrakech, was a member of the illustrious family of the Akit who, like so many of the *literati* of Timbuktu, were of Jedala origin. He was the son of a jurist of more than usual distinction. It is interesting to learn that he completed his education under a learned negro named Muhammad Barhayorho, a Mandingo who had been one of his father's pupils and had attained a considerable reputation as a scholar. Most of the scholars of Jenne, which was widely recognized as a centre of learning, were negroes, whereas those of Timbuktu were

THE LATER PASHAS 193

nearly all of Berber blood. Although none of Ahmed Baba's works have survived he is still remembered in the Sudan as a great scholar. Es Sadi had been too young to come under his direct influence, but he benefited greatly from the cultured society of which Ahmed Baba had for long been the leader.

In the second part of the *Tarikh*, Es Sadi describes events under the later Pashas in which he himself frequently played an important part. It is far more graphic and easier reading than the first. The period it covers was less eventful than the preceding one, but it was perhaps the saddest in the history of the Western Sudan.

From the year 1618, when Mulay Zidan finally washed his hands of the Sudan, the Moorish troops on the Niger became absolute masters of their own destiny. They chose their own Pashas and Kaids, whom they removed at the slightest whim and obeyed or not as they pleased. They at first selected only officers who had been sent out from Morocco, but as these gradually dwindled in number vacant posts were filled by degenerate mulattoes who were known as Arma. As it was always the object of each of the three divisions into which the army was still divided to secure the Pashalik for one of its own officers, these appointments frequently provoked violent dissensions. The disappointed factions would refuse to serve under the duly elected commander whose removal they sought to contrive at the earliest opportunity. Nor were officers ambitious for advancement scrupulous in the methods they employed to remove those who stood in their way. Pashas rose and fell with the utmost frequency.

The general policy of every Pasha was to satisfy at all costs the avarice of the troops on whom he depended for his position and the opportunities it gave for personal gain. Consequently the civil population became the perpetual victims of the most infamous extortion from which there was no escape. Under the Arma conditions became worse. When a Pasha began to feel his enemies in the army growing too strong for him he did not hesitate to summon to his aid one or other of the enemies of his country whose reward was liberty to plunder the peasantry at will. This state of hopeless anarchy and general insecurity inevitably led to reduced cultivation with the result that the country was swept by a series of devastating famines.

Timbuktu remained the Moorish capital and the seat of the Askias of the North who succeeded each other nearly as frequently as the Pashas. Garrisons commanded by Kaids were maintained in Gao,

o

THE LATER PASHAS

which was in an almost constant state of mutiny, at Bamba and at Jenne. In spite of their entire freedom from restraint and the atmosphere of anarchy in which they lived, the Moors still gave formal recognition to the suzerainty of the Sultan of Morocco and the Friday prayer continued to be said in his name in the mosques. There is even reason to believe that tribute was still sometimes paid to the Sultan. About the year 1645 a Frenchman who had spent twenty-five years in Morocco reported that 'the king of Gago', doubtless meaning the Askia of the North who was always the puppet of the ruling Pasha, 'hath so great a veneration (for the Sultan) that some have assured us he pays tribute to the King of Morocco: But I cannot credit it, only this is certain, that he sends him presents'.[1]

The political condition of the Sudanese Moors at this time was little better than that of the surrounding tribes. The muskets, with which they were still armed and which had hitherto ensured the continued subjection of the tribes on whom they had imposed their yoke, did not compensate for the collapse of their military organization. Gradually the peoples who for so long had been forced to endure the intolerable burden of Moorish tyranny began to rise against their oppressors and revolts became increasingly frequent.

In 1629 the newly elected Ardo, or Fulani king of Massina, refused to accept formal investiture at the hands of the Pasha, Ali ben Abdelkader,[2] and throughout his long reign of thirty-six years he successfully resisted the repeated attempts of the Moors to re-impose vassalage on him and his people. By the middle of the century the Moors exercised little authority beyond the immediate neighbourhoods of Timbuktu, Gao, and Jenne, and the river connecting these garrison towns.

In 1660 Muhammad ech Chetuki, commonly known as Buya, the twenty-seventh Pasha since Judar, finally repudiated the suzerainty of the Sultan of Morocco and thenceforward the Friday prayer was said in the name of the ruling Pasha. All future Pashas were Arma who, as time went on, approached in all respects ever closer to the general type of the negroid population by whom they were ultimately absorbed. According to the *Tedzkiret en Nisian**[3] during the next ninety years there were no less than 128 different Pashas. There could be no more convincing proof than this of the hopeless incapacity of the

---

* Of the anonymous author of this work, which is principally composed of biographies of the Pashas, we know nothing except that he was born in 1700 and stopped writing in 1751.

THE LATER PASHAS

Arma to govern. The period was one of ever increasing anarchy and chaos, and by 1670 the Pashas of Timbuktu had fallen into subjection to the pagan Bambara king of Segu.

Just when the renewal of the old associations between the Sudan and Morocco seemed least probable a political upheaval in the latter country brought them together once more. In the year 1664 the Saadian dynasty was replaced by the Hassanids or Filalians who still rule in Morocco. Mulay Er Rechid, the third Sultan of the new dynasty, was compelled to spend the whole of his reign in struggling with formidable adversaries most of whom were interested in the restoration of the old imperial family. The chief rallying point of the insurgents was a fortress in Sus where a certain Ali ben Haidar had his head-quarters. In 1670 Er Rechid captured the rebel stronghold, but Ali ben Haidar escaped and made his way with a handful of followers to the Sudan where he secured, at the price of two Andalusian virgins, the protection of Biton, the powerful Bambara king of Segu, whose extensive dominions now included the city of Timbuktu.

As soon as Er Rechid learnt where Ali ben Haidar had fled he sent an envoy to the Sudan demanding his surrender, but this was refused by Biton.[4] According to unconfirmed tradition Er Rechid thereupon led an army in person across the desert and invaded Massina, but when he was confronted with the formidable array of the Bambara forces he beat a hasty retreat.

Ali ben Haidar remained in Timbuktu where, in consequence of his friendship with Biton and of a reputation for piety, he enjoyed a position of considerable influence. He devoted his energies to assembling a negro army with which to avenge himself on the Sultan. Having collected a force which was said to number several thousand, but was probably very much smaller, he set out for Morocco and arrived in 1672 just as Er Rechid died. His quarrel being with the Sultan personally rather than with his house he disbanded his army. Mulay Ismail,* the new Sultan, hearing of this and seeing the opportunity which it offered to acquire a ready-made army, promptly ordered Ali ben Haidar's troops to reassemble and he formed them into a sort of praetorian guard. This was the origin of the famous Abid or Bokhari, the negro troops who were destined in later years to become by their arrogance such a baneful influence in the political life of Morocco which for a time they entirely dominated.

---

* Mulay Ismail died in 1727 after a brilliant reign of fifty-five years and was survived by no less than 548 sons and 340 daughters.[5]

O 2

THE LATER PASHAS

Like the *Frendji* of former times the black troops could, on account of their aloofness from local politics, be depended upon for loyal service. So well pleased was Ismail with them that he decided greatly to increase their strength and to establish them as a permanent institution. He drafted into their ranks all the Haratin he could collect and all the descendants of the negroes whom Judar and Mahmud had sent as captives to El Mansur. He also encouraged his black army to beget children who from early childhood were carefully prepared for a military life.[6] Perceiving, however, that further means would have to be devised to keep it permanently up to strength he sent his nephew Ahmed to the Sudan to secure more recruits and to arrange for a regular supply of drafts.

Ahmed, accompanied by a large escort, arrived in Timbuktu in 1672, probably during the Pashalik of Muhammad Ed Dara'i. He occupied the city in the name of the Sultan and required the Pasha to take the oath of allegiance. This change of régime was welcomed by the natives who had recently been much harried by Berabish raiders against whom the Bambara king afforded them insufficient protection.

Ahmed spent several years in Timbuktu. Whether he confined his activities to enlisting recruits is uncertain, but El Ufrani, who is not a reliable authority on events outside Morocco, tells us that at this time the Moors conquered many provinces of the Sudan. Ahmed eventually returned to Morocco with his recruits. He left behind him a garrison to uphold the authority of the Sultan, but no sooner had he quitted the city than it was re-occupied by the Bambara. The garrison was gradually absorbed by the native population and went to swell the ranks of the Arma.[7]

The history of the middle Niger during the next few decades is obscure. The lower the Arma sank the more acute became the disruption in their ranks. As long as they paid tribute to the king of Segu they were little interfered with and did much as they liked in Timbuktu. In spite of the anarchy and insecurity which prevailed along all the caravan routes the ancient trade in gold and salt between Barbary and the Sudan continued to flourish. Numbers of Barbary merchants resided permanently in Timbuktu, still obtaining their gold by dumb barter from the mysterious pagans of Wangara, and assuring to Morocco a continuous and bountiful supply of the precious metal. Besides gold and slaves they now exported ivory, the trade in which had hitherto been confined principally to the Central and Eastern Sudan.[8] It was the resources provided by the large foreign

THE LATER PASHAS   197

mercantile community of Timbuktu which held the Arma together and prevented their troops from dispersing. From the *Tedzkiret en Nisian* it would appear that the only way the troops were ever paid was by a levy on the merchants whose payments were made in gold, salt, or cowries. Although these imposts were a heavy burden there was never much difficulty in collecting them. Defaulters were simply thrown into gaol. But so inadequate was the security which the payments secured that the foreign merchants had to make private arrangements with the troops for the protection of themselves and their caravans. Each division of the army had its regular clients who paid agreed sums for the services of guards.

In 1647 Hamed el Haguzui, who was then Pasha at Timbuktu, received a report from the Kaid at Gao that he was being severely harassed by the Aulimmiden Tuareg. In his answer, which was written down by Es Sadi and delivered by him in person to the Kaid at Gao, the Pasha warned his subordinate against the futility of half measures with such perfidious enemies as those who were pressing him. They must be exterminated; and if the Kaid's own forces were not sufficient the Kaid of Bamba would send him reinforcements. If he wished to master these Tuareg on no account must they get wind of his plans.[9] The situation was evidently critical, but Es Sadi unfortunately does not tell us what happened next. For some time we hear no more of these Aulimmiden, but they were the forerunners of a movement which was destined to terminate for ever Moorish domination in the Sudan.

The desert to the north and west of Gao was at this time much disturbed. Owing to pressure from the west the tribes of Tuareg who inhabited this desolate region were competing with each other for the inadequate pastures. Consequently the necessity for the weaker folk to migrate elsewhere was becoming increasingly apparent. These disturbed conditions may be traced back to the accession to the throne of Bornu of a redoubtable warrior, Mai Idris Alooma, in the year 1571. Mai Idris, after conquering much of Hausa, had organized three expeditions against the Tuareg. The third had been directed against Air, where he broke the power of the Kel Geres and made room for his vassals the Kel Owi. By their commercial ability and efficient organization the Kel Owi had won for themselves control of the ancient north and south caravan route which runs through Air, with the result that the whole of the desert trade between Ghat and the Sudan passed through their hands. Their neighbours on the north-west were the Ahaggaren who controlled the

THE LATER PASHAS

routes between Tuat and Ahaggar, and on the north-east the dreaded Azger, to-day the least known and probably the purest of the Tuareg. The Azger were masters of the roads running from Ghat northwards to the Maghreb and eastwards to Fezzan. The Kel Geres, forced to give way before the Kel Owi, moved into Adrar, which borders Air on the west and should not be confused with the district of the same name north of the Senegal. Some of the Kel Geres later moved into Gobir where we find them to-day.[10]

At the time of these migrations Adrar was occupied by two nearly related but hostile clans. The stronger of these were the Aulimmiden who, finding themselves in need of more pastures owing to the arrival of the Kel Geres, drove out their weaker brethren who made their way towards the Niger. The riverain people gave the latter the name of Kel Tadmekket because they had come from the direction of Tadmekka. In 1655 the Tadmekket, accompanied by their women and children and their flocks and herds, presented themselves before the Pasha and, concealing the fact that they were homeless exiles, announced their desire to place themselves under his jurisdiction. Flattered by the unexpected compliment to his administration, which must have been without precedent in the whole history of the Moorish occupation, the Pasha consented to take them under his benevolent wing. Thus were the Tadmekket, to the lasting regret of the Moors and of the sedentary peoples of the Niger, allowed to settle in the neighbourhood of Timbuktu.[11]

Meanwhile the Aulimmiden, compelled like the Tadmekket to abandon Adrar, had followed hard on the heels of their despised relatives and had settled round Bamba and Gao where the abundant grazing made them well content. In 1680 they captured Gao, but eight years later the Moors drove them out and captured much of their stock.[12] Severely shaken by this reverse and reluctant to abandon the Goshen they had so recently made their home, they decided to submit to the authority of the Moors. In 1690 their chief, Kari Denna, sought investiture at the hands of the Pasha. The ceremony took place in Timbuktu amid great solemnity and pomp and in the presence of the whole garrison. At the conclusion of the elaborate formalities a magnificent procession conducted the new Amenokal of the Aulimmiden to his tent outside the city. Once more official recognition had been given to the paralysing grip of a horde of homeless nomads.

The sedentary Songhai population offered an easy prey to the pre-

THE LATER PASHAS

datory instinct of the Tuareg who very soon began to assert themselves. From Timbuktu to Gao the river villages were constantly exposed to Tuareg raids against which there was no protection. The Moors sent punitive expeditions against the raiders which at first were not wholly without effect. But as time went on the incompetence of the Arma increased and the failure of their counter measures only served to advertise their own growing weakness and to encourage their elusive enemies.

At this time the Arma probably formed a very small part of the army. El Mansur Pasha laid it down that only a tenth of an expedition against Tuareg should be Arma, the rest being Arabs, Fulani, Bambara, and above all Tuareg from the friendly tribes. Thus, he naïvely explained, the brunt of the fighting would fall on the mercenaries, but the honour and glory would go to the Arma.[13]

By the end of the century the Kaids of Jenne had fallen into permanent tutelage, sometimes to the Bambara, sometimes to the Fulani. Gao had again been lost to the Aulimmiden and was never recovered. In 1716, while the country was being ravaged by a famine which had already lasted five years, two rivals for the Pashalik called in respectively the Bambara and the Tadmekket to their aid. There was no bloodshed, but both factions entered Timbuktu, each occupying a separate quarter of the city, where they lived in comparative luxury at the expense of the already famished population. In 1720 the Amenokal of the Aulimmiden cut off the city from its port of Kabara and had to be bought off with 3,000 *mitkal* of gold. In 1726 Bamba was destroyed as the result of a battle between the Kaid, who was supported by the Tadmekket, and his own mutinous troops who had allied themselves with the Aulimmiden. All that remained to the Arma was the city of Timbuktu. Curiously they had not wholly lost the prestige of conquerors, for the Amenokal of the Aulimmiden continued to seek formal investiture at the hands of their Pasha.

In 1737 the Tadmekket, led by their chief Oghmor and reinforced by some Arab Berabish from Arawan, pillaged Timbuktu itself and then withdrew into the desert.[14] This thoroughly alarmed the Arma who perceived that their very existence was threatened. Realizing that their only hope of salvation was to rid the Niger of the Tuareg and to drive them back into Adrar they set about assembling the largest force they could muster. While the main body was completing its preparations troops were sent ahead to re-occupy Bamba and Gao.

At last the rest of the army prepared to move. The oracles were

THE LATER PASHAS

consulted, but the omens were declared unfavourable. Nevertheless they marched resolutely out of the city. Meanwhile Oghmor, the Amenokal of the Tadmekket, who had assembled a large force consisting of his own and other tribes of Tuareg, set out in pursuit. He came up with the Moors at Togahia, only a few miles east from Timbuktu, and there he destroyed them.[15]

The strength and spirit of the Arma was for ever broken. They reassembled in Timbuktu, but were forced to pay tribute to the Tadmekket. Till the year 1780 they continued to elect their own Pashas. After that they kept only their Kaid whose position was virtually that of mayor of the city. Although the Arma continued to survive in Gao, Timbuktu, and Jenne, by the end of the eighteenth century they were indistinguishable from the rest of the population.

The only good that had come of the calamitous Moorish occupation was the development of certain domestic arts. On the upper Niger Moorish influence is still discernible in the pottery, the dress, and the diet of the people, but nowhere is it more clearly seen than in the architecture, notably at Jenne where the builder's art reached its zenith.[16] Such were the paltry advantages which had cost several generations of a once prosperous people almost everything that made for human happiness.

REFERENCES

1. Mons. A. ✳✳✳✳, op. cit., p. 17.
2. *Tarikh es Soudan*, p. 351.
3. *Tedzkiret en Nisian*, trad. O. Houdas, Paris, 1901.
4. Ibid., p. 257.
5. Sir H. H. Johnston, *A History of the Colonization of Africa*, Cambridge, 1899, p. 23.
6. O. Houdas, *Le Maroc de 1631 à 1812*, pp. 21–3.
7. M. Delafosse, *Hespéris*, Paris, 1923, pp. 1–11.
8. P. Masson, op. cit., p. 233.
9. *Tarikh es Soudan*, p. 437.
10. F. R. Rodd, op. cit., p. 390.
11. *Tarikh es Soudan*, p. 484.
12. *Tedzkiret en Nisian*, p. 9.
13. Ibid., p. 43.
14. Ibid., p. 176.
15. Ibid., p. 181.
16. Charles Monteil, *Une Cité Soudanaise, Djénné*, Paris, 1932, p. 83.

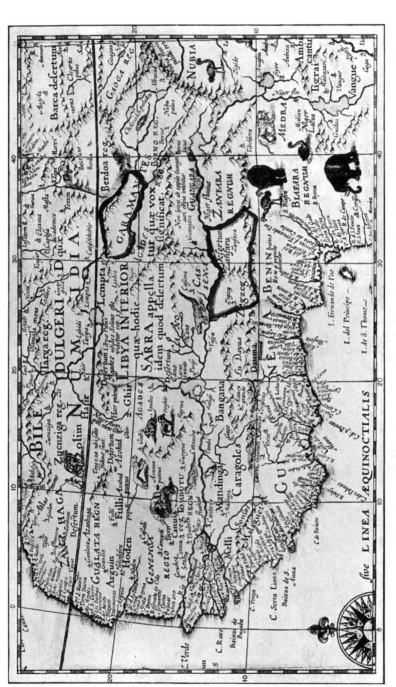

X. THE *AFRICAE NOVA DESCRIPTIO* OF BLAEU (1665)

THE SUDAN UNVEILED

XVIII

THE VEIL

'For surely, those interiour parts of Affrica are little knowen to either English, French, or Dutch, though they use much the Coast.'—CAPT. JOHN SMITH.
'And pray what is Cape Verde? A stinking place!'—CHARLES II.

AT the beginning of the last decade of the eighteenth century the ignorance of Europe regarding the interior of northern Africa was still profound, and in striking contrast with its wide knowledge of the rest of the habitable globe. If we compare de Lisle's *Carte de la Barbarie de la Nigritie et de la Guinée*, published by Elwe in 1792,* with such well-known maps as the *Africae Tabula Nova* of Ortelius of 1570† and Blaeu's *Africae Nova Descriptio* of 1665, we find that since Leo Africanus there had been practically no advance in knowledge, and that European ideas about the interior of Africa were still archaic.

Ortelius shows the Niger rising near the equator in a lake which he calls the *Lac Niger*. Thence it flows northwards and dives under ground. *Hic Niger flu*: we read, *per 60 mill: se sub terram condit*. It enters the *Borno Lacus* (Lake Chad) and then turns westwards leaving *Guangara* (Wangara), *Casena*, and *Cano* on the north and *Zanfara*, *Zegzeg*, and *Mandinga* opposite them on the south. It continues its westerly course through the great *Lacus Guber*. This imposing sheet of water (which long continued to figure prominently in all maps of Africa) was probably the result of an attempt to identify the floods which Leo had described in Gobir with the great lake which Diego Gomez had heard of in the interior and which was almost certainly Lake Debo. Beyond the *Lacus Guber* the Niger, still following a westerly course, is joined by a tributary from the south coming from the direction of *Gago*. Flowing still westwards past *Cabra* and *Tombotu* the Niger empties itself into the ocean through five different channels, two of which are the *Senega* and the *Gambra*. Scattered over the Sahara (the northern part of which Ortelius calls the *Biledulgerid*—a corruption of Beled el Jerid, the Dry Country) are such familiar

---

* Opposite p. 210.   † P. 129.

THE VEIL

names as *Hayr* (Air), *Tegazza, Gualata* (Walata), *Hoden* (Wadan), and, far removed from *Hayr, Agadez.*

Blaeu's map of 1665 follows Ortelius closely as far as the Niger is concerned. *Guangara, Cassena, Cano, Zanfara* and *Zegzeg* occupy approximately the same positions, but to *Guangara* is appended the note *Non longe ab oppido Guangara auri copia invenitur.* The *Lacus Guber* of Ortelius has become, probably by corruption, *Lacus Guarde,* * and *Mandinga,* doubtless on information received from merchants trading on the coast of Guinea, has been moved to a less incorrect position farther west. *Cabra* has disappeared, but *Tombotu* survives. Although the northern Sahara retains the name of *Biledulgerid* it is traversed by several imposing rivers and at the source of one of these we find the words *Niger fluvi ptol nunc Ghir.* Blaeu makes up for lack of fresh geographical knowledge by adorning his map with grotesque representations of beasts and reptiles.

A marked advance in the methods of reproduction gives the de Lisle map of 1792 an air of scientific precision which lends emphasis to the archaic geographical ideas it perpetuated. De Lisle places the source of the Niger a little to the south-east of Lake Chad, and to it he appends the note *Quelques uns croyent que le Niger est un bras du Nil et l'appellent à cause decela le Nil des Nègres.* Before reaching the *Lac de Bournon* the Niger dives under a range of mountains. Beyond the lake it follows much the same course as that given it by Ortelius and Blaeu. Wangara, however, has changed places with Zanfara so that we find them south and north of the Niger respectively. *Ouangara,* we read, is *d'où l'on tire l'Or du Sene et des esclaves.* In order to conform to Idrisi's description of Wangara as an island the Niger is made to divide and flow completely round it through two different channels. South of Wangara lies the *Desert de Zeu,* the Desert of Seu of Leo. Kano has disappeared owing to the belief then current that it was really the ancient Ghana. But we find *R. de Cassena ou de Ghana,* and astride the Niger *les 2 Villes de Ghana,* the Muslim and pagan towns of El Bekri. The *Lac du Guarde* has assumed immense proportions and beyond it the *Niger Flu* becomes the *Ica R. ou Senegal. Cabra* has reappeared and is correctly shown as the port of *Tombouctou.* The Niger finally flows out as the Senegal into the *Mer Sargasse nommé par quelques uns Mer Verte à cause des herbes qui y flottent continuellement,* the Green Sea of Darkness of Masudi and Idrisi.

---

* It should be noted, however, that in a map by G. Gastaldi, published in Venice in 1564, we read *Laguarde Lago de Guber.*

THE VEIL 203

It was no fault of de Lisle, nor of the rest of the eighteenth-century cartographers, that they were still so blindly ignorant of the interior of Africa. Their ignorance was due in part to the apathy of Europeans, but chiefly to the 'closed-door' policy of the natives of Africa for which the white man had only himself to blame.

Since the early African voyages of the Portuguese the conquest of India and of the New World had almost wholly absorbed the oversea activities of the maritime nations of Europe. The gold of Africa, till then so alluring, had paled before the dazzling wealth which the spectacular achievements of the Conquistadors had revealed to an astounded world. Human wealth was now judged by new standards and avarice no longer looked to Africa.

Nevertheless, although the world had lost much of its interest in Africa, European trade with the Barbary and Guinea coasts had continued to increase. The failure of Europeans to penetrate the mysteries of the interior till so late in the history of geographical discovery is usually attributed to such physical obstructions as unnavigable rivers, impenetrable forests, waterless deserts, and pestilential climate. In the northern and western parts of the continent it was rather the character of the political associations of Europe with the coast peoples than inability to overcome natural obstacles which arrested the advance of the discovery of the interior.

At the beginning of the sixteenth century an extraordinary increase in the activities of the Barbary pirates completely revolutionized the friendly relationship which had so long existed between Europe and the coast of North Africa. For the next three centuries the petty pirate princes were allowed to harass the whole of the carrying trade of the Mediterranean, to raid the shores of Europe and to enslave hundreds of thousands of Christians with almost complete impunity. With contemptible meekness the Powers of Europe accepted the profound humiliation of having to secure safety for their vessels and redemption for their nationals by paying blackmail and ransoms to the pirates.

Throughout the Middle Ages piracy, both Christian and Muslim, had been an ever-present condition of maritime life in the Mediterranean; but, as we have already seen, it was never permitted seriously to hamper trade. Its sudden and violent growth at the beginning of the sixteenth century was brought about by the unhappy synchronization of the expulsion of the Moors from Spain with the rise of Ottoman sea-power in European waters.

The exiled Moors formed settlements all along the North African

THE VEIL

coast whence they sought to avenge themselves against their hated oppressors by raiding the familiar shores of Spain and by harassing Christian shipping, especially in the Straits of Gibraltar and the Malta Passage. The African coast, abounding in sheltering creeks and inlets, was admirably suited to their purpose. They succeeded, moreover, in enlisting the very active assistance of the Turks who quickly became the predominant partners in the trade. So profitable did piracy prove that within a few years every harbour from Jerba in the east to Salee* in the west held its pirate fleet.

Early in the century two Greeks from Lesbos, known as the Barbarossa brothers, arrived on the African coast with a large Turkish following. Piracy, now placed under the control of master minds, was organized on a grand scale and the 'Scourge of Christendom' commenced. From his head-quarters at Algiers, which the Morisco pirates had already made notorious, Urūj sent his galleys to raid Christian shipping in every part of the Mediterranean. His brother, Khair-ed-din, at the bidding of Sulayman the Magnificent, re-organized the Ottoman navy to such effect that it quickly made itself master of the eastern waters of the Mediterranean. The defeat of the Turkish fleet at Lepanto robbed the great corsair princes of their chief protection and they degenerated into petty pirates. But, sup-ported by the Turkish Deys of Barbary, their nefarious trade continued with unabated rigour. The pusillanimous governments of the European trading powers were unable to compose their differences and unite to stamp out the intolerable menace to civilization. They pre-ferred with bribes to set the pirates against each other. They even accredited diplomatic representatives to the African courts to arrange these matters and to secure the redemption of the more influential of the thousands of Christian slaves who endured the purgatory of the galleys or languished in the bagnios.

In the seventeenth century the galley was superseded by the square-rigged sailing ship and the corsairs were enabled greatly to extend the radius of their activities. They were further assisted in distant enter-prises by the numbers of English seamen thrown out of employment, when the peaceful reign of James I took the place of the bellicose days of Elizabeth, who sought service under corsair chiefs to save them-selves from starvation.[1] In 1650 an independent band of English rovers

---

* No port had a worse reputation than Salee which owed its pre-eminence in piracy to the organization established by 3,000 to 4,000 Moriscos who had settled there after being expelled from Spain in 1610.

THE VEIL

were constantly sheltering in Tunis where they were warmly welcomed. That their Tunisian rivals should have given them so much encouragement may be attributed to the Englishmen's habit of selling all their prizes in Tunis, which they never left till they had spent all their earnings in debauchery, in the course of which most of the money found its way into the pockets of the local pirates.*[2] The African pirates, however, now equipped with better ships and more skilful navigators, began to raid the shores of Britain, Denmark, and Iceland, and as late as the reign of Charles II the people of Cork shuddered as they heard the Muslim call to prayer echoing over the peaceful waters of their harbour.

With the growth of European naval power the corsairs were gradually forced once more to confine their activities to the Mediterranean. There they continued to be an intolerable menace till the close of the Napoleonic wars when, at the Congress of Utrecht in 1818, the Powers decided to unite against the common foe. Such were the humiliating circumstances which for three centuries had made impossible the penetration of the interior of Africa from the north.

Even more discreditable were the associations of Europe with the Guinea coast during these same centuries. Between their discovery of the Cape route and the loss of their independence the Portuguese devoted the whole of their enterprise and energy to India where their triumphs were more brilliant, though of shorter life, than in Africa. Although they had lost much of their interest in Africa, which came to be regarded merely as a convenient half-way house to India, they jealously guarded their monopoly of the Guinea trade. In their hands it tended more and more to be restricted to the export of slaves for which the West Indies had now become the chief market. With the approval of the Pope a slave market was opened in Lisbon, and in 1537 as many as 10,000 to 12,000 negro slaves were brought to the city for re-export across the Atlantic.

The neglect by the Portuguese of such important commodities as gold, ivory, and gum attracted rivals. By the middle of the sixteenth century the French and English were actively participating in the African trade at the expense of the Portuguese. Later the Dutch, having freed themselves from the yoke of Spain, also entered the field and before long they made themselves supreme. Scattered along the

---

* In England, as in Africa, piracy knew no class distinctions. In 1597 Robert Cecil, who afterwards became James's Chief Minister, sent his ship the *True Love* to Morocco to engage in trade and piracy.[3]

206   THE VEIL

coast there still survive many imposing relics of this period of international rivalry. Forts, which had been built as prisons for slaves and
as a protection against the fierce onslaughts of outraged tribes, grew
into great castles designed to resist the attacks of European rivals by
land and by sea. Their military garrisons, when not engaged in fighting
each other, greatly facilitated the quest for slaves in obedience to the
ever-increasing demand for negro labour overseas.

The export of gold from the coast of Guinea was also considerable,
but the source from which the gold came was as much a mystery as
ever. The Dutchman Bosman described the coast at the end of the
seventeenth century:

'There is no small numbers of Men in *Europe*', he wrote, 'who believe that
the Gold Mines are in our power; that we, like the *Spaniards* in the *West-
Indies*, have no more to do but to work them by our Slaves: Though you
perfectly know we have no means of access to these Treasures; nor do I
believe that any of our People have ever seen one of them: Which you will
easily credit, when you are informed that the *Negroes* esteem them Sacred,
and consequently take all possible care to keep us from them.'[4]

What the Barbarossas did in North Africa for piracy the Hawkinses
of Plymouth, later in the same century, did for the slave trade in
West Africa. They demonstrated how greatly profits could be increased by careful organization and the introduction of business
methods, and this did much to popularize the trade. The family
connexion with the coast began with William who enjoyed the patronage of Henry VIII. His more famous son John reorganized the trans-
Atlantic traffic in slaves and served the pressing needs of the Spanish
settlers in the West Indies with an efficiency which their fellow
countrymen, who till then had controlled this part of the trade, had
never attained. 'One regrets', wrote Froude, 'that a famous Englishman should have been connected with the slave trade; but we have
no right to heap violent censure upon him because he was no more
enlightened than the wisest of his contemporaries.' When in the
following century some 'over-scrupulous persons', concerned at
the alarming proportions which the slave trade had assumed, questioned the morality of the traffic, the Protestant Church of France, like
the Catholics of two centuries before, defended it on the ground of the
opportunity it gave for the saving of negro souls. As the trade increased the civilized world became ever more deeply interested in its
continuance. One of the most valued privileges which England gained

THE VEIL 207

under the Peace of Utrecht of 1712 was the right to supply Spain's American colonies with negro slaves.

Although gold, ivory, and other commodities continued to be exported from West Africa in large quantities, slaves were the primary concern of all the nations engaged in the Guinea trade. In the middle of the eighteenth century it was estimated that there were a million negroes in America and that during the whole of the century six million slaves were shipped from different parts of Africa. When, towards the close of the century, the infamous traffic first began to disturb the conscience of Europe the annual export amounted to 200,000.

The European slave merchants depended for their supplies of slaves on the coast chiefs who obtained them from the interior which was consequently in a permanent condition of inter-tribal strife. As the demand outgrew the supply the Europeans tried to stimulate the trade by providing the middlemen with fire-arms. This added fresh terrors to tribal warfare and greatly increased the already vast area of Africa subject to slave raids. When the great explorers of later years began to penetrate into the far interior they discovered that so insistent was the demand for slaves on the coast that tribes living hundreds of miles from the sea were constantly being raided to maintain the supply. When the slaves reached the coast, suffering intense mental anguish from the conviction that their fate was to be fatted and eaten by white men, they were branded with irons and, under the most revolting conditions, were stowed into the reeking holds of the slave ships. The suffering and mortality of the slaves during the Middle Passage was appalling. At one time a vessel sailing from Guinea with 500 negroes was considered to have done well if she landed 300 in Jamaica.

The slave trade largely accounted for the failure of Europeans to penetrate the interior from the coast of Guinea. Not only did it engender the bitterest hatred for the white man among the suffering tribes of the interior, but it so enriched the coastal chiefs that they offered determined opposition to any move which threatened their privileged positions as middlemen. When England eventually proceeded to abolish the trade the hostility of these wealthy coast chiefs was at once excited, greatly to the prejudice of her legitimate commercial interests. The patroling of African waters by gunboats added a fresh terror to the Middle Passage, for captains of slave ships did not hesitate, on finding themselves pursued, to jettison their incriminating human cargoes in order to facilitate their escape from their pursuers

THE VEIL

and in the hope of establishing their innocence in the event of capture. Another tragic effect of abolition was the recrudescence of human sacrifice on a vast scale which, owing to the high export value of prisoners of war, had been in abeyance for a long time.

Added to the hostility of the natives there were serious natural obstacles to any attempt by Europeans to explore the interior. Almost everywhere along the coast the dense forests of the tropical rain belt pressed hard upon the shore. Not only did the forest present a serious impediment to human movement but conditions of life within it were, before the discovery of the prophylactic use of quinine, highly inimical to the well-being of the European. How lethal the climate was in those days is well illustrated by the mortality experienced by the early expeditions sent to explore the Niger. Even as late as 1841 a British government expedition, equipped with all the precautions which medical science could devise for the preservation of health, lost in two months on the lower Niger forty-eight men out of a total European strength of 145,[5] while the MacGregor Laird expedition of 1832 lost thirty-nine out of a total white personnel of forty-eight.

'Thus,' wrote Lady Lugard, 'when Europe approached West Africa, it was upon the coast that her adventurers landed. It was with the coast natives that she had to deal—natives who had from time immemorial been enslaved—and it was in the coast climate that her settlements were made. The coast belt was too broad for her to traverse. Its inhabitants were savage, its climate deadly, its jungle impenetrable without auxiliary force of steam. For upwards of 400 years Europe held the coast. Slaves were hunted for her in the far interior. Ivory was shot for her, gold was washed for her; but Europe herself, the civilization, the order, the justice for which her name now stands, penetrated no farther than perhaps twenty miles inland.'[6]

If the slave trade had not embittered the natives with a deadly hatred for the white man, the natural obstacles would have been more easily overcome and the penetration of the interior would not have been so long delayed. But with conditions as they were it is small wonder that during the sixteenth, seventeenth, and eighteenth centuries the activities of the European communities on the Guinea coast were practically restricted to the narrow limits of their trading beaches. This and the contemptible failure of western civilization to crush the petty pirate princes of the northern littoral account for European knowledge of the Western Sudan being still limited in the closing years of the eighteenth century to the little that had been learnt from the vague and often misleading reports of Arab travellers

THE VEIL

and geographers, supplemented by such information as filtered through to the coast in the course of trade.

Happily there were men in England who had already recognized that

'the map of the interior of Africa is still but a wide extended blank, on which the geographer, on the authority of Edrisi and Leo Africanus, has traced, with a hesitating hand, a few names of unexplored rivers and uncertain nations. The course of the Niger, the places of its rise and termination, and even its existence as a separate stream, are still undetermined. . . . It is certain', they declared, 'that while we continue ignorant of so large a portion of the globe, that ignorance must be considered as a degree of reproach upon the present age. Sensible of this stigma, and desirous of rescuing the age from a charge of ignorance, a few individuals, strongly impressed with a conviction of the practicability and utility of their enlarging the fund of human knowledge, have formed a plan of an Association for promoting the discovery of the interior part of Africa.'

Thus in the year 1788 there came into existence in London the Society Instituted for Exploring the Interior of Africa, commonly known as the African Association. Under the vigorous direction of a small body of men of learning, of whom Sir Joseph Banks was the most illustrious, the African Association succeeded after years of disappointment in penetrating the veil of mystery in which the interior of northern Africa had so long been wrapped. Its outstanding achievement was the discovery of the Niger.

REFERENCES

1. Capt. John Smith, op. cit., ii. 202–5.
2. P. Masson, op. cit., p. 90.
3. Hatfield House, Cecil MSS. 38, f. 59; *apud* de Castries.
4. William Bosman, op. cit., p. 70.
5. Capt. W. Allen and Dr. T. R. H. Thomson, *A Narrative of the Expedition to the River Niger in 1841*, 2 vols., London, 1848.
6. Lady Lugard (Flora L. Shaw), *A Tropical Dependency*, London, 1905, p. 320.

XIX

THE NIGER QUEST

'The supposition of the wise man is better than the certainty of the ignorant.'—MOORISH
PROVERB.

HERODOTUS had reported the existence of a great river running
from west to east, dividing Africa as the Danube does Europe.[1]
This was believed to be the Niger of Pliny and Ptolemy. Idrisi in the
twelfth century, however, declared that this river flowed to the west,
confusing it (like the Portuguese in the fifteenth century) with the
Senegal. He called it the Nile of the Negroes and derived it from the
same origin as the Nile of Egypt. Ibn Battuta[2] described it flowing
eastwards. Leo Africanus,[3] as we have already seen, with inexcusable
carelessness declared the Niger flowed from east to west. At the end
of the eighteenth century, almost 300 years later, Leo's was still the
last first-hand report and accordingly was widely accepted.

In the seventeenth century the French traders on the Senegal made
many unsuccessful attempts to penetrate the interior to exploit the
goldfields of Bambuk and discover Timbuktu. In 1690 they satisfied
themselves that the Senegal was a different river from the Niger and
this discovery gave increased popularity to the theory that the Niger
and the Nile were one. It is hardly surprising that with so much
contradictory information the mystery of the course of the Niger
became a source of bitter controversy and a scarcely less popular
subject for speculation than the problem of the North-West Passage.
Some thought it flowed west, others east; some declared the Niger
was the Nile, while others still sought to identify it with the
Senegal.

The African Association began its work by making exhaustive inquiries about the interior from British Consuls and native traders
engaged in the caravan traffic of North Africa. These investigations
produced a great mass of inaccurate information which stimulated
speculation, but did nothing to advance geographical knowledge. The
Association, realizing the futility of these inquiries, wisely decided to
send out explorers. The first two they chose were Ledyard and Lucas.
They instructed the former to set out from Egypt in search of the
Niger, but he died in Cairo before the commencement of his journey.
Lucas, who had had curiously varied experiences in Morocco first as

THE NIGER QUEST

a slave and later as British Vice-Consul, made an unsuccessful attempt to reach the Sudan from Tripoli.

Having failed in the north the Association made its next attempt from the west. In 1790 it sent Major Houghton to the Gambia with instructions to traverse the continent from west to east. Houghton, with Timbuktu as his first objective, travelled up the Gambia and crossed the Faleme, but he died at Jara, probably at the hands of the natives. His death was a severe blow to the Association, but they resolved to continue their work if, and when, a man hardy enough to brave the inevitable perils could be found.

At this juncture Mungo Park, a Scottish yeoman only twenty years of age, offered his services which were eagerly accepted. He sailed from Portsmouth in May 1794 and spent some time on the Gambia at Pisania studying the Mandingo language and completing his arrangements for the hazardous journey he had undertaken. The special object of the Association in sending him out had been to dispel the mystery which surrounded the Niger.

'My instructions,' he tells us, 'were very plain and concise. I was directed, on my arrival in Africa, to pass on to the river Niger, either by way of Bambouk, or by such other route as should be found most convenient. That I should ascertain the course, and, if possible, the rise and termination of that river. That I should use my utmost exertions to visit the principal towns or cities in its neighbourhood, particularly Tombuctoo and Houssa.'[4]

He left Pisania early in December accompanied by a native servant and a boy. Passing north of Bambuk he crossed the Senegal and reached Jara safely. But he here found himself in grave peril. The country was overrun with predatory bands of Moors—probably Arabised Berbers from Hodh—at whose hands it was believed Houghton had met his death. His servant refused to accompany him farther, so he continued his journey with his faithful boy as his sole companion. Robbed and reviled by all he met he was in hourly expectation of a violent end. He at last reached a village of friendly negroes whose kindliness was in striking contrast to the barbarity of the Moors.

Just when he appeared to have escaped the gravest peril and when no serious obstacle seemed to stand between him and the object of his journey, he was seized by a party of Moors and carried off to their encampment where he had to suffer every form of indignity. 'Never did any period of my life', he wrote, 'pass away so heavily: from sunrise to sunset was I obliged to suffer, with an unruffled countenance, the insults of the rudest savages on earth.'[5]

P 2

212   THE NIGER QUEST

It was nearly four months before Park was able to escape. After intense suffering he managed to reach the Bambara country where hospitable negro villages were numerous. At last, on 20 July 1796, as he was approaching Segu, the Bambara capital, he saw, he tells us, 'with infinite pleasure the great object of my mission; the long sought for, majestic Niger, glittering to the morning sun, as broad as the Thames at Westminster, and flowing *to the eastward*. I hastened to the brink, and, having drank of the water, lifted up my fervent thanks in prayer, to the Great Ruler of all things, for having thus far crowned my endeavours with success.'[6]

Continuing his journey downstream he crossed over the river to Silla where the state of his health and the exhaustion of his resources made it evident that if his discoveries were not to be lost to the world by his own death he must turn back without further delay.

'Worn down by sickness,' he wrote, 'exhausted with hunger and fatigue; half naked, and without any article of value, by which I might procure provisions, clothes, or lodging; I began to reflect seriously on my situation. I was now convinced, by painful experience that the obstacles to my further progress were insurmountable. . . . I was apprehensive that, in attempting to reach even Jenné . . . I should sacrifice my life to no purpose; for my discoveries would perish with me. The prospect either way was gloomy.'[7]

Before leaving Silla he collected from Moorish and negro traders as much information as possible about the further course of the Niger. These inquiries were not helpful and failed to throw any light on the termination of the river which was generally declared to 'run to the world's end'.

His return journey up the Niger was rendered difficult by the flooded state of the country. He made his way painfully to Bamako, supporting himself by writing and selling charms. He eventually reached Kamalia where he was befriended by a negro trader named Karfa Taura who was collecting slaves for sale to the European traders on the Gambia. Park remained under Karfa's protection for no less than seven months. During this period he was tormented with fever and undoubtedly owed his life to the kindly care of his host. When the rains abated Park set out with Karfa's slave caravan for the coast where he secured a passage on an American slave ship which took him to Antigua. Here he trans-shipped into a British vessel and arrived back in London on Christmas Day 1797.

Park's return to England, where he had long since been given up for dead, caused a deep sensation. The news of the discovery of the Niger

THE NIGER QUEST

was received with the utmost enthusiasm, not only by the African Association who, after long years of failure, had begun to doubt whether their endeavours would ever bear fruit, but by the whole country. His eagerly awaited narrative was published in 1799 with a long memoir on the scientific results of his work by Major James Rennell, F.R.S., the most distinguished geographer of the day. Besides very carefully working out Park's routes and reconstructing the geography of the upper Niger in the light of the new discoveries Rennell plunged boldly into the problem of the termination of the river. After studying the accounts of Idrisi and other Arabic authors he declared that: 'On the whole, it can scarcely be doubted that the Joliba or Niger terminates in lakes, in the eastern quarter of Africa; and those lakes seem to be situated in Wangara and Ghana.'[8] These two countries he regarded as the 'sink of North Africa', in which the waters of the Niger became so widely spread that they evaporated. With all the weight of Rennell's name behind it this theory, which was not, however, quite a new one, found very wide acceptance. Although it was so far from the truth as to appear to us almost ridiculous there was considerable excuse for Rennell's mistake. It was primarily due to the old blunder of Leo Africanus in placing Wangara in Hausa to the confusion of geographers for nearly three centuries. Rennell's reasoning was based on the assumption that Idrisi's Wangara and Leo's Wangara were the same. His acceptance of the current belief that the Hausa city of Kano was the ancient Ghana* added greatly to the confusion, for, like Leo's Wangara, it was an essential point in his attempt to reconcile the geography of the medieval Arab scholars with the results of the recent discoveries of Park and other explorers.

While Park had been discovering the Niger the African Association had sent out a young German, named Frederic Hornemann, to penetrate the interior by way of the caravan routes of the Sahara starting from Egypt. When he was in Cairo completing his arrangements to accompany a pilgrim caravan to Fezzan the city was captured by Napoleon who, however, with characteristic magnanimity, did all he could to facilitate the enterprise. Disguised as a Muhammadan trader Hornemann reached Murzuk whence he intended continuing his journey to Katsina.

The last communication received from him was dated from Murzuk in April 1800 when he was about to set out for Bornu. It was after-

---

* 'Of course Ghana,' he wrote, 'which in the 15th century was paramount in the centre of Africa, is now become a province of Kassina.'[9]

THE NIGER QUEST

wards ascertained that he reached the Niger, probably at Say, and followed it downstream to Nupe where he died.[10] The world was thus robbed of the fruits of one of the most remarkable journeys in the history of African discovery which, had Hornemann lived, would have placed him in the first rank of the world's great explorers.

Through the good offices of Napoleon, Hornemann's account of his journey as far as Fezzan, which contained the considerable amount of information he had collected about the interior, was safely delivered to the African Association. This journey, together with a memoir by Rennell, was published in 1802.[11] Hornemann's chief contribution to the controversy still raging over the termination of the Niger was to revive the old theory of its junction with the Nile.[12] Rennell's pet theory was now gravely threatened by a new heresy that sought to identify the Niger with the Congo of which only the vast estuary was known. But he had little difficulty in finding in Hornemann's *Journal* fresh evidence of 'the termination of the Niger, by *evaporation*, in the country of Wangara'.

Spurred by the African Association the British Government now began to interest itself in African exploration. In 1803 it was resolved to send an expedition to penetrate to the Niger from the west and to navigate it to its termination. Mungo Park, who had married and settled down to the uncongenial life of a medical practitioner in Peebles, eagerly accepted the post of leader. In a memorandum submitted to the Colonial Office he proposed first making his way to Segu and there building a boat in which he would sail down the Niger, past Jenne and Kabara and 'through the kingdoms of Haussa, Nyffe (Nupe) and Kasna (Katsina), to the kingdom of Wangara'. If the river ended there he might return either up the Niger, or across the Sahara, or by the Nile, or, more probably, through the Bight of Benin. If, however, as he himself now firmly believed, the Niger proved to be the Congo then he would follow it to its termination.[13]

In January 1805, after many irritating delays, Park sailed from Portsmouth. He was accompanied by two fellow Scots and five naval artificers who were to build the boat at Segu. At Goree the expedition was joined by an escort of an officer and thirty-five men from the garrison, and two seamen. Except for a Mandingo guide named Isaaco not a single native could be induced to join the expedition.

In attempting to lead into the interior of Africa an expedition of forty-six Europeans, unaccompanied by native servants, Park com-

THE NIGER QUEST

mitted a serious error of judgement. He was also seriously handicapped by the unfitness of the troops whose health had already been gravely shaken by the appalling conditions then inseparable from military service in the tropics. The expedition soon met with misfortune. The enervating climate, the lack of relief from heavy menial work, and the hostility of the native population quickly undermined their resistance to disease. At the very beginning of the journey men started to collapse from dysentery and fever and before long despondency settled down on every one except Park whose resolute determination alone kept the expedition moving towards its goal.

The route they followed was approximately that by which Park had returned from his previous journey. Soon after crossing the Faleme, the rains burst upon them and deaths became alarmingly frequent. More than half those who struggled on were sick. A band of plunderers clung to the heels of the expedition, ever ready to cut off a straggler or seize a lagging beast. At night the exhausted travellers were constantly the prey of thieves.

In August the shattered remnant of the expedition derived some slight pleasure from arriving within sight of the Niger. By the time they entered Bamako the artificers and three-quarters of the soldiers were dead. The remainder struggled on downstream to Sansanding where they set to work to construct a boat in which to continue the journey down the Niger. By the middle of November Park's preparations were complete. On 17 November 1805 he wrote his last dispatch to Lord Campden, the Colonial Secretary, dating it from: 'H.M.Schooner Joliba, at anchor off Sansanding'.

'I am sorry to say', he wrote, 'that of forty-four Europeans who left the Gambia in perfect health, five only are at present alive, viz. three soldiers (one deranged in his mind) Lieutenant Martyn, and myself.

'From this account I am afraid that your Lordship will be apt to consider matters in a very hopeless state; but I assure you I am far from desponding. With the assistance of one of the soldiers I have changed a large canoe into a tolerably good schooner on board of which I this day hoisted the British flag, and shall set sail to the east with the fixed resolution to discover the termination of the Niger or perish in the attempt. I have heard nothing that I can depend on respecting the remote course of this mighty stream; but I am more and more inclined to think that it can end no where but in the sea.

'My dear friend Mr. Anderson and likewise Mr. Scott are both dead; but though all the Europeans who are with me should die, and though I were myself half dead, I would still persevere; and if I could not succeed in the object of my journey, I would at last die on the Niger.'[14]

216 THE NIGER QUEST

This and a letter to his wife, carried back to the coast by the faithful Isaaco, were the last communications received from Park. He had expected to be back in England in May or June of the following year. When 1807 arrived without any news having been received the Government sent Isaaco to the Niger to make inquiries. At Segu he was fortunate enough to meet the guide who had embarked with Park at Sansanding.

According to this man, in spite of the repeated attempts of hostile natives to intercept the expedition, they had arrived safely at Yauri on the frontier of Hausa. Here his agreement with Park terminated and he left them. He knew, however, that Park and his companions had continued their journey down stream, unconscious of the dangerous rapids at Busa which lay close ahead. Arrived at the rapids they had found the banks thronged with armed natives who made a landing impossible. The canoe, swept on by the current, had plunged down the most dangerous of the three channels and jammed between two rocks. The natives, according to the guide's story, seeing the plight of the Europeans had then attacked their canoe. Park and the three other white men, the only survivors of the original expedition, had made a last desperate effort to save themselves by leaping into the river, but all four had been drowned.

Such was the sad story with which Isaaco returned to the coast. How closely it represents the truth will never be known. Years later Barth, following in Park's wake, complained bitterly of the hostility to white men caused by his predecessor's unprovoked attacks on native canoes.[15] It is not improbable that Park, driven desperate and determined, as he had said in his last letter to his wife, not to stop or land anywhere, mistook friendly natives, who had come out to welcome him, for enemies bent on his destruction. Similarly there are doubts about the last tragic scene at Busa. It is certain that Park and his companions perished there, but some have thought that the wild gesticulations of the armed natives who thronged the banks were only intended to warn the white men of the perils ahead of them. Against this must be set the extreme reluctance of the natives in later years to discuss the incident at all.[16]

Park's second expedition had been a tragic failure in every sense. Not a single member of the expedition had escaped death, and in spite of the heavy loss of life and the immense distance covered by Park, no fresh light had been thrown on the riddle of the termination of the Niger. Owing to an unfortunate belief that Busa was only 80 miles

THE NIGER QUEST

below Timbuktu, instead of 800, neither the coastward direction of the river nor the magnitude of Park's achievement were recognized. Meanwhile the theory that the Niger and Congo were one, with the great explorer's authority to support it, gained ever wider acceptance.

REFERENCES

1. Herodotus, ii. 32, 33.
2. Ibn Battuta, trans. H. A. R. Gibb, p. 323.
3. Leo Africanus, i. 124; iii. 1096.
4. Mungo Park, *Travels in the Interior Districts of Africa*, London, 1799, p. 3.
5. Ibid., p. 125.
6. Ibid., p. 194.
7. Ibid., p. 211.
8. Ibid., p. lxxvii.
9. Ibid., p. lxiv.
10. Major Dixon Denham, and Capt. Hugh Clapperton, *Narrative of Travels and Discoveries in Northern and Central Africa*, London, 1826, ii. 264.
11. Frederick Horneman, *Journal of Travels from Cairo to Mourzouk*, London, 1802.
12. Ibid., p. 103.
13. Mungo Park, *Travels in the Interior Districts of Africa, with an Account of a Subsequent Mission in 1805*, London, 1816, vol. ii, p. lxvi.
14. Ibid., p. cxxi.
15. H. Barth, *Travels*, iv. 453; v. 201.
16. Denham and Clapperton, op. cit., i. 244; ii. 305.

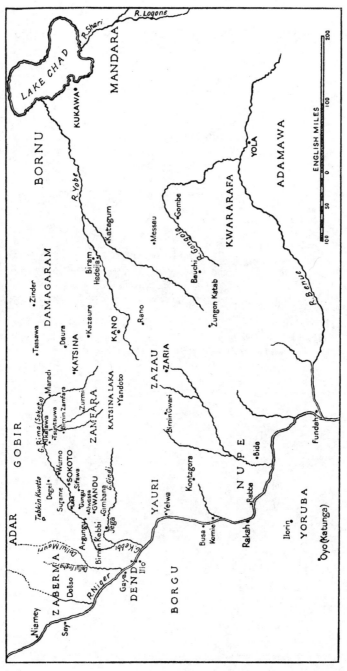

XII. The Hausa States.

XX

THE SOKOTO FULANI

'There is one more people dwelling and abiding among these Maudingoes. . . . *These are called* Fulbies, *being a* Tawny *people, and have a resemblance right unto those we call* Egiptians.'—RICHARD JOBSON.

WHILE Mungo Park was engaged on his last tragic journey the chief focus of political interest in the Western Sudan moved eastwards to Hausa where, unknown to the explorer, events of great consequence were taking place.

Many explanations of the origin of the name Hausa have been offered but none seems wholly satisfactory. It is perhaps of the same root as the Arabic *habesh*, meaning 'mixed', and possibly shares a common origin with the names Asben and Abyssinia.* In the Western Sudan the name Hausa is applied by the natives to the country known to us as the Hausa States and (rather loosely, as some think) to its inhabitants who call themselves Hausawa. It is, however, essentially the name of the language they speak which appears to be a mixture of Zaghawa and Temajegh, much modified by Arabic.[1] Leo tells us that the people of Gobir, Kano, Katsina, and Zegzeg spoke the Gobir language.[2] Nowhere does he use the word Hausa, which is surprising and has led some to suppose that the name is a comparatively recent introduction.[3]

The Hausa-speaking peoples are of mixed origin and, in spite of a common language and a common culture, they have never achieved political unity. They have been aptly described as a 'nation-in-the-making'.[4] Although they are negroid in general appearance Berber blood is one of the most important elements in their composition. According to their traditions a Berber hero, Abu Yazid, arrived in the ancient town of Daura from Bornu, slew the sacred serpent and married the queen. From this union sprang the founders of the Hausa Bokwoi or Seven Hausa States—Daura, Kano, Zazau or Zegzeg, Gobir, Katsina, Biram, and Rano. The lesser kingdoms of Kebbi, Nupe, Gwari, Yelwa, Illorin, Kwararafa, and Zamfara were known as the Banza Bokwoi, the bastard or upstart seven. Daura was always considered the senior kingdom and was to some extent regarded by the others as sacrosanct.[5]

---

* It may also be noted that Abyssinia includes a Sultanate of Aussa.

THE SOKOTO FULANI

The similarity between the story of Abu Yazid, the serpent slayer, and that of Aliamen who slew the Songhai river-god is striking. Both traditions have their origin in the great Berber or Zaghawa invasion of the Sudan which probably took place in the tenth century. The Zaghawa invaders introduced into Hausa a new form of worship and substituted patrilineal for matrilineal descent. The introduction of the horse and the art of sinking wells in rock have also been attributed to them. The invaders were probably few in numbers, but being pastoral nomads they were better organized and more skilled in the arts of war and of leadership than the Sudanese agriculturists over whom they easily established themselves as a ruling aristocracy, as did other Zaghawa on the upper and middle Niger and in Kanem. The descendants of these Shepherd Kings continued to rule in Hausa for many centuries and are the people usually called Habe.

The invading Zaghawa were of two classes, Imajeghan or nobles and Imghad or serfs. The former who are referred to as Kiptawa, or Copts, from Egypt settled in Gobir.* The latter occupied the rest of Hausa. For this reason the Gobirawa have always been regarded as a free people in contradistinction to the rest of the inhabitants of the Hausa States who are looked upon as slaves.[6] The Sarakuna or ruling family of Gobir still have under one eye a tribal mark, the *takin kaza*, which is found under the eyes of certain Pharaohs of Egypt.

Unfortunately most of the local historical records were destroyed by the Fulani when they conquered the country, but one important source of Hausa history survived. This is the *Kano Chronicle*[7] in which are recorded the reigns of forty-eight Sarkis or Kings of Kano, from Bagoda (A.D. 999–1063) to Muhammad Bello (1883–92). Its accuracy as an historical record has been proved to be much above the average for a document of this nature. Tradition attributes the foundation of Kano to ironworkers known as Abagazawa, a tribal name still used in Kano by families of blacksmiths who have practised their craft for countless generations. According to tradition Bagoda, the first Habe king, was a son of the serpent slayer of Daura.

The Muhammadan religion reached Kano in the fourteenth century, introduced by Wangarawa or Mandingoes from Mali. Although Hausa culture was profoundly influenced by Muhammadanism, especially in the systems of government and administration of justice, the people were never wholly won over from their ancient religion

---

* According to Mr. H. R. Palmer (*Journal of the African Society*, xxxi (1932), 163) Kipti does not mean 'Copts' but 'people of Avalis' on the Somal coast.

THE SOKOTO FULANI

which usually took some form of tree or serpent worship. They frequently relapsed into paganism and many clung, as they do to-day, to the old heathen beliefs of their ancestors.

Kano probably attained the height of its power under Muhammad Rimfa (*c.* 1463–99) who, like Askia the Great of Songhai, came under the influence of the Muslim preacher El Maghili. In the following century Kano was conquered by a Songhai army under Kanta of Kebbi, but as Askia the Great had no wish to occupy the country his general contented himself with exacting tribute. About the year 1600 Kano, together with the greater part of Hausa, became tributary to the Kwararafawa, Jukuns from the Gongola-Benue basin. In 1671 they actually occupied the city. About 1680 they were severely defeated by Bornu of which Kano shortly afterwards became a vassal.

Katsina, according to tradition, was founded by Kumayo, a grandson of Abu Yazid. The Berber or Zaghawa dynasty, known as the Durbawa, ruled for about 200 years and ended with Sanau, who was slain by Korau, a wrestler from Yandoto.* The Emir of Katsina is still acclaimed as Magajin Korau, successor of Korau, and the sword with which Korau slew Sanau forms part of his regalia.†

The Muslim religion probably reached Katsina in the fourteenth century at the end of which we find a Sarki named Muhammad. It seems to have relapsed into paganism, but was reconverted in the following century by El Maghili. In the fifteenth century, during the reign of Muhammad Rimfa, a war broke out between Kano and Katsina which lasted eleven years without a decisive result. Rimfa's successor, Abdullahi, however, defeated Katsina in several battles.

It is often stated that Katsina was at one time a fief of the Mali empire, but there is little evidence that this was ever the case. In the sixteenth century, as we have already seen, it was twice attacked by the Songhai; in 1513 by Kanta, who was then a general of Askia the

---

* Yandoto, which was situated between Chafe and Kotorkoshi, is now in ruins.

† 'The Sword of State is an ancient blade suggesting Moorish or possibly Eastern workmanship. The hilt and scabbard of silver were made to the order of the present Emir. The blade itself is engraved with an inscription in Arabic characters which has been translated as under:

Obverse. Help comes from God and victory is near so announce glad tidings to the Faithful O Muhammad.

Reverse. There is no sword save Dhul Fiqar and no hero save Ali.

'The sword Dhul Fiqar was captured from the Koreish at the battle of Badr and became henceforth the Sword of the Prophet. From him it passed to Ali.'[8]

THE SOKOTO FULANI

Great, and later by the Hi-koi and his gallant band. According to the *Tarikh es Sudan* the Hi-koi's raiders were defeated at a place called Karfata by 400 horsemen of 'Libti' who were possibly Lemtuna Tuareg.[9] Before the end of the century Katsina became a vassal of Bornu and remained so for 200 years. During the seventeenth century there were frequent wars with Kano which were terminated by the increasing menace of a common enemy in the Kwararafawa from the Benue. After the latter had captured Kano they attacked Katsina. Although they actually breached the walls they unexpectedly withdrew without capturing the city.

In the eighteenth century Katsina became one of the leading cities in the Western Sudan with a considerable reputation as an important market and as a seat of learning and of culture. Its boundaries extended in the north to Maradi and Tassawa, in the west to Zamfara, and in the south to Birnin Gwari. Its prosperity at this period was chiefly due to the importance it had acquired as an entrepôt for desert trade. This position, which it owed to its geographical situation as the northern gate of the prosperous Hausa States, it was later forced to yield to Kano. The names of the present city wards, most of which probably date from this period, indicate how far flung were its associations. There is the Tudun Mali, the Tawatinke or quarter of the people of Tuat, the Wangarawa quarter, the Sararin Tsako or encampment of the Kel Owi; other less distant peoples who had their own quarters were the Kebbawa, the Beri-Beri of Bornu, and the Gobirawa. In the middle of the century the Gobirawa, probably yielding to pressure from the Tuareg who some time previously had driven them from their home in Asben,* moved southward into Zamfara which brought them into conflict with the Katsinawa. A long period of war between Gobir and Katsina followed, but without any decisive result.

The early history of Zazau or Zegzeg is obscure. In the fifteenth century it became a powerful state under the vigorous rule of Queen Amina. As the result of constant warfare with her neighbours she extended the frontiers of her kingdom considerably. She is popularly supposed to have first introduced eunuchs and kola nuts into Hausa, but this is probably untrue. She constantly toured her kingdom, building walled towns and taking a new lover wherever she stayed and, like the notorious Dowager Empress of China, murdering him when she left. Zaria, the capital of Zazau, was probably built in the six-

* The Gobirawa have been traced back to a still earlier home in Bilma.

THE SOKOTO FULANI

teenth century by Bakwa, revered as the great ruler who delivered his people from the terrors of the Kwararafa invasions.[10]

Though farming has always been the principal occupation of the Hausa-speaking peoples, they are justly renowned as skilled craftsmen and as enterprising and intelligent traders. The wares of the Hausa smiths, weavers, dyers, tanners, and leather-workers always attracted foreign merchants, and many of their walled towns became important markets. Their trade was also fostered by hordes of enterprising traders who peddled the wares of Hausa craftsmen throughout the neighbouring countries, and made their language the *lingua franca* of a great part of the Western Sudan. The walls with which their towns and villages are surrounded often attain imposing proportions. The walls of Kano, which enclose a large area of cultivable land, have a circuit of no less than thirteen miles.

As we have already seen, the Hausa was accustomed to alien domination. As long as he was allowed peacefully to cultivate his fields, manufacture his trade goods, and hold his markets he cared little who were his masters. Although in almost constant subjection to foreign rulers the Hausa people seem usually to have enjoyed local autonomy and seldom had to suffer interference in their local affairs. They were consequently able to develop an elaborate social organization, naturally much influenced by Muslim culture. Their machinery of government by a hierarchy of officials, whose titles are still in use, and their system of taxation are still the basis of administration under British rule.

At the close of the eighteenth century the Gobirawa were all-powerful in the north-west. Bornu was the undisputed master of the north-east, dominating both Kano and the Jukun kingdom of Kwararafa which had sunk into insignificance. In the south Nupe retained its independence, though it had been much weakened by civil strife. Zaria and Katsina were nominally independent, but they were probably under the influence, if not the tutelage, of Bornu. Such briefly was the political situation of the Hausa States when the Fulani *jihad* burst upon them.

The Fulani, or Fulbe as they call themselves, whose eastward migrations had brought them into Hausa as early as the thirteenth century, are divided into the Bororoje or Cow Fulani and the Fulanin Gidda or Town Fulani. The former are shy pastoral nomads and generally pagans. Preferring the bush to settled habitations of man they have retained a high degree of racial purity

224 THE SOKOTO FULANI

though even they are gradually losing the light complexion and the finely chiselled features characteristic of the race. The Fulanin Gidda are Muslims, racially much modified by intermarriage with the many different peoples among whom they have sojourned, and, as their name indicates, prefer the sedentary life of towns and villages.

The Fulani, like the Jews and the Gipsies with both of whom some have sought to identify them, are a people without a home and, again like the Gipsies, they have never disbanded tribally in spite of centuries of a wandering life. Their peaceful penetration of the Sudan is typical of most great ethnic movements which seldom attained the spectacular speed usually attributed to them. (Even the Vandals took two and a half centuries to reach Africa from their original home to the south of the Baltic.)

The entry of the Fulani into Hausa did not disturb the rest of the population. The Bororoje maintained their customary aloofness, but the Fulanin Gidda settled in the towns and lived amicably among the people of the country with whom they intermarried. According to the *Kano Chronicle* the Fulani brought with them books on Divinity and Etymology, but they 'passed by and went to Bornu leaving a few men in Hausa, together with some slaves and people who were tired of journeying'.[11] By the end of the eighteenth century these settlers had been so increased in numbers by later arrivals from the west that the Fulani formed a considerable element in the population and were to be found, as the result of their intellectual superiority, occupying high positions in every department of life. Although they held aloof from the Hausawa, whom they regarded with the customary contempt of pastoral nomads for agriculturists and of white for black, they were welcomed by the dark tillers of the soil for the butter they provided and for the manure of their herds.

One of the most powerful of the clans of the Fulanin Gidda who had settled in Hausa were the dark-skinned Torobe, Toronke, or Toronkawa. The name signifies people of Toro in the Senegal basin, the earliest habitat to which they can be traced, which has given its name to a Tucolor clan who are consequently sometimes confused with them. From Toro, where they acquired their dark complexion through intermarriage with the negroid inhabitants, they moved eastwards, settling round the shores of Lake Debo. After a while they continued their eastward migration. Some settled in Liptako, some in Yatenga, others crossed the Niger and settled in Gobir, while

THE SOKOTO FULANI

another section of the clan pushed on into Adamawa in the Benue basin.

Usuman dan Fodio, whom the Nigerian Fulani recognize as their great national hero, belonged to the Toronke of Gobir. Born in 1754 Usuman was brought up as a strict Muhammadan of the Maliki school. As he grew up he became filled with a deep religious enthusiasm which found its outlet in the career of a preacher, upon which he embarked at a very early age. His piety and fervour quickly won him recognition, and many of those who fell under the influence of his personal magnetism became devoted disciples. His constant journeys among the people of Gobir produced a religious revival, and he soon exercised a profound influence on a large part of the population who called him Shehu, or Sheikh, the name by which he became generally known.

Since the days of El Maghili the Hausa people had become increasingly lax in their religious observances and there was a strong tendency to revert to the pagan rites of their Habe ancestors. In some districts this process had become so marked that paganism had completely replaced the Muhammad religion. The principal object of Shehu's fervent preaching was to denounce this lamentable reversion. This quickly brought him into opposition to Nafata, Sarkin Gobir, who was then the champion of paganism. Nafata decreed that none except those who had been born Muslims should practise the Muhammadan religion, and forbade the wearing of turbans by men and of veils by women.

Yunfa in his childhood had been taught by Shehu. When he succeeded his father Nafata he became openly hostile to his old tutor whose growing influence among the people he regarded as a menace to his throne. Yunfa first took up arms against Gimbana, where lived a certain Abdu Salame, a disciple of Shehu, who had incurred his special displeasure. The town was captured and its inhabitants were led away to slavery. On the way they encountered Shehu who, perceiving many Muslims among the prisoners, had their chains struck off. Yunfa, furious at the affront, sought to put Shehu to death, but according to tradition the interposition of divine power caused the plot to fail.

The undisguised hostility of Yunfa increased the sympathy for Shehu who now became a popular hero. The most prominent among those who supported him were the Fulani clan of the Sulebawa. Thoroughly alarmed at the growth of the movement Yunfa now summoned his captains and marched against Degel, Shehu's town. A

226 THE SOKOTO FULANI

memorable date in Fulani history is 21 February 1804 which marked the *Hijra* or Flight of Shehu from Degel. He sought refuge in Gudu where his disciples rallied round him in such numbers that he quickly found himself at the head of a considerable body of warriors, all fired with the dauntless religious fervour of their master.

On 21 June the army of Yunfa met the preacher and his followers on the shores of Tabkin Kwotto and were severely defeated. The victorious Muslims solemnly swore a *jihad* against the infidels on the field of battle. They proclaimed their leader Amir ul Muminina, in Hausa Sarkin Musulmi, Commander of the Faithful, the title still borne by his descendant, the reigning Sultan of Sokoto. 'Let no man', declared Shehu, 'think that I accept this office that I may be greater than another or that my slave may lord it over others'.

The Fulani victory caused widespread consternation. Warned by Yunfa of the peril which threatened to spread into all parts of Hausa, the kings of Katsina, Kano, Zazau, Daura, and Adar attacked the followers of Shehu in their own dominions. A general rising of the Fulani followed and the whole country was thrown into a state of war. It has been said that Yunfa ordered all Fulani in Gobir to be killed and that he urged the other Hausa chiefs to do the same. This is probably untrue for many Fulani fought on the side of Gobir and many Hausas were to be found in the ranks of Shehu's army.[12]

Shehu gave to each of his most trusted followers a flag, which he blessed, and sent them out into the world to conquer. The emirates which they won for themselves were Katsina, Kano, Zaria, Bornu, Hadeija, Adamawa, Gombe, Katagum, Nupe, Illorin, Daura, Kazaure, Bauchi, and Messau. In nearly every case a descendant of the original flag-bearer still rules as emir over the lands won by his ancestor.[13]

Shehu had gained a signal victory over the Gobirawa but Alkalawa, their capital, offered a stubborn resistance. His first expedition against it was unsuccessful. The Tuareg, with characteristic perfidy, played traitor to both sides. Shortly afterwards he was severely defeated at Tsuntsuwa, but he soon reorganized his forces and gained fresh strength as ardent supporters arrived from the more distant parts of Hausa.

Zaria fell in 1804. Katsina was captured after a long siege in 1805 and later in the year the Fulani forces met the Sarkin Kano in battle. The Kano army of 10,000 spearmen, clad in mail and quilted armour,

THE SOKOTO FULANI

must have presented an awe-inspiring array, but they were an ill-disciplined rabble and no match for the Fulani bowmen by whom they were routed. Kano was occupied without further opposition, but later in the same year Shehu's forces were severely defeated at Alwassa, near Gwandu, by a combination of Kebbawa and Gobirawa who were supported by a great number of Tuareg. The enemy pressed their victory and for a time the Fulani were placed in a very critical situation.

In 1806 another unsuccessful attempt was made to break the power of the Gobirawa by seizing their capital, but in 1808, after elaborate preparations, Shehu's son Bello captured the city and slew Yunfa. The fall of Alkalawa was a blow from which Gobir never recovered. It placed the Fulani in a position of unchallenged authority and made their cause secure. Shehu's prestige was further increased by the arrival in Hausa of the Sarkin Air of Agades, a Targui of the Kel Owi tribe, who came south especially to do homage to him.

Meanwhile several Hausa chiefs had appealed to Bornu which the Fulani invaded in 1808. The Bornu army, led by the Waziri, was defeated and the Fulani occupied the capital. The Shehu of Bornu fled and appealed to his relative Shehu Lamino of Kanem, more generally known as El Kanemi, to come to his aid. El Kanemi, a leader of outstanding ability, placed himself at the head of the Bornu forces and drove out the Fulani. Two years later the latter renewed their attack but El Kanemi again saved the country. Although the Fulani continued to make serious inroads into Bornu and successfully occupied considerable areas on its western marches they never conquered the country. An important ethnic result of the intervention of El Kanemi in the affairs of Bornu was the arrival of many Kanembu tribes who settled there permanently and inter-married with the Kanuri.[14]

From the early days of the *jihad* Shehu had usually made his head-quarters at Sokoto. Although posterity has sought to endow Sokoto with a respectable antiquity and scholars have identified it with the Zogde of the Catalan map of 1375 and with the Sagoto of Malfante, before the *jihad* it had never been more than a hunters' camp at the foot of the tamarind tree which still stands in the enclosure of the mosque. It remained a mere camp till the year 1809 when Bello built the present town.

The year 1809 was also memorable for an incident known as the miraculous crossing of the Niger. While Shehu's brother, Waziri

228 THE SOKOTO FULANI

Abdullahi, was fighting in Dendi some of the enemy fled across the river. 'When we came to this river', wrote Bello, 'the river was obedient to us so that we forded it. Again we crossed it a second time, on our going and on our return the water did not pass the soles of our feet.'[15] This incident inevitably recalls the passage of the Israelites through the Red Sea, but, as Sir James Frazer has pointed out,[16] there are other well authenticated instances of similar passages over which later generations have thrown a veil of mystery; for example the passage of Alexander the Great and his host over the Pamphylian Sea, and the unexpected capture of New Carthage by Scipio the Elder as the result of a spectacular crossing of an arm of the sea at ebb-tide.

That Bello's statement was probably not altogether fanciful is indicated by a passage in Barth's *Travels* where he describes the Niger between Tosaye and Gao. 'The river being here so broad', he tells us, 'it did not at all surprise me to hear from these people that in average years, during the lowest state of the river, it is fordable in several places.'[17] Moreover Capt. Hill of the Laird-Oldfield Expedition declared that at a point near the confluence of the Benue with the Niger the latter was so low that he could walk across it.[18] That the Fulani forces did ford the river is therefore not wholly improbable. That in doing so they scarcely wetted their feet may be dismissed as an excusable adornment of posterity.

Shehu had many sympathizers beyond the Niger where there was a considerable Fulani population many of whom belonged to his clan, the Toronke. The extent of his influence within the Bend of the Niger was probably never very great, but he exercised nominal suzerainty over the district of Liptako, of which Dori is the chief town.[19]

Among Shehu's early followers there had been a certain Ahmadu Lobo, a Fulani Malam or Ulema of Massina, afterwards known as Seku or Shehu Ahmadu. When he returned from Gobir to Massina he and his disciples were persecuted by the Arma of Jenne and by the Ardo. This excited the sympathy of a large part of the population and he soon found himself at the head of a considerable following. His career continued, as it had commenced, following a course very similar to that of his master. The Ardo, alarmed at the growing influence of Seku, appealed to his suzerain, the Bambara king of Segu. Seku's retort was to declare a *jihad*. In spite of the inferior numbers of his force he took the field and defeated his enemies so completely that, for the first time since 1670, Massina was freed

THE SOKOTO FULANI

from the tutelage of the Bambara of Segu. Seku now sent two of his brothers to Shehu Usuman to ask for his blessing and for a flag, both of which were granted. This incident has given rise to the erroneous belief that Seku Ahmadu was one of Shehu's original flag-bearers.

Shehu's cordial sympathy added greatly to Seku's prestige. The rest of the Fulani population of Massina who had held aloof rallied round him and delivered up the Ardo. Seku Ahmadu was now the undisputed master of Massina, but instead of calling himself Ardo he, like Shehu, adopted the title of Amir ul Muminima, or Commander of the Faithful. Making his head-quarters at a village which he called Hamdallahi, he organized his kingdom and embarked on a career of conquest which ultimately made him master of a vast territory which for a time included Timbuktu in the north and extended to the Black Volta in the south.[20]

Early in 1810 Shehu Usuman's *jihad* was practically complete. He had established his rule over more than 100,000 square miles and was recognized as sovereign by four to five million people. Like every other conquering race who had advanced southwards through the parklands of the Sudan the Fulani were eventually held up by the forests. This natural barrier was further strengthened in the south-west by the not inconsiderable military power of the Yoruba, and along the course of the Benue by pagan hill tribes such as the Sura and the Tangale. In the east the Fulani reached as far as Yola which they occupied. In the north-east, as we have already seen, they made serious inroads into Bornu but never became masters of the country. The arid and sparsely populated plains of the north presented no attractions. In the west the Kebbawa, amongst whom the spirit of Kanta still survived, continued to defy them in spite of their proximity to the principal Fulani strongholds. Birnin Kebbi, the chief town of the Kebbawa, had fallen in the second year of the *jihad*, but their power remained unbroken and they played a leading part in the defeat of Shehu at Alwassa a few months later. Eventually numbers of Kebbawa submitted to the Fulani, but the irreconcilables, led by a chief named Ismaila, preserved their independence at Argungu, situated between the twin capitals of Sokoto and Gwandu, and continued incessantly to raid the Fulani. Their spirit was indomitable and they remained unconquered till the arrival of the British almost a century later.

Well content with the measure of his achievement Shehu now turned his attention to the organization and administration of his

THE SOKOTO FULANI

empire. He divided it into two parts. To his son Bello he gave the east and to his brother Waziri Abdullahi the west. Bello's head-quarters were at Sokoto, Abdullahi's at Gwandu in Kebbi. For a century the Fulani empire continued to be administered from these twin capitals. Shehu wisely adopted the elaborate machinery of government and taxation, based on Quranic law, which he found already existing throughout the Hausa States. Tribute in slaves and other goods had to be paid annually to Sokoto and Gwandu, and the emirs had to furnish any troops which might be required. As long as these services were punctually carried out the central govern-ment interfered little in the affairs of the emirates.

'Shehu', writes Mr. Daniel, 'lived to see the conclusion of his life's work. He had found Muhammadanism under a ban: he left it supreme. The Fulani, from a tribe of nomad herdsmen, had become the ruling race throughout the Hausa states. A man of sincere faith and deep religious convictions, he had implicit confidence in his Divine call, and his personality inspired his followers with a confidence similar to his own. His simple habits and austere life made a profound contrast to the barbaric pomp affected by the pagan rulers. No soldier himself, he attributed his successes solely to the hand of God. After the partition of his empire, he withdrew from the active conduct of affairs and devoted himself to a life of study, first at Sifawa, and later in the city of Sokoto. Here he died in 1817, and was buried within the city walls, where his tomb is still a place of pilgrimage.'[21]

The Fulani were naturally accused by their enemies of making religion an excuse to seize political power. El Kanemi of Bornu, himself a fervent Muslim, directly charged them with this in corre-spondence which he exchanged with Bello. He admitted many of the charges of pagan practices which the Fulani brought against their adversaries, but he denied that they were sufficiently grave to justify a *jihad*. Nevertheless the *Infaku'l Maisuri*[22] of Bello, who was the political, as his father had been the religious, founder of the Sokoto empire, demonstrates clearly the absolute sincerity of Shehu. That the *jihad* was in its origin purely a religious movement is beyond doubt. The racial consciousness, however, which it inevitably awakened among the widely scattered Fulani population of the Hausa States soon gave the *jihad* a national character and this has doubtless led many to forget the high purpose with which it was launched. Shehu's *jihad*, moreover, was not the only occasion on which the Fulani, after making a peaceful entry into a country and acquiring political power, had finally seized supreme control by force of arms.

THE SOKOTO FULANI

At Shehu's death Bello was made Sarkin Musulmi. Bello's reign of twenty years was largely occupied in putting down revolts in different parts of the great dominions he had inherited. He proved himself a statesman and an able administrator and was unquestionably the greatest of the Sokoto Sultans. He warned his people against the Hausa superstition that the Fulani inherited wisdom at their birth. 'That is a lie and an illusion', he declared, 'for knowledge can only be preserved by study and the Ulemas are nearer to knowledge than anyone else.'[23] Bello encouraged science and learning and his court became the resort of scholars from many distant countries. El Hadji Omar, the Tucolor *jihadi* who, in the middle of the century, won for himself a large kingdom on the upper Niger, owed much to the influence of Bello. As a young man returning from the pilgrimage to Mecca he had first visited El Kanemi in Bornu and had then settled for a time in Sokoto where he married a kinswoman of Bello.

With the death of the original flag-bearers the religious enthusiasm of the Fulani soon began to evaporate. The enjoyment of the fruits of victory, as so often before in history, brought with it a weakening of all the qualities which had brought them success. As a Tripolitan Arab remarked to Clapperton, when they were poor the Fulani chiefs led their people into battle; since they had become rich they lagged behind and sent their men forward alone.[24] Their leaders became fief-holders, living in luxury surrounded by slaves, eunuchs, and concubines, and farmed the taxes of large districts where their relations and favourites acted as their deputies. The *jihad* against their pagan neighbours still went on, but it had degenerated into simple slave-raiding.[25]

With the loss of their martial zeal the Fulani became the constant prey of insurrection and revolt. When they grew too feeble even to raid their neighbours they fell to the depths of enslaving their own peasantry. Both within and without their frontiers they depopulated and ruined vast areas. The central government lacked both the will and the power to check these abuses, and when the British entered the country at the beginning of the following century the Sarkin Musulmi was being openly defied by many of his powerful subjects.

Although the degradation of the Fulanin Gidda was profound there were happily still some amongst their leaders who preserved the nobler traditions of the race for the inspiration of later generations. That the Fulani are to-day as capable as they have ever been of great

THE SOKOTO FULANI

achievements is abundantly proved by the distinction with which many of them are occupying responsible positions requiring a high degree of personal integrity and real administrative ability. The Bororoje, who had taken little interest in the political upheaval which had brought power and wealth to their relatives, continued to pasture their herds in the seclusion of the bush. There we still find them, leading the life of their remote ancestors and preserving a high degree of racial purity.

REFERENCES

1. H. R. Palmer, *Journal of the African Society*, xxii (1922–3), p. 125.
2. Leo Africanus, i. 134.
3. C. K. Meek, op. cit., i. 85–7; F. R. Rodd, op. cit., p. 363; H. R. Palmer, *Mai Idris of Bornu*, p. 76.
4. C. K. Meek, loc. cit.
5. A. E. V. Walwyn, *apud* H. R. Palmer, *Sudanese Memoirs*, iii. 132.
6. H. R. Palmer, op. cit., iii. 96.
7. Ibid., p. 97.
8. F. de F. Daniel, *Historical Notes, Katsina Emirate*, 1928. See also *Journal of the African Society*, xxxi (1932) p. 80.
9. F. de F. Daniel, *Katsina Emirate*.
10. E. J. Arnett, *Gazetteer of Zaria Province*, London, 1920, p. 8; C. K. Meek, op. cit., i. 90.
11. H. R. Palmer, op. cit., vol. iii, p. 111.
12. E. J. Arnett, *The Rise of the Sokoto Fulani*, Appendix, p. 16.
13. Ibid., Appendix, p. 29.
14. C. K. Meek, *op. cit.*, i. 81.
15. *Infaku'l Maisuri*, *apud* E. J. Arnett, op. cit., p. 97.
16. Sir J. G. Frazer, *Folk-Lore in the Old Testament*, London, 1919, ii. 457.
17. H. Barth, *Travels*, v. 196.
18. MacGregor Laird and R. A. K. Oldfield, *Narrative of an Expedition into the Interior of Africa by the River Niger, 1832–1834*, London, 1837, p. 176.
19. M. Delafosse, op. cit., ii. 367.
20. Ibid., p. 231.
21. F. de F. Daniel, 'Shehu dan Fodio', *Journal of the African Society*, xxv (1925–6), p. 282.
22. E. J. Arnett, loc. cit.
23. Al Hadji Said, *Tarikh es Sokoto, apud, Tedzkiret en Nisian*, p 319.
24. Denham and Clapperton, op. cit., ii. 214.
25. Lord Lugard, *The Dual Mandate in British Tropical Africa*, London, 1923, p. 232.

XXI

THE LIFTING OF THE VEIL

*And yet may Africa have a Prerogative in Rarities, and some seeming incredibilities be true—*SAMUEL PURCHAS.

IN 1803 a German geographer named Reichard had declared his conviction that the Niger discharged its waters through the channels of an immense delta in the Bight of Benin.[1] Owing to the widely held belief that the Kong Mountains, which Leo Africanus had reported lying south of Mali, extended so far to the east that they prohibited the possibility of the Niger reaching the Bight of Benin, Reichard's hypothesis was rejected by his contemporaries. A few years later James McQueen, a resident in the West Indies whose interest in the Niger had been stirred by Park's work, instituted inquiries among the West African slaves who were under his care. Among them were Mandingoes and Hausas from whom he industriously collected a mass of information about the Niger which he compared very carefully with what had been learnt from Arab and European traders on the North and West African coasts. As the result of these researches McQueen was able to reconstruct the geography of the interior of West Africa and to demonstrate, with a convincing array of facts, that the termination of the Niger could be nowhere else but in the Gulf of Guinea. He was also the first to report the existence of the great confluent of the Niger which we now know as the Benue.[2] But the world had been too deeply moved by repeated tragedies in the field to heed the teachings of a mere theorist, so the fruits of McQueen's industry were wasted.

Meanwhile there was no lack of men prepared to go out to Africa and continue the work of Park. In 1810 London was diverted by the arrival of an enthusiastic German named Roentgen, who, having first been circumcised, was in training on a diet of spiders, ants, and grasshoppers in preparation for a journey to Timbuktu. In spite of these elaborate preparations he lost his life shortly after first setting foot on African soil.

In 1816 the British Government attempted to test the Niger-Congo theory by sending expeditions to each of these rivers. The one, under a Capt. Tuckey, was to ascend the Congo; the other, under Major Peddie with Capt. Campbell as his assistant, was to follow Park's route into the interior and descend the Niger. Both expeditions came

THE LIFTING OF THE VEIL

to a disastrous termination without throwing any fresh light on the problem of the Niger.

In 1818 the British Government, profiting by the friendly relations which they had recently established with the Basha of Tripoli, whose influence extended far to the south, sent a mission to attempt the penetration of the Sahara from that country. The expedition, led by a Mr. Ritchie with Capt. F. G. Lyon as his companion, only got a little beyond Murzuk where Ritchie himself died. From Lyon's narrative we learn that they had not been wholly without hope of hearing something of Park whom a few believed to be 'still confined by the Sultan (of Timbuktu) on account of his skill in surgery'. Lyon's own inquiries regarding the Niger led him to the conclusion 'that by one route or other, these waters join the great Nile of Egypt, to the southward of Dongola'.

Lyon's comments on Wangara demonstrate how easily Leo may have been misled by the wide application of the name, and how closely the natives still associated it with the silent trade in gold.

'Wangara', he tells us, 'is a place of which we cannot obtain any decided account; it is, however, generally supposed to be a low country, and sometimes inundated. One person states it to be twenty days south of Tembuctoo; another places it south of Kashna; and many even assert, that it is beyond Waday: but it is quite impossible from the varied accounts given of it, to form any idea as to its actual situation, or even existence.

'Should there really be three places so called, may it not be probable that it is a general name for marshes and swamps? In the one spoken of behind Tembuctoo, the capital is said to be Battagoo, and is a large town, near which much gold is reported to be found. An invisible nation, according to our informant, inhabit near this place, and are said to trade by night. Those who come to traffic for their gold, lay their merchandise in heaps, and retire. In the morning they find a certain quantity of gold dust placed against every heap, which, if they think sufficient, they leave the goods; if not, they let both remain until more of the precious ore is added. These traders in gold dust are by many supposed to be devils, who are very fond of red cloth, the favourite article of exchange.'[3]

Modest though the results of the Ritchie-Lyon mission had been, the British Government regarded them as sufficiently encouraging to warrant another attempt from the north. In 1821 they sent out an expedition of Dr. Denham, R.N., Lieut. Clapperton, R.N., Dr. Oudney, who was to become Political Agent in Bornu, and a ship-wright named Hillman. They reached Murzuk where they found every obstacle put in the way of further progress. After months of

THE LIFTING OF THE VEIL

waiting the Basha was induced to provide the necessary escort and in
February 1823 they sighted Lake Chad where they had hoped to find
at least a clue to the solution of the Niger problem. 'My heart bounded
within me at the prospect', Denham tells us, 'for I believed this lake
to be the key to the great object of our search.' A fortnight later they
entered Kukawa, the capital of Bornu, where they were welcomed by
Muhammad El Kanemi who by this time had taken the government
into his own hands.

Denham, with characteristic enterprise, accompanied a slave raiding
expedition against the pagans of Mandara who were still nominally
subject to the Fulani of Sokoto. He had the misfortune to fall into
the hands of the pagans but, although wounded and stripped naked,
he contrived to make good his escape while his captors were wrangling
over the division of his clothes.

Meanwhile Clapperton had set out with Oudney to explore Hausa
and search for the Niger in the west. Oudney died near Katagum, but
Clapperton, himself in ill health, continued his journey alone and
reached Kano in January 1824.

'Arrayed in naval uniform,' he tells us, 'I made myself as smart as circumstances would permit. . . . At eleven o'clock we entered Kano, the great
emporium of the kingdom of Haussa; but I had no sooner passed the gates,
than I felt grievously disappointed; for from the flourishing description of it
given by the Arabs, I expected to see a city of surprising grandeur: I found,
on the contrary, the houses nearly a quarter of a mile from the walls, and in
many parts scattered into detached groups, between large stagnant pools of
water. I might have spared all the pains I had taken with my toilet; for not
an individual turned his head round to gaze at me, but all, intent on their
own business, allowed me to pass by without notice or remark.'[4]

The Emir, however, to whom El Kanemi had given him a letter of
introduction, welcomed him cordially and the Ghadamsi merchants
were embarrassingly pressing in their offers of financial accommodation to any amount in exchange for a bill on the British Consul
at Tripoli,[5] Mr. Frederick Warrington. The readiness of North
African merchants trading in the Sudan to provide Clapperton and
later travellers with financial assistance was probably partly due to
their anxiety to seize a rare opportunity to remit funds to the north,
for the absence of banking facilities made the transference of credits
a very difficult matter. On the other hand the accommodation was
only made possible by the unbounded confidence which the Arabs had
in the British Consul who was held in the highest repute over an

236 THE LIFTING OF THE VEIL

immense area. Barth tells us he was 'the most amiable possible specimen of an Arabianized European'.

In Kano Clapperton was led to believe that the Niger, or Kworra as it was called by the natives in its lower course, flowed into the sea at a place called Rakah,* in Yoruba, which was visited by the ships of the Christians. He attributed the reticence of the natives to their fear that if strangers learnt the course of the Kworra they would make their way from the coast to the interior and seize the country. In Kano he heard that Hornemann had died of dysentery in Nupe.

From Kano he travelled westwards to Sokoto, where his reception was wholly gratifying to his vanity. It is surprising to find that Clapperton, who had just arrived from the now far more imposing Kano, considered Sokoto the most populous city he had visited in the interior of Africa, an opinion which he still held on his second visit some years later.[7] Muhammad Bello, in spite of slight annoyance at Denham's escapade in Mandara, gave Clapperton a cordial welcome. He was very anxious to establish friendly relations with the British whose ships he wanted to visit Rakah and open up trade with his country. He was particularly insistent that the King of England should send a consul and a physician to reside permanently at Sokoto.

Clapperton's intention was to continue his journey to Yauri and Nupe to explore the Niger, and Bello promised his assistance. Unfortunately the Arab merchants of Sokoto, perceiving how prejudicial to their own interests Bello's project of opening the country to British trade would be, persuaded the Sultan to change his attitude with the result that Clapperton soon found every sort of hindrance put in the way of further progress. His oft repeated insistence that the price of the King of England's friendship would be the abolition of the slave trade with the coast probably contributed not a little to his difficulties.

At Clapperton's request Bello had a map prepared showing the course of the lower Niger. Although the Sultan had stated it flowed into the sea at Fundah, which, he said, was a little below his port of Rakah, the map showed it flowing into the Nile of Egypt. This accorded with what Denham had learnt in Bornu, but Clapperton still felt sure that the termination of the Niger really lay in the Gulf of Guinea.

Reluctantly forced to abandon his project of reaching the Niger, he rejoined Denham in Bornu and returned with him to England. He

---

* Rakah, which has disappeared from modern maps, was situated near the junction of the Moshi with the Niger.[6]

THE LIFTING OF THE VEIL

carried a friendly letter from Bello addressed to George IV in which the Fulani Sultan agreed to prohibit the export of slaves to the coast and proposed that a British ship should go to Rakah and open up trade with his country.

The British Government had every reason to be well satisfied with the excellent work accomplished by Clapperton and Denham. Not only had they added considerably to the geographical knowledge of the interior, but they had reported very favourably on the opportunities for commercial expansion which had now become the primary reason for the Government's interest in African exploration.

Accordingly in 1825 the Government sent out another mission under Clapperton accompanied by four Europeans including his servant Richard Lander.[8] Finding to their disappointment that no one on the coast had ever heard of Rakah or Fundah, both of which Bello had said were seaports, they landed at Badagry and set off for the north. Of Clapperton's companions one had landed at Whydah and was never heard of again and two others died soon after leaving Badagry. There remained only Lander with whom he travelled northwards through the great Yoruba town of Oyo or Katunga to the Niger, which they reached at Busa, where he was unable to obtain any information regarding Park's death.

The journey through the forest belt had left Clapperton and Lander so badly shaken in health that had they been men of less determination they would certainly have turned back. They made their way to Kano and after spending a month here Clapperton set out alone for Sokoto, where the lack of cordiality in his reception was in marked contrast with the friendliness he had enjoyed on his former visit. The change was largely due to a rumour (probably put about by his old enemies the Arab merchants) that the English meant to dispossess the Fulani and that Clapperton was their spy. Clapperton was soon rejoined by Lander who found his master completely broken in health. He died on 13 April 1827 and was buried in the neighbouring village of Jangebe. Although his achievements had been less spectacular than those of his fellow countryman, Mungo Park, his contributions to human knowledge were scarcely less important. In his two journeys he had traversed the continent from Tripoli to the coast of Guinea and had been the first European to reach the Western Sudan from the south.

Richard Lander, in failing health and almost destitute, made his way back to Kano. From there he set out for Fundah, which was situated at the confluence of the Niger and the Benue, where he

238 THE LIFTING OF THE VEIL

intended to embark and follow the river to its termination which he, like his master, believed to be in the Bight of Benin. When nearing the river in full expectation of solving the greatest geographical problem of the day he was compelled to return to Zaria. He eventually reached the coast at Badagry, secured a passage, and arrived in England in April 1828.

The expedition had been costly in human life and disappointing in results. Hopes of establishing trade with the Fulani had been shattered and little additional light had been thrown on the mystery of the Niger. Although both Clapperton and Lander had been convinced that it flowed into the Bight of Benin, many still believed that a 'deep range of granite mountains' intervened between the sea and the lowest known point on its course, and they therefore refused to accept such an hypothesis. Amongst them was General Sir Rufane Donkin whose *Dissertation on the Course and probable Termination of the Niger*, published in 1829, lent a certain amount of humour to the controversy. Completely regardless of all that the great explorers had lately accomplished in the field, he sought to prove with a wealth of quotations from the classics that the Niger flowed into the Mediterranean in the Gulf of Syrtis! This was too much even for *The Quarterly Review* which had interested itself deeply in the controversy and had enthusiastically championed every theory in turn. It heaped ridicule on the General who replied 'with a great deal of very coarse language', but he was happily silenced by the final solution to the problem in the following year.

Richard Lander, without advantages of birth or education, was eager to return to Africa to complete the work which he had commenced in the service of Clapperton. With the promise of a paltry reward of £100 on his return and of an allowance of £25 a quarter to his wife during his absence, he entered the service of the Government and set out for Africa accompanied by his brother John who was refused any sort of remuneration. His orders were to make his way to Busa and from there to follow the river to Fundah where he was to see whether the river flowed into any lake or swamp. If he should explode the old Wangara myth he was to follow the river to the sea, or, if the river turned eastwards, to Lake Chad.

The two Landers reached Busa in the middle of 1830 and after considerable delay set out down the Niger. They reached the confluence of the Benue without opposition but near Asaba they were captured by Ibos. They at last recovered their liberty and made their

THE LIFTING OF THE VEIL 239

way down the river to the sea. They reached England in June 1831 and announced the solution to the problem which had puzzled the world for so many centuries.[9]

. . . .

In the meantime a solution had also been found to the only other West African mystery which really interested the civilized world. This was the situation of the mysterious city of Timbuktu. Till then nothing had happened to dispel the highly coloured picture which Leo had painted of this remote city. The public imagination had been further excited by exaggerated accounts of the arrival in Morocco of gold-laden caravans and its discovery was eagerly awaited on both sides of the Atlantic.

In 1825 another adventurous Scot, Major Gordon Laing, set out from Tripoli to discover Timbuktu and explore the upper waters of the Niger. From Tripoli he travelled across the desert through Ghadames to In Salah, where he struck an important caravan route running south-west to Timbuktu. After nearly dying of wounds received in an affray with Tuareg, he entered Timbuktu in August 1826, fifteen months after leaving Tripoli. Unfortunately his arrival coincided with the capture of the city by the fanatical Fulani of Massina. Shehu Ahmadu resented the presence of the infidel, and Laing, after spending a month in the city, was ordered to leave. Forced to abandon his project of continuing his journey up the Niger he set out again for the north. Two days from Timbuktu he was treacherously murdered by the Berabish escort who had undertaken to conduct him safely across the desert. All the papers of this gallant explorer perished with him, and, except for the information contained in letters sent back on his outward journey and in native reports collected by subsequent explorers, we know little about his fine journey which ended so tragically. The world consequently had still to wait for the long-hoped-for account of Timbuktu.

But it did not have to wait long. The year after Laing's death Réné Caillié, an impecunious young Frenchman of humble origin, started out from the Rio Nunez to realize his long-cherished ambition of discovering Timbuktu. Disguising himself as an Arab he crossed Futa Jallon and made his way to Jenne. From there he continued his journey by canoe down the Niger to Kabara whence he rode into Timbuktu a year after he had left the coast.

Caillié's conception of Timbuktu had been that of the masses, and his satisfaction at reaching his goal was inevitably tinged with

240

THE LIFTING OF THE VEIL

disappointment. 'I had formed', he tells us, 'a totally different idea of the grandeur and wealth of Timbuctoo. The city presented, at first view, nothing but a mass of ill-looking houses, built of earth.'[10] There was no sign of Leo's 'stately temple' nor of the 'princely palace also built by a most excellent workman of Granada'. Nor was there any evidence of the king of Timbuktu possessing 'many plates and sceptres of gold . . . and a magnificent and well-furnished court'. In almost every respect reality fell far short of what Leo had described, but that 'salt is verie scarce heere' proved to be true enough. Caillié found Barbary merchants amassing fortunes by importing salt from Taodeni and European trade goods from Morocco, Tunis, and Tripoli.

After spending a fortnight in Timbuktu he continued his journey northwards, travelling through Arawan and Taghaza in company with a caravan of 1,400 camels taking slaves, gold, ivory, gum, ostrich feathers, and cloth to Tafilelt. After enduring intense privations in the desert and more than once narrowly escaping death he reached Fez in safety and from there made his way to the coast where he secured a passage to Toulon. Although those who are ever ready to discredit any traveller's tale were not wanting, his remarkable journey —for which he had been singularly ill equipped—received the recognition it so richly deserved.

.   .   .   .

Up to the middle of the eighteenth century every attempt by Europeans to explore the interior of northern Africa had been inspired by desire for gain and had failed miserably. Then had come the more worthy appeal of scientific research. A brilliant band of explorers penetrated, but did not lift, the veil which had for so long obscured the interior. These stirring achievements had excited the interest of the whole civilized world. But after curiosity had been satisfied by the solution of the problems of the course and termination of the Niger and by the disappointing discovery that Timbuktu was in reality only a large collection of mud huts, interest in this part of Africa quickly evaporated. It was forgotten that vast areas, which included the greater part of the course of the Niger, had yet to be revealed.

The remoter parts of the continent provided strong counter attractions. In the south Livingstone was exploring the Zambezi, and Krapf and Redmann were revealing to an astounded world snow-capped peaks on the equator. Equally sensational were the reports of east coast Arabs of a great inland sea in the heart of the continent

THE LIFTING OF THE VEIL

which had been supposed to be 'a scene of everlasting drought, under the perpetual, unclouded blaze of a vertical sun'.

While the gaze of the civilized world was directed upon the band of intrepid explorers who were revealing the secrets of the southern part of the continent, there arrived in England, almost unnoticed, a weary traveller who had spent five perilous years in the interior of north-western Africa exploring the unknown lands of the Niger basin. This man was Dr. Henry Barth, a young German whose remarkable book, *Travels and Discoveries in North and Central Africa*, still remains the most valuable contribution ever made to the literature of north-western Africa. The importance of Barth's work has never received the recognition it deserves, and therefore we shall do well to consider it here in greater detail than might otherwise seem justified.

In 1849 the British Government had decided to send an expedition under James Richardson to negotiate commercial treaties with the chiefs of north-western Africa. Their offer to allow a German traveller to join the expedition had been eagerly accepted by Barth, a young lecturer at the University of Berlin who had a remarkable gift for languages.

The mission left Tripoli for the interior in March 1850, and was joined at the last moment by another young German, a geologist named Overweg. In the middle of the Sahara the three travellers separated with the intention of meeting again in the Sudan. Barth travelled to Air and spent some time in Agades whence he continued his journey to Hausa. Here he realized his long-cherished ambition of visiting Kano, 'the emporium of Central Africa', as he called it.

Barth arrived in Kano almost destitute, but he persuaded the Emir to give him 60,000 cowries which enabled him to buy camels and so to continue his journey to Bornu. Kano and Bornu were at war and the caravan road was so notoriously unsafe that only one of his men, a stranger to the country, would accompany him. Before he reached Kukawa he received news of Richardson's death and assumed command of the expedition. One of the principal objects of the mission was to negotiate a commercial treaty with the powerful Sultan of Bornu, and Barth spent much of his time in Kukawa studying the trade of the country. He quickly found that a keen desire for commercial intercourse with Europe, as a means of obtaining firearms, was tempered by fear of the well-known hostility of the English to the slave trade for which the arms were required.

THE LIFTING OF THE VEIL

Overweg rejoined Barth in Kukawa and was sent to explore Lake Chad with a boat which had been brought with great difficulty across the Sahara. Meanwhile Barth set out for Adamawa in search of the upper waters of the Benue, the Niger's greatest tributary, then only known in its lower reaches. He reached Yola and set eyes upon the upper Benue, an incident which he described as one of the proudest moments of his life. Unfortunately he carried only Bornuese credentials which were ill received by the Fulani of Yola, so he had to retreat precipitately. His discovery of the upper Benue, however, was an event of importance, and constituted one of his chief contributions to geographical knowledge.

Barth returned to Kukawa and spent some time exploring Kanem, Mandara, and Bagarmi, and witnessed some of the horrors of the slave trade and the intense human misery it caused. He now found himself again in a state of extreme destitution, and decided to abandon his plan of travelling eastwards to the Nile. But just as he was preparing to return to England he unexpectedly received dispatches from Lord Palmerston and a supply of dollars which enabled the mission to continue its work. The dispatches blandly invited Barth to endeavour to reach Timbuktu. He was entirely unprepared for this proposal, but it appealed to his enterprising spirit and he dwelt with delight upon the thought of 'succeeding in the field of the glorious career of Mungo Park'.

Before Barth was able to set out for Timbuktu, Overweg fell suddenly ill and died. Having buried the last of his companions, Barth travelled westwards from Kukawa, passing through Zinder, Katsina, and Kano to Sokoto and Gwandu. It was in Gwandu that he discovered a copy of the now famous *Tarikh es Sudan*, till then unknown to students. In June 1853 Barth crossed the Niger at the important town of Say. Finding himself in a very turbulent country, he was forced to continue his journey in disguise. Although he had habitually travelled in Arab dress under the name of Abdul Karim, he had never attempted to conceal his faith. But greater caution was necessary in the Bend of the Niger. The fanatical Fulani of Massina were at war with their Tuareg and Arab neighbours, and the country was consequently so disturbed that there was no hope of an undisguised Christian being allowed to pass through it.

Barth reached Timbuktu safely, but his health, which had already caused him anxiety, now grew rapidly worse. Moreover, the fact of his being a Christian soon became known and he again found him-

THE LIFTING OF THE VEIL 243

self in a position of grave peril. His spirited defence of his own faith and his profound knowledge of both the Christian and Muslim religions won him the respect of the more cultured citizens, so that he came to no physical harm. Happily he also enjoyed the protection of El Bekkai, the powerful sheikh of the Kunta Arabs who, with their Berabish and Tuareg allies, were for the time being in the ascendancy over the Fulani. He was able to apply himself to exploring Timbuktu, of which Caillié had brought back very little information, but he was gravely hampered by the ferment which his presence was causing.

Political feeling in Timbuktu was running very high. The control of the city was at the time, as so frequently in its history, a matter of dispute between the desert tribes, now under the leadership of El Bekkai, and the Fulani of Massina. Open warfare was prevented by a fairly equal division of forces, neither side daring to risk an engagement. The advent of a Christian threw the town into a worse turmoil. The Fulani leader, a son of Seku Ahmadu, demanded his surrender from El Bekkai, who fortunately for Barth, more or less controlled the situation within the city and refused to comply. Attempts were made to take Barth dead or alive but they all failed.

He spent altogether eight months in Timbuktu and the surrounding solitudes. During the whole of this period he enjoyed the friendship of El Bekkai who, in spite of every consideration of self-interest, stubbornly refused to withhold his protection from the Christian. Six years later, when the victorious Tuculor warrior, El Hadj Omar, was threatening Timbuktu, El Bekkai sent a mission across the Sahara to Tripoli to seek help from Queen Victoria, whom he had learnt from Barth to be the most powerful European monarch.[11] To-day his body lies in a tomb which the French erected in recognition of his services to civilization as the protector of Barth. It is also the resort of pilgrims, for his services to his own people were not less than those he rendered to the lonely Christian.

Barth was eventually able to seize an opportunity of setting out on his homeward journey. Travelling down the left bank of the Niger he made his way to Hausa which, he declared, 'amongst all the tracts that I have visited in Negroland I had found the most agreeable for a foreigner to reside in'. He continued his journey eastwards to Bornu and recrossed the Sahara. He arrived in Tripoli in August 1855 after over five years' absence during which he had done as much as any of his predecessors to reveal the secrets of the interior.

The extent of Barth's achievement was little appreciated in

THE LIFTING OF THE VEIL

England. On his return to London a kindly reception by Lords Palmerston and Clarendon was the only mark of favour shown him by the Government he had served so well and which had spent little over £1,000 on the expedition. (There could be no more striking proof of Barth's loyalty to his alien masters than El Bekkai's attempt to enlist the sympathy of Queen Victoria in his hour of need.) To its lasting credit the Royal Geographical Society accorded him their highest award.

But Barth's name remained unknown to the general public. The departure of the expedition had received some notice in the press, and a rumour of Barth's death had subsequently been reported and afterwards denied in *The Times*. But that newspaper, like the rest of the press, recorded neither the successful termination of the mission nor Barth's return to London. So slight was the interest of the British public in western Africa at this period that the publishers printed only 2,250 copies of the first three volumes of Barth's *Travels* and only 1,000 copies of the last two.[12]

Yet those five volumes provided an extraordinarily complete account of the Western Sudan. The great mass of geographical, ethnological, and linguistic information which they contained was presented with truly marvellous accuracy. The same scholarly discrimination had been exercised in compiling the abundant historical data which greatly enhanced the value of the work.

The purely geographical results of Barth's expedition alone should have ensured him lasting fame. Besides discovering the upper Benue he was the first to describe the middle course of the Niger which none but Park had seen. With great accuracy he had plotted on the map rivers and mountains and scores of towns, many of which had never been heard of before. His itineraries of the trade routes of the interior were singularly complete. But he unfortunately could offer no spectacular discovery to excite the interest of the public. It remained for later generations to realize that it was Henry Barth who had finally lifted the veil which others had only penetrated.

THE LIFTING OF THE VEIL

REFERENCES

1. C. G. Reichard, *Ephémérides Géographiques*, Weimar, August 1803.

2. James McQueen, *A Geographical and Commercial View of Northern Central Africa*, Edinburgh, 1821.

3. Capt. F. G. Lyon, R.N., *A Narrative of Travels in Northern Africa*, London, 1821, p. 148.

4. Denham and Clapperton, *Travels*, ii. 237.

5. Ibid. 244.

6. E. A. Reeves. Letter to the Author.

7. Capt. Hugh Clapperton, *Journal of a Second Expedition into the Interior of Africa*, London, 1829, p. 207.

8. Ibid., p. xi.

9. Richard and John Lander, op. cit.

10. René Caillié, *Travels through Central Africa to Timbuctoo*, English trans., London, 1830, ii. 49.

11. M. Delafosse, op. cit., ii. 317.

12. Longmans, Green & Co. Letter to the Author.

XXII

THE GREAT CARAVANS

'*Trading is the true test of man, and it is in the operations of trade that his piety and religious worth become known.*'—KHALIF 'UMAR.

THE foregoing chapters have shown what an important part trade played in the history of the interior. It bridged the Sahara, linking Barbary with the Sudan, it was the chief vehicle by which civilization reached the Sudanese and it largely inspired the achievements by which, after centuries of disappointment, the interior was ultimately revealed to Europeans. But in the subversive effects of the European occupation, now fast approaching, no sphere of human activity was more completely revolutionized than trade. That this should have been so was inevitable, for the European had always been rigorously excluded and only by right of conquest was he finally able to open new outlets to the coast and thus divert trade from the ancient caravan routes.

As long as the peoples of the interior remained masters of their own destiny trade continued to follow with little interruption the channels through which it had flowed since before the dawn of history. Moreover, because politics were seldom allowed seriously to disturb its course, the conditions of commercial life had probably changed very little since their stimulation by the Arab invasions. We shall do well therefore to take a brief glance at the trade of the interior as the great explorers found it, and while its general conditions remained much as they had been throughout history.

In the first half of the nineteenth century the greater part of the caravan traffic between Barbary and the Western Sudan was still concentrated on the three great trade routes which must be numbered among the oldest highways in the world—the Taghaza–Timbuktu road in the west, the Ghadames–Air road to Hausa in the centre, and in the east the Fezzan–Kawar road to Bornu. On each of these roads there were long waterless stages which heavily laden caravans could only cross at great peril. Nevertheless the test of time had proved them the safest routes for merchants, besides being also the shortest. Each represented about two months' journey for a camel caravan. Lesser roads came into use periodically only to be abandoned

THE GREAT CARAVANS
247

through failure of wells or pasturage, or through the hostility of the nomads. On the three ancient highways there was greater certainty of finding water where it was expected, and in the face of this compelling circumstance neither desert politics nor blackmail could force the toiling caravans of merchants permanently to forsake them. They had endured through the ages and were the channels along which culture reached the Sudanese.

The greatest of the three was the Taghaza–Timbuktu road, pre-eminent as a trade route, and still more important as a cultural highway. The destruction of Sijilmasa in the closing years of the previous century had deprived this road of its historic northern terminus. Its place had to some extent been taken by the neighbouring town of Abuam, but much of the trade had left Tafilelt and gone to In Salah, the capital of Tuat. The rest, and perhaps the greater part, of the old trade of Sijilmasa had been diverted westwards to Wady Nun, which was situated near the coast a few miles from Cape Nun.

Merchants trading from Wady Nun and Abuam with the Sudan travelled through Akka, which had inherited from Sijilmasa the business of fitting out and equipping the trans-Saharan caravans, and thence along the old road through Taghaza and Taodeni to Timbuktu. Instead of turning westwards at Taodeni to Walata (which was now in decay, like Wadan, though still noted for the skill of its goldsmiths) the road followed the more direct route through Arawan. Here it was joined by two other roads; one running from Tuat to Timbuktu through Mabruk; another coming from Sansanding on the upper Niger. Centuries of traffic had not lessened the dangers of this road. In 1805 a caravan of 2,000 men and 1,800 camels perished of thirst in the desert when returning from Timbuktu, not a man or beast being saved.[1]

The Taghaza road, which was controlled by the Berabish Arabs, owed its long-continued prosperity to the unequal distribution of gold and salt in the interior. Medieval Europe knew that the gold of the Saharan caravans came from an unknown country in the Sudan which they called Wangara. We now know that this Wangara was the country which extends across the upper Senegal basin from the Faleme to the Niger and includes the provinces of Bambuk, Bure, Manding, and Gangaran, the last being a variant of the name Wangara. Alluvial gold is very widely distributed throughout this region which was the principal, but not the only, source of the gold which for so many centuries flowed freely northwards across the Sahara and not less

248 THE GREAT CARAVANS

abundantly, though for a shorter period, through the European trading factories on the western Guinea coast.

Some of this gold probably came also from Lobi on the Black Volta river where there are gold workings of great age. Farther south, moreover, there were the famous Ashanti goldfields. Since the fifteenth century the principal outlet for Ashanti gold has been the sea-coast, but before that much must have found its way into the Sudan, especially to Gao, by the roads which since very early times have been used by the kola nut traders.

But of all the districts which contributed to the Saharan gold trade Bambuk was the richest. Early in the history of the exploration of the coast reports of the wealth of this district had reached European ears. We have already seen that in the sixteenth century it had been visited by a band of Portuguese adventurers who had perished without turning their discovery to account. It was not till the first half of the eighteenth century that it was rediscovered by the French, then actively trading on the Senegal, but their repeated attempts to exploit the goldfields all ended in failure.

Neither Park nor Caillié nor the pioneers who had preceded them realized that these goldfields were the Wangara of history. So the discovery of the African El Dorado continued to exercise men's minds, exciting nearly as many conflicting theories as the problem of the termination of the Niger. In 1824 Dupuis, influenced and consequently misled by Leo, announced his opinion that the ancient Wangara extended along the coast from Ashanti in the west, across Dahomey, to the Cross river in the east. 'Wonderful as it may seem,' he declared, 'that we should have actually colonized the country for many ages past, without every having known it even by name.'[2] A year or two later Denham came to the conclusion in the course of his travels that there was no such place as Wangara. 'All gold countries,' he wrote, 'as well as any people coming from the gold country, or bringing Goroo nuts, are called Wangara.'[3] This was half true for Wangara is the name by which Mandingo traders, whose enterprise carries them very far afield, are widely known in the Sudan, especially to the Hausas. Even Barth failed to realize that Wangara was Bambuk. In one map he sought vaguely to identify it with Lobi and Ashanti; in another he placed it with fair accuracy on the Senegal.

The comparative silence which followed the discovery of the Bambuk goldfields was in striking contrast with the keen interest which they had excited in Europe for so many centuries. This was not so

THE GREAT CARAVANS

much due to the failure of Europeans to recognize them as the famous Wangara, nor was it due to lack of gold, but rather to failure to exploit them profitably owing to their remoteness from the coast, the difficulties of transport, and the necessity of having to restrict work, as Idrisi had described, to four months in the year.

It is unlikely that so many centuries of trade had not reduced the richness of the Wangara mines. Nevertheless gold was, and still is, constantly being washed down from the highlands by the Faleme and its tributaries so that gravels which have been worked to exhaustion are found after three or four years' rest to have become rich again. This gave rise to the native belief that gold travelled mysteriously of its own accord; it may also be the origin of the legend, mentioned by Yaqut, that gold grew like carrots. After the seventeenth century we hear less about gold passing through Jenne and Timbuktu to Morocco; but the trade continued, though on an ever-dwindling scale, for the next 200 years.[4]

El Bekri's statement that the Ferawi used to exchange gold for an equal amount of salt[5] was probably not a gross exaggeration. We find a similar statement about Mali on certain Jewish maps of the early sixteenth century,[6] which may or may not have been a repetition of El Bekri. But less than a century ago a European traveller in these parts found himself so short of salt that he was fully prepared to make such a bargain.[7] It is impossible for those who have not witnessed it to realize how intense is the craving for salt amongst those to whom an adequate supply is denied. In the Western Sudan it was universally a luxury which only the rich could regularly enjoy.

With the exception of the salt pans of the Dallul Fogha in Dendi, which were only capable of supplying the requirements of a very small area, scarcely any natural salt occurs in the Western Sudan. Where the natives were unable to import it they obtained it from the ashes of grasses, millet stalks, and shrubs, and also from cattle dung. But these inadequate sources of supply were never equal to the needs of the people.

Up to the end of the sixteenth century the countries of the middle Niger were almost wholly dependent on the salt pans of Taghaza for their supplies. It will be recollected that in 1585 the Songhai, driven out of Taghaza by the Moors, began to work the now famous deposits at Taodeni, which thereafter became the principal source of salt for the middle Niger. It was carried at least as far upstream as Bamako, which Park found being supplied from Taodeni and with sea salt from

THE GREAT CARAVANS

the Rio Grande.[8] Salt was also obtained from Sebka d'Ijil in the north-west, which was known as Taghaza el Gharbie or West Taghaza.[9]

Although Taghaza and Taodeni had inexhaustible stores of salt their customers often found them very unreliable sources on which to depend for this essential to the well-being of man. Being situated in the heart of the desert and defenceless against marauders, the salt pans were often the prey of raiders so that in times of turbulence there was grave risk of no salt reaching the Sudan. Moreover the labourers who dug the salt were wholly dependent for their subsistence on passing caravans whose comings and goings were necessarily very irregular. Their miserable lot at Taghaza was graphically described by Leo. 'Neither haue the said diggers of salt any victuals,' he wrote, 'but such as the merchants bring vnto them . . . insomuch that oftentimes they perish for lacke of foode, whenas the merchants come not in due time vnto them.'[10] The passage of time does not seem to have brought much improvement. As recently as the year 1910 no less than fifty-six people died of starvation at Taodeni owing to the failure of a caravan to arrive in time to save them.[11]

Timbuktu owed as much to gold and salt as did the great highway of which it was the southern terminus. Neither growing nor manu-facturing anything, it depended on imports for its food and on foreign trade for its prosperity. It was essentially an entrepôt. The important position it had for so long held in the commercial life of the interior was chiefly due to its situation at the point where the Niger is most accessible from the Maghreb and its outpost, the oasis of Tuat.

Timbuktu was served by three important routes. Firstly the water-way of the Niger from Sansanding and Jenne, the two markets on which the city depended for its supplies of rice and millet, and whence came gold and slaves and ivory and kola nuts; secondly the ancient Taghaza road; and lastly the Tuat road which led through Ghat to Ghadames, the merchants of which occupied a predominant position in the trade of the interior. In Barth's time Timbuktu was importing kola nuts from Tangrela, far away in the *hinterland* of the Ivory Coast, Manchester cottons and English cutlery from Mogador, and it was in touch with the trading factories on the Senegal and Gambia rivers through Sansanding and Bamako. Such was the imposing scale on which this desert city conducted its foreign trade.

The Ghadames–Air road is probably not less ancient than the Taghaza road. Where it passes over rocky ground the deeply worn tracks clearly indicate its immense age and the great amount of traffic

THE GREAT CARAVANS

it carried. The route it followed seems never to have varied. Between Ghadames and Ghat it was, in the first half of last century, controlled by the fierce Azger Tuareg. Between Ghat and Air, where it passes over one of the worst bits of desert in the world, it was controlled by the Kel Owi. Half-way it was joined at In Azawa, or Asiu, by the Tuat road to Air which passed through the Ahaggar massif and was controlled by the Ahaggar Tuareg. The main road entered Air at Iferuan. This was an important junction, for here the road was joined by the old pilgrim way from Timbuktu which entered Air at In Gall, passing thence through In Azawa, Ghat, Murzuk, Augila, and Siwa to Cairo. Agades, which dates only from the fifteenth century, lies off the main road, a few miles to the west. Owing to the country surrounding the city being unsuitable for heavily laden camels the road has never been diverted to pass through the capital. This road used to end at Katsina. But when, as the result of the Fulani *jihad*, Kano rose to occupy the predominant commercial position, the latter became the southern terminus of the road which was diverted eastwards through Zinder. Between Kano and Air it was controlled by the Kel Geres.

In the days when Gao was the capital of a rich empire, Agades occupied an important position, for it was the chief entrepôt for the gold trade between Gao and Tripoli. The capture of Gao by the Moors killed this trade and Agades consequently fell into decay. Politically it continued to occupy an important position and its situation close to the great trans-Saharan caravan road between Ghadames and Hausa always ensured it a certain amount of foreign trade.

What little prosperity remained to Agades in the nineteenth century was derived principally from the salt trade. The grazing grounds of Air were constantly thronged with camels and it was this abundant supply of transport which enabled the people of Agades to control the salt trade with Hausa. A remarkable feature of this trade was the gigantic caravan, known as the *Taghalam* or *Azalai*, which set out from Air every autumn to bring salt from Bilma, the chief town of the Kawar oasis. Probably nowhere else in the world could be found a commercial enterprise comparable with the spectacular scale on which the *Azalai* was conducted. As recently as 1908, when it was in its decline, it numbered no less than 20,000 camels.[12]

Elaborate preparations preceded the departure of the *Azalai*. The assemblage of so many camels took a long time. They congregated at Tabello in central Air where there was sufficient grazing to condition

THE GREAT CARAVANS

the animals for the arduous journey before them. Although the round journey to Kawar and back took only three weeks, the endurance which it demanded was so great that the losses of camels were very heavy and vast numbers of skeletons marked the route of the *Azalai*. This immense caravan, moreover, was such a vulnerable body that it was frequently raided by those Tuareg who were not participating, and it sometimes suffered heavy losses at their hands. Most of the camels of the Azalai belonged to the Kel Geres and the Itesan.*

One of the principal duties of the Amenokal's vizier, the Sarkin Turawa of Agades, was to conduct the *Azalai* in person. It set out in October and carried, besides corn and cloth to barter for the salt, immense quantities of forage, for there was no grazing in Kawar where the few local camels were fed on dates. Fachi, an outpost of Kawar, was reached in five days, and there the *Azalai* was joined by a caravan from Damagaram. It entered Bilma three days later. By a curious and unexplained phenomenon the 'singing' of a neighbouring peak used to give the people of Bilma two days' warning of the approach of the *Azalai* or of any other exceptionally large caravan coming from the west.[14]

The return to Air was made by the same route, the camels carrying a few dates besides immense quantities of salt. After a rest in Agades a large part of the *Azalai*, with the Sarkin Turawa still at its head, travelled south to Sokoto and thence to Kano where salt was sold for distribution all over Hausa and beyond. The camels returned from Kano to Air loaded with cloth and corn.

Kano was at this time by far the most important commercial city in the interior, not excepting Timbuktu. The population, predominantly Hausa, but with a large foreign element which included a rich colony of Tripolitan Arabs, was estimated by Barth at 30,000, but with the coming of the dry season and the opening of the trade routes this number was doubled by the influx of traders. Kano enjoyed the advantage of being the centre of a rich agricultural district which produced all the requirements of a teeming native population and a considerable surplus of corn for export. But the real foundation of its extraordinary commercial prosperity was the industry and skill of the Hausa craftsmen whose wares were in demand all over northern and western Africa. The most important trade was that in cotton cloth, woven and dyed in Kano, Katsina, Zaria, and neighbouring towns.

* All the older and more remarkable buildings in Air are attributed to the Itesan.[13]

THE GREAT CARAVANS

253

'The great advantage of Kano', wrote Barth, 'is that commerce and manufactures go hand in hand, and that almost every family has its share in them. There is really something grand in this kind of industry, which spreads to the north as far as Murzuk, Ghat, and even Tripoli; to the west, not only to Timbuktu, but in some degree even as far as the shores of the Atlantic, the very inhabitants of Arguin dressing in the cloth woven and dyed in Kano; to the east, all over Bornu, although there it comes into contact with the native industry of the country; and to the south it . . . is only limited by the nakedness of the pagan *sans-culottes*, who do not wear clothing.'[15]

The slave trade was a considerable item in the commerce of Kano, about 5,000 slaves being exported annually to Ghat, Fezzan, Bornu, and southwards to Nupe, whence some probably found their way to the Christian slave ships on the coast.

Most of the imports into Kano came down the Air road and the rest through Kawar and Bornu. They consisted principally of a coarse kind of silk from Tripoli and a wide range of European trade goods. The latter included cottons from Manchester, French silks, glass beads from Venice and Trieste, paper, mirrors, and needles from Nuremberg, sword blades from Solingen,* razors from Styria, besides quantities of spices, sugar, and tea. Kano was also the chief entrepôt in this part of the Sudan for the important trades in salt from Bilma, already described, kola nuts from Gwanja in the *hinterland* of the Gold Coast, and natron from Lake Chad.

The valuable trade in kola nuts, most of which came from Gwanja, was largely controlled by the people of Kano. This nut, known to the natives and the early Arab explorers as *goro*, had been in use in the Western Sudan since very early times.† The twin interlocking kernels were regarded as symbolic of friendship and no present was complete unless it included kolas. Consequently they acquired a kind of ceremonial importance and it became customary to swear oaths on a kola nut. The curiously bitter flavour not only appeals strongly to the palate of the native, but it has the property of making the foulest water taste sweet after chewing the nut. Kolas are undoubtedly very sustaining and they are widely regarded among the natives as a cure for impotency. They are transported immense distances, but they need great care for they perish easily if neglected and this always kept their price high. Nevertheless so greatly were they appreciated that

---

* Many of the sword blades still used in the Western Sudan bear such well-known Solingen marks as the 'wolf' and the 'orb and cross.'

† Leo seems to have thought that kola nuts were the fruit of the baobab tree.[16]

THE GREAT CARAVANS

from at first being only a luxury of the rich, they became virtually a necessity to a very large part of the population.

The kola nut was one of at least three articles which used to travel the whole distance from the coastal belt of Guinea to the shores of the Mediterranean, where the nuts were sold at a dollar apiece. Glass beads from Venice and unwrought silk from Tripoli found their way to Gwanja, where they were exchanged for kolas, and to Badagry on the Slave coast. The latter was the most important trading port on the west coast of Africa and had become the chief centre of the European slave trade. It was divided into British, Spanish, Portuguese, and French quarters and there was a large Hausa colony trading between Kano and the coast.

Between Kano and Badagry there was no single well-defined trade route. These two places were separated by a belt of dense bush and rain forest, peopled by Yorubas and many lesser pagan tribes, mutually hostile and constantly in a state of political instability. The tracks running through this belt were consequently liable to be closed to traders at frequent intervals. Instead of flowing freely along a well-known road trade tended to percolate along a variety of ill-defined tracks. It was this belt of pagan forest which for so many centuries proved an impenetrable barrier to Europeans trading on the coast.

In these disturbed regions, as in the Sahara, it was necessary for traders to travel together in large bodies for mutual protection. The caravans thus formed were sometimes several thousand strong with immense numbers of pack animals. The crossing of the Niger was a serious undertaking for such huge companies of traders and could only be accomplished where the necessary facilities existed. The riverain tribes had established ferries at suitable points and made large profits by levying tolls on the heavy traffic they attracted. The two principal ferries used by Hausa traders were at Rabba, near the modern Jebba, and at Komie (Wonjerque), just below Busa. There was a less important ferry upstream at Illo.

From the ferry at Komie one road ran north-east through Birnin Gwari and Zaria to Kano. Another well-known route followed the left bank of the Niger through Yauri into the north-western districts of Hausa, where it converged on an important kola route running in a north-easterly direction from Gwanja. The latter was an alternative route from the kola district to Kano, the crossing of the Niger being effected probably at Illo. These two, with a third coming from Wagadugu and Fadan Gurma, were the chief trade routes leading

THE GREAT CARAVANS

into Hausa from the west; they converged and met in the valley of the Gulbin Gindi, probably at or near Jega.

Barth tells us that Jega was 'the important place which, . . . on account of its mercantile importance, had attracted attention in Europe a good many years ago'.[17] Diligent search has failed to reveal how and when Jega came to attract attention in Europe at a period when so little was known of this part of Africa. It undoubtedly was an important place, but neither Clapperton nor Lander mentions it.

Jega occupied in Hausa and the surrounding country a commercial position second only to that of Kano. Like Bamako, Wagadugu, Fadan Gurma, Gaya, and Kano it was situated in very close proximity to the twelfth parallel of north latitude. It cannot be by mere coincidence that we find these six important markets and several lesser ones strung out along the same parallel. This line runs through the zone of parklands which separates the savannas from the forests. It roughly divides the *hyphaene* and date palms of the north from the oil palms of the south, and the humped from the humpless cattle. It approximately marks the southern limit of camel transport and the northern limit of the tsetse-fly. To the north of this line the population is predominantly Muhammadan, to the south mostly pagan.

Generally speaking this intermediate zone of parklands was peopled by tribes of mixed origins who made an outward display of Muslim culture, but at heart had strong pagan sympathies. The breadth and elasticity of their religious views generated in their towns an atmosphere favourable to trade between the slave raiding Muhammadan and the hunted pagan. The necessity for trade, which transcended all considerations of race and creed and politics, had to be satisfied and it seems that the twelfth parallel offered exceptionally favourable advantages for the growth of the necessary entrepôts. Here kolas, gold-dust, and slaves were exchanged for salt and natron and European trade goods from the far-distant north.

The position of Kano was not comparable with that of the other important markets on the twelfth parallel. Owing to the elevation of the plain of which it is the centre, Kano belongs geographically to the savannas rather than to the parklands. Although the greatest entrepôt of the interior it was primarily a centre of production and its prosperity was based on the skill and industry of its people and on the fertility of its soil rather than on the accident of geographical situation to which Jega owed its importance.

All the conditions which made it desirable as an entrepôt were to be

256 THE GREAT CARAVANS

found in Jega. Being free from tsetse it could be safely visited by the animal transport of the savannas. Situated at the head of perennial navigation on the Gulbin Gindi it could at all times be reached from the Niger by water and on this account was exceptionally accessible from the forests. Its inhabitants, the Gimbanawa, were an unprogressive people who professed Islamism but had marked pagan sympathies. The exceptional prosperity which they enjoyed cannot be said to have been due to any special effort on their part, for the whole of the trade of Jega was in the hands of foreign brokers.

Jega enjoyed the further advantage of being close to the salt mines of the Dallul Fogha. Its situation also enabled it to tap the trade of Gwanja and Badagry and to profit by the political importance of the twin Fulani capitals. Sokoto and Gwandu were too frequently disturbed by the clash of arms and the marshalling of troops to generate the tranquil atmosphere so necessary to trade. The religious fervour of the Fulani, moreover, was definitely discouraging to the cosmopolitan hordes of small traders who throng the great markets of the Sudan. With fanaticism within and turbulence without there was little enough to attract trade to Sokoto and Gwandu. But as they gradually became the centres of a wealthy population there was a need for a large and easily accessible market where the foreign trade of the country could be handled. This need was largely satisfied by Jega.

The ancient Fezzan–Kawar road was the last of the three great desert highways leading to the Western Sudan. This was the old Roman road from the Garamantes to the Aethiopians and its route can have altered little since Septimus Flaccus and Julius Maternus first led their troops down it into the interior.

The caravan traffic on this road had always been subject to periodical interruption owing to the turbulence of desert politics. The road was nominally controlled by the negroid Tebu of Tibesti whose hereditary and bitterly hated enemies were the Tuareg of Air. Raids and counter raids were constantly taking place across the road and when the Tuareg failed to capture Tebu herds they not infrequently consoled themselves with robbing passing caravans.

Although the salt of Bilma played a part in its life the Fezzan–Kawar road was essentially a slave route. Every European who travelled this bloodstained highway was profoundly impressed by the thousands of human skeletons, mostly those of women and girls, with which it was strewn.

Until the intervention of Christian powers in the middle of last

THE GREAT CARAVANS

century there had always been a large demand for negro slaves in the countries of the North African littoral. They were partly required for the local markets, but large numbers were exported to Egypt and Turkey. In the North African markets the highest prices were always paid for Hausa slaves on account of their good looks and their superior industry and intelligence. The Taghaza and the Ghadames–Air roads were both used by slave traders, but the part they played in the trade was small compared with the Fezzan–Kawar road; so much was this so, that in Denham's time foreign merchants trading with Bornu refused to accept payment for their trade goods in anything but slaves which consequently became the chief currency of the country.

The slave merchants took care in their own interests that their slaves were in good condition before they set out across the Sahara. The men, mostly youths, were coupled with leg-irons and were chained by the neck, but the women and girls were usually allowed to be free. Only the most robust survived the desert march and these were little better than living skeletons when they reached Fezzan. Here they were rested and fattened for the Tripoli market where prime slaves were sold at a profit of 500 per cent. Appalled though we may be by the horrors of the trans-Saharan slave traffic they were not equal, in the opinion of those qualified to draw the comparison, to those of the trade which Europeans carried on between the coast of Guinea and the West Indies.

The traffic in eunuchs was a particularly hideous branch of the slave trade of the interior. In the Sudan there was always a good demand for eunuchs as harem attendants. Consequently it was customary for the healthiest boys and youths captured in a slave raid to be gelded, and in Mossi it was the punishment meted out to incorrigible thieves. Owing to the hopeless lack of surgical skill not more than 10 per cent. survived.* The most noted sources of supply were Mossi and Bornu both of which enjoyed an international reputation in the trade. The Mossi people were supposed to be especially skilled in the operation and kept their methods a carefully guarded secret.[19] They and the Bornuese, besides supplying a considerable local demand, did a large export trade with Turkey and Egypt which, with the Barbary States, were the principal foreign markets. Perhaps it was

---

* Barth tells us that less than one in ten survived. A native of Kano once related to the author how he remembered a hundred Ningi pagans being gelded and ten surviving, which was considered as many as could be expected.[18]

THE GREAT CARAVANS

a deal in eunuchs which brought an embassy from the Sultan of Turkey to Bornu in the sixteenth century.[20] Leo once took part in this trade and tells us how he bought eunuchs from some wild tribes on the coast of Tripoli.

Repulsive though this trade seems we should remember before condemning the Sudanese for their barbarity that not only was it common throughout the Muhammadan world, but that it was long practised in Europe. During the Middle Ages large establishments, mostly under the direction of Jews, were maintained in France, notably at Verdun, for the supply of eunuchs to Muslim Spain.[21] A still more deplorable example were the *Soprani* of the Sistine chapel, 'the musical glory and the moral shame' of the papal choir. Although the *Soprani* were not finally abolished till late in the nineteenth century by Pope Leo XIII, the gelding of boys continued to be practised in Italy till even more recent times.

As the result of the enormous demand for slaves for export and for domestic use locally, the raiding of the hill and forest pagans became one of the principal dry-weather occupations of the Muhammadan tribes throughout the length and breadth of the Western Sudan. The young men and women would all be carried off to the slave markets, but usually the grown men, who always commanded a poor price, and often also the aged and infirm, who were unsaleable, were massacred in cold blood. All this ruthless savagery was perpetrated in the name of religion. As Lord Lugard has truly said, 'It is the most serious charge against Islam in Africa that it has encouraged and given religious sanction to slavery'.[22]

The abolition of the slave trade was one of the changes wrought by the coming European occupation which caused the decay of the trans-Saharan caravan routes. It was not that these roads relied so much on the traffic which the trade provided, but the oases depended on slave labour to hold back the encroaching desert which was always threatening to engulf them. It was the negro Haratin and Bella, not the nomads, who carried on the cultivation by which the oases were preserved. Consequently with the increasing difficulty of securing fresh negro labour the Sahara crept in and the oases began to disappear.

A more potent factor in the destruction of the caravan routes was the competition of sea-borne trade. Once the interior had been thrown open from the coast of Guinea the gold, ivory, and ostrich feathers which had been the principal exports across the desert were conveyed

THE GREAT CARAVANS

to the northern markets by the more circuitous but safer and cheaper sea route. At the same time European salt began to flood the Sudanese markets, and this further sapped the trade of the ancient desert highways.

This reversal of the course of trade profoundly affected the political situation in the Sahara. The modest attempts at agriculture in the oases had always been an important economic factor in the life of the Tuareg and one which they could ill afford to lose. As transport agents and as convoyers, blackmailers, and raiders of caravans they were also very dependent on the carrying trade of the Sahara for a part of their livelihood. When these resources began gradually to melt away the narrow margin which in the desert divides starvation from plenty quickly vanished.

When the local means of subsistence became inadequate desperate need compelled the people of the desert to prey on each other and on the sedentary tillers of the oases and of the peripheral areas. A period of chronic disturbance supervened and the roads became so insecure that what little remained of the carrying trade of the Sahara was completely destroyed. Oases dwindled, wells fell in, and waterholes silted up. Through human neglect the sterility of the Sahara became more profound than ever before, and the ties which for countless ages had bound Barbary to the Western Sudan were for ever broken.

S 2

THE GREAT CARAVANS

REFERENCES

1. J. G. Jackson, *Empire of Morocco*, p. 239.
2. Joseph Dupuis, *Journal of a Residence in Ashantee*, London, 1824, p. xli.
3. Denham and Clapperton, *Travels*, ii. 85.
4. J. G. Jackson, op. cit., pp. 23, 116, 245.
5. El Bekri, p. 327.
6. De la Roncière, op. cit., i. 138.
7. A. Raffenal, *Nouveau Voyage dans le Pays des Nègres*, Paris, 1856, i. 284.
8. Mungo Park, *Travels*, 1816, i. 446.
9. J. G. Jackson, op. cit., p. 241.
10. Leo Africanus, iii. 800.
11. Meniaud, ii. 207.
12. M. Abadie, op. cit., p. 292.
13. F. R. Rodd, op. cit., p. 377.
14. Hanns Vischer, *Across the Sahara from Tripoli to Bornu*, London, 1910, p. 266.
15. H. Barth, *Travels*, ii. 126.
16. Leo Africanus, i. 174.
17. H. Barth, *Travels*, v. 325.
18. Ibid., ii. 290.
19. L. Marc, *Le Pays Mossi*, Paris, 1909, p. 171; *L'Anthropologie*, 1904, p. 679. F. Horneman, *Travels*, p. 114.
20. H. R. Palmer, *Sudanese Memoirs*, i. 69, 76.
21. R. Dozy, op. cit., p. 430.
22. Sir F. D. Lugard, *The Dual Mandate*, p. 365.

XXIII

SHEPHERD KINGS

'Every shepherd is an abomination unto the Egyptians.'—GENESIS xlvi. 34.

THE Sahara and the northern fringes of the Sudan form part of a zone of deserts and steppes which extend right across the Old World. This belt presents a striking example of geographical and historical uniformity. It has one story to tell—the conquest of agriculturalists by nomad herdsmen.

The vast steppes of Central Asia have repeatedly sent out hordes of pastoral nomads—Scythians, Aryans, Avars, Huns, Arabs, and Turks —whose conquests have shaken the world. The conquest of tillers by nomads has been an equally persistent feature of the history of the Western Sudan, but the preponderance of desert over steppe and the consequent paucity of pasture prevented the formation of vast hordes. Africa therefore never achieved a great historical movement.

A distinguished American writer has aptly described the Sudan as the Broadway of Africa.[1] Confined between two great barriers to ethnic movement—the Sahara on the north and the tropical forests on the south—the Sudan itself is strikingly free from physical obstructions. The dominating geographical feature is the immense course of the Niger which, far from being a barrier, is a great natural highway for land and water transport. The climate, always a factor of historical importance, is as unvarying as the relief. With no physical or climatic barriers to hinder them people have always travelled with ease up and down this vast corridor.

Such geographical uniformity is unfavourable to the early growth of civilization. It restricts the possibilities of development and tends towards a monotonous uniformity in human life, and towards ethnic fusion. It is because of their physical diversity, giving rise to a wide variety of peoples and cultures, that Europe and Asia have contributed to the history of civilization all its most stirring episodes. In Africa structural sameness has produced historical monotony and ill-defined ethnic frontiers.

In the western parts of the continent there were no small isolated habitats (such as, for example, Phoenicia and Nepal in Asia, and Abyssinia in East Africa) to encourage the growth of independence

262 SHEPHERD KINGS

and national character by keeping out foreign infiltration, and to foster the early growth of civilization and the development of the embyro state. This advantage was wholly denied to the peoples of the Western Sudan.

Whereas the forest, physically and climatically unfavourable to the well-being of Sudanese man, was an almost impenetrable barrier, the desert, although imposing severe restrictions on the movement of peoples, presented a limitless horizon whence came trade and culture. Clapperton found that although the geographical knowledge of Sultan Bello of Sokoto extended east and north to Mecca and Stambul, southward it was so limited that he believed the Niger's mouth was at Fundah which was on his own frontier and several days' march from the sea.[2] Other explorers found that some of the powerful peoples of the interior, such as the Mossi who raided northwards right into the Sahara, had never heard of the sea. The forest stood for darkness and savagery, the desert for light and culture.

'Everything that was interesting, its new races, its religions, its science, its literature, its commerce, its wars, had come to the Soudan from the north,' wrote Lady Lugard. 'It faced north to civilization. And behind it to the south there had always been the unknown, the barbaric, the uninhabitable. . . . From about the latitude of 7° southwards the climate of the Western Soudan became practically uninhabitable for those finer races which . . . required a good climate in which to attain to their natural limits of perfection.'[3]

But the light was rather dim and the culture somewhat tarnished by the time they had filtered through the desert. Nomadism, which the barren regions of the earth impose on their inhabitants, is incompatible with progress, and deserts are therefore always regions of arrested development. Since biblical times there has been no improvement in the social and economic life of the Arabian desert. Similarly there has been no change in the manner of life of the inhabitants of the Sahara since the revolution caused by the introduction of the camel.

Even under favourable conditions life in a desert is precarious and the unreliable local resources have to be supplemented from outside. Seasonal migrations to the peripheral areas in search of trade and pasture are a normal feature of desert life. Every summer the Kirghis of Russian Turkistan drive their herds up into the Altai Mountains and the nomads of the Arabian and Syrian deserts move, like the sons of Jacob, into the valleys of the Nile and the Euphrates. Similarly

SHEPHERD KINGS

in the Sahara, as the hottest months approach, Bedawin and Tuareg move out of the desert, northwards into the high plateaux of the Atlas and southwards into the rolling pastures of the Sudan.

The northward movement follows a few well-defined routes, for the high plateaux are only accessible from the desert by certain passes, the most notable being the gorge of El Kantara. On these routes the migrations of nomads in spring and autumn, to and from their summer pastures, assume spectacular proportions. But the southward movement, which has no obstacles to circumvent, takes place on a vast and uninterrupted front. The nomads come and go as suddenly and as unobtrusively as flocks of migrating birds.

These annual migrations from the desert to the sown usually take place without disturbance to the sedentary agriculturalists to whom the nomads are welcome for the trade they bring and for the manure of their herds. But unfortunately seasonal migrations always tend to increase their range. Not infrequently they are a prelude to marauding expeditions which in turn may culminate in the permanent occupation of fields and cities.

Covetousness is seldom the origin of ethnic movements among nomads. Far more frequent causes are failure of supplies through natural increase of population, and the pressure of more powerful neighbours. Deterioration of climate is another. Owing to the nomad's helpless dependence on rain a slight decline in the already inadequate mean annual fall compels him to move. Finally there is the spur of religious enthusiasm to the development of which deserts are peculiarly favourable. The fanaticism and intolerance of nomads, who have given the world its three great monotheistic religions, have always been potent factors in the history of civilization. Nomads, owing to lack of attachment to the soil and extreme mobility, yield easily to pressure, whether economic or political, but the forces thus set in motion are not easily controlled.

Proximity to deserts, therefore, has always been fraught with danger to sedentary tillers of the soil. The Great Wall of China was built against the constant menace of advancing nomads, and the same peril made the Romans build Lambaesis (Lambessa), the Bridle of the Desert Tribes, commanding the head of the El Kantara gorge; later the pressure became so great that they had also to hold the entrance to the pass and therefore they built Vescera (Biskra).

Although backward in developing the arts of civilization, desert nomads have always shown themselves capable of political organization

264 SHEPHERD KINGS

and martial achievement. In the desert there is no margin for waste. This necessitates a carefully ordered life for the individual and military organization for the tribe which must be ever ready to resist encroachment at the point of the sword. Consequently nomads make formidable enemies and as conquerors they build well-organized states.

Agriculture is the basis of all permanent advance in civilization, but the tiller of the soil lacks enterprise, mobility, wide vision, and political ability.[4] These, however, are the very qualities most strongly developed in the nomad. Hence we find that the union of pastoralists and agriculturalists makes for stable government and imperial expansion. Nomad conquerors put iron into the blood of the conquered, but in so doing they absorb their superior culture. It was to such unions that the Western Sudanese owe their gift for political organization which enabled them more than once to achieve imperial greatness.

Probably no event in the history of the Western Sudan had more far-reaching consequences than the Zaghawa invasion. Unfortunately we know nothing of its circumstances—how it came about, or the manner of its achievement. According to Ibn Khaldun, the Zaghawa were Muleththemin and probability indicates that the period at which they overran the Sudan was subsequent to the first Arab invasion of the Maghreb. They succeeded in establishing themselves as a ruling aristocracy—as Shepherd Kings—throughout nearly the whole length and breadth of the Sudan. In the west the political achievements of the Mandingoes, the Songhai, and the Hausas must be attributed to the infusion of Zaghawa blood into their negro veins. Kanem, which lies outside the scope of this work, came under the same stimulating influence.

Although nomads frequently figure in history as conquerors and as the architects of powerful states their rule seldom endures for very long. For this there are three principal reasons. First nomads usually content themselves with evicting the rulers of the conquered, leaving the general mass of the population undisturbed. The result is the same as that which follows when a numerically weak force conquers a population too large to be dislodged. The vanquished absorb their conquerors. This is what happened to the Hyksos in Egypt, the Vandals in Africa, and the Normans in England. It was equally the fate of the Moors in the Sudan.

Another weakness inherent in nomad rule is the habit of wide

SHEPHERD KINGS

dispersion which the herder never leaves behind him in his desert home and which leads inevitably towards dismemberment and the collapse of the political organization. It was this weakness that ruined the empires of the Arabs and the Tartars. Like so many of the great empires of antiquity they lacked cohesion and broke up along lines of ethnic cleavage.

The third principal cause of the evanescence of shepherd dynasties is the enervating effect of unaccustomed ease and luxury. All the sturdy qualities which the herder acquires in the desert and which enable him to conquer his fellow men evaporate when he abandons a nomadic life and frees himself from its rigours and restraints. None of the nomad conquerors of history escaped this weakness.

If we look back at the history outlined in this volume we find that one dynasty after another succumbed to the weaknesses inherent in nomad rule. The Almoravids present a striking example of the evanescence of the shepherd state. Directly the austere desert warriors experienced the fatal allurements of life in southern Spain their great empire evaporated. The mysterious white dynasty of Ghana, herders of an unknown race, were absorbed by their Mandingo subjects, the black Soninke. But the latter, defenceless against the turmoil of desert life, soon succumbed to another nomad invasion, that of the southern Almoravids led by Abu Bekr. In a few years this new dynasty crumbled before the fatal tendency to wide dispersion. Dissensions among the Lemtuna, Jedala, and Mesufa, which had long kept the Almoravids on the point of disruption, gave the Soninke another chance to reassert themselves.

The persistence with which the Mandingoes held the stage in western Africa is very striking. Their tenacious hold on Ghana, the expansion of Mali into a great empire which received recognition far beyond the shores of Africa, and the brilliant Soninke dynasty of the Askias place the Mandingoes above all other races of the Western Sudan. The qualities which enabled them to achieve so much they owed to their nomadic Zaghawa blood.

Although the Zaghawa probably provided the greatest stimulus which the Sudan has ever received, and although they established themselves as rulers over an immense area it was very rare for a Zaghawa dynasty to survive into historical times. Throughout the Western Sudan these and the other virile tribes of nomads were absorbed by their negro subjects. It has been said of the Fulani *jihad* that the Hausas, in a truer sense than the Greeks, 'captured

266 SHEPHERD KINGS

their rude conquerors',[5] and it is equally true of other Sudanese peoples.

The Za or Lemta kings who ruled for many centuries over the Songhai were one exception to the general rule of the evanescence of nomad dynasties. There is reason to suppose, however, that long before their eviction by the Soninke in the fifteenth century they had so intermarried with their negro subjects that they were scarcely to be distinguished from them. The Sokoto Fulani, like the Almoravids, are an example of the heights to which the pastoralist can rise before the spur of religious enthusiasm. For although most of the leaders of the *jihad* had abandoned the nomadic mode of life, they had preserved their nationality and with it some of the discipline of the pastoral tribe. When, however, the British conquered Sokoto they found that a century of power had sufficed completely to demoralize the Fulani and that their empire was on the verge of dissolution. The fatal effects of ease and luxury and of intermarriage with the negroes and the characteristic tendency towards wide dispersion had virtually destroyed their character, their nationality, and their empire. As administrators they had grown incompetent and corrupt, in appearance they were scarcely distinguishable from the Hausa population, and many of the emirs were openly defying the Sarkin Musulmi.

The disintegrating weakness for wide dispersion which the Sudanese inherited from their conquerors was fostered by the absence of confining natural frontiers. It showed itself in a marked tendency towards premature political expansion. The law has been laid down that 'the more closely the territorial growth of a state keeps pace with that of its people, and the more nearly the political area coincides with the ethnic, the greater is the strength and stability of the state'.[6] Natural increase of population played no part in the conquests of the Mandingoes, the Songhai, and the Fulani. In each instance political expansion preceded the development of a central government sufficiently strong to hold what had been conquered. Easily defensible frontiers would have lent strength to the central control, but these were wholly lacking from the boundless horizon.

The difficulty of communications was another source of weakness. That 'a long reach weakens the arm of authority' has been recognized by all the great empire builders of the world who consequently have always sought to annihilate distance by improving means of communication. The Romans did not permit the Alps, nor the Incas the Andes, to prevent the building of roads to knit the outposts of the

SHEPHERD KINGS

empire closer to the central government. But neither the Sudanese, nor any other African people, ever rose sufficiently high on the ladder of civilization to build roads or to develop efficient systems of runners. Consequently no African race has ever been able to control a widely flung empire. In the Sudan the task of the empire builder was made especially difficult by the rains which, in the absence of made roads, paralysed communications for several months of the year.

Although the Sudanese states were capable of conquests and political organization they never overcame the handicap of lack of natural frontiers and the difficulties of communication. Each empire was infected at birth with the germs of its own decay, and each fell an easy prey to its enemies within and without its always nebulous frontiers.

Where imperial aspirations were either lacking or were checked by overwhelmingly powerful neighbours a remarkable degree of political stability was sometimes achieved. The present rulers of the Mossi kingdoms of Yatenga and Wagadugu belong to dynasties which have ruled for a thousand years. The Kebbawa of Argungu are another example of dynastic stability lasting several centuries. In Yatenga, Wagadugu, and Kebbi martial enterprise was strongly developed, but attempts were seldom made permanently to occupy territory belonging to others. The political frontier consequently coincided with the ethnic boundary and stability resulted. In none of these instances could this be attributed to the advantages of a naturally protected habitat. Yatenga and Wagadugu were exposed to invasion from every direction and Kebbi was only partially protected by its extensive marshes.

If the absence of natural frontiers was unfavourable to political stability it was stimulating to trade and consequently to the spread of culture. That the rains paralysed most of the trade routes for six months in the year mattered little, for during this period agriculture wholly absorbed the activities of the Sudanese. During the rest of the year a large proportion of the population was free to devote itself to trade. In the absence of geographical barriers there were throughout the length and breadth of the Sudan a constant coming and going of foreign caravans and endless streams of negro traders travelling to and fro between the great markets.

The buying and selling of commodities is always accompanied by the exchange of ideas, and the cultural influences which drifted across the Sahara were quickly disseminated over the Sudan, carried from market to market by the throngs of traders. These influences, which

SHEPHERD KINGS

were mainly Muhammadan, taught the cultivation of economic, as opposed to alimentary, plants—notably cotton and indigo; they taught the building of substantial dwellings and of walled towns; they stimulated the development of political organization and the cultivation of letters; they banished cannibalism, human sacrifice, and other sinister pagan rites. The only barrier to the spread of these civilizing influences were the great forests of the south. In the Sudan itself a number of isolated groups of highlands, such as the Hombori Mountains and the Bauchi Plateau, or swamps, such as fringe the shores of Chad and the great lakes of the middle Niger, became islands of survival where hardy mountaineers or shy fisherfolk sturdily resisted the intrusion of new thought and learning. Elsewhere trade and culture went hand in hand, developing the great natural wealth of the country, and building cities and states which enjoyed intimate relations with the commercial and intellectual centres of the Maghreb.

There was one incalculable factor which contributed very materially to the closeness of the associations which bound the Sudan to the Maghreb. This was the temperament of the Sudanese. They had all the likeable characteristics of the negro, but the qualities which distinguished them from the rest of their race and which excited the admiration of all who visited their country were their industry, their love of peace and justice, and their rare gift of human sympathy. We have seen how Ibn Battuta was first convinced that no good could be expected from such people, but eventually wrote enthusiastically of their love of justice and the security of their roads. These same qualities also excited the admiration of Leo Africanus. The sincerity of such spontaneous tributes to the black race from travellers so strongly prejudiced cannot be questioned. Not less striking was the relief experienced by every one of the great white explorers on reaching the Sudan where the friendliness and the kindliness of the people were in marked contrast to the undisguised hostility of the brutal desert tribes.

The constant circulation of the population in pursuit of trade encouraged tolerance to foreigners and created an atmosphere favourable to the maintenance of commercial intercourse with Barbary. But the distinctive characteristics of Sudanese man were essentially the direct result of the conquest of negro farmers by Berber herdsmen. The vanquished absorbed their rude conquerors and Africa gained a people in whom all the finer qualities of the negro race are seen to the best advantage.

SHEPHERD KINGS

REFERENCES

1. Ellen Semple, *Influences of Geographic Environment*, London, 1914, p. 118.
2. Denham and Clapperton, *Travels*, ii. 304.
3. Lady Lugard, op. cit., p. 316.
4. F. Ratzel, *History of Mankind*, London, 1896–8, i. 28.
5. A. H. Keane, op. cit., p. 67.
6. Ellen Semple, op. cit., p. 190.

CHRONOLOGY

A.D.

428 The Vandals invade Africa.
477 Death of Genseric.
533 The Byzantines under Belisarius land in Africa.
642 The Arabs invade the Maghreb.
647 Defeat of the Byzantines at Sufetula.
711 The Arabs invade Spain.
890 The Lemta capture Gao.
1020 The Sanhaja unite against the Soninke.
1028 Birth of El Bekri.
1042 Ibn Yacin declares a *jihad*.
1050 The Beni Hillal and Beni Soleim invade the Maghreb.
1054 Fall of Audogast.
1057 Death of Ibn Yacin.
1062 Yusuf founds Marrakech.
1076 Abu Bakr captures Ghana.
1086 Yusuf invades Spain.
1087 Death of Abu Bakr.
1100 Birth of Idrisi.
1203 The Soninke recover Ghana.
1235 Sundiata defeats the Soninke at Kirina.
1307 Accession of Mansa Musa.
1324 Mansa Musa's pilgrimage to Mecca.
1325 The Mandingoes capture Gao.
1332 Death of Mansa Musa.
       Birth of Ibn Khaldun.
1333 The Mossi sack Timbuktu.
1335 Liberation of Gao.
1352 Ibn Battuta visits the Sudan.
1394 Birth of Prince Henry the Navigator.
1413 D'Isalguier returns from Gao.
1434 Gil Eannes rounds Cape Bojador.
1445 Nuno Tristam discovers Guinea.
1447 Malfante reaches Tuat.
1454 Cadamosto enters Prince Henry's service.
1460 Death of Prince Henry.
1464 Accession of Sonni Ali.
1468 Sonni Ali sacks Timbuktu.
1480 The Mossi sack Walata.
1487 The Portuguese occupy Wadan.

CHRONOLOGY

A.D.

1492 Death of Sonni Ali.
     Massacre of Jews in Tuat.
1493 Battle of Angoo.
     Accession of Askia the Great.
1502 El Maghili travels through Hausa to Gao.
1513 Askia invades Hausa.
     Leo Africanus visits the Sudan.
1516 Revolt of Kanta.
1528 Askia abdicates.
1546 The Songhai refuse to cede Taghaza to the Moors.
1578 Battle of El Ksar el Kebir.
     Accession of Mulay Ahmed el Mansur.
1585 El Mansur seizes Taghaza.
1590 El Mansur's expedition leaves for the Sudan.
1591 Judar Pasha captures Gao.
1595 Defeat of Askia Nuh.
1596 Birth of Abderrahman es Sadi.
1600 Kano becomes tributary to the Kwararafawa.
1603 Death of El Mansur.
1618 Mulay Zidan abandons the Sudan.
1620 Jobson's expedition to the Gambia.
1655 The Kel Tadmekket migrate to the Niger.
1660 Buya repudiates Moroccan suzerainty.
1670 Ali ben Haidar seeks refuge in Timbuktu.
1671 The Kwararafawa occupy Kano.
1680 The Aulimmiden capture Gao.
     Kano becomes tributary to Bornu.
1737 The Kel Tadmekket destroy the Arma at Togahia.
1754 Birth of Shehu Usuman dan Fodio.
1788 The African Association founded.
1796 Mungo Park discovers the Niger.
1804 The *Hijra* of Shehu.
1817 Death of Shehu.
1830 The Landers discover the termination of the Niger.

A SELECT BIBLIOGRAPHY

Abadie, M. *La Colonie du Niger*, Paris, 1927.

Aboulfeda. *Géographie*, 2 vols., Paris, 1848.

Allen, Capt. W., and Dr. T. R. H. Thomson. *A Narrative of the Expedition to the River Niger in 1841*, 2 vols., London, 1848.

D'Anville. *Géographie ancienne abrégée*, Paris, 1768.

Arnett, E. J. *The Rise of the Sokoto Fulani, Kano 1929.*
Gazetteer of Zaria Province, London, 1920.

A. x x x x, Mons. *A Letter Concerning the Countrys of Muley Arxid King of Tafiletta*, Englished out of French, London, 1671.

Azurara, Gomes Eannes de (Zurara), *The Chronicle of the Discovery and Conquest of Guinea*, 2 vols. Hakluyt Society, London 1896–9.

Barges, Abbé. 'Mémoire sur les relations commerciales de Tlemçen avec le Soudan' (*Revue de l'orient*), Paris, 1853.
Tlemçen, ancienne capitale du royaume de ce nom, Paris, 1859.

Barros, J. de. *Da Asia*, 24 vols., Lisbon, 1777–8.

Barth, Henry. *Travels in North and Central Africa*, 5 vols., London, 1857–8.

Bates, Oric. *The Eastern Libyans*, London, 1914.

Batouta, Ibn. *Voyages*, trad. Defrémery et Sanguinetti, 5 vols., Paris, 1853–9.

Battuta, Ibn. *Travels in Asia and Africa*, trans. H. A. R. Gibb, London, 1929.

Bekri, El. *Description de l'Afrique septentrionale*, trad. de Slane, Algiers, 1913.

Béthencourt, J. de. *The Conquest of the Canaries*, edited by R. H. Major, Hakluyt Society, London, 1871.

Bosman, William. *A New and Accurate Description of the Coast of Guinea*, English trans., London 1721.

Brown, Dr. Robert, *see* Leo Africanus.

Cadamosto (Alvise de Ca' da Mosto). *Relation des voyages à la côte occidentale de l'Afrique (1455–7)*, trad. J. Temporal, Paris, 1895.

Caillié, René. *Travels through Central Africa to Timbuctoo*, English trans., 2 vols., London, 1830.

Castries, H. de. *Les Sources inédites de l'histoire du Maroc*, Paris, 1918–25.
Hespéris, Paris, 1923.

Charlesworth, M. P. *Trade Routes and Commerce of the Roman Empire*, Cambridge, 1926.

Chudeau, R. *Missions au Sahara*: ii, *Sahara soudanais*, Paris, 1909.
Annales de géographie, xxv, 1916.

Clapperton, Capt. Hugh. *Journal of a Second Expedition into the Interior of Africa*, London, 1829.

A SELECT BIBLIOGRAPHY

Cooley, W. D. *The Negroland of the Arabs*, London, 1841.
Cosmas. *Christian Topography*, Hakluyt Society, London, 1897.

Daniel, F. de F. *Historical Notes, Katsina Emirate*, 1928. (*Unpublished*)
Journal of the African Society, xxv, 1925–6; xxxi, 1932.
Dapper, O. *Description de l'Afrique*, Amsterdam, 1686.
Delafosse, Maurice. *Haut-Sénégal-Niger*, 3 vols., Paris, 1912.
Le Gâna et le Mali (*Bull. du Comité d'Études historiques et scientifiques de l'Afrique Occidentale Française*), 1924.
Hespéris, Paris, 1923.
Denham, Major Dixon, and Capt. Hugh Clapperton. *Narrative of Travels and Discoveries in Northern and Central Africa*, 2 vols., London, 1826.
Desplagnes, L. *Plateau central nigérien*, Paris, 1907.
Diehl, C. *L'Afrique byzantine*, Paris, 1890.
Dozy, R. *Spanish Islam*, trans. F. G. Stokes, London, 1913.
Dupuis, Joseph. *Journal of a Residence in Ashantee*, London, 1824.
Duveyrier, H. *Les Touareg du Nord*, Paris, 1864.

Edrissi. *Description de l'Afrique et de l'Espagne*, trad. R. Dozy et M. J. de Goeje, Leyden, 1866.
P. A. Jaubert, *Géographie d'Edrissi, Recueil de voyages*, vols. v and vi, Paris, 1836.
Edwardes, H. S. W. *Geographical Journal*, liii, 1919.

Gaden, H. 'Les Salines d'Aoulil' (*Revue du monde musulman*), Paris, 1910.
Gautier, E. F. *Missions au Sahara*, I. *Sahara algérien*, Paris, 1908.
La Conquête du Sahara, Paris, 1925.
Les Siècles obscurs du Maghreb, Paris, 1927.
Le Sahara, Paris, 1928.
Gharnati. *Roudh el Qarthas*, trad. Beaumier, Paris, 1860.
Grierson, P. H. Hamilton. *The Silent Trade*, Edinburgh, 1903.
Gsell, Stéphane. *Histoire ancienne de l'Afrique du nord*, 8 vols., Paris, 1921–9.

Hakluyt, Richard. *Principal Navigations of the English Nation*, 12 vols., Glasgow, 1903–5.
Haoukal, Ibn. 'Description de l'Afrique', trad. de Slane, *Journal asiatique*, Paris, 1842.
Harris, Walter B. *Tafilet*, London, 1895.
Haukal, Ibn. *The Oriental Geography*, trans. W. Ouseley, London, 1800.
Horneman, Frederick. *Journal of Travels from Cairo to Mourzouk*, London, 1802.
Houdas, O. *Le Maroc de 1631 à 1812*, Paris, 1886.
Hubert, Henri. *Annales de géographie*, xxvi, 1917.

T

274 A SELECT BIBLIOGRAPHY

Idrisi, *see* Edrissi.

Infaku'l Maisuri, apud E. J. Arnett, *The Rise of the Sokoto Fulani.*

Jackson, J. G. *An Account of the Empire of Morocco*, London, 1809.
  An Account of Timbuktoo and Housa, London, 1820.
Jean, C. *Les Touareg du Sud-Est l'Aïr*, Paris, 1909.
Jobson, Richard. *The Golden Trade*, Teignmouth, 1904.

Kati, Mahmoud. *Tarikh el Fettach*, trad. O. Houdas et M. Delafosse, Paris,
  1913.
Keane, A. H. *Man Past and Present*, Cambridge, 1920.
Khaldun, Ibn. *Histoire des Berbères*, trad. de Slane, 2 vols., Paris, 1925.
Kilian, Conrad. *Au Hoggar*, Paris, 1925.
King, W. J. Harding. *Geographical Journal*, liii, 1919, p. 49.

Laird, MacGregor, and R. A. K. Oldfield. *Narrative of an Expedition into the
  Interior of Africa by the River Niger, 1832–4*, 2 vols., London, 1837.
Lander, Richard and John. *Journal of an Expedition to Explore the Niger*,
  3 vols., London, 1833.
Leo Africanus. *The History and Description of Africa done into English by
  John Pory*, edited by Dr. Robert Brown, Hakluyt Society, 3 vols.,
  London, 1896.
Léon l'Africain. *Description de l'Afrique*, trad. Jean Temporal, 4 vols., Paris,
  1830.
Lugard, Lady (Flora L. Shaw). *A Tropical Dependency*, London, 1905.
Lugard, Sir F. D. *The Dual Mandate in British Tropical Africa*, London,
  1923.
  Geographical Journal, vi, 1895.
Lyon, Capt. F. G., R.N. *A Narrative of Travels in Northern Africa*, London,
  1821.

MacMichael, H. A. *A History of the Arabs of the Sudan*, 2 vols., Cambridge,
  1922.
Maçoudi. *Les Prairies d'Or*, trad. Barbier de Meynard et Pavet de Courteille,
  9 vols., Paris, 1861.
MacQueen, James. *A Geographical and Commercial View of Northern Central
  Africa*, Edinburgh, 1821.
Major, R. H. *The Life of Prince Henry of Portugal, Surnamed the Navigator*,
  London, 1868.
Makrizi. *Description historique et topographique de l'Égypte*, trad. P.
  Casanova, Cairo, 1906.
Mangeot, Col. *L'Afrique française*, 1922.
Marc, L. *Le Pays Mossi*, Paris, 1909.
Marmol Caravajal. *L'Afrique*, trad. Perrot d'Ablancourt, 3 vols., Paris, 1667.

A SELECT BIBLIOGRAPHY

Martin, A. G. P. *Les Oasis sahariennes*, Algiers, 1908.

Mas Latrie. *Relations et commerce de l'Afrique septentrionale ou Maghreb avec les nations chrétiennes du moyen âge*, Paris, 1886.

Masson, Paul. *Histoire des établissements et du commerce français dans l'Afrique barbaresque*, Paris, 1903.

Massoudi, *see* Maçoudi.

Mauroy, M. *Du Commerce des Peuples de l'Afrique Septentrionale*, Paris, 1845.

Meek, C. K. *The Northern Tribes of Nigeria*, 2 vols., London, 1925.

Meniaud, J. *Haut-Sénégal-Niger*, 2 vols., Paris, 1912.

Monteil, Charles. *Les Bambara du Ségou et du Kaarta*, Paris, 1924.

Une Cité soudanaise, Djénné, Paris, 1932.

Les Empires du Mali (*Bull. du Comité d'Études historiques et scientifiques de l'Afrique Occidentale Française*), 1929.

Newton, A. P. *Travel and Travellers of the Middle Ages*, London, 1926.

Nozhet-Elhadi, see El Ufrani.

Omari, Al. *Masalik el Absar*, Paris, 1927.

Palmer, H. R. *Mai Idris Alooma of Bornu (1571–1583)*, Lagos, 1926.

Sudanese Memoirs, 3 vols., Lagos, 1928.

The Carthaginian Voyage to West Africa in 500 B.C., Bathurst, 1931.

Journal of the African Society, xxii, 1922–3; xxvi, 1926–7; xxix, 1929–30; xxxi, 1932.

Park, Mungo. *Travels in the Interior Districts of Africa*, London, 1799.

Travels in the Interior Districts of Africa, with an Account of a Subsequent Mission in 1805, 2 vols., London, 1816.

Pellow, Thomas. *The Adventures of Thomas Pellow*, London, 1890.

Purchas, Samuel. *Purchas His Pilgrimes*, 20 vols., Glasgow, 1905–7.

Raffenel, A. *Nouveau voyage dans le pays des nègres*, 2 vols. Paris, 1856.

Reichard, C. G. *Éphémérides géographiques*, Weimar, Aug. 1803.

Reygasse, M. *Gravures Rupestres et Inscriptions Tifinar' du Sahara Central. Cinquantenaire de la Faculté des Lettres d'Alger*, Algiers, 1932.

Richer, A. *Les Oulliminden*, Paris, 1924.

Rodd, F. R. *People of the Veil*, London, 1926.

The Times, 30 March 1928.

Roncière, Charles de la. *La Découverte de l'Afrique au moyen âge*, 3 vols., Cairo, 1924–7.

Roudh el Qarthas, see Gharnati.

Sa'di Es (Abderrahman-es-Sa'di et Timboukti). *Tarikh es Soudan*, trad. O. Houdas, Paris, 1900.

276 A SELECT BIBLIOGRAPHY

Said, Al Hadji. *Tarikh es Sokoto*, apud *Tedzkiret en Nisian*.

Sauzey, *La Géographie*, Paris, 1926.

Sayous, A. E. *Le Commerce des Européens à Tunis*, Paris, 1929.

Semple, Ellen. *Influences of Geographic Environment*, London, 1914.

Shaw, Flora L., *see* Lady Lugard.

Smith, Capt. John. *Travels*, 2 vols., Glasgow 1907.

Tarikh el Fettach, *see* Kati.

Tarikh es Sokoto, see *Tedzkiret en Nisian*.

Tarikh es Soudan, *see* Sa'di.

Tauxier, L. *Nouvelles Notes sur le Mossi et le Gourounsi*, Paris, 1924.

Tedzkiret en Nisian, trad. O. Houdas, Paris, 1901.

Tilho, M. A. J. *Documents scientifiques de la Mission Tilho*, Paris, 1906–9.
    Geographical Journal, lvi, 1920.

Tohfut ul Alabi, apud H. R. Palmer, *Sudanese Memoirs*, ii.

Ufrani, El. *Nozhet Elhadi*, trad. O. Houdas, Paris, 1889.

Vidal. *Bull. du Comité d'études historiques et scientifiques de l'Afrique Occi-
    dentale Française*, 1923.

Vischer, Hanns. *Across the Sahara from Tripoli to Bornu*, London, 1910.
    Geographical Journal, xxxiii, 1909.

Walckenaer, C. A. *Recherches géographiques sur l'intérieur de l'Afrique
    septentrionale*, Paris, 1821.

Walwyn, A. E. V., *apud* H. R. Palmer, *Sudanese Memoirs*, iii.

Wüstenfeld, F. *Jacuts Geographisches Wörterbuch*, Leipzig, 1866–70.

Yaqut, *see* Wüstenfeld.

Zurara, *see* Azurara.

INDEX

'Abagazawa, and the founding of Kano, 220.

Abd el Mumen, 55; conquers the Maghreb, 120.

Abdalla abu Muhammad, 47.

Abdel Wadites of Tlemcen, 21, 55.

Abdu Salame, 225.

Abdul Karim (= Henry Barth), 242.

Abdul Malek, Sultan of Morocco, 151.

Abdullah ibn Yacin, and the Jedala, 47–8; founds the Almoravids, 48; organizes them, 48–9; attacks Audoghast, 49; his death, 50.

Abdullahi, King of Kano, 221.

Abdullahi, Waziri, 227–8; his share of Shehu's kingdom, 230.

Aben Ali, at Toulouse, 131–2.

Abid, the 195–6.

Abu Amran, 47.

Abu Bakr, Emir of the Almoravids, 50, 265; and Yusuf, 51; spreads Muhammadanism among the negroes, 64; and the overthrow of Ghana, 64; his death, 65.

Abu Bakr II, 71 & n.

Abu Fares, 175; succeeds El Mansur, 178.

Abu Hafs Omar, Qadi of Timbuktu, 171; sent as a prisoner to Morocco, 174.

Abu Hammen, 79.

Abu Inan, 39, 76.

Abu'l Hassan, 38, 76.

Abu Yazid, legend of, 219, 220.

Abuam replaces Sijilmasa, 247.

Abulfeda, his *Geography*, 36, 40, 65–6.

Abyssinia, gold trade in, 61; Prester John in, 140; origin of the name, 219.

Adahu, 144.

Adamawa, 225; captured by the Fulani, 226.

Adar, 226.

Addax gazelle, 106 n.

Adrar (Central Sahara), 85; the Kel Geres and, 198.

Adrar (Mauritania), 27, 50, 63, 64.

Aethiopians, the Greeks and the, 15, 17, 23; the Romans and the, 19, 256.

Africa, the Church in, 115–16; her trade with Europe, 119–25; Christian interests in, 121–2; her imports, 124; the knowledge of her interior, 127–9, 201–3; effect of Turkish spread in her trade, 130; European exploration of, 130–6; fishing fields of, 146; effect of new discoveries on, 203; exploration of, 240–1; effect of her wide dispersion on development, 266–7.

Africa, Central, and the slave trade, 106.

Africa East, dumb barter in, 61.

Africa, Northern, its natural zones, 1; change of climate in, 3, 5, 10; under Roman occupation, 3–4; extinct fauna of, 4; early attempts to penetrate, 13–22; dumb barter in, 14; introduction of camels into, 20–2; inhabitants of, in pre-Arab times, 23–7; effect of Arab invasions on, 27–30; Arab writers and its geography, 33–40; under the Almoravids, 48–55; under the Almohads, 55; her trade with Europe, 119–25; reasons for exploring, 240; demand for slaves in, 256–7.

Africa, West, Carthaginian expedition to, 14–16; dumb barter in, 61; difficulties of trading in, 168; dangers of exploration of, 208–9.

Africa, West Central, Leo Africanus and, 104.

African Association, its genesis, 209; sends explorers to Africa, 210; and Mungo Park, 211; and Frederic Hornemann, 213, 214.

African native, the, causes of his migration, 6–7; his knowledge of agriculture, 7; his hostility to exploration, 207–8; his geographical knowledge, 262.

Agades, 95, 202; Sultan of, 96; captured by Askia, 97; and the caravan routes, 107, 251; Leo Africanus and, 110; Sarkin Air of, 227; Barth at, 241; and the salt trade, 251, 252.

Agadez, 202.

Agadir, 185.

Aghmat, 50.

Agriculture, the basis of civilization, 264.

278 INDEX

Agisymba, its identity with Air, 19–20.

Ahaggar, 128, 198; Tuareg of, 251.

Ahaggar Mountains, the, 8.

Ahaggaren, the, 197–8.

Ahmadu Lobo, 228.

Ahmed, nephew of Mulay Ismail, in Timbuktu, 196.

Ahmed Baba, the historian, 73; his birth, &c., 192–3; his imprisonment and death, 174.

Air, 25, 26, 27, 202; its identity with Roman Agisymba, 19–20; Mali and, 74; Ibn Battuta and, 78; El Maghili and, 92; Askia and, 95; the Muleththemin of, 96; Songhai conquest of, 97; and the caravan trade, 107, 251, 253; expedition against, 197; Barth and, 241; the *Azalai* and, 252.

Air Mountains, the, 9.

Akil ag Malwal, 86, 87.

Akit, the, 192.

Akka, 247.

Al Adalet, attacked by Askia, 96.

Al Hassan Ibn Muhammad, *see* Leo Africanus, 103.

Al Makkari, the brothers, their commercial house, 78–9.

Al Morabethin, *see* Almoravids.

Alexander VI, Pope, and the Portuguese trade, 185.

Alfonso VI, King of Castile, 52.

Algeciras, Yusuf and, 53.

Algiers, the eastern limit of Almoravid Empire, 52; trade with Timbuktu, 128; Florentine monopolies in, 135.

Aliamen, *see* Za Aliamen.

Ali ben Abdelkader, 194.

Ali ben Haidar, his rebellion, 195.

Ali et Tlemcani, 179; defeated by the Songhai, 179–80; declares himself Pasha, 180; tortured to death, 181.

Ali Ghaji Dunamani, 95.

Ali Kolen, 72, 75, 86.

Alkalawa, Shehu and, 226; fall of, 227.

Almina Walo, death of Mahmud at, 175.

Almohads, the, 55; and Christian mercenaries, 116–17; their conquest of the Maghreb, 120; as wine drinkers, 124.

Almoravids, the, 38; origin of, 48; organized under Ibn Yacin, 48–9; cross the Atlas mountains, 49–50; under Abu Bakr, 50–1; under Yusuf,

51, 57; extent of the Empire, 52; and the Spanish Muslims, 52–4; annex Muhammadan Spain, 54; their decline 54–5, 65; under Yahia in Adrar, 64; and Ghana, 64; and Christian mercenaries, 116–17; and Pisa, 121; as wine drinkers, 124; their weakness, 265.

Alwassa, Shehu defeated at, 227, 229.

Amalfi, 121; pirates of, 123.

Ambergris, 46, 106, 119.

Amenokal (== Sultan), an, 97; of Aulimmiden, 198, 199.

America, export of slaves to, 207.

Amina, Queen, 222.

Amir ul Muminina, title of, 226, 229.

Ammar Pasha, sent to Timbuktu, 177; succeeded by Sulayman, 178; sent out to the Sudan, 180–1.

Andalusians, the, 51–2; Yusuf and, 53–5; in the Moorish troops, 156.

Andalus, white slaves from, 119.

Angelino Dulcert of Majorca, 74.

Angoo, battle of, 91, 92.

Ansaman, 96 n.

Anu Maqaran valley, 20 n.

Aquilegi, 3.

Arabs, the, 19, 60; and the camel in Africa, 20; and the races of Africa, 23; their invasion of Africa, 27, 28–30, 96; development of their learning in Middle Ages, 32; at Biru (Walata), 65; motive of their invasion, 115; and the corn trade with Europe, 118; and trade with Europe, 119–20; piracy amongst, 122–3.

Arawan, the Moorish invasion and, 157; Caillié and, 240; and the caravan routes, 247.

Archudia, 136.

Ardo, the, 194; and Shehu Ahmadu, 228.

Aretnenna, building of, 48.

Argui, 50.

Arguin, 15, 46, 49, 187; the Portuguese at, 90; and the road from Wadan, 107; discovery of the island, 142, 144 n.; as a fishing centre, 146; and the Sahara trade, 149.

Argungu, 84, 98, 229.

Aribinda-Fari, office of, 93.

Arma, the, as governors, 193, 194–5, 196; their payment of troops, 197; their incompetence, 199; defeat of, 199–200; of Jenne, 228.

INDEX

279

Arms of war, trade in, 109, 186; for slaves, 207, 241.

Arnett, E. J., 61.

Arzuges, 24.

Asaba, 238.

Asben (Air), 95, 219; the Gobirawa and, 222.

Ashanti, and the gold trade, 184, 248.

Asia, Leo Africanus in, 104; early European travellers in, 125; Christians in, 140; nomads from, 261.

Asiu, 251.

Askias, the, foundation of their dynasty, 92; Leo Africanus and, 108; appointed by the Moors, 165.

Askia Muhammad Bani, 101.

Askia Bengan Korei, 99.

Askia Daud, 83 n., 98; his reign, 100.

Askia Muhammad El Hadj, and El Mansur, 100–1.

Askia Ishak I, 99; and Sultan Mulay el Aarejd, 99.

Askia Ishak II, his accession, 101; El Mansur and, 155; and the Moorish invasion, 158; flees across the Niger, 160; reorganizes in Gurma, 161; offers terms to Judar, 151; meets Mahmud Pasha at Bamba, 164–5; his murder, 165.

Askia Muhammad I (Askia the Great), his character, 92; his reforms, 93; goes to Mecca, 93; his expedition, 94–5; eastern campaign, 95–6; abdicates in favour of Musa, 98–9; evicted by Askia Bengan, 99; his death, 99; Leo Africanus and, 109; bans commerce with Jews, 130; and Kano, 221.

Askia Muhammad Gao succeeds Askia Ishak II, 165.

Askia Nuh, the Songhai leader, 165; his struggle with Mahmud Pasha, 166–8, 175; at Kolen, 173; his defeat and disappearance, 175; as a leader, 175–6.

Askia of the North, appointed by the Moors, 165; in Timbuktu, 193–4.

Askia Sliman, 175.

Astacures, *see* Azger.

Atlantic, the, exploration of, 136–44.

Atlas Mountains, 1, 43, 74; elephants in, 4; on the Catalan Map, 127–8; Judar crosses, 156.

Attila, 28.

Audoghast, 34; the Lemtuna capital, 46–7; attacked by Ibn Yacin, 49.

Aujila, 73; and the caravan routes, 251.

Aukar, district of, 45, 70; as part of Mali, 79; the *literati* in refuge at, 90.

Aulil, island of, 44; salt in, 62, 63.

Aulimmiden, the, 83, 197; submit to the Moors, 198.

Auriga, the, 26, 83.

Aussa, 219 n.

Ausuriani, 24.

Avalis, people of, 220 n.

Awni of Ife, the, 148.

Ayoru, captured by Askia, 94.

Azalai, the, 251–2.

Azaneguys, 142, 143.

Azger, the, 24, 198; and Ghadames-Ghat road, 251.

Azores, the, 141.

Azugui, 50.

Azurara, Gomes Eannesde, his *Chronicle of Guinea*, 138, 145; and the ivory trade, 146 n.

Bab-el-Mandeb, Straits of, 23.

Bab Ras el Hammada, 20.

Badagry, 237, 238; and the European trade, 254; and Jega, 256.

Bagana, 45, 79; attacked by Askia, 94; rebels against Moors, 172.

Bagarmi, 27, 242.

Baghdad, 33, 34, 36.

Bagoda, 220.

Bakari Da'a, succeeds Sonni Ali, 91; in refuge, 94.

Bakhoy, the, 67.

Bakwa, 223.

Balama (= Chamberlain), office of, 93.

Baldaya, 141–2.

Bamako, 82, 212, 215, 255; supply of salt to, 249–50.

Bamba, 84, 133, 158; battle at, 164–5; fort of, 168; the Kaids in, 194, 197; destruction of, 199.

Bambaras, the, overcome by Sundiata, 68; ravage Jenne, 170, 199; as kings of Segu, 195, 196, 228; Mungo Park and, 212.

Bambuk, 60, 210, 247; becomes an apanage of Mali, 70; discovery of gold mines at, 150, 248–9; its identity with Wangara, 248.

Bango-Fari, 93.

280 INDEX

Bani, the, 82, 88; the Sorko and, 84.
Banks, Sir Joseph, 209.
Banza Bokwoi, 219.
Baramendana, 67–8.
Barbarossas, the, 204.
Barbary, 1, 2; changes of climate in, 3, 4; fauna of, 4–5; and the Sudan in Roman times, 10; the merchants of, and Ghana, 57; and the gold trade, 59–60, 73; and Takedda, 75; trade with the Sudan, 101, 105; Leo Africanus and, 103; trade with Jenne, 109; trade with Bornu, 111; and the Frankish militia, 117, 118; Christian trade with, 119–25; goods handled in her ports, 124; and trade with Italy, 130; English seamen and, 186; and the salt trade with Sudan, 196; effect of her pirates on trade, 203; Caillié and her merchants, 240; her link with the Sudan, 246; demand for eunuchs in, 257.
Bardai, 20.
Bardetus, 19.
Barros, J. de, 141, 149; Governor-General of Guinea, 149–50.
Barth, Henry, 63, 216, 257 n.; and the *Tarikh es Sudan*, 192; and the Niger, 228; and the British Consul at Tripoli, 236; joins Richardson's expedition, 241; discovers the upper Benue, 242; reaches Timbuktu, 242–3; his achievements, 243–4; and Wangara, 248; and Kano, 252–3; and Jega, 255.
Bassi, 50–1, 57.
Bassikunu, 89.
Bastions, the, 185.
Basur-Kayin, 85.
Bauchi, won by Shehu's emirs, 226; plateau of, 268.
Baule river, 45, 65.
Beads, coral, industry in, 62.
Beads, glass, import of, 76, 76, 253, 254.
Bedawin, the, 30, 263.
Beibei, 84.
Beirut, 135.
Beled el Jerid, 201.
Beled es Sudan, 1, 23.
Belisarius, 28.
Bella (= Buzu), the, 9.
Bello, Sultan, 25, 227; on the miraculous crossing of the Niger; his share of Shehu's kingdom, 230; his reign, 231;

and Clapperton, 236; his geographical knowledge, 262.
Bembo, 133.
Bemoy, 149.
Bendugu, 99.
Bengan Korei, Askia, 99.
Beni Hillal, 30.
Beni Soleim, 30.
Bentia, island of, 83.
Benue, the, 222, 225; and the Niger, 228, 233, 237, 238; upper reaches of discovered by Barth, 242.
Berabish, the, 25, 101.
Beranes, the, 25–6.
Berbers, the, 20, 23, 63; division of, 25–6; their revolts against invasion, 28, 29–30; purity of their stock, 30; sources of their history, 36, 40; Tilutane and, 45; of Audoghast, 46; and the Muslims in Spain, 52–4; a new sect, 55; and the Mandingoes, 80; of Adrar, 85; of Timbuktu, 87; and the Arab invasion, 115; of the Hausa country, 219; their influence on the Sudanese, 268.
Berdeoa, the, 26.
Berghwata, the, 50.
Beri-Beri, the, 95; Kanta and, 98; of Katsina, 222.   [137.
Béthencourt, de, conquers the Canaries,
Bight of Benin, voyages into, 148, 149; and the gold trade, 187; Mungo Park and, 214; the Niger and, 233, 238.
Biledulgerid, the, 201, 202.
Bilma, 222 n.; salt from, 251, 256; the *Azalai* and, 252.
Biram, 95, 219.
Birnin Gwari, 111, 219, 222; and the ferry road, 254.
Birnin Kebbi, 98, 229.
Birnin Zamfara, 110.
Biru (= Walata), 65.
Biskra, 8, 29; and the caravan routes, 107; building of, 263.
Biton, King of Segu, 195.
Bitu, 88.
Bleau, 201; and the course of the Niger, 202.
Bofon, 133.
Bojador, Cape, 136, 141.
Bokar, Governor of Bagana, 172.
Bokhari, the, 195–6.
Bona, 135

INDEX

281

Bonduku, 88; and the gold trade, 184.

Boniface, Count, 28.

Books, trade in, 106.

Book of Roger ('Rogerian Description of the World'), 35.

Borgawa, the, 167.

Borgu, 27; harried by Sonni Ali, 89; attacked by Askia, 94; the Moors and, 166–7, 173.

Borgu aquatic grass, 82, 89 n.

Bornu, 6, 133, 222; Christianity in, 24–5; and Takedda, 75, 87; Musa II and, 79; and the Hausa States, 95; shepherd kings of, 96; and the caravan routes, 107; and trade with Agades, 110; and trade with Barbary, 111; Mai Idris of, 197; Kano a vassal of, 221; its power in the north-east, 223; won by Shehu's emirs, 226; and the Fulani, 227; Barth and, 241; caravan road to, 246; export of slaves to, 253, 257; eunuchs in, 257;

Bororoje (= Cow Fulani), the, 223, 224, 232.

Bosman, William, 206.

Botr, 26.

Bozo, the, 84.

Brass, trade in, 46, 62, 63, 109.

British Government, the, decides to explore the Niger, 214; tests the Niger-Congo theory, 233; sends out Clapperton, 234, 237; sends out the Landers, 238; and Henry Barth, 241.

Buda, 128.

Bugie, 117, 128, 135.

Bu Ikhtiyar, 174.

Bure, 60, 247.

Busa, rapids of, 82, 83, 254; attacked by Askia Daud, 100; Mungo Park's death, at, 216; Clapperton reaches, 237; the Landers reach, 238.

Butter, trade in, 78.

Buya, 194.

Buzu, *see* Bella.

Buzurgaiyin, 85.

Byzantines, the, 21, 22, 97; their invasion of N. Africa, 28; end of their rule, 29.

Cabra, 201, 202.

Cadamosto, 60; voyages to Guinea, 146; explores the Gambia, 146–7.

Caesarea, *see* Cherchel.

Caillié, Réné, and Timbuktu, 239–40.

Cairo, Mansa Musa and, 71–2; Bornu and, 95; and Arab commerce, 120; as an ivory market, 146 n.; caravan routes to, 251.

Camel, the, its introduction into N. Africa, 20–2, 27, 262; trade in, 134; and the *Azalai*, 251–2.

Cameroon Mountain, 15.

Campbell, Capt., sent to the Niger, 233–4.

Campden, Lord, 215.

Canaries, The, their discovery, 137.

Cannibals, 62 n.; of Wangara, 77.

Cannon, Moorish, 156, 161.

Cano (= Kano), 201, 202.

Canoes, Songhai, 82.

Cantor reached by Gomez, 147, 148.

Cape Blanco, 142; and the fishing trade, 146.

Cape Cantin, 14.

Cape Ghir, 14.

Cape Nun, 247.

Cape St. Vincent, 140.

Cape Verde, 143, 145, 187.

Capsa, *see* Gafsa.

Caravajal, *see* Marmol.

Caravans, their dependence on water stages, 1–2, 8; in Roman times, 10; and the arrival of the camel, 22; the Tuareg and, 25; and Timbuktu, 73; the *takshif* and, 76; the route of the Sudan traders, 106, 107; their route marked on Catalan Map, 128; chief routes of, 246–58; the *Azalai*, 251–2; on the Kano-Badagry route, 254; effect of abolition of slave trade on, 258; sea-borne trade and, 258–9.

Carthage, 3; its occupation by Genseric, 28; its destruction by Hassan, 29; the seat of the Primate of All Africa, 116; Charlemagne and, 118–19; Dei and, 135.

Carthaginians, the, their expedition to W. Africa, 14–16; their trade with the Sudan, 16; and traffic with the natives, 13–14.

Casena (= Katsina), 201.

Cassena (= Katsina), 202.

Castilia, colony of, 116.

Castilians, the, and the Spanish Muslims, 53–4; mercenaries, 117.

Castries, Col. H. de, 157 n., 160 n.

282 INDEX

Catalan Atlas, 74; of Africa, 127, 133, 137, 141, 227.
Catalans, the, 137.
Cattle, trade in, 134.
Cecil, Robert, 205 n.
Cellaba (= Cilliba), *see* Zuila.
Centurione, Benedetto, 132, 135.
Centurione, Luigi, 132.
Cerne, *see* Herne Island, 15.
Ceuta, 51; chief industry of, 62; coral fisheries of, 119; Henry the Navigator and, 138, 140; held by Portuguese, 185.
Chafe, 221 n.
Charlemagne, 115, 118–19.
Charles V, Catalan atlas of, 74, 127.
Cheraga, Moorish troops from, 156.
Cherchel, 3.
'Chigguiya', manufacture of, 63.
China, Ibn Battuta visits, 37; European trade with, 130.
Chipp, Dr. T. F., 9.
Chretes, the, *see* the Senegal.
Christianity, among the Tuareg, 24–5; and Arabic learning, 32; and the Muslims in Spain, 52; Leo Africanus converted to, 104; in the Sahara, 115–16; and the maritime trade of Mediterranean, 118; and trade with Muslims, 120; her interest in African ports, 121–2; in Asia, 140; and the Barbary pirates, 204.
Cintra, Pedro de, discovers Sierre Leone, 148.
Circumcelliones, the, 115.
Cirta, *see* Constantine.
Civet, 106, 184.
Clapperton, Capt. Hugh, 6, 231, 255; his first expedition to the Niger, 234–5; at Kano, 235–6, 237; travels to Sokoto, 236; returns to England, 237; his second expedition, 237; his death, 237; and Bello's geographical knowledge, 262.
Clarendon, Lord, and Barth, 244.
Climate, its importance in the Sahara, 2; change of, in N. Africa, 1–10; effect of forests on, 7; its effect on human development, 261.
Cloth, trade in, 109, 110, 119, 240, 252; imported into Africa, 124, 186.
Columbus, Christopher, 132.
Company of Adventurers, &c., the discovery of gold mines, 188–90.

Congo, the, identified with the Niger, 214, 217, 233.
Congo, Pygmies of, and dumb barter, 61.
Congress of Utrecht, 1818; and piracy, 205.
Constantine, 3, 107; Christian merchants and, 125.
Constantinople, 37; Leo Africanus and, 104; supply of eunuchs from, 119.
Copper, trade of, in Takedda, 75; imported into Sudan, 124, 134; exported to England, 186.
Copts, the, 220.
Coral, fisheries, 119; as a currency, 130.
Cordova, El Bekri and, 34; El Idrisi and, 35.
Corn, trade in, 118, 252.
Cosmas of Alexandria, 61.
Cotton, production of, 119.
Cotton, trade in, 109, 250; imported into Africa, 253.
Cotton cloth, Kano and, 252–3.
Cowry shells, as a currency, 86.
Craftsmen, English, in Morocco, 185.
Cresques, Abraham, 127.
Crucifix found in Gao, 161.
Crusades, the, and European trade with Africa, 120; their effect on piracy, 123.
Cutlery, English, import of, 250.
Cydamus, *see* Ghadames.
Cyrenaica-Kufra-Wadai road, 25.

Dallul Fogha, salt-pans of, 249, 256.
Dallul Mauri, 84.
Damagaram, 252.
Danakil, the, 71.
Daniel, F. de F., 111 n.; on Shehu 230.
Dar el Bideea, palace of, 185.
Darfur, 27.
Daura, 95, 98, 219; captured by the Fulani, 226.
Daw (Dao), 62 & n.
Degel attacked by Yunfa, 225–6.
Dei, Benedetto, his travels, 135–6.
Delafosse, M., 77, 79.
De Lisle, 111, 201; and the source of the Niger, 202.
Demdem, 62.
Dendi, 27, 72, 77; traditional home of the Songhai, 83, 84; attacked by the Askias, 99; Malfante and, 133; the

INDEX

283

Songhai flight to, 165; rise of the kingdom of, 166; the Songhai advance from, 180.

Denham, Major Dixon, sent to the Niger, 234–5; returns to England, 236–7; and Wangara, 248; and the slave trade, 257;

Desert of Seu, 202.

Desiccation, 1–10.

Desplagnes, L., 83.

Dhul Fiqar, sword of the Prophet, 221 n.

Diaz, Dinis, reaches Guinea by sea, 143; discovers the Senegal, 145.

Dinar, 46 n.

Dirma, country of, 89.

Donatists, the, 28, 115.

Dongola, 77, 234.

Donkin, General Sir Rufane, 238.

Dori, 99, 180; Shehu and, 228.

Dra'a, 49, 59, 73; raided by Tuareg, 100; Valley of the, 128; Fernandez in, 146 n.; Judar and, 156; Judar's envoy in, 162.

Dried fruit, import of, 46.

Drums, Soninke, 58.

Dumb barter, *see* Silent trade; and the gold trade, 14, 33, 59–60, 61, 196, 234; other examples of, 61; Jobson and, 189–90; E. J. Arnett on, 61.

Dungula (=Dongola), 77, 234.

Dupuis and Wangara, 248.

Durbawa, the, 221.

Dutch, the, and the slave trade, 205–6.

Eannes, Gil, rounds Cape Bojador, 141.

Easterlings, *see* Hansa merchants.

Ebony, trade in, 119, 124, 184.

Ed Daher Bibers, 70.

Egypt, Arabs' invasion from, 28–30; Mansa Musa and, 71–2, 73, 74; settles from, 220; export of slaves to, 257.

El Baghdadi, *see* El Maghili.

El Bekkai, and Barth, 243; and Queen Victoria, 244.

El Bekri, 33, 116; his works, 34, 57; and Sijilmasa, 43; and Taghaza, 44; and Audoghast, 46; and Mu'tamid, 53; and Ghana, 57, 63, 202; and Tekrur and Lemlem, 63; and Gao, 84–5; and Tadmekka, 85; and Kanem, 95; and the gold trade, 249.

El Besatin, 185.

El Cala, Christian community of, 116.

Elches in the Moorish army, 156.

El Dzehebi, *see* Mulay El Mansur.

El Ghaba, 57.

El Hadjar, Nuh and, 175.

El Hadji Omar, 231, 243.

El Hamma, 116.

El Hassan, 179.

El Idrisi, 33; as a geographer, 35, 43; and Ghana, 58, 202; and Wangara, 60, 202; and Kukia, 83; and Tirekka, 86; and the Niger, 210.

El Jem, 2.

El Kanemi, 227, 230; and Denham, 235.

El Kantara, gorge of, 107, 263.

El Kheber, work of Ahmed Baba, 192.

El Ksar el Kebir, battle at, 151, 155, 185.

El Maghili, 92–3, 130; and Muhammad Rimfa, 221.

El Mamer, 72.

El Mehedia, 120, 121.

Elmina, *see* San Jorge da Mina.

El Motawekkel, Askia and, 93.

El Mustapha, Kaid, 171; and the Sanhaja Tuareg, 172–3; and the townspeople of Timbuktu, 174; murder of, 176.

El Omar, 33; his *Masalik el Absar,* 36; and Ghana, 70; and Abu Bakr, 71 n.; and Mansa Musa, 72. .

El Ufrani, and the Moorish invasion, 151 n., 157 n.; and the date of Tondibi, 160 n.; and the gains of the Sudan expedition, 183, 196.

Elephants, in N. Africa, 4–5; in Morocco, 184; transported across the Sahara, 184.

Elizabeth, Queen, and El Mansur, 152, 156, 162 n.; and saltpetre, 186.

Elmina, 144, 148; Barros at, 149–50.

Emagadezi, the, 97.

Enedi, the, 8.

England, and Morocco, 152; troops from, in Moorish army, 156; merchants of, in Morocco, 185; and the Portuguese, 185–6; and piracy, 204–5; and the slave trade, 205–7, 237; Bello and, 236; and Henry Barth, 244; her merchants in Badagry, 254.

Erg, 7.

Eritrea, 71.

Es Sadi, 86; and Ghana, 45; and Ahmed Baba, 73; and Sonni Ali, 87, 90; and

284 INDEX

Askia, 95; and Askia Daud, 100; and the Moorish invasion, 151 n., 156, 159; and the date of Tondibi, 160 n.; and anarchy amongst the Songhai, 170; and the Moorish losses, 183; his *Tarikh es Sudan*, 192–3; and the later Pashas, 193; and Hamed el Haguzui, 197.

Es Saheli, 72; builds mosques, 73, 109; tomb of, 78.

Es Suk, 85.

Eunuchs, 28, 156, 163, 181; demand for, 119, 257.

Europe, and trade with Africa, 105, 107, 109, 110; Christian mercenaries from, 117; maritime trade with Barbary, 119–25; export of slaves to, 124; her ignorance of interior Africa, 127, 130, 201, 203; effect of Turkish advance on her trade with Africa, 130; shortage of gold in, 130; and the Moorish invasion, 151; and El Mansur, 152; and the African gold trade, 187–90; and the Barbary pirates, 203–5; effect of her occupation of N. Africa, 246; goods imported from, 253, 255; Badagry and her trade, 254; the gelding of boys in, 258; effect of her trade on the caravan routes, 258–9.

Fachi, 252.

Fadan Gurma, 254, 255.

Fa-Hein, and dumb barter in Ceylon, 61.

Faleme, the, 60, 247; Mungo Park and, 215; gold washed down by, 249.

Faran Ber, 84.

Fari-Mondio (= Treasurer), office of, 93.

Fatimite Khalif of Cairo, 30.

Fauna, of N. Africa, 4; of the Sahara, 8.

Ferawi, the, 63–4; and the gold trade, 249.

Ferdinand III, 117.

Fernandez, Alvaro, 145.

Fernandez, John, 143, 144, 146 n.

Fernandez, Peroz, 150.

Ferries on the river Niger, 254–5.

Fez, 37, 38, 39, 43; Merinides of, 21, 55; entered by Yusuf, 51, 52; and Timbuktu, 73; Mari Jata II and, 79; Leo Africanus and, 103–4; as a market, 105, 106; the mint at, 107; Moorish troops from, 156; El Mansur's fort at, 185; Caillié at, 240.

Fezzan, 17, 23, 96; occupation under Roman rule, 18, 19–20; the Arabs in, 29; and the caravan trade, 73, 198; Hornemann and, 213, 214; export of slaves to, 253, 257.

Fezzan-Kawar road, 246; a Roman road, 256; as a slave route, 256–7.

Figuig, 8.

Filalian dynasty, 195.

Firearms, their introduction into Bornu, 159.

Fishing off the African coasts, 146.

Florence and African exploration, 135.

Fonduk, the, 121–2.

Fono, the, 84.

Frederick of Castile, 117.

French, the, their influence on the Sahara, 9; and Morocco, 152; their trade with the Moors, 186; and the route to the gold mines, 188, 210; and the slave trade, 205; and El Bekkai, 243; Frankish militia, *see* Frendji; and the Bambuk goldfields, 248; their silk imported into Africa, 253; and the Badagry slave trade, 254.

Frendji, 117–18; their importance to Europe-Africa relation, 118.

Fulani, the, Jewish blood in, 27; ancestors of, 45; raided by Sonni Ali, 89, 90; and the Mandingoes, 90; assist Bagana, 94; Koli and, 95; in modern times, 98; Askia Daud and, 100; arrest of their progress, 168; ravage the Songhai, 170; Ali et Tlemcani and, 179, 180; king of Massena, 194, 242; the Kaids of Jenne, and divisions of, 223–4; and the Hausa states, 224–9; general rising of, 226; their victories, 226–9; administration of, 229–30; loss of martial zeal amongst 231; of Massina, 242, 243; Jega and, 256; effect of ease on, 266.

Fulanin Gidda (= Town Fulani), 223, 224, 231.

Fulbe, *see* Fulani.

Fundah, 236, 237.

Futa, 27, 63, 90; Jolof kingdom of, 95.

Futa Jallon, 68, 239.

Gabes, 119.

Gabibi, the, 83.

Gaboon river, the, 15.

Gadiaro, 63.

INDEX

285

Gaetuli, the, 17, 23.

Gaetulia, 22.

Gafsa, 4.

Gago, 201.

Galam, 79.

Gama, Vasco da, 149.

Gambia, the, 15, 70, 201; discovery of, 146–7; as a route to gold mines, 188–90; Major Houghton and, 211; trading factories of, 250.

Gangara (= Gangaran), 60, 111; becomes an apanage of Mali, 70; variant of Wangara, 247.

Gao, 77, 78, 83, 128, 147 n.; Songhai of, 71; capture of, 72, 74, 281; freed by Ali Kolen, 75; the Sorko kingdom of, 84; its king becomes Muhammadan, 84; El Bekri and, 84–5; visited by Ibn Battuta, 86; el Maghili and, 92; visited by Leo Africanus, 110; d'Isalguier at, 131; the Moorish invasion and, 157 n., 158–9, 160; Judar enters, 160–1; his disappointment with, 161; held by Judar, 175; tribute from, 183, 184; gold mines near, 188, 189; commanded by Kaids, 193–4, 197; captured by Aulimmiden, 198; as a gold market, 248.

Gaphara, 16.

Gara, 23, 26, 45.

Garama, 18, 20; ruins of, 23.

Garamantes, the, as convoyers of caravans, 17; the Romans and, 19, 20, 23, 256.

Garamantian caravan road, 18.

Garawan, the, 23.

Gastaldi, G., 202.

Gau, 71.

Gautier, E. F., 3.

Gaya, 255.

Gbangara, 60.

Genoa, and trade with Africa, 119, 120, 121, 122; export of slaves to, 124; export of ships from, 124; and African exploration, 132; expedition to India, 137.

Genseric, his occupation of Fezzan, 18, 28.

Geography, Arabic contribution to, 32; travel and trade as an incentive to, 32–3; Arabic writers and, 34; Roger II of Sicily and, 35.

Germany, goods imported from, 253.

Geugeu, *see* Gao.

Ghadames, 18, 73, 85, 133; as a market, 105; and the caravan routes, 107–8, 250, 251; Laing at, 239.

Ghadames–Air road, 246; route of, 250–1; slave traffic on, 257.

Ghadames–Ghat road, 25, 250.

Ghana, 34, 144; and the gold trade, 43; and the salt supply, 44–5; kingdom of, 45; Tilutani and, 45–6; and Audoghast, 47; Abu Bakr and, 50–1; El Bekri and, 57; life of the court of, 57–8; people of, 58–9; and the gold trade, 59–62; and slavery, &c., 62; imports of, 62; markets of, 63; overthrow of, 64–6, 70; under the Susu, 65; trade with Tadmekka, 85, 86; difficulty of its southward expansion, 168; Kano confused with, 202; white dynasty of, 265.

Gharian, 20.

Ghat, 18, 96; and the caravan routes, 197, 198, 250, 251; export of slaves to, 253.

Ghomara, the, 51.

Gimbana, 225.

Gimbanawa, the, 256.

Gipsies, the, the Fulani compared with, 224.

Glass, its export to Africa, 124.

Glawi pass, 49, 51.

Gobir, 78, 95, 198; captured by Askia, 96; ruled by Kanta, 98; visited by Leo Africanus, 110; language of, 219; settlers in, 220; and Katsina, 222; the Torobe and, 224; Shehu and, 225; fall of her capital, 227.

Gobirawa, the, 25, 96 & n., 220; move to Zamfara, 222; their power in the north-west, 223; defeated by Shehu, 226; at Alwassa, 227.

Gold, trade of, in Africa, 43, 44, 46, 59, 110, 196, 234, 240, 258; Mansa Musa and, 72, 74; Morocco and, 106, 124; as a currency in the Sudan, 109, 111; shortage of, in Europe, 130; quest for, in Africa, 132; Malfante and, 134; the mystery of its source, 134–5; Cadamosto and the trade in, 147; Gomez and, 147–8; the Moors and, 154–5; from the Sudan invasion, 183–4; exported to England, 186; stimulation of the trade, 186–7; expeditions for its discovery, 187–90;

286 INDEX

exported from Guinea, 206; source of, 247-9.

Gold, River of, quest for, 137-8; its imagined discovery, 142.

Gold dust, trade of, in Timbuktu, 73; in the Sudan, 119; brought back by Tristam, 142; Portuguese trade in, 145.

Gombe won by Fulani, 226.

Gomez, Diego, explores the Gambia, 147-8, 201.

Gonçalvez, Antam, 142, 144.

Gongo Musa, *see* Mansa Musa.

Gongola-Benue basin, the, 221.

Goree, 214.

Goro, see Kola nuts.

Granada, entered by Yusuf, 54; Es Sahili of, 72; Leo Africanus and, 103; renegades from, 156.

Granary of Rome, the, 2, 3.

Greeks, the, and the use of African elephants, 4; and the condition of the desert, 10; and commerce with Africa, 14-17; as pirates, 123, 204.

Green Sea of Darkness, 137, 141, 148, 202.

Gregory, Prefect, 29.

Gsell, Stéphane (quoted), 3, 5, 10.

Gualata, *see* Walata.

Guangara, *see* Wangara.

Guber, *see Lacus Guber*.

Gudu, Shehu and, 226.

Guedala, *see* Jedala.

Guides, blind, in the Sahara, 76.

Guinea, 125, 254; gold of, 130; its exploration by Henry the Navigator, 138; reached by sea, 143; derivation of name, 144; Cadamosto sails to, 146; Portuguese interest in, failing, 149; England and trade with, 186; and the gold trade, 187, 188, 206, 248; and the slave trade, 205, 207, 257.

Guinea, Gulf of, termination of Niger in, 233, 236.

Gulbin Gindi, the, 255, 256.

Gulbin Kebbi, the, 83, 110.

Gulbin Rima, the, 110.

Gum, trade in, 240.

Gungia, 165.

Gungu, 97.

Guraan, *see* Garawan.

Gurara, 8.

Gurma, right bank of Niger, 83, 84;

attacked by Bengan Korei, 99; people of Gao flee to, 160; Askia Ishak at, 164-5.

Gurma-Fari, office of, 93.

Gurmanche, the, 75.

Gwandu, 98, 192; Abdullahi and, 230; Barth and, 242.

Gwangara, 60.

Gwanja, kola nuts from, 253, 254; Jega and, 256.

Gwari, Birnin, 111, 219, 222, 254.

Gwozaki, Wangara's identity with, 111 n.

Habe, 220, 225.

Habesh, 219.

Hadeija captured by the Fulani, 226.

Hadj, the, 32.

Hadrumentum (= Susse), 4.

Hafsids of Tunis, 38-9, 55.

Hakluyt Society, 112, 113.

Hamdallahi, Seku and, 229.

Hamed el Haguzui, 197.

Hamites, 23.

Hammada el Homra, 20.

Hanno, Carthaginian expedition under, 14-16.

Hansa merchants, the, and English pilots, 186.

Haratin, the, 9; in the Abid, 196.

Harris, Walter B., 179 n.

Hartebeest, Bubal, 2 n.

Harun el Raschid and Charlemagne, 118.

Hassan, 29.

Hassanid dynasty, 195.

Hausa country, 25, 27; and Takedda, 75; name for left bank of Niger, 83, 84; divisions of, 95; attacked by Askia, 96; attacked by Askia Daud, 100; visited by Leo Africanus, 110-11; faction in, 154; Mungo Park and, 214; origin of the name, 219; invaded by Zaghawa, 220; history of, 220-1; Muhammadanism in, 220-1; occupation of, 223; the Fulani and, 223; Barth and, 243; road to, 246; salt trade with, 251; chief trade routes to, 254-5; demand for slaves from, 257; their debt to the Zaghawa, 264.

Hausa Bokwoi, 219.

Hausa, Seven States of, 95, 219; history of, 219-23; the Fulani and, 223.

Hawkinses, the, and the slave trade, 206.

INDEX

287

Hayre, *see* Air.

Heawood, Edward, 19.

Hellenistic culture, its effect on Arabic learning, 32.

Henry the Navigator, Prince, 16; and Atlantic exploration, 138–44; at Sagres, 140; his accomplishments, 140–1; his successes, 141–2; and the Venetians, 146; and the Gambia river, 147–8; his death, 148.

Herne Island, 15.

Herodotus, and the exploration of the Sahara, 13–14, 17; and the Niger, 210.

Hides, trade in, 186.

High Plateaux, the, 1, 22.

Hi-Koi (= High Admiral), office of, 93, 100; attacks Katsina, 222.

Hill, Capt., and the Niger, 228.

Hillalian Arabs, 119.

Hillman sent to the Niger, 234–5.

Himalayas, the, dumb barter in, 61.

Himyarites, the, in Africa, 25, 26.

Hoden, *see* Wadan.

Hodh, 45.

Hoggar, *see* Ahaggar.

Ho-Koi(= Chief Fisherman), office of, 93.

Hombori, 175, 179, 180.

Hombori-Koi, office of, 93.

Hombori Mountains, 90, 268.

Honein, 132.

Honey, trade in, 46, 119.

Horn, Southern, *see* Gaboon river.

Horn, Western, *see* Sierra Leone.

Hornemann, Frederic, 213–14, 236.

Horses, trade in, 105, 109, 110, 146.

Houdas, O., 155, 160 n.

Houghton, Major, 211.

Hundred Years War, 131, 132.

Ibadites, 77.

Ibn Battuta, 32, 33; his birth and early life, 36; visits India, 37; crosses the Sahara, 37; in Fez, 37–8; and Taghaza, 44; and Mali, 67, 76–8; visits Gao, 86; and the Niger, 210; and the Sudanese, 268.

Ibn el Faqih, 60.

Ibn Ghania, 24.

Ibn Haukal, 33–4; and Sijilmasa, 43, 46; and Gao, 84; and the Maghreb, 119.

Ibn Juzayy and Ibn Battuta, 38.

Ibn Khaldun, 25, 26–7, 33, 36; birth and early life, 38–9; his *Prolegomena*,

&c., 39–40; and Tamerlane, 40; and Ghana, 45, 58, 66, 70 & n., 148 n.; and Mali, 72, 74, 75, 79, 80; and the Lemta, 83; and the Atlantic Ocean, 137; and the Zaghawa, 264.

Ibn Said, 40, 143.

Ibos capture the Landers, 238.

Ibrahim Sal, 64.

Ibuzahil, 97.

Idenan, the, 171.

Ifernan, 251.

Ifoghas, 24.

Ifrikia, 16, 71, 119.

Ifuraces, 24.

Igdem, 133.

Illo, 84; ferry at, 254.

Illorin, 219; won by Shehu's emirs, 226.

Imajeghan, 24, 220.

Imbert, Paul, accompanies Amman to Sudan, 180–1.

Imghad, 24, 220.

Immedideren, 171.

In Azawa, 251.

Infaku'l Maisuri, the, of Bello, 230.

In Gall, 97; and the caravan routes, 251.

In Salah, 239; replaces Tafilelt, 247.

In Ziza, 128.

India, Ibn Battuta in, 36–7; European trade with, 130; discovery of a sea-route to, 137, 138, 147, 148, 149, 150, 203; the Portuguese and, 205.

Indigo, trade in, 119.

Isa, 110.

Isaaco, 214, 216.

Isalguier, Anselm d', his exploration of Africa, 131–2.

Islam, schism in, 29; and geographical research, 32; Jedala converted to, 48; in Spain, 52–5; in Tekrur, 63; in Goa, 85; its revival under Askia, 92; the Berbers and, 115; and Christianity in the Sahara, 116; and Christian trade with Africa, 120, 121; and the Moorish king, 152; in the Hausa States, 220–1, 225; Shehu and, 230; and the slave trade, 258; cultural influences in Africa, 268.

Ismail, 94; rebels against Askia, 98; his reign, 99; Ismaila, 229.

Italy, her trade with Barbary, 119; piracy among her merchants, 123; and maps of Africa, 130; goods imported from, 253.

288 INDEX

Itesan, the, 252.
Ivory, trade in, 111–12, 119, 124, 145–6, 196, 207, 240, 250, 258.
Ivory Coast, 250.
Iwalatan, *see* Walata.

Jaga, 77, 79.
Jangebe, 237.
Jara, 79, 95.
Jaressi, 63.
Jata, 79.
Jaula, the, 60.
Jawambe, 27.
Jaye, 189.
Jayme, Maistre, 140.
Jebba, 254.
Jedala (= Guedala), 26, 265; Ibn Yacin and, 47–50, 64; scholars of, 73, 192.
Jega, and the caravan routes, 255; its important position, 255–6.
Jenne, 73, 82, 144, 180, 189; its independence, 74; captured by Sonni Ali, 88–9; on a caravan route, 107; visited by Leo Africanus, 108–9; ravaged by the Bambara, 170; submits to the Moors, 172; Es Sadi Imam of, 192; the Kaids in, 194, 199; Mungo Park and, 214; Caillié and, 239; and the caravan routes, 250.
Jenne-Koi, office of, 93.
Jerba, 204.
Jerba, Leo Africanus captured off, 104.
Jeriba, capital of Mali, 67, 68, 70.
Jerma, 18, 20.
Jewellery, trade in, 59, 62, 63.
Jews, the, in Northern Africa, 27, 47, 85; inter-marriage with Arabs, 29; massacre of, at Tuat, 92; as goldsmiths, 107; persecuted by Askia, 109, 130; and the knowledge of Africa's interior, 127–9; of Tuat, 133; and the export of sequins, 186; the Fulani compared with, 224; and the supply of eunuchs, 258.
Jihad, Fulani, against the Hausa States, 226, 227, 228, 229, 265, 266; character of, 230.
Jobson, Richard, and the Gambia, 189–90.
John II, as Lord of Guinea, 144; and African exploration, 148; and Prester John, 149.

Judar Pasha, in command of the Moorish expedition, 156; crosses the Sahara, 157; reaches the Niger, 157–9; enters Gao, 160; his disappointment, 161; relinquishes command to Mahmud Pasha, 164, 168; quarrels with Mansur, 176; murders El Mustapha, 176; returns to Morocco, 177.
Jukuns, the, 221, 223.

Kabara, port of Timbuktu, 73, 82, 109, 172, 199; Karabara mistaken for, 157 n.; Mungo Park and, 214; Caillié and, 239.
Kaids, the, and the Moorish invasion, 156, 162, 163; in Gao, 193–4, 197; of Jenne, 199.
Kairwan, Roman remains in, 18–19; building of, 29; Yahia at, 47; its trade with Tadmekka, 85; and the caravan routes, 107; Christian colony at, 110; sugar from, 119; and the slave trade, 119; the Sicilians and, 121; Christian merchants and, 125.
Kala, Askia Ishak at, 158.
Kamalia, 212.
Kamba, 79.
Kanda, royal title, 85.
Kanem, 24–5; capital of Bornu, 95, 220; Barth and, 242; its debt to the Zaghawa, 264.
Kanembu, the, their arrival in Bornu, 227.
Kankan Musa, *see* Mansa Musa.
Kano, 92, 95, 96, 168, 202; and trade with Agades, 110; supposed to be the ancient Ghana, 202; language of, 219; Muhammadanism in, 220; at the height of its power, 224; and Katsina, 222; Bornu and, 223; captured by the Fulani, 226–7; reached by Clapperton, 235, 237; visited by Barth, 241; and the caravan routes, 251; the *Azalai* and, 252; the Hausa craftsmen of, 252–3; and the slave trade, 253; and the kola nut trade, 253–4; importance of its position, 255–6.
Kano Chronicle, 220, 224.
Kanta of Kebbi, 96, 221; revolts against Askia, 97; his territory, 98; defeats Bengen Korei, 99; attacks Katsina.
Kanuri, the Kanembu and the, 227.
Karabara, the Moorish invasion and, 157 and n., 158.

INDEX

Karengia, burr grass, 85.
Karfa Taura and Mungo Park, 212.
Karfata, 222.
Kari Denna, 198.
Katagum conquered by the Fulani, 226.
Katsina, 92, 95, 98, 110, 201, 202; attacked by Askia Daud, 100; Mungo Park and, 214; language of, 219; foundation of, 221; attack on, 221–2; in the eighteenth century, 222; conquered by the Fulani, 226; Barth and, 242; and the caravan routes, 251; and the cotton cloth trade, 252.
Katunga, *see* Oyo.
Kaukau, 84.
Kawar, oasis of, 29; the *Azalai* and, 251, 252, 253.
Kawar, Bornu empire extended to, 95; and the caravan routes, 107.
Kaza-Maghan Sisse, 45.
Kazaure won by Shehu's emirs, 226.
Kebbawa, the, 98, 222; the Fulani and, 227, 229; their dynastic stability, 267.
Kebbi, king of, 96, 175; Askia Daud quarrels with, 100; stability of the kingdom, 154; a lesser Hausa state, 219; dynastic stability in, 267.
Kel Geres, the, 97, 197, 198; and the caravan routes, 251, 252.
Kel Owi, the, 197, 198, 222, 227; and the Ghat-Air road, 251.
Kel Tadmekket, 85, 198; settle in Timbuktu, 198, 199; pillage Timbuktu, 199–200.
Kénié, rapids of, 82.
Ketama, the, 26, 83.
Khair-ed-din the pirate, 204.
Khalif, title of Christian bishop, 116.
Khurasan, 37.
Kinuku, silent trade in, 61 n.
Kiptawa, 220.
Kirina, 68.
Koceila, 29.
Koceilata, 85.
Kola nuts, 73, 250; trade in, 253–4, 255.
Kolen, fort of, 166; invested by Nuh, 173–4.
Koli founds a Fulani dynasty in Futa, 95.
Komie, ferry at, 254.
Kong Mountains, 233.
Konkodugu, 70.
Korau, 221.

Kore-Farima (=High Priest), office of, 93.
Kotorkoshi, 221 n.
Krapf, 240.
Ksar el Kebir, 128.
Kubar, *see* Gobir.
Kugha, 63.
Kuka, Leo Africanus and, 111.
Kukawa, 235; Barth and, 241, 242.
Kukia, its situation, 83–4; Musa attempts to form a kingdom at, 98; Gomez and, 147 n.
Kulikoro, 68, 82.
Kumayo, 221.
Kundafi Pass, 49, 51.
Kunta Arabs, 29, 243.
Kwararafa, 219; Kano tributary to, 221 222; Bakwa and, 223.
Kworra, *see* Niger.

Labe, 68.
Lac de Bournon, 202.
Lacus Guarde, 110, 202.
Lacus Guber, 110, 202.   [140.
Lagos (Portugal), the naval arsenal at,
Laird-Oldfield expedition, 228.
Laing, Major Gordon, and Timbuktu, 239.
Lake Chad, 1, 25, 26, 27, 95, 201, 202, 235, 268; exploration of, 242; natron from, 253.
Lake Debo, 84, 89, 90, 93, 175, 201, 202; the Toronke and, 224.
Lake Fagbine, 6, 86; Sonni Ali and, 89–90.
Lambessa (=Lambaesis), 18, 263.
Lander, Richard, 237–8; joined by his brother, 238.
Landers, the, 61, 255; solve the Niger problem, 238–9.
Lanza, Frederick, 117.
Laraiche, 185.
Lead, its export from Barbary, 122.
Leather, its export from Morocco, 124.
Lebbi, 64.
Ledyard, 210.
Leka, 96, 97, 175.
Lekawa, the, 98.
Lektawa, 156.
Lemlem, 62; tribes of, 63–4.
Lemta, 26, 266; and the Almoravids, 64–5; and the Gabibi, 83; and the Sorko, 84; end of their dynasty as kings, 91; and the new dynasty, 94.

INDEX

290

Lemtuna tribe, 26; and Ghana, 45–7 Ibn Yacin and, 48, 49; Abu Bakr and, 50; and the Almoravids, 64, 265; and the Hi-koi raiders, 222.

Leo X, Pope, and Leo Africanus, 104.

Leo Africanus, 65, 128, 201, 202; his division of the Sahara, 26; and blind guides in the desert, 76; and Timbuktu, 88; and Askia, 93, 95, 97, 99, 101; his birth, &c., 103–4; his early travels, 104; settles in Rome, 104–5; and the Barbary-Sudan trade, 105; and the exports of Sudan, 106; and the Sahara caravan routes, 107; and the kingdom of the Negroes, 108; visits Timbuktu, 109–10; visits Gao and Gobir, 110; and the Hausa States, 110–11; his error over the Niger, 112–13, 210; and the Christian mercenaries, 117 n.; and the native merchants, 125; on Tuat, &c., 132–3; and the ivory trade, 146 n.; and the fate of rebels, 152 n.; the languages of W. Sudan, 219; and the Kong Mountains, 233; and the salt labourers of Taghaza, 250; and the kola nut, 253 & n.; and the eunuch trade, 258; and the character of the Sudanese, 268.

Leptis Magna, 16, 18, 19; the camel in, 21.

Levant, the, 130.

Libya, 13; in ancient times, 19, 21.

Libyans, the, 230; *see also* Tuareg.

Liptako, 224; Shehu and, 228.

Lisbon as a slave market, 205.

Livingstone, David, 240.

Lixitae, the, 14, 15, 16 & n.

Lixus, River, 14.

Lobi, 249.

Lorenzo the Magnificent, 104.

Luata (= Levata), 26, 36.

Lucas, 210–11.

Lugard, Lady, 208, 262.

Lugard, Lord, 167, 258.

Lyon, Capt. F. G., and the Niger, 234.

Mabruk, 247.

Macgregor-Laird expedition, 1832, 208.

MacMichael, H. A., 27 n.

McQueen, James, and the Niger, 233.

Madeira, 141; as a fishing centre, 146.

Madghis, 25–6.

Madoc, Laurence, on the spoils of the Sudan invasion, 183.

Magha III, 80.

Maghan succeeds Mansa Musa, 75.

Maghcharen, 86.

Maghreb, the, 21, 29, 46, 73; Arab invasion of, 29–30, 45; invaded by Yusuf, 41, 57; and Ghana, 59, 62; and Tekrur, 63, 64; and Mali, 71; and Gao, 84; and the Christian mercenaries, 116–17; famines in, 118; prosperity in, 119–20; conquered by the Almohads, 120; the Jews of, 127; spread of Turks to, 130; export of ivory from, 146 n.; its link with the Sudan, 268.

Mahmud ben Zergun, sent to the Sudan 163; arrives in Timbuktu, 164; and Askia Muhammad Gao, 165; and Askia Nuh, 166–8; returns to Timbuktu, 168; departs for the south, 170, 171; in Timbuktu again, 173; his death ordered, 174; dies in battle, 175; his success as a leader, 175–6; 183–4.

Mahmud Kati and the Moorish invasion, 151 n., 157 n., 159.

Mahmud Lonko, succeeds Sulayman, 179; his removal, 180.

Mai Ali, Sultan of Bornu, 98.

Mai Dunama Dabalemi, 95.

Mai Idris of Bornu, 197.

Maistre Jayme, 140.

Majorca, and maps of Africa, 127, 130, 138.

Makrizi, 40.

Maldive Islands, Ibn Battuta in, 37.

Malfante, Antonio, his exploration of the Sahara, 132–5, 227.

Mali, Emperor of, 36, 37, 63.

Mali, Empire of, 65, 128; its prestige, 67; and the Susus, 68; Sundiata, king of, 68–70; successive kings of, 70; under Sakura, 70–1; under Mansa Musa, 71–4; cartographical reference to, 74; under Maghan, 75; under Sulayman, 75; visited by Ibn Battuta, 75–8; civil war, 79; in the fifteenth century, 79–80; attacked by Askia, 94, 95; attacked by Askia Ishak, 99; and by Askia Daud, 100; as a market, 107; visited by Leo Africanus, 108; Portuguese mission to, 150; the

INDEX

291

Songhai and, 154; difficulties of its expansion, 168; influence of Mandigoes on, 265.

Malinke, the, and the Susu, 65.

Malinke gold-diggers, 61.

Malakite Mufti of Cairo, Ibn Khaldun appointed, 39, 40.

Malik es Sudan, 80.

Malikite Qadi of Delhi, Ibn Battuta appointed, 37.

Mallel, 62.

Malli, *see* Mali.

Mamadu, 71.

Mami ben Barun Kaid, and the Timbuktu rebellion, 171–2; and other rebellious tribes, 172, 173–4.

Mamun, 117.

Mandara, 27; Denham and, 255; Barth and, 242.

Mande, *see* Mali.

Manding, 247.

Mandinga, 201, 202.

Mandingo kingdom, the, 67; *see also* Mali.

Mandingo tribes, the, 23, 45, 47, 60; and Timbuktu, 86; the Mossi and, 90; raid the Moors, 177–8; and Muhammadanism in Kano, 220; their debt to the Zaghawa, 264; their persistence in the Sudan, 265.

Mansa Musa, 36; and the gold trade, 60; his fame, 71, 74; his pilgrimage to Mecca, 71–2; and the capture of Gao, 72; and Timbuktu, 73; his death, 74; his mosques, 109.

Manse Ule succeeds Sundiata, 70.

Mansur ben Abderrahman, sent to supersede Mahmud, 174; defeats Askia Nuh, 175; quarrels with Judar, 176.

Mappae-mundi, 74.

Marabouts, 48.

Maradi, 222.

Mari Jata, *see* Sundiata.

Mari Jata II, 79.

Marmol Carvajal, 66, 73; his *Descripcion de Africa*, 187.

Marrakech, 43, 50, 100; founded by Yusuf, 51; intellectual life of, 103; Christian mercenaries at, 117; Christian merchants and, 125; and Taghaza, 154; Moorish troops for, 156, 163; Judar's envoy arrives at, 162; Omar imprisoned at, 174; palace of, 185; Barbary Company in, 188.

Marseilles and trade with Africa, 119, 121.

Massa, port for the gold export, 124.

Massina, 158; the Fulani king of, 194, 242; attacked by Er Rechid, 195; Ulema of, 228; Seku and, 228–9.

Masmuda, the, 51.

Massufa, *see* Mesufa.

Masud, 49.

Masudi, 43, 202; his *Meadows of Gold, &c.*, 33; and the gold trade, 60.

Mayma, 128.

Mazaghan held by Portuguese, 185.

Mazices, 24.

Meat, trade in, 78.

Mecca, pilgrimage to, 32, 70 & n., 71, 75; Ibn Battuta in, 36, 37; Mansa Musa and, 71–2, 74; Askia and, 93.

Mediterranean, maritime trade in, 118; effect of Turkish conquests on, 130; ivory trade in, 146 & n.

Mehedia, 14.

Mekron river, district of, 166.

Mellahs of Barbary, 127.

Mellestine, the, *see* Mali.

Menin, Tunka, king of Ghana, 57.

Mercenaries, Christian, and the Maghreb, 116–17; their character, 117–18; and the Moorish invasion, 151.

Merchants, Christian, 116; and trade with Barbary, 119–25; piracy amongst, 123; and the African interior, 125.

Merinids of Fez, the, 21, 55; Mansa Musa and, 74.

Mesche, 19.

Messau won by Shehu's emirs, 226.

Mesufa, the, 26, 44, 50; and the Almoravids, 64–5, 265; desert messengers, 76; of Taghaza, 101.

Metals, precious, shortage of, in Europe, 130.

Middle Passage, the, 207.

Millet, 250.

Mima, 79.

Mirrors, import of, 253.

Miski, 20.

Mitkal (Mithqal), 44 n.

Mizda-Murzuk road, 18, 20.

Mogador, 250.

Moors, the, Henry the Navigator and, 138, 143; and Taghaza, 155; appoint

U 2

INDEX

their own Askia of the North, 165, 193; the Tuareg and, 171; make peace under Mami, 171–2; domestic dissension amongst, 174–9; defeated by the Songhai, 180; their losses in the Sudan, 183; supply of arms to, 186; under the later Pashas, 193; rebellion against, 194, 199; as pirates in N. Africa, 203–4; and Mungo Park, 211.

Moorish invasion, accounts of, 151 n.; sets off, 156–7; reaches the Niger, 157–9; at the battle of Tondibi, 159–60; enters Gao, 160–1; its disillusionment, 161–2; retires to Timbuktu, 162; contemporary opinion of, 163–4; and Askia Nuh, 165–8; reinforcement of, 168; abandoned, 181; its strain on Morocco, 184; results of, 200.

Mopti, 89.

Morho-Naba (Mossi king), the, 94.

Moriscos, 204 n.

Morocco, 27, 62; the Almoravids and, 49–50; and the Taghaza salt mines, 99–100, 100–1; seizes Taghaza, 101; and the gold of the Sudan, 101, 106; at the time of Leo Africanus, 103; Pisa's trade with, 121; gold trade in, 124; the Jews in, 127; internal strife in, 180; relinquishes the Sudan, 181; her tribute from the Sudan, 183–4; the Moors in the Sudan and, 194; its suzerainty repudiated, 194; internal troubles in, 195. *See also* Moorish invasion.

Moshi, the river, 236 n.

Mossi, the, raid Timbuktu, 75; attack Walata, 89; Sonni Ali and, 90; Askia conducts a *jihad* against, 94; attacked by Askia Daud, 100; their king as Prester John, 149; gelding as a punishment amongst, 257; their geographical knowledge, 262; their dynastic stability, 267.

Msila and cotton, 119.

Muhammad the Prophet, 32.

Muhammad XI, Sultan, and the recovery of his throne, 151–2.

Muhammad Abd el Kerim el Maghili, *see* El Maghili.

Muhammad Barhayorho, 192.

Muhammad Bello, 220.

Muhammad Bengan Korei, 99, 100.

Muhammad ech Chetuki, 194.

Muhammad Ed Dara'i, 196.

Muhammad Naddi, 86, 87.

Muhammad uld Benchi, 167.

Muhammad Rimfa, 221.

Muhammad Taba, appointed Pashalik of the Sudan, 176.

Muhammad Ture, 91; proclaims himself King of the Songhai, 92. *See* Askia.

Muhammadanism, *see* Islam.

Mulay Ahmed El Mansur, 181; and Askia Daud, 100; his desert expedition, 101; succeeds to the throne, 152–3; determines to invade the Sudan, 154; at Taghaza, 155; date of his manifesto, 160 n.; his reception of Judar's terms, 162; his triumphant proclamation, 162–3; follows up Judar's expedition, 163; contemporary opinion of, 163–4; and Mahmud Pasha's failure, 168; sends reinforcements, 173; and the *literati* of Timbuktu, 174; appoints Muhammad Taba, 176; and Judar, 176–7; his death, 178; called El Dzehebi, 183; his revenue from the Sudan, 183–4; and the constitution of the army, 199.

Mulay el Aarejd and Taghaza, 99–100.

Mulay Er Rechid and Ali ben Haidar, 195.

Mulay Ismail, forms the Abid, 195–6; his large family, 195 n.

Mulay Zidan, 174, 180, 193; and the Moorish losses, 183.

Muleththemin, the, 23, 43; divisions of, 26, 83; their arrival in Africa, 26; and the Mandingoes, 80; of Tadmekka, 85; of Bornu, 95; Lemta division of, 96; Christianity amongst, 115.

Murzuk, 213; death of Ritchie at, 234; and the caravan routes, 251.

Musa, son of Askia the Great, 94; rebels against his father, 98; his reign, 99.

Musa II, King of Mali, 79.

Musa ibn Noceir, 29.

Muslims, the, and the court of Ghana, 57–8.

Mu'tamid, King of Seville, 53.

Mzab, 62, 77; as a trading centre, 128.

Nafata and Shehu, 225.

Naples and trade with Africa, 119, 121.

Napoleon and Hornemann, 213, 214.

INDEX

293

Nasamones, 96 n.

Nassere, attacks Walata, 89; Sonni Ali and, 90; summoned by Askia, 94.

Natron, trade in, 253, 255.

Needles, import of, 253.

Nefta, 116.

Negroes, in N. Africa, 23; Muhammadanism amongst, 64; Ibn Battuta on, 77–8; Leo Africanus on, 105; as an enemy, 145; formed into the Abid, 195–6; their absorption of the nomads, 265.

Negroland, the ancients and, 17, 19, 44; the Ghadamsi merchants and, 107.

Nema, 45.

New World, the, 203.

Niamey, 128.

Niani, 70, 74; Ibn Battuta and, 76, 77–8.

Niger, the, 13, 45, 65, 67, 68, 73, 148; the Romans and, 20; Ibn Haukal and, 34; as the 'Nile' of Ibn Battuta, 77; its importance to the Songhai, 82; Leo Africanus and, 108, 112–13; Malfante and, 133–4; the Moorish invasion and, 157 & n., 158–9; in the hands of the Moors from Jenne to Gao, 175; and the gold mines, 188; eighteenth-century cartographers and its course, 201–2, 210; Mungo Park and, 211–12; James Rennell and, 213; reached by Hornemann, 214; the Zaghawa and, 220; miraculous crossing of, 227–8; theories of, 233; British expedition to, 234–8; Clapperton and, 236–8; Donkin and, 238; the Landers and, 238–9; the problem solved, 239; Laing and, 239; as a waterway, 250; ferries on, 254; its importance to the Sudan, 261.

Niger, Bend of the, 6, 27; Nuh and, 175; Shehu and, 228; Barth and, 242.

Niger, Middle, 72; character of, 82; the Fono and, 84; the Songhai and, 154; history of, under later Pashas, 196–7; Barth and, 244; salt supply of, 249.

Niger, Upper, 6, 25, 60.

Nigeria, encroachment of desert in, 6.

Nile, the, 13, 26; Ibn Battuta and, 77; the Senegal confused with, 140–4; the Niger confused with, 210.

Nobatae, 23.

Nomads, their effect and development, 261, 262; migration of, 263; political

organization of, 263–4; their temporary influence, 264; weakness of, 264–5.

Ntoba, attacked by Askia Ishak, 99.

Nuba, 77.

Nubia, 111.

Nupe, 77, 219; Hornemann dies at, 214, 236; Mungo Park and, 214; its independence, 223; won by Shehu's emirs, 226; export of slaves to, 253.

Nyam-Nyam (cannibals), 62 n.

Oases, the, decay of, 8, 259; people of, 9; of Tafilelt, 43.

Oden, 133.

Oea, 16.

Ogane believed to be Prester John, 148–9.

Oghmor, Amenokal of the Tadmekket, 199–200.

Okba ibn Nafi, 29.

Olive, its cultivation in N. Africa, 4.

Olive oil, trade in, 119.

Omar, Qadi of Timbuktu, see Abu Hafs Omar.

Omar, and Akil the Targui, 86–7; pursues Nassere, 89; becomes Timbuktu-Koi again, 92.

Omar ben Idris, 79.

Omar Komdiago, 94.

Ommayyads, the, of Kanem, 95.

Oran, 135.

Ortelius, 110, 111; and the course of the Niger, 201–2.

Oudney, Dr., sent on a Niger expedition, 234–5.

Overweg, joins Richardson's expedition, 241; rejoins Barth, 242.

Ostrich feathers, trade in, 240, 258.

Ottoman Empire, Khalif of, and El Mansur, 152; use of her sea-power 203–4.

Oyo (Katunga), 237.

Palmer, H. R., 16 n., 83 n., 111 n., 220 n.

Palmerston, Lord, and Barth, 242, 244.

Palola, island, 137 n.

Palolus, river, 137 n.

Paper, import of, 253.

Park, Mungo, 113; explores the Niger, 211–12; returns to England, 212–13; sets out again, 214; trials of the

294   INDEX

expedition, 214–15; his death, 216; later explorers and, 234.

Pashas, the, assume their own authority, 193–4; finally repudiate the suzerainty of Morocco, 194.

Pelele, the, 190 n.

Pepper, malaguetta, imported into Europe, 124; Portuguese trade in, 149.

Petoney, Melchior, and the African gold trade, 187.

Phazania, Fezzan, 17.

Philip II and El Mansur, 185.

Pillars of Hercules, 13, 14.

Piracy, off Barbary, 122–3; its effect on trade, 203.

Pisa, and trade with Africa, 119, 120–1; export of slaves to, 124; a rival of Florence, 135.

Pisania, Mungo Park and, 211.

Pizzigani of Venice, the, 74, 137.

Pliny, 18.

Podo, the, 88.

Podor, 63.

Pomponius Mela, 61.

Popes, the, and the Christian Berbers, 115; and the *Frendji*, 117; and trade with Muslims, 120, 124, 152 n.; and the slave trade, 205.

Portinari, the, 135.

Porto Santo, 141.

Portolano Mediceo, 137.

Portuguese, the, and the history of Mali, 80; the Mandingoes and, 90; and the pepper trade, 124 n., 149; and Wadan, 136; and Atlantic exploration, 138–44; and the slave trade, 142, 145; and Prester John, 148–9; and the exploration of the Sahara, 149–50; Dom Sebastian of, 151; and the Moorish sultan, 152; ports held by, 185; controversy with England, 185–6; and the sea route to India, 205; and the Badagry slave trade, 254;

Pory, John, 124 n.

Pottery, trade in, 119.

Prester John, his identity with Mansa Musa, 74, 137; Henry the Navigator and, 138–9; identified with Ogane, 148–9; identified with the Mossi king, 149; Dom Sebastian and, 151 n.

Ptolemy, and the Romans in Africa, 19, 20; and Arab geography, 32.

Pygmies, 61.

Qoraysh, 155.

Rabba, ferry at, 254.

Rakah, as the termination of the Niger, 236 n., 237.

Rano, 95, 219.

Ras el Ma, 89; Moorish garrison massacred at, 172.

Razors, import of, 253.

Red Sea, 1.

Redmann, 240.

Reichard, C. G., his theory of the Niger, 233.

Reinel, Pero, 149.

Religious fanaticism, nomads and, 263.

Rennell, Major James, and the source of the Niger, 213, 214.

Rice, its cultivation in Gobir, 110; trade in, 250.   [241.

Richardson, James, sent to N.W. Africa,

Rio Grande, the, 147, 250.

Rio Nunez, the, 239.

Rio d'Ouro (Rio de Oro), its discovery, 142; Fernandez and, 143.

Ritchie, Mr., Sahara expedition under, 234.

Roberts, Henry, and the conquest of Morocco, 188.

Robes, import of, 46, 105.

Rodd, F. R., 19, 20 n., 24, 26, 96 n.

Roentgen, 233.

Roger II of Sicily and El Idrisi, 35.

Romans, remains of, in the Sahara, 1, 2; their irrigation of the Sahara, 3; and the granary of Rome, 3; and the fauna of N. Africa, 5; and commerce in N. Africa, 18–22; and Arabic literature, 32; and dumb barter, 61.

Roncière, Charles de la, 131, 133.

Saadian dynasty replaced by the Hassanids, 195.

Sabratha, 16.

Safi, 185.

Saghmara, the, 85.

Sagoto, 133, 227.

Sagres, Henry the Navigator at, 140–1.

St. Cyprian, 119.

St. Louis, 117.

Sakura, king of Mali, 70–1.

Salee as a pirate centre, 204 & n.

Salt, supply of, in Sudan, 44, 59, 60–1, 85, 134, 249–50; tax on, in Ghana,

INDEX

62; El Mansur and, 155; Barbary merchants and, 240; exchanged for gold, 249; trade of, in Agades, 251; carried by the *Azalai*, 252; trade of, in Kano, 253, 255.

Saltpetre, trade in, 152, 156, 186.

Sahara, the, 1; its political importance, 1; change of climate in, 2–3, 9–10; its encroachment on the Sudan, 6–8; residual fauna of, 8; people of, 8–9; effect of abolition of slave trade on, 9; traffic in, in ancient times, 10; early penetration of, 13–17; in Roman times, 18–22; inhabitants of, in pre-Arab times, 23; the Tuareg and, 24–6; its division by Leo Africanus, 26; and the importance of Sijilmasa, 43; water supply in, 59; Mansa Musa and, 74; and the Mandingo influence, 80; traffic in Leo Africanus's time, 106; Christianity in, 115; on the Catalan map, 128; crossed by d'Isalguier, 131; Portuguese exploration of, 149–50; the Moorish army crosses, 156–7; value of astronomical instruments in, 181; early cartographers and, 201, 202; British expedition to, 234, 241; crossed by Barth, 243; importance of trade to, 246; traffic of slaves across, 257; effect of decaying caravan routes on, 259; seasonal migrations from, 263.

Sanau, 221.

Sangaran, taken by Sundiata, 68.

Sanghana, 63.

Sanhaja, the, 24, 26, 27, 45, 60, 80, 83, 143; and the Soninke, 47; in Air, 97; Fernandez and, 144; and the slave trade, 145; and the Moors at Timbuktu, 172–3.

San Jorge da Mina (Elmina), building of, 144; European settlement at, 148.

Sankarani, 68.

Sankore, mosque of, 73; university of, 87.

Sansanding, Park's despatch from, 215; and the caravan routes, 247, 250.

Santa Cruz du Cap de Ghir, 185.

Sao-Farima (= Chief Verderer), 93.

Sarakuna, the, of Gobir, 220; of Kano, 220.

Sararin Tsako, 222.

Sarkin Air of Agades, 227.

Sarkin Gobir, *see* Nafata.

Sarkin Kebbi Samma, 98.

Sarkin Musulmi, 226, 231.

Sarkin Sudan, 80 n.

Sarkin Turawa of Agades, and the *Azalai*, 252.

Say, 84, 94, 166, 214; Barth and, 242.

Sbeitla, 29.

Sealskins, trade in, 119, 145.

Sebab, 119.

Sebastian of Portugal, Dom, and the Moorish invasion, 151.

Sebka d'Ijil, 250.

Segu, 113; the Bambara king of, 195, 196, 228–9; Mungo Park and, 212, 214, 216.

Seku, 228, 243; his *jihad*, 228–9.

Senegal, advance of desert in, 6; gold trade in, 14, 25.

Senegal river, 15, 27, 45, 57, 60, 63, 201, 247; country of, 25; as the 'Nile' of Wangara, 59; as the Niger, 112; reached by sea, 143; confused with the Nile, 143–4, 145; Cadamosto and, 146–7; and the gold mines, 188; distinguished from the Niger, 210; trading centres of, 250.

Setif, 4, 116.

Seven Hausa States, 95, 219.

Sfax, 119, 135–6.   [239.

Shehu Ahmadu, 228; and Major Laing, Shehu Lamino of Kanem, 227.

Shehu, *see* Usuman dan Fodio.

Shepherd Kings, the, their descendants, 220; their establishment, 264; their weakness, 264–5.

Shama, 26, *see also* Zaghawa.

Shigge, 63.

Sicily, Normans of, 121.

Sidi Mahmud, 173.

Sierra Leone, 15; discovered by de Cintra, 148.

Sifawa, 230.

Sijilmasa, 32, 46, 50, 76, 78, 128; ruins of, 43; and the salt supply, 44; and Dra'a, 49; rebellion in, 49; and the gold trade, 59, 60; and Timbuktu, 73; and the Saharan caravan trade, 79, 105, 106; Christian merchants and, 125; destruction of, 247.

Sijilmasa–Walata road, 25; Judar and, 157.

Silent trade (*see* Dumb Barter for references).

Silk, trade in, 119, 146, 253, 254.

296 INDEX

Silla, 63; Mungo Park at, 212.
Silver as a currency, 130.
Siwa, 251.
Skins, trade in, 186.
Slave trade, its abolition in the desert, 9, 258; in Ghana, 62; in Tekrur, 63; in the Sudan, 106, 119; in Bornu, 111; among Christian captives, 116; in the Maghreb, 119; the Portuguese and, 142, 145; and the Abid, 196; in Timbuktu, 196, 250; among the pirates, 204; Europeans and, 205–9; horror of, 207–8, 242; in Tafilelt, 240; England and, 241; in Kano, 253; in Badagry, 254; on the Fezzan–Kawar road, 256–7; Muhammadans and, 258.
Smith, Capt. John, and El Mansur's kingdom, 185.
So, *see* Su.
Sokoto, 6, 25, 97, 98, 128, 133; Shehu and, 227; Bello and, 230, 231; Clapperton and, 236; Barth and, 242; the *Azalai* and, 252; Jega and, 256; the Fulani of, 266.
Solingen, sword blades from, 253 & n.
Solomon, 28.
Songhai, the, 71; capture of their capital, 72; freed by Ali Kolen, 75; the Mandingoes and, 79–80; importance of the Niger to, 82–3; their history, 83; capital of, 83–4; capital removed to Gao, 84; lack of early history of, 86; attack Timbuktu, 87; capture Jenne, 88–9; termination of the Za dynasty of, 91; under Askia, 92; and the Tuareg, 96–7; Kanta's defiance of, 97–8; attack Katsina, 100; and Taghaza, 100–1; and political stability, 105; Moorish invasion of, 154, 155, 158–9; at the battle of Tondibi, 159–60; a new leader of, 165–8; outbreak of anarchy amongst, 170; revival of nationalism amongst, 179–80; victory of, 180; the Tuareg and, 199–200; and Kano, 221; their debt to the Zaghawa, 264.
Soninke, the, 23, 45, 49, 60; and the Lemtuna, 47, 50; capture of their capital, 64; division amongst, 65; and the caravan trade, 65; the Sorko and, 84; and Jenne, 88; and the white dynasty of Ghana, 265.
Sonni, 86.

Sonni Ali of Songhai, 6, 87; Es Sadi and, 87–8; captures Jenne, 88–9; at Ras el Ma, 89; his canal, 89; and Walata, 89–90; his death, &c., 90–1; the Portuguese and, 149.
Sonni Sulayman Nar, 86.
Sorko, the, 83; found a kingdom at Gao, 84.
Sotuba, rapids of, 82.
Spain, Muslims in, 52–5; Moorish exodus from, 103–4; her trade with Africa, 124; and the Moorish invasion, 151 n., 152, 157 n., 163; raided by Moorish pirates, 203, 204; and the Badagry slave trade, 254.
Spice Islands, 130.
Spices, trade in, 78, 253.
Stambul, the Tuareg and, 97.
Stukeley and the Moorish invasion, 151 & n.
Su (= So), the, 23, 65 n.; Bornu and, 95.
Sudan, the, records of the past in, 5–6; encroachment of the desert in, 6–7; its relationship with Sahara in Roman times, 10; Carthaginian trade with, 16–18; Roman trade with, 18–22; importance of Zaghawa influence in, 26–7; Jews in, 27; Arabic writers and, 34, 40; and the gold trade, 43, 59, 106; its lack of salt, 44; and Timbuktu, 73; Ibn Battuta and, 76–8; trade with Barbary, 101, 105; imports of, 105–6; Leo Africanus and, 104–13; trade with the Maghreb, 119; export of pepper from, 124; export of beads, to 124; on the Catalan map, 128; Muslim states of, 133; Moorish invasion of, 151, 154–65; difficulties of its expansion, 167–8; raided by the Mandingo, 177–8; relinquished by Morocco, 181; invasion of, by Zaghawa, 220; Barth and, 244; importance of trade to, 246; the caravan routes and her culture, 247; demand for eunuchs in, 257; geographical features, 261; their effect on its development, 261–2; wide dispersion of its inhabitants, 266–7; dynastic stability in, 267; cultural influences in, 267–8; character of her people, 268.
Sudan, Central, ivory trade in, 146.
Sudan, Eastern, 63, 71.
Sudan, Western, 1; progressive desicca-

INDEX

297

tion in, 7; importance of Zaghawa influence in, 27; Jews in, 27; early history of, and the Arabs, 33–4, 40; sometimes called Tekrur, 63; people of, 67; importance of Timbuktu to, 73; under Askia, 92–3; Moorish invasion of, 154–68; famine in, 165; characteristics of inhabitants, 170; under the later Pashas, 193; and the name Hausa, 219; value of Leo Africanus's account of, 112; Clapperton and, 238; shortage of salt in, 249; kola nuts in, 253; the raiding of, for slaves, 258; influence of nomads on, 261; influence of its geographical features on, 261–2; effect of Zaghawa invasion on, 264.

Sufetula, *see* Sbeitla.

Sugar, trade in, 119, 132, 156, 186, 253; traded for marble, 185.

Sulayman, 75; visited by Ibn Battuta, 75–6, 77.

Sulayman the Magnificent, 204.

Sulayman Nar, 72, 75, 86.

Sulayman Pasha sent to Timbuktu, 178–9.

Sulebawa, the, 225.

Sumanguru, 65; and the ruling house of Mali, 68; his death, 68–9.

Sundiata, 65, 71; acquires Sangaran, &c., 68; victorious over Sumanguru, 68–70; removes his capital to Niani, 70; his death, 70.

Sura, the, 229.

Surame, Kanta's capital, 97–8.

Sus, 50, 65, 73, 128; valley of, 74; sugar from, 105.

Susse (=Susa), 4.

Susu, the, and Ghana, 65 and n.; and Mali, 68; *see also* Su.

Sword blades, import of, 253.

Syrtica Regio, 16, 17.

Syrtis the Greater, 16.

Syrtis the Lesser, 16.

Tabelbert, 128.

Tabello and the *Azalai*, 251.

Tabkin Kwotto, defeat of Yunfa at, 226.

Tabonie, 18.

Tabudium, *see* Tabonie.

Tadjurah, 71.

Tadmekka, 84; its position, 85, 86.

Tadmekket, the, *see* Kel Tadmekket.

Tafilelt, oasis of, 43, 240, 247.

Tagant, 45, 46, 47.

Taghaza, salt mines of, 44, 59, 62, 76, 88, 128, 249–50; limit of Askia's dominion, 94; their control, 99–100; moved to Taghaza el Ghizlan, 100–1; Leo Africanus at, 107; Cadamosto, 146; the Moors and, 154–5, 157; Caillié, 240.

Taghaza el Gharbie, 250.

Taghaza el Ghizlan (=of the Gazelles), 100, 101.

Taghaza-Timbuktu road, 246; route of, 247; slave traffic on, 257.

Tagost, 128.

Taghalem, see *Azalai*.

Takedda, and the caravan trade, 75, 84; Ibn Battuta and, 78; el Maghili and, 92.

Takshif, 76.

Tamentit, 128; Malfante at, 133, 134.

Tamerlane, 40.

Tangale, the, 229.

Tangier, 51; Dom Sebastian lands at, 151; held by Portuguese, 185.

Tangrela, 250.

Taodeni, salt mine at, 100–1, 240, 249; and the caravan routes, 247.

Taotek, 85.

Targa, 26.

Targui, *see* Tuareg.

Tasarahla, *takshif* sent out from, 76.

Tassawa, 222.

Tawatinke, the, 222.

Taxes, in Ghana, 62–3.

Tea, trade in, 253.

Tebu (=Teda), 23, 26; intermarriage with Ommayyads, 95; and the Ghadamsi merchants, 108; and the Fezzan-Kawar road, 256.

Tedzkiret en Nisian, the, 194, 197.

Tegazza (=Taghaza), 202.

Tekarir, the, 63.

Tekrur, loosely applied term, 63; kingdom of, 50, 63, 70, 74, 133; and Abu Bakr, 64; the Mandingoes and, 79; Askia and, 95.

Tell, the, 1; elephants in, 4.

Temajegh language, the, 24, 219.

Tenbuth, *see* Timbuktu.

Tendirma, 89; Askia at, 94.

Tenes, 119.

298 INDEX

Tensift Valley, 51.

Thompson, George, and the exploration of gold mines, 188–9.

Thora, 133.

Thymiaterium, *see* Mehedia.

Thysdrus, *see* El Jem.

Tibar, gold dust, 73, 186.

Tibesti, 17, 23, 26; in Roman times, 19–20; Bornu empire extended to, 95.

T'ifnagh script, the, 24.

Tilaberi, 83.

Tilemsi, the, 85.

Tilutane, 45–6, 47.

Timber, destruction of, in N. Africa, 30; scarcity of, on Middle Niger, 82; England's trade with Morocco in, 152 & n., 186.

Timbuktu, 45, 63, 77, 82, 151 n.; its commercial position, 73; raided by the Mossi, 75; Ibn Battuta and, 78; as part of Mali, 79, 80; Akil ag Malwal and, 86; taken by the Songhai, 87; compared with Jenne, 88; Sonni Ali and, 90; return of the *literati* to, 92; visited by Leo Africanus, 104, 108, 109, 112; and the Saharan routes, 106, 107, 128; its prosperity under Askia, 109–10; Dei at, 136; Portuguese mission to, 149; the Moorish invasion and, 157 n., 158; evacuation of, 160; the Moors retire to, 161–2; Mahmud Pasha arrives at, 164; Mahmud Pasha returns to, 168, 170; rebellion in, 171; return of order in, 172; attacked by Sanhaja Tuareg, 172–3; and El Mustapha, 174; under Muhammad Taba, 176; under successive Pashas, 176–81; Moorish spoils from, 184; Es Sadi and, 192; Scholars of, 192–3; the seat of the Askias of the North, 193, 194; Ahmed and, 196; the Tadmekket and, 198–200; the French and, 210; Seku Ahmadu and, 229; the problem of its situation, 239–40; Laing and, 239; Caillié and, 239–40; Barth and, 242; and the caravan routes, 247, 250.

Timbuktu-Koi, post of, 86; Omar becomes, 92; under Askia, 93.

Timgad, 2.

Tin Shaman, 96.

Tindo Galadio, 95.

Tinkisso, 60, 68.

Tirekka, 59, 73; its importance, 86.

Tlemcen, the Wadites of, 21, 55; the Zenata capital, 52; a commercial house of, 78–9; el Maghili and, 92; as a market, 105; caravan route from, 107; Christian community of, 116; Christian mercenaries of, 117–18; Christian merchants and, 125.

Tobacco, its introduction into Maghreb 184.

Togahia, Moors defeated at, 200.

Tombo, the, 90, 175.

Tombotu, 201, 202; *see also* Timbuktu.

Tomson, Jasper, and Judar's return to Morocco, 177.

Tondibi, battle of, 157 n., 159–60; date of, 160 n.; news of, in Morocco, 162–3.

Toro (people of), 224.

Torobe (Toronke or Toronkawa), 224–5; Shehu Usuman of, 225, 228.

Tosaye, 82.

Tozeur, 116.

Toulouse, d'Isalguier and, 131–2.

Trade, its stimulus to geography, 32–3; its importance to N. Africa, 246; its overruling importance, 255; effect of, absence of natural frontiers on, 267.

Traditionists, the, 55.

Tripoli, 1, 119; the Pasha of, 234, 235; British Consul at, 235–6; Laing sets out for, 269; Richardson's mission leaves, 241; Barth and, 243.

Tripoli–Kawar–Chad road, 17, 25; and the silk trade, 253; as a slave market, 257.

Tristam, Nuno, passes Cape Blanco, 142; reaches Guinea by sea, 143.

Tsuntsuwa, Shehu's defeat at, 226.

Tuareg, the, 6, 9; characteristics of, 23–4; in Roman times, 24; their religion, 24–5; as caravan drivers, 25; division of, 26, 83; their arrival in Africa, 26; raid Timbuktu, 86, 87; of Air, 96–7; of Tamentit, 133; as Portuguese prisoners, 142; and the Moors, 159; outbreak of licence among, 170; and Timbuktu, 171, 179, 197; and the Songhai, 198–9; and the Gobirawa, 222, 226, 227; and Major Laing, 239; and the Fulani, 242; and the *Azalai*, 252; and the Tebu, 256; and the decay of the caravan routes, 259; seasonal migrations of, 263.

INDEX

299

Tuat, 26, 78, 250; Arabs in, 29; and Timbuktu, 73; el Maghili and, 92; and the caravan routes, 107, 128, 198, 247; massacre of Jews in, 130; Malfante at, 132–3, 134.

Tuckey, Capt., sent to explore the Congo, 233–4.

Tucolor kingdom, the, 50, 63, 224; attacked by Sakura, 70; and Timbuktu, 243.

Tudun Mali of Katsina, the, 222.

Tuggurt, and the caravan routes, 107, 128; massacre of Jews at, 130.

Tunis, Hafsids of, 38–9, 55; Leo Africanus dies in, 105; and the caravan routes, 107; St. Louis and, 117; renewed prosperity in, 119; her trade with Pisa, 121; Venetian trade with, 125, 135; spread of Turks to, 130; and piracy, 205.

Tunisia, 16.

Turawa, 85.

Turks, the, 19; and the Arab pirates, 123; and the Moorish king, 152; as pirates, 204; export of slaves to, 257; Turks, Seljukian; westward movement of, 130.

Twelfth parallel, significance of, 255.

Two Shores, the, 54.

Ubritenga, 75.

Uld Kirinfil and El Mansur, 155.

Ulema of Massina, the, 228.

Ulimmiden, *see* Aulimmiden.

Uruj the pirate, 204.

Usuman dan Fodio (Shehu), 225; and Yunfa, 225–6; his flight from Degel, 226; his victories, 226–7; and Seku, 228–9; his *jihad* completed, 229 his administration, 229–30.

Utzila, 26.

Vandals, the, their invasion of N. Africa, 27–8.

Venice, and trade with Africa, 119, 122; 124, 125, 132; export of glass to Barbary, 124; and the Guinea voyage, 146.

Vescera (= Biskra), 263.

Victoria, Queen, El Bekkai and, 243.

Viladestes, Mecia de, 128.

Virgin, Holy, statue of, found in Gao, 161.

Volta, the, upper, 75; Black, 229, 248.

Wad Mihero, the, 8.

Wadai, the Zaghawa of, 26.

Wadan, 133, 202; the Portuguese and, 90, 107, 136; El Mansur to attack, 101; as a caravan centre, 107; as a desert market, 146; Portuguese factory established at, 149.

Wadi Tilemsi, 84.

Wady Nun, 247.

Wady Sebu, 14.

Wagadu, district of, 45.

Wagadugu, 75, 254, 255; dynastic stability in, 267.

Wagag, 47; and Ibn Yacin, 48, 49.

Wahiguya, 75.

Walata, 6, 44, 45, 87, 202; made a caravan centre, 65; Jenne and, 73; and the desert caravans, 76; gold trade in, 79, 247; attacked by the Mossi, 89; Sonni Ali and, 89–90; as a caravan junction, 107; Leo Africanus and, 108; Christian merchants and, 125.

Wangara, 23, 45, 47, 70, 201, 202; and the gold trade, 43, 59–61, 150, 184, 196; its identity, 60, 62, 247, 248; cannibals of, 77; Leo Africanus and, 111, 234; as the termination of the Niger, 213, 214; Capt. Lyon and, 234.

Wangarawa, the, 220, 222.

Wargla, 62, 75; as a market, 105; and the caravan route, 107.

Warrington, Frederick, British Consul at Tripoli, 235–6.

Waziri, the, 227.

Waziri Abdullahi, 227–8; his share of Shehu's kingdom, 230.

West Indies as a slave market, 205, 206, 207, 257.

Wheat, import of, 46.

Whips, trade in, 63.

Whydah, 237.

Wine imported into Africa, 124.

Wonjerque, 254.

Wool, trade in, 63.

Yahia (brother of Askia), 98.

Yahia, Tuareg chief attacks Timbuktu, 171.

Yahia ibn Ibrahin, 47.

Yahia ibn Omar, 50, 64.

Yandoto, 221 & n.

Yaqut, 23; and the Sudan, 35; and

INDEX

Sijilmasa, 43; and the gold trade of Ghana, 59, 60, 249.
Yatenga, 75, 90; the Toronke and, 224; dynastic stability in, 267.
Yauri, 216; and the ferry roads, 254.
Yelwa, 219.
Yola, 229, 242.
Yorubas, the, 229, 236, 254.
Yufi (= Nupe), 77.
Yunfa, Sarkin Gobir, and Shehu, 225; defeat of, 226; his death, 227.
Yunis Amenokal of Air, 97.
Yusuf ibn Tashifin, 50, 67; commands the Maghreb, 51, 57; founds Marrakech, 51; and the Spanish Muslim, 52–4; becomes master of Seville, 54.

Za kings, 83, 91.
Za Aliamen, first Berber king of the Songhai, 83, 220.
Za Kossoi, 84.
Zaberma, 94.
Zafcu, the, 63–4.
Zaghari, 77.
Zaghawa, the, 26, 83, 133; importance of, in Sudan, 26–7; of Bornu, 95; their language, 219; their invasion of the Sudan, 220, 264; the influence of their blood, 264–5.

Zaghay, 78.
Zaghrani, the, 90.
Zagrana ravage the Songhai, 170.
Zakzak, 95.
Zallaqa, battle of, 53.
Zamfara, 201, 202, 210, 222; captured by Askia, 96; Leo Africanus and, 110, 111.
Zanziga, 26.
Zazau, 95, 101, 219; early history of, 222–3.
Zegzeg, 95, 201, 202, 219; early history of, 222–3.
Zaria, 95, 96; building of, 222–3; won by Shehu's emirs, 226; Lander and, 238; and the cotton cloth trade, 252; and the ferry roads, 254.
Zenata, the, 49; their arrival in Africa, 21–2, 25; Tlemcen their capital, 52.
Zinder, 242; and the caravan routes, 251.
Zogde, 128, 133; and Sokoto, 227; Zogoran, 27.
Zohri, 144.
Zoromawa, 27.
Zugu, 27.
Zugurma, 27.
Zuila, 18.
Zurmi, 98.
Zurara, see Azurara.

PRINTED IN GREAT BRITAIN AT THE UNIVERSITY PRESS, OXFORD
BY JOHN JOHNSON, PRINTER TO THE UNIVERSITY